The Deluge

2 *Serv.* Why, then we shall have a stirring world again. This peace is good for nothing but to rust iron, increase tailors, and breed ballad-makers.

I *Serv.* Let me have war, say I; it exceeds peace as far as day does night; it's spritely, waking, audible, and full of vent. Peace is a very apoplexy, lethargy; mulled, deaf, sleepy, insensible; a getter of more bastard children than war's a destroyer of men.

2 *Serv.* 'Tis so: and as wars, in some sort, may be said to be a ravisher, so it cannot be denied but peace is a greater maker of cuckolds.

I *Serv.* Ay, and it makes men hate one another.

3 *Serv.* Reason; because they then less need one another. The wars for my money.

(Shakespeare, *Coriolanus*, Act IV, Scene V)

ARTHUR MARWICK

The Deluge

BRITISH SOCIETY AND THE FIRST WORLD WAR

Reissued Second Edition

with a new Preface by
Joanna Bourke

palgrave
macmillan

First edition 1965
Second edition 1991
Reissued second edition published 2006 by
PALGRAVE MACMILLAN

Palgrave Macmillan in the UK is an imprint of Macmillan Publishers
Limited, registered in England, company number 785998,
of Houndmills, Basingstoke, Hampshire RG21 6XS.

Palgrave Macmillan in the US is a division of St Martin's Press LLC,
175 Fifth Avenue, New York, NY 10010.

Palgrave Macmillan is the global academic imprint of the above
companies and has companies and representatives throughout
the world.

Palgrave® and Macmillan® are registered trademarks in the
United States, the United Kingdom, Europe and other countries.

ISBN-13: 978-0-230-00245-6
ISBN-10: 0-230-00245-5

This book is printed on paper suitable for recycling and made
from fully managed and sustained forest sources. Logging, pulping
and manufacturing processes are expected to conform to the
environmental regulations of the country of origin.

A catalogue record for this book is available from the British Library.

Printed and bound in Great Britain by
CPI Antony Rowe, Chippenham and Eastbourne

Contents

Illustrations

Preface to the Reissued Second Edition of *The Deluge* by Arthur Marwick

Joanna Bourke

On 11 April 1917, *The Tatler* published a cartoon entitled 'The Key of the Situation'. It shows a female munitions worker standing in front of a door to the Houses of Parliament. On the door are the words 'The Vote'. At her side is a discarded axe, marked 'Militancy', while the key she is using to open the door is labelled 'National Work'. John Bull is seen greeting the munitions worker with the words: 'It was no good axe-ing for it, but now you've worked for it and earned it, it's a different matter.'[1]

Arthur Marwick's book addresses the issue hinted at in this cartoon: to what extent did the First World War precipitate a deluge of social change? Were the lives of women and workers, as well as the relationship between the state and its citizens, dramatically altered as a direct result of the waging of war? The title of Marwick's book gives away his answer, evoking a cataclysmic flood, sweeping away the last remnants of Victorian culture. In Marwick's words, in the inter-war years Britain was a 'better place to live in' than it had been in 1914.[2] Although Marwick insists time and again that the war was a tragedy, his central argument is that most of the changes on the home-front were positive and lasting.

This provocative thesis, argued with passion and embedded within a vast array of evidence, has been profoundly influential. Throughout the world, teachers in schools and universities have set versions of the examination question: 'To what extent was the First World War a watershed in British social life?' The question owes its long life to Marwick.

The Deluge, fist published in 1965, has remained a central textbook on British society in the aftermath of the war. It has also provided Marwick with 40 years of debate. Marwick has elaborated and refined his thesis in innumerable articles and books. In particular, his *Women at War, 1914–1918* (1977) extended his analysis of the effect of war on women and his *War and Social Change in the Twentieth Century* (1974) introduced a much needed comparative dimension by investigating not only Britain, but also the United States, France, Germany, and Russia.[3] *The Deluge* was not Marwick's first book, nor (by any means), his last, but it has spurred a remarkable career.

When Marwick published *The Deluge*, he was a 29-year-old Scottish historian, with two books and a number of articles already in the public domain. In 1969, he was among the first batch of 'academics of the air' to be named by the Open University (originally known as the University of the Air) and he brought his love of football, sports cars, and history into what he called this 'young and swinging institution'.[4] In those less regulated times, it was not unknown of him to bring a pint of beer into lectures in order to quench both his thirst as well as his students' appetite for knowledge.[5] Marwick is now Emeritus Professor of History at the Open University.

The Deluge was published to rave reviews. *The Times* praised it for its 'biting scepticism and challenge to established authorities'.[6] *The American Historical Review* observed that many other people had written social histories of the First World War (the reviewer mentioned Caroline Payne, Irene Willis, and Robert Graves), but registered delight at 'the freshness and the perception of this sensitive survey'. Marwick's book was 'an absorbing narrative' that 'stamps him as one of the most interesting of the new breed of British historians who have finally discovered that the twentieth century is, after all, as much a part of their history as is the seventeenth', the reviewer pronounced.[7]

Certainly, the timing of publication was impeccable. 1964 had heralded in the fiftieth anniversary of the war. The British reading public had been deluged with histories, plays, and poetry about the war. And their appetite showed no signs of being sated. Both within and without academe there was widespread curiosity about the ways in which the *second* world war of the century had affected British society and culture. Scholars such as Quincy Wright in *A Study of War* (1942) argued that it 'cannot be said that war in its present form has promoted progress'. Indeed, 'in the most recent stage of world-civilisation war has made for instability, for disintegration, for despotism, and for unadaptablity, rendering the course of civilisation less predictable and continued progress toward achievement of its values less probable'.[8] Arnold Joseph Toynbee went further, making the grandiose claim in *War and Civilization* (1950) that war had 'proved to have been the proximate cause of the breakdown of every civilization which is known for certain to have broken down'. Not only was military conflict and revolution 'man's principal engine of social and spiritual self-defeat', but Toynbee lamented that its spectres 'once again stalk abroad'.[9]

Marwick was also writing in the aftermath of R. M. Titmuss's work on the Second World War. Titmuss's 'War and Social Policy', first published in *The Listener* on 3 November 1955, and later republished in *Essays on 'The Welfare State'* (1958), sought to examine the ways in which 'war and social policy influence each other'. He observed that one of the major characteristics of war in modern times was 'the fact that modern war casts its shadow long before it happens and . . . its social effects are felt for longer and longer periods after armed conflict has ceased'. He concluded by arguing that modern war was only tolerable for the population if social inequalities were not intolerable. Although Titmuss concluded by saying that war was not 'the whole story in the evolution of social policy' (after all '[m]an does not live by war alone'), he asserted that British society had been profoundly shaken by the experience of the Second World War.[10]

Provoked into dialogue with these intellectual giants, Marwick turned to examine the war of 1914–18. He was especially caustic about his competitors in First World War history. 'In general those who have talked the most about war's impact have presented the least strict analysis and the fewest hard facts', he brusquely observed: popular historians of war seemed content to simply write 'blithely' about 'social revolution, short skirts, and the vulgar manners of the *nouveau riche*'. Frank P. Chambers's *The War Behind the War, 1914–1918* was 'a worthless narrative', Marwick insisted.[11] He showed as little respect for the 'higher ground of solid scholarship' as well. Although praising the work of A. L. Bowley (an economic historian who argued that the war was influential in raising the wages of the lowest paid workers),[12] Marwick was adamant that scholars such as Francis W. Hirst, author of *The Consequences of the War to Great Britain* (1934), 'set a fashion in naivety of analysis which many have imitated but few have equalled'. Much of the scholarship on the impact of war was really simply 'patriotic polemic', he lamented.[13]

So what did Marwick think was the correct way to address questions about the impact of war? One of his most decisive acts – and one that most other historians addressing similar questions to Marwick continue to follow – was to insist that 'war' and 'society' could not be categorically differentiated. 'War is not something separate from society, like an alien invasion', Marwick contended in the Preface to the 1991 edition of *The Deluge*. Rather, the two entities were wholly entangled.

Equally important was Marwick's insistence on shifting attention to so-called ordinary people (who inevitably turned out to be quite extraordinary). For Marwick, it was obvious that a history of war must be a history of *all* participants, and not simply of elites and leaders. Instead of writing the history of war as the history of battlefields and generals, Marwick explored a vast range of individual and group experiences. Variations by class and gender were meticulously distinguished; the political and the economic, painstakingly surveyed; technological and cultural variables given a balanced weighting. Marwick insisted that the only way to understand the impact of the war was to appreciate its cumulative effect. Leisure and collectivism; the advance of the Labour Party and the retreat of the Liberal Party; food shortages and state-directed distribution; military versus industrial conscription; science and technology – all were transformed. In *The Deluge*, readers were instructed in the major upheavals taking place in the history of food, leisure, dress, housing, the arts, and so on. Finally, although easy to exaggerate, Marwick's judicious mixture of statistics, official reports, newspaper reports, letters, memoirs, and novels was much more novel in 1965 than it is today. Marwick's history became one of 'mentalities' as much as seemingly more objective indicators.

I will let the book tell its own story, but basically *The Deluge* makes the case that the war permanently transformed British society, and that most of the changes were positive. Marwick acknowledged the suffering of war: this book certainly does not glorify war and its effects. Fifteen per cent of males aged between 15 and 29 years in 1911 were killed in the First World War; 1.2

million were sufficiently disabled to receive disability pensions in the 1920s. In the silence of their homes as well as in front of the war memorials that sprang up in villages, towns, and city neighbourhoods throughout the nation, millions of individuals mourned the brutal deaths of their loved ones. The emotional and psychological impact of the war was colossal.

Nevertheless, Marwick points out that destruction and distress constitute only a part of the historical story. Mass dislocation (particularly in the economic sphere) demanded major programmes of social reconstruction. The exigencies of war directly challenged the most prominent social and political institutions in the country: they were forced to operate more efficiently and adopt the latest scientific and technological innovations. The need to ensure that lower-status groups and classes participated in the war effort proved to be a compelling means by which relatively powerless groups could improve their position. Women and the working classes, for instance, won increased recognition as a result of their war work. For women, 'emancipation' became a reality. For workers, great strides were made. Working-class income increased by an average of 100 per cent between 1914 and 1920 and, in the aftermath of war when price levels dropped, this war-enhanced wage level was successfully defended. In line with the latter work of Jay Winter, in his classic, *The Great War and the British People* (1985), the lives of British civilians improved during the war because of full employment, rationing, and rent control, as well as improved social provision more generally.[14] As Marwick put it, in 1914, the working class was large and poor; by the 1920s, 'it was not quite so large, and it was not quite so poor'.[15] For women, 'emancipation' became a reality.

This was all provocative stuff, and historians quickly took sides. Critics were particularly incensed by Marwick's notion of dramatic change. Instead of a revolution, weren't the post-war years characterised by a conservative backlash against the changes of those years between 1914 and 1918, they asked? In answering this question, a lot depended upon the time-frame adopted. For instance, in deciding about the political impact of war, different conclusions might be reached if the time-frame was 1914 to the 1920s, compared with the 1870s to the 1930s. As Rodney Lowe argued, in the first case, the 'rapid abandonment of many wartime innovations' could be seen as a 'lost opportunity for the modernisation of British government', but in the longer term the war was 'the occasion that forced choices to be made from a wide range of options long debated but largely evaded during late Victorian and Edwardian England'.[16]

Culturally, too, some historians stepped forward to argue that Britons responded to the end of the war by looking backwards – nostalgically – to a mythic image of pre-war harmony and stability. In *Blighty* (1996), Gerald DeGroot wrote:

> War was tragic, in some ways catastrophic. But for most people it was an extraordinary event of limited duration which, as much as it brought change, also inspired a desire to reconstruct according to cherished patterns. If war is the locomotive of history, the rolling stock in this case was typically British: slow, outmoded, and prone to delay and cancellation.[17]

Jay Winter, too, in *Sites of Memory, Sites of Mourning* (1995), pointed out that the search for a 'meaning' to the war led individuals to turn to the past. Rather than attempting to invent new ways of understanding their experiences, people sought to 'return to older patterns and themes'. Classical strophes, religious motifs, and romantic forms had almost universal appeal in the face of catastrophe. They provided a way for the bereaved to 'live with their losses, and perhaps to leave them behind'.[18] Finally, a lot of attention focused upon gender ideologies (both masculine and feminine), suggesting that traditional roles were much more resilient than Marwick postulated. In the words of Eric Leed in *No Man's Land* (1979): 'war experience is nothing if not a transgression of categories . . . war offered numerous occasions for the shattering of distinctions that were central to orderly thought, communicable experience, and normal human relations.'[19] In its aftermath, people yearned to restore 'traditional' order. In the case of gender relations, this meant a return to an order 'based on national biological categories of which sexual differences were a familiar and readily available expression'.[20] In the post-war world, there was a powerful current urging a return to social conservatism.

Indisputably, the most trenchant critique of the Marwick thesis came from a new generation of historians interested in the experiences of women. The new wave of feminists of the 1970s and

1980s were dismayed by Marwick's approach to 'the women question'. While, on the one hand, they lauded the fact that (unlike many other historians of the time) Marwick devoted considerable space to women's experience of war. On the other, however, they were dismayed by the tone of some of his work. A number of examples could be given, but the most quoted one was Marwick's quip that the 'one of the pleasantest by-products of the new female self-confidence' was women's 'new pride in personal appearance, especially among a class of women who had formerly become ill-kempt sluts by their mid-twenties, if indeed they had ever been anything else'.[21]

Many of the new generation of scholars analysing the role of women in wartime also disagreed with Marwick's conclusions. At one level, the disagreement was what might constitute 'emancipation' and 'modernisation'. For Marwick, the fact that the war led to changes in social mores, which enabled women to smoke in public, wear shorter skirts, and seek employment in jobs previously barred to them, represented a shift away from subordinate forms of femininity. For feminists writing in the 1970s and 1980s, this was simply not good enough. In the words of Gail Braybon and Penny Summerfield, authors of *Out of the Cage* (1987):

> the belief that men and women naturally occupy separate spheres within which they pursue quite different tasks was not shaken during either war: men were not expected to take an equal share of domestic responsibilities; nor was it considered proper that women, like men, should die for their country.[22]

Historians of women asked Marwick to square his account with the continued exploitation of female labour within the home. Female wages remained substantially lower than men's: how could Marwick reconcile that fact with emancipation? At times, the accusations got decidedly heated.

The debate continues. No one suggested that the war did not have *some* major social and economic effects on women's lives. Time and again, historians have quoted the feminist and suffragist Millicent Garrett Fawcett who said, in 1920, that the 'war revolutionalized the industrial position of women. It found them serfs and left them free.' She went on to assert that the war 'not only opened to [women] opportunities of employment in a number of skilled trades, but, more important even than this, it revolutionized men's minds'.[23] As Marwick pointed out, many women *did* find themselves freer to act in a greater variety of ways during the war. Female factory workers challenged the gender order: they were earning much more than previously (three times more in some cases), were able to demonstrate their ability to carry out skilled work in areas previously barred to them, and were allowed greater leeway in the way they comported themselves publicly. In making these points, Marwick has many supporters. In the words of Angela Woollacott in *On Her Their Lives Depend* (1994), financial autonomy and mobility amongst female munitions workers fostered 'the ambition, independence, and assertiveness that were reflected in their desire to emigrate at the end of the war, their higher level of labor organization, and their refusal of prewar conditions and servitude of domestic service'. Significant female unionisation and a newly forged assertiveness

> all suggest a new conception of their own interests as distinctly different from those of men workers (and those of middle- and upper-class women). Their awareness of the importance of their efforts to the national cause gave them a basis on which to ground their expectations for future consideration.[24]

For Woollacott, it was essential to evaluate the impact of the war through women's eyes: for this generation of women, new-found confidence might not have been 'revolutionary' in the way that modern feminists might define it, but should not be sniffed at nonetheless.

Others disagreed, painting a more pessimistic story that coalesced around the argument that any changes to women's lives were always 'for the duration'. Indeed, even during the war, there were severe tensions between the need to preserve the domestic sphere (especially maintaining the birth rate) and the urgent requirements of the war economy for labour. Penny Summerfield called this a tension between 'production and patriarchy'.[25] In the words of Susan R. Grayzel, in *Women's Identities at War* (1999):

> Rather than completely undermining specific assumptions about gender in each nation, the war, from its outset, paradoxically both expanded

the range of possibilities for women and curtailed them by, among other things, heightening the emphasis on motherhood as women's primary patriotic role and the core of their national identity . . . the maintenance of gender order in society via an appropriate maternity became a fundamental tactic of the war.[26]

By emphasising the role of women as mothers, the war cemented rather than freed up traditional gender roles.[27]

These scholars admitted that there were dramatic changes in women's lives during the war, but argued that, because of entrenched assumptions about gender roles, the changes did not survive the post-war backlash. Indeed, proof that women were capable of jobs that had previously been the exclusive domain of men, made women even more dangerous to male-dominated trade unions.[28] As Deborah Thom argued, there were no permanent changes to 'the organisation of production': 'The effect of war work was to demonstrate that women were capable of a great variety of tasks; it did not demonstrate that they should be able to do them', she noted.[29] Furthermore, the pre-war definition of 'femininity' was not merely an attitude forced on women by state agents, employers, and husbands, but was frequently accepted by women themselves. Having grown used to self-sacrifice, they lacked the economic and political power after the war to transform their world.

This more pessimistic school of thought also introduced the element of class to discussions about the effect of the war on women. It was an element that Marwick amply acknowledged in *The Deluge*, but these historians wanted to elaborate on the theme. They accepted that middle-class women may well have seen long-term improvements in their lives. The Eligibility of Women Act of 1918 which enabled women to stand for parliament, the Sex Disqualification (Removal) Act of 1919 which opened all branches of the legal professions to women, and the Matrimonial Causes Act of 1923 which eliminated the double standard in divorce all arose out of the war and helped middle-class women establish themselves more securely in the inter-war years. In contrast, working-class women found themselves pushed out of those well-paid jobs they had performed during the war. Domestic service remained a form of servitude. Laundries and sweat-shops continued to pay abysmal wages. Even the 1918 Maternity and Child Welfare Act, which

introduced ante- and post-natal reforms and might have been
expected to improve working-class women's lives, placed 'greater
emphasis on the health of the child than the mother'.[30] In fact,
maternal mortality actually rose between the wars.

What about the effect of the war in winning women the vote?
Here, again, there is still no consensus. Historians, like Marwick,
who want to tie female suffrage to their war-work, tend to appeal to
the changing rhetoric of prominent politicians. As Marwick
observed, former Prime Minister Herbert Henry Asquith (that
'bastion of the resistance to the women's claims' in the years prior
to the war) acknowledged the war in his conversion to the cause.
'Some of my friends may think that . . . my eyes, which for years in
this matter have been clouded by fallacies and sealed by illusions, at
last have been opened to the truth', he admitted to Parliament.[31]
The war converted die-hard misogynists to grant women the vote.

Dissenters to this view tended to fall into two camps. On the one
side were those who insisted that the suffrage issue had been
resolved by 1914 and the war might have even delayed its
progression through parliament. Thus, in her meticulously argued
book, *Feminism and Democracy* (1986), Sandra Stanley Holton was
able to show that the main influence of the war was simply to
eliminate the remaining dissent against female suffrage by
demolishing the basis of most of their claims.[32] On the other side,
historians drew attention to the striking limitations of the
Representation of the People Act of 1918. The Act had only been
introduced because of a crisis in *male* suffrage. The fact that so
many men were out of the country due to the war necessitated
reform of male suffrage (otherwise, these men would have been
unable to vote). Reform of male suffrage 'thereby precipitat[ed] the
bill that suffragists insisted had to include women'.[33] More to the
point, the 1918 Act only enfranchised some 6 million women out
of a total of 11 million. While the Act granted universal manhood
suffrage, it allowed women to vote only if they were over the age of
30 years and were householders or wives of householders. As a
result, most of the women who had worked in war industries were
ineligible. Equality in voting had to wait another ten years.

In addition, the feminist movement seemed to falter after the
war. Gone was their confident and assertive tone. A new
defensiveness crept in.[34] A demoralising gap opened up between

returning servicemen and civilians (particularly female civilians). As Vera Brittain put it in her memoir, *Testament of Youth* (1933), she was afraid lest the war would 'come between' her and her fiancé, Roland, 'as indeed, with time, the War always did, putting a barrier of indescribable experience between men and the women they loved . . . Quite early I realised this possibility of a permanent impediment to understanding.'[35] The historian, Susan Kingsley Kent put it even more fiercely, insisting 'the soldiers on the line felt a greater sense of solidarity with Germans sitting across No Man's Land than with their compatriots at home'. While this was an exaggeration, Kent rightly observed that the 'hostility and anger directed toward the home – symbolized and epitomized by women – got played out after the war'.[36] Face-to-face with mutilated veterans begging for work on the streets of cities throughout the United Kingdom, insisting upon equal pay and employment rights could seem churlish.

Of course, it is important to recognise that Marwick's book was first published in 1965: inevitably, there has been a great deal of further research since that time. At the very least, a lot more documents have been released. More importantly, there has been what can only be described as a revolution in historical mentalities since the 1960s. When Marwick wrote *The Deluge*, social history was in its infancy and cultural history still at an embryonic stage. Even the topics of historical enquiry have been transformed. Since the 1960s, masculinity has taken its place alongside femininity.[37] Histories of 'memory' and commemoration have boomed. As Jay Winter and Emmanuel Sivan insisted in their decisive *War and Remembrance in the Twentieth Century* (1999), 'memory' is the 'socially-framed property of individuals (or groups of individuals) coming together to share memories of particular events, of time past'. Collective memory is 'the process by which individuals interact socially to articulate their memories'.[38] The range of ways men and women in the past 'remembered' the dead profoundly changed their societies, yet, being a modern fascination within the academy, it is a topic Marwick barely addresses. Finally, the infusion of cultural and literary approaches to war has transformed the ways military history is written. The 'new military history' spawned by this work has been breathtaking – and arguably as controversial as Marwick's work.[39]

The Deluge remains a central book in the social history of war. Marwick draws attention to previously neglected actors in the past; he takes memoirs and diaries sources seriously; he attempts to combine more objective measurements with more subjective ones. Most importantly, Marwick reminds historians that the war was a symbolic crisis that affected everyone, whether combatant or civilian. The emphasis on war as imagined has had a profound effect on war studies to this day. Marwick's research initiated a wave of research in social history. Indeed, the question about whether the First World War was a watershed in the history of modern Britain has dominated discussions precisely because of the complexity of the discussions and the passions they inspire. Debate, in conjunction with evidence and exegesis, is at the heart of what it means to be an historian: for this, we owe Marwick gratitude.

NOTES

1. 'Pictorial Politics: The Key of the Situation', *The Tatler*, 11 April 1917, 40.

2. Arthur Marwick, *The Deluge: British Society and the First World War*, 2nd edn, first published in 1965 (Basingstoke: Palgrave Macmillan, 1991), 52.

3. Arthur Marwick, *Women at War, 1914–1918* (London: Croom Helm, 1977) and Arthur Marwick, *War and Social Change in the Twentieth Century* (London: Macmillan, 1974).

4. 'The Times Diary', *The Times*, 8 February 1969, 8.

5. Ken Gosling, 'University Where a Lecture Begins with a Beer', *The Times*, 6 September 1973, 11.

6. 'Ordeal by Battle', *The Times*, 11 March 1965, 17.

7. 'HRW' (Henry R. Winkler), review of 'The Deluge: British Society and the First World War', in *The American Historical Review*, 71.2 (January 1966), 569.

8. Quincy Wright, *A Study of War*, vol. 1 (Chicago: University of Chicago Press, 1942), 272.

9. Arnold J. Toynbee, *War and Civilization: From a Study of History* (New York: Oxford University Press, 1950), vii–viii and 165. Also see John U. Nef, *War and Human Progress: An Essay on the Rise of Industrial Civilization* (London: Routledge & Kegan Paul, 1950).

10. R. M. Titmuss, *Essays on 'The Welfare State'* (London: George Allen & Unwin, 1958), 77–8 and 85–6.

11. Arthur Marwick, 'The Impact of the First World War on British Society', *Journal of Contemporary History*, 3.1 (January 1968), 51–2.

12. Arthur Lyon Bowley, *Some Economic Consequences of the Great War* (London: Thornton Butterworth, 1930); and Arthur Lyon Bowley and Margaret H. Hogg, *Has Poverty Diminished?* (London: P. S. King & Son, 1925).

13. Francis W. Hirst, *The Consequences of the War to Great Britain* (Oxford: Oxford University Press, 1934); Marwick, *The Deluge*, 2nd edn (1991), 52.

14. Jay Winter, *The Great War and the British People* (Basingstokes: Macmillan, 1985).

15. Arthur Marwick, *The Deluge*, 2nd edn (1991), 344.

16. Rodney Lowe, 'Government', in Stephen Constantine, Maurice W. Kirby, and Mary B. Rose (eds), *The First World War in British History* (London: Edward Arnold, 1995), 50.

17. Gerald DeGroot, *Blighty: British Society in the Era of the Great War* (London: Longman, 1996), 311.

18. Jay M. Winter, *Sites of Memory, Sites of Mourning: The Great War in European Cultural History* (Cambridge: Cambridge University Press, 1995), 6–7. Also see Joanna Bourke, *Dismembering the Male: Men's Bodies, Britain, and the Great War* (London: Reaktion, 1996).

19. Eric J. Leed, *No Man's Land: Combat and Identity in World War I* (Cambridge: Cambridge University Press, 1979), 21.

20. Susan Kingsley Kent, 'The Politics of Sexual Difference: World War I and the Demise of British Feminism', *Journal of British Studies*, 27 (July 1988), 247.

21. Marwick, *The Deluge*, 2nd edn (1991), 153.

22. Gail Braybon and Penny Summerfield, *Out of the Cage: Women's Experiences in Two World Wars* (London: Pandora, 1987), 2.

23. Millicent Garrett Fawcett, *The Women's Victory – and After: Personal Reminiscences* (London: Sidgwick & Jackson, 1920), 106.

24. Angela Woollacott, *On Her Their Lives Depend: Munitions Workers in the Great War* (Berkeley: University of California Press, 1994), 215–16.

25. Penny Summerfield, *Women Workers in the Second World War: Production and Patriarchy in Conflict* (London: Routledge, 1989).

26. Susan R. Grayzel, *Women's Identities at War: Gender, Motherhood and Politics in Britain and France During the First World War* (Chapel Hill: University of North Carolina Press, 1999), 3.

27. Deborah Thom, *Nice Girls and Rude Girls: Women Workers in World War I* (London: I. B. Tauris, 1998), 25.

28. Gail Braybon, *Women Workers in the First World War: The British Experience* (London: Croom Helm, 1981), 208.

29. Deborah Thom, 'Women and Work in Wartime Britain', in Richard Wall and Jay Winter (eds), *The Upheaval of War: Family Work and Welfare in Europe, 1914–1918* (Cambridge: Cambridge, University Press, 1988), 317.

30. Braybon and Summerfield, *Out of the Cage* 282–3.

31. House of Commons Debates, 28 March 1917, in Marwick, *The Deluge*, 2nd edn (1991), 144.

32. Sandra Stanley Holton, *Feminism and Democracy: Women's Suffrage and Reform Politics in Britain, 1900–1918* (Cambridge: Cambridge University Press, 1986).

33. Angela Woollacott, *On Her Their Lives Depend*, 189.

34. Kent, 'The Politics of Sexual Difference', 236; and Harold Smith, 'British Feminism in the 1920s', in Smith (ed.), *British Feminism in the Twentieth Century* (Aldershot: Edward Elgar, 1990), 47.

35. Vera Brittain, *Testament of Youth*, first published 1933 (London, 1978), 143.

36. Kent, 'The Politics of Sexual Difference', 247. Also see Susan Kingsley Kent, *Making Peace: The Reconstruction of Gender in Interwar Britain* (Princeton: Princeton University Press, 1993).

37. For instance, see Bourke, *Dismembering the Male*; Joanna Bourke, *An Intimate History of Killing: Face-to-Face Killing in Twentieth Century History* (London: Granta, 1999); and George L. Mosse, *The Image of Man: The Creation of Modern Masculinity* (New York: Oxford University Press, 1996).

38. Jay Winter and Emmanuel Sivan, 'Setting the Framework', in Winter and Sivan (eds), *War and Remembrance in the Twentieth Century* (Cambridge: Cambridge University Press, 1999), 6–40.

39. For an excellent, critical summary, see Gail Braybon (ed.), *Evidence, History, and the Great War: Historians and the Impact of 1914–18* (Oxford: Berghahn, 2004). Also see Joanna Bourke, 'Critical Military History', in Matthew Hughes and William J. Philpott (eds), *Palgrave Advances in Modern Military History* (London: Palgrave, 2006).

War and Social Change in Twentieth-Century Britain

[I] THE PLACE OF *THE DELUGE*

WHEN a government declares war, or responds in kind to another's declaration, it usually has certain purposes in mind, perhaps simply the preservation of national independence, perhaps the removal of a persistent threat, perhaps to acquire territory of strategic or economic value. Depending upon its military prowess, upon the efficiency with which it organizes its economy, upon the performance of its allies, and of its enemies, it may or may not achieve some or all of its aims. When the fighting is over it will be possible to identify 'consequences' of the war: some countries will be strengthened relative to others; some will have gained territory, some will have lost it; possibly new independent nation states will appear on the map for the first time. There will also have been much havoc: precise figures will usually prove hard to establish, but large numbers of soldiers will have been killed, and possibly also civilians, men, women and children. Towns and villages may have been destroyed; certainly much capital will have been used up in getting the armies into the field and in furnishing them with weapons. Here too the war has identifiable consequences.

The political and military consequences of war, and also its destructiveness, are relatively easy to plot. But what of the social consequences of war? According to the celebrated French feminist Simone de Beauvoir the winning of the vote by British women 'was in large part due to the services they rendered during the war' (i.e. the First World War).[1] According to Robert Roberts, whose parents at the time ran a corner-shop in a working-class area, women at the end of that war 'were more alert, more worldly-wise'. They then discovered that their husbands, returned from the war, 'were far less the lords and masters of old, but more comrades to be lived with on something like level terms'. [2] According to the novelist Evadne Price, in her fictional autobiography based on the genuine reminiscences of a nurse who served on the battle front, the war destroyed old-style sexual reticence:

We, who once blushed at the public mention of childbirth, now discuss such things as casually as once we discussed the latest play; whispered stories of immorality are of far less importance than a fresh cheese in the canteen; chastity seems a mere waste of time in an area where youth is blotted out so quickly. What will they expect of us, these elders of ours, when the killing is over and we return? [3]

In 1918 an Education Act was passed, and a Maternity and Child Welfare Act; in 1919 a major Housing Act, and an Act establishing a Ministry of Health. There were Unemployment Insurance Acts in 1920 and 1921. Before the war, the distinguished statistician A. L. Bowley had declared raising 'the wages of the worst-paid workers' to be 'the most pressing social task' then facing the country; after the war he wrote, 'it has needed a war to do it, but that task has been accomplished. . .' [4]

How could a war possibly be responsible for raising wages, or for giving women the vote, let alone for bringing about an Education Act or a Housing Act, or altering family relationships? Wars are about killing, maiming, and starving the enemy, conquering land and destroying resources. Military victory, military defeat, military exhaustion obviously bring certain consequences. But what connection could there be between military events and social changes – the products surely of long-term economic developments, movements of ideas, and the decisions of whatever politicians happen to be in office? Evidently in seeking the social consequences of war one is dealing with a different order of causation: it would certainly seem that such short-hand phrases as 'the war brought votes for women', 'the war brought a rise in wages', or 'the war brought educational reform' could only have meaning if the phrase 'the war' is taken to include the whole complex of social, economic and political reorganization necessitated by the war effort.

Undoubtedly many of those who lived through the First World War thought that it had brought considerable social change. Factually, there was a cluster of reforms enacted in the closing years of the war and the first post-war years. How did one establish what, if any, were the connections? Those historians who, before the 1960s, had suggested a connection between war and change had tended to take refuge in metaphor: war it was said, 'accelerated' existing trends, or war was a 'catalyst' for change. But metaphors of this sort drawn, respectively, from the physical and the chemical sciences, do not *explain* anything. They are essentially *assertions*, though they may possibly also be *descriptions* of what actually happens though, on reflection, it would seem just as reasonable to *assert* that wars disrupt and slow down existing trends.

These were the sorts of problem which, back in 1964, began to trouble me as I tried to bring *The Deluge* to a satisfactory conclusion. My approach, save in so far as I was dealing with social and cultural, rather than political and military, matters, and had made some attempt to quantify changes in social structure, had been a pretty traditional one, accumulating as much evidence as possible till patterns and correlations began to emerge, trying above all to pin down the different chronological phases of change as well as the relationship between immediate effects and longer-term consequences. Readers will quickly see how the book is divided into the following chronological phases: August 1914–March 1915; 1915–1916; 1917–1918; and how the two major topics of 'The Challenge to Laissez-faire', and 'Science and Collectivism' run across the chronological divisions. Sorting out the structure of the book caused many problems, and one big crisis, only resolved when I realized that I had to put together material scattered throughout the book into an analytical chapter not envisaged in my original plan (Chapter Five). But that was nothing compared to the problem of distilling my discoveries into a satisfactory concluding chapter. As readers will see, what I came up with was this:

. . .in summarizing analytically the material presented chronologically in the course of this book, we find that there are not many topics in which we can say this or that was caused by the war, *and nothing but the war*. If we attempt to list the bed-rock direct consequences of the war, we shall find that we are dealing as much with the *method* by which the war affected society as with the actual effects in society.

The direct consequences, which we can limit to seven, reacted with a multiplicity of other forces creating a tremendous range of side effects and indirect consequences. (See below, Chapter Nine)

The direct consequences are then listed as loss of life and limb, destruction of capital, the disruption of international trade and finance, the huge physical demand for manpower and machines creating an irresistible pressure for reorganization and reorientation of society, the manner in which the war brought to Britain a sharp sense of her deficiencies and a sharp determination to remedy them, the mass of domestic problems piled up by the interruption of normal social development and finally, the scale, horror, and excitement of the war, calling forth all sorts of different responses. It amazes me now that, in this listing, I made no separate mention of the question of participation of under-privileged groups in the war effort, taking this to be subsumed within the phrase 'huge physical demand for manpower'; certainly in the body of the book there is a great deal on the changing status of labour and the changing role of women. The fact is that it was only subsequently, while I was still puzzling over how, if at all, one *established* relationships between the different aspects (mainly non-military) of war, and the social changes which appeared undoubtedly to be accompanying and following the war, that I encountered Stanislav Andreski's *Military Organisation and Society* (1954), with its concept of the 'military participation ratio'.

In the article which embodied my first effort to codify further what I was grappling with in the final chapter of *The Deluge*, I remarked upon the enormous timespan covered by Andreski, quoting him as stating:

It is nevertheless significant that the two world wars, fought with conscript armies, strengthened immensely these levelling tendencies. The end of the First saw the introduction of universal adult suffrage; the Second brought to power the Labour Party, with its programme of soaking the rich.

Though later critics preferred to ignore this (and indeed to use Andreski's words against me) I immediately distanced myself from Andreski by appending to this quotation the comment that:

The last phrase, sufficient to send shudders down the historian's spine, perhaps suggests that, vitally important as Andreski's contribution undoubtedly is, the parade of sociological precision conceals a goodly amount of historical imprecision.[5]

I came very quickly to see that it is military conscripts who benefit least, if at all, from participating in any war, though, of course, they may on their return to peacetime life benefit as citizens from changes which have meantime taken place in domestic society; it is those who participate in the relatively free conditions of the home front who have the greatest opportunities for benefiting from that participation. The notion of *participation* (stripped of the irrelevant encumbrances of 'military' and 'ratio'), the notion that war offers opportunities to under-privileged groups not available in time of peace, became central to all my subsequent thinking. In taking further my reading in relevant sociological works, I also paid a great deal of attention to studies of catastrophe and disaster, following the line that in some of its aspects war could be likened to such natural phenomena. Thus I was able to issue the following declaration of intent for my next book, *Britain in the Century of Total War: War, Peace and Social Change 1900–1967* (1968):

There will be no attempt to generalize about the 'consequences' of war, for to talk of a war having consequences — save at the most direct level of 'so many killed', 'so many houses destroyed', and so on — is really a wrong use of language. War is, in its very essence, negative and destructive; it cannot of itself create anything new. What I shall try to do is to isolate the four *aspects* of war which are relevant to social change, and thereby endeavour to demonstrate the four *modes* through which war affects society. The consequences — so-called — of the war will be the final identifiable products — Acts of Parliament, new wage rates, changes in the social structure — resulting from war's fourfold reaction with existing society, and with the agents of change already apparent in that society. Obviously the whole exercise is valueless without a deep knowledge of the nature of a society on the eve of the war it is proposed to study.[6]

From the very start of this exploration, it may be noted, I was absolutely categorical about the need to begin by analysing society on the eve of war, and the agents of change already apparent in that society; never have I in the faintest degree suggested that war itself, independently, initiates change. In this new declaration the unsatisfactory words *methods* from the final chapter of *The Deluge* had gone, but I was now hung up between *aspects* and *modes*. Seven headings, excluding participation, had become four: progress of a sort! As I moved on to a comparative study of *War and Social Change in the Twentieth Century* (1974) I retained the notion of the four *aspects* of war, but, mistakenly, as I have long felt, I brought these together in what at that time I called a 'four-tier model'. My starting point had been the *complexity* of war and *difficulty* of pinning down simple cause-effect relationships; by adopting the jargon term 'model' I may well have given the opposite impression, particularly to those who found the book too tiresome actually to read.

Behind all the fiddling with phraseology, the key point, implicit in *The Deluge*, and which I have been clarifying over the past ten years, is that we will make little progress in exploring the possible relationship between war and social change if we persist in thinking of war on the one side, and society on the other, as two distinct variables, with the first 'impacting' on the second, and producing 'consequences'. War is not something separate from society, like an alien invasion, nor even like a catalyst (catalysts, it may be remembered, remain *unchanged* after a chemical reaction has taken place – a very curious metaphor for a war). Wars spring out of society. Societies *engage* in war. Thus, instead of thinking of society here, and war 'out there', we should envisage a continuum of 'society at war'. This continuum of 'society at war' can then be contrasted with 'society not at war' (see diagram). It then becomes possible to isolate the processes taking place in 'society at war' which do not take place in 'society not at war': new levels of participation, for instance, and certain effects akin to those of natural disaster. It is these processes (*reacting* with pre-existing agents of change, though not necessarily *accelerating* them) which (in my view) account for the social changes widely detected at the end of, and immediately after, wars. The exact detail of these changes, and whether they are merely temporary or whether they have long-term effects in post-war society, are matters which remain to be determined upon a careful examination of the evidence.

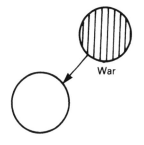

War

(b)

(a)

Society

Conventional image of war 'impacting' on society

My images of (a) 'Society not at War', and (b) the continuum of 'Society at War'. 'Society at War' is 'bigger', in that activities, expenditures, etc., multiply in wartime

Diagram

How one summarizes the processes taking place in 'society at war' which are not taking place in 'society not at war' is of far less moment than the basic principle of treating society at war as a continuum. Personally, I still think that the four headings (to use as neutral a term as possible) which I developed immediately after completing *The Deluge*, are as useful, in that they are both concise and comprehensive, as any other list that might be offered. My four headings will be familiar to many readers (they have recently been discussed by Ian F. W. Beckett in his chapter on 'Total War', in *Warfare in the Twentieth Century: Theory and Practice*, edited by Colin MacInnes and G. D. Sheffield (1987),[7] but I shall set them out here in their latest form. The purpose of these headings, let me repeat, is to identify the processes which come into play when society is at war and which, interacting with existing processes and circumstances, account for such change as does take place, short-term and long-term. The headings are: (1) *Destruction–Disruption*; (2) *War as Test*; (3) *Participation*; (4) *War as Cataclysmic Psychological Experience.*

Destruction–Disruption. The first and inescapable fact about war is that it is a great catastrophe, destroying lives, destroying resources; destroying, in the case of the First World War, the delicate mechanism of trading and financial relationships constructed in the later nineteenth century; bringing a stop to the developments of peacetime, the accumulation of capital, say, or the cultivation of crops, or (these are specific examples from Britain in 1914 and after) aborting proposed educational reform, and bringing to an end the building of new houses. In looking at any particular society in any particular war it is necessary to see first whether the total destructive effect outweighs any other more positive effects which may be detected. The inhabitants of Austria in the First World War (where there was immense deprivation[8]) or Poland in the Second (where havoc was wrought by both Germans and Russians[9]) might well gasp in horrified disbelief over any suggestion that war might bring positive social change. Even if one does gain new political rights, new welfare systems, what does that matter if one is starving? For the historian there will be a complex balance sheet to work out. The disruptions of war may be acutely painful for some, but they may be liberating for others. Men leaving the quiet, God-fearing villages of, let us say, Wales or Scotland, to fight in the trenches may encounter new ways and feel unable ever again to settle back into the old life. The disruption of war forces people into new life-styles and new patterns of living and behaviour; it will be necessary, of course, to scrutinize these very carefully to see whether they are long-lasting or merely temporary.

War as test of existing institutions and ways of doing things. Studies of war of all types are full of references, overt or covert, to the way in which, as their writers see it, war tests social organizations, institutions, ideas, as well as personal qualities. Another way of expressing the same general notion would be to speak, as A. J. Toynbee used to do, of 'Challenge and Response'.[10] The trouble with both 'challenge' and 'test' is that they may imply a kind of value judgement, perhaps even suggesting that it is an important function of social organization to be prepared to meet the challenge of war, that societies are to be judged by their success in war. That is not my argument at all. The concept of *test* should be taken to include the connotations of stress and strain (perhaps I should have coined a new word, '*strest*'). The argument is simply that in the new conditions of society at war adaptations and changes will be enforced, if victory, or even survival, is to be attained. Some changes may well be highly undesirable (in the longer term, if not from the point of view of immediate survival):

the granting of dictatorial powers to the government, or to the military, for instance; or, in the case of Britain in the First World War, over-emphasis on the traditional heavy industries, essential to the war effort, but faced with shrinking markets in the post-war years. Generally, however, the experience of war has been that more egalitarian organization is more efficient organization, and that the exploitation of science and technology is more productive than the redoubled application of old methods. The question at issue, in any case, is simply that of change, not exclusively 'desirable' or 'progressive' change.

War as involving the participation of hitherto under-privileged groups. This is my more cautious formulation of Andreski's original concept. Caution is needed because much depends upon the circumstances under which participation takes place. There has been some implied criticism of my own work for concentrating on home fronts rather than directly studying the experiences of fighting men. My view, in fact, has always been that men participating under strict conditions of military discipline are likely to make far fewer (if any) direct gains from their participation than those participating in the much more permissive atmosphere of the home front. This point is supported by those who actually have studied the experience of the fighting men. [11] However, this does not invalidate the general thesis: conditions for the under-privileged may well, nonetheless, improve on the home front (and as suggested above, soldiers, on rejoining civilian life, *may* find that they too can now share in the benefits of the changed conditions). Much, again, depends upon the nature of the domestic regime. If the home front is controlled with anything akin to the autocratic and military rigour of the war front, then scope for change will probably be very limited (as for instance in Russia in the Second World War). All qualifications made, the fundamental fact remains that in participating in the non-military aspects of the war effort, hitherto under-privileged groups find themselves in a very strong market position: government, and private employers, *need* them; hence improvements in wages and conditions (sometimes largely paper ones, which may then be torn apart by the destructiveness of war). Both military and non-military participants gain in prestige, as having been vital to the national effort. Less important, though more noticed by traditionalist historians, is the manner in which governments may feel bound to offer direct rewards for participation. The precise processes at work have to be scrutinized very closely, but on a broad appraisal across Europe it would seem that in the First World War the participation effect did have benefits for women, sections of the working class, and various national minorities.

War as cataclysmic psychological experience. With this heading we, as it were, 'seal' the continuum, joining up with the first heading, relating to war as catastrophe, or disaster. Social science studies of natural disaster have shown that they tend in human communities to inspire a determination, not just to make good the damage, but to build better than before.[12] The very destruction of war tends, of course, to make pre-existing social problems stand out more starkly: housing is a particularly good example. There is plenty of evidence (much of it cited in *The Deluge*) to show that people from all sections of society, finding war so horrific, so cataclysmic, feel that it must be part of some greater purpose, that it must result in changes commensurate with the tremendous sacrifices being made and suffering being endured. The waging of war, at the same time, tends to intensify 'in-group' feelings, and to intensify hostility to 'out-group' (among which, of course, the military enemy is the most significant). A general sense of national solidarity can encourage the promulgation of social welfare policies; solidarity among the working class, or among women, can make them more determined to fight for their rights. Often, the catastrophe of war is felt most intensely by intellectuals and artists: this may have quite profound results within their own spheres, for example, a growing acceptance during the First World War of the techniques of modernism.

From all the reactions and interactions suggested by these four headings will come the actual 'consequences' of the war: the merely short-term will have to be distinguished from the long-term. Not only will comparisons have to be made with the state of society on the eve of the war, the only true comparison will be between how things are after they have settled down after the war with how, in any case, they would have been had there been no war. Full weight will have to be given to all the negative influences. Where a country has suffered very serious direct losses (through, perhaps, invasion and occupation) the possibilities for beneficial change will be severely curtailed; as they will also be in a country subject to very strict autocratic control.

[II] THE DEBATE

Early critics of the ideas I was developing were Henry Pelling and Angus Calder (both writing on Britain and the Second World War). [13] As new documents became available in the 1970s and 80s (particularly, of course, with respect to the Second World War) a new generation of historians began an intensive study of different aspects of the two wars, almost with one voice denouncing the idea that the wars had any noteworthy social consequences. In many cases, as it seemed to me, the meticulous work of these authors did actually expose certain specific consequences, while they, as authors, almost in the same breath denied this very thing (often employing the 'Certainly/undoubtedly . . . 'however/but' technique, whereby specific consequences *are* recognized, then somehow conjured away by the magic 'however' or 'but'). [14]

Why was there this very powerful wave of hostility to the thesis of war producing certain identifiable social consequences? Many of the younger writers were strongly feminist, or strongly socialist in sympathies. Since women still manifestly do not enjoy full equality with men, while anything like a true socialist society is still very far away, these writers reckoned it absurd to talk of war fostering change when, in fact, so little change had actually taken place. If change as between, say, 1914 and 1925, and between 1939 and 1950 is judged by the standards of the classless society or the feminist paradise, then indeed it will seem trivial. This wave of historians, in any case, tended to have a Marxist or Marxist-derived sense of the long-term imperatives said to govern social change: compared to such imperatives wars are untidy interruptions. Thus, any changes in women's employment were to be attributed to secular trends in economic organization and technological innovation, not to the needs of war. In addition, feminist and socialist historians had a special interest in the conscious actions of suffragists, suffragettes, the working-class movement, and labour activists. If women, or the working class, did make specific gains, these had to be credited to militant action by the workers or by the women themselves, not to the unguided processes of war. One might add that most of the newly released materials were of the traditional, political sort. Thus much attention focused on the attitudes of politicians and civil servants, rather than on forces generated within the broader society: since politicians and civil servants are, on the whole, a conservative lot this focus tended to yield a view of lack of change, while ignoring the manner in which politicians were often pressured against their own personal inclinations.

There is, in certain educational circles, a liking for the historical debate, or controversy, as an end in itself. One can write a whole book on the 'war and social change thesis', summarizing the views of those who are for, and those who are against; this is much easier than doing the serious research required to extend 'real' historical knowledge; easier still is to put together a collection of essays by alleged representatives of the different sides in the debate. In 1986 the American historian Harold L. Smith produced a collection of first-class research papers by many of the new wave of historians, all of which, he claimed, cast doubt upon there being any connection between war and lasting social change. In fact (as it seemed to me) the individual authors were so scrupulous in their presentation of the evidence that they often referred to specific instances which looked incredibly like the war's having had a clear effect on social change.[15] Taking up a monolithic position on one side of an alleged debate, irrespective of what the detailed evidence actually shows, is scarcely the best way of contributing to historical knowledge. Despite its stated intentions the Smith collection rather stimulates the reflection that most historians would agree that social change in the twentieth century has been the product of a number of forces, among which, in certain areas and in certain respects, war has been an important one. This, in effect, is exactly the conclusion of The Deluge.

Very genuine controversy, of course, continues over the relative weights to be given to the different possible factors, and in particular, naturally, the weight to be given to war. Much then turns on how one conceives the historian's tasks. History, in my view, is concerned with the real lives of real human beings, not just with generalizations about the long-term processes to which human societies are subject. Some writers are content to see what I conceive of as the rather important participation of under-privileged groups in the war effort simply as a demonstration of the enlistment of what Marx called 'the reserve army of the proletariat', being more preoccupied with showing that the capitalist system indeed works as Marx said it did, than in exploring the human implications for those involved in this participation. It does also sometimes seem to me that those who focus only on long-term processes lack the human perspective. Whether major educational reform takes place at a certain date, or twenty years later, will be of critical importance to a whole generation; similarly with reforms relating to the opportunities open to women. It simply isn't good enough to keep on repeating that all reforms and changes would, because of long-term forces, have happened anyway; there is a responsibility to explain why a particular development took place *when* it did, and in the *way* it did. The ultimate concern of the historian is not with what might have happened, or what would have happened, but with what actually did happen. As a matter of inescapable fact there were clusters of reform measures at the end of each war in all the European countries: this needs to be explained.

Lately, a sense of balance seems to have returned to the discussion. J. M. Winter has been a pioneer in using detailed studies of mortality and public health statistics to demonstrate a connection between the First World War and a general improve-ment in health and life expectancy in Britain.[16] The particular form of analysis I am setting out in this Introduction may not have been very widely adopted, but certainly the broad con-clusions arrived at in *The Deluge* (and also the later *Women at War, 1914–1918*), have been cited and endorsed. I note in particular Noel Whiteside's chapter, 'The British Population at War' in John Turner's collection, *Britain and the First World War* (1988), Alastair Reid's chapter 'The impact of the First World War on British workers' in R. Wall and J. Winter (eds), *The Upheaval of War* (1989) and J. M. Bourne in his splendidly comprehensive yet concise *Britain and the Great War 1914–1918* (1989). Two recent works seem unaware that there ever has been any sort of debate. About the only hint of an awareness of wider issues in

Trevor Wilson's *The Myriad Faces of War: Britain and the Great War 1914–1918* (1986), a volume of nearly 900 pages (and no bibliography), is his insistence that it is 'absurd' to call this war a 'total war', on the grounds, apparently, that women were not actually subject to compulsion; given the fact that masses of women *were* involved, and once involved usually subject to some form of control, this seems to me an absurd quibble. The dry monograph, *War, Law, and Labour: the Munitions' Acts, State Regulation, and the Unions, 1915–1921* (Oxford, 1987), by Gerry R. Rubin never looks outside its purely legalistic concerns, but does recognize that the Munitions' Acts, while obviously restrictive, could be manipulated to the advantage of the workers.[17]

[III] OTHER COUNTRIES

All that said, it has to be admitted that set upon the world's stage and compared, say, with Germany or Russia, Japan or China, Britain in the twentieth century must seem a country which has undergone remarkably little change in political or social structures. Partly, of course, this is because Britain was already in 1914 an advanced industrial country, with long-established and highly sophisticated forms of representative (though certainly not yet democratic) government; quite obviously, the less developed the country, the greater the potential scope for change. To some historians the crucial facet of the British experience in the twentieth century is her 'eclipse' as a great power: in such a perspective the effects of war may seem marginal (though they should not, I believe, be totally ignored).[18]

It is also true that, while I have referred to war as catastrophic and cataclysmic, Britain's experience of war in the twentieth century was far less cataclysmic than that of many other countries. An interesting discussion point arises here: should we argue that it is in the countries where war was most cataclysmic that most change will take place; or, on the contrary, should we argue that cataclysm simply means greater destruction and more negative effects, and that it is in Britain, with relatively liberal regimes in both wars, and no utterly catastrophic impact of war (no occupation, no tracts of utter devastation, no atomic bombs) that we should expect the more positive effects of war to work themselves out most fully? This certainly was the line taken by the German Marxist historian Gerd Hardach who, in his general study of the First World War, warned against taking the British example as characteristic of war's effects everywhere (which he saw as destructive, and tending to the consolidation of monopoly capitalism — Russia being the exception, and the Russian revolution being the only really important social consequence of the First World War). It is, I think, fairly easy to give a general answer: war did not bring to Britain the great upheavals in regime or social order experienced by some other countries; but, because less destructive, it allowed full scope for the other processes, particularly the participation effect, to bring about improvements in wages, living conditions, and so on. Specialist essays in the Winter and Wall collection show how overwhelmingly destructive the First World War was in such countries as Austria and Belgium, with positive consequences (for example the establishment of social democracy and welfare provisions in Austria), being outweighed by conditions of serious deprivation. Everywhere on mainland Europe at the end of the Second World War there were conditions of squalor and near-starvation, although, it has to be added, economic recovery got going very quickly. [19]

What of the countries which remained neutral in either, or both, wars? Sweden, for instance, is widely recognized as perhaps the most advanced social democracy in the world; doesn't her example invalidate all arguments about change being brought by war? To this very important and relevant question, I would give two responses. The first is that it was not really possible for a neutral country in Sweden's geographical location to be unaffected by the war raging nearby: for example, her steel industry enjoyed a boom, while at the same time the country as a whole endured a blockade more complete than that of any other country save Germany. The second is that the war experience changed values and standards throughout Europe; Sweden could not remain isolated from these. The new standards can be seen in the Treaty of Versailles, which though fundamentally concerned with redrawing the map of Europe, also laid down basic labour standards and basic democratic rights, above all for women. It is true that neither France nor Italy at this stage granted votes to

women, but I think it can fairly be said that in basic reforms
Sweden rather followed other countries than led them; universal
manhood suffrage and votes for women were not granted till
1921. It is highly relevant that the two countries which were
most insulated from both wars, Switzerland and Spain, were the
last in Europe to grant votes to women.

[IV] BRITAIN AND THE FIRST WORLD WAR

The book (written in the early 1960s, remember) which follows
this introductory essay expounds in some detail the experiences of
the British during the First World War, and the longer term
effects of that experience. Here, with the benefit of a further 25
years' reading and reflection, I am going to identify in schematic
fashion six areas of change in which the effects of the war can be
most clearly seen: the first expresses the most important negative
consequences, the other five indicate the kind of positive consequences war can have.

1. International and Economic Dislocation
The economic history of Britain in the interwar years has been
subject to much revision since *The Deluge* was originally published: attention has been drawn both to the areas where very real
economic growth took place, and to the genuine problems
governments faced as they responded with the deflationary
policies which have subsequently been so much criticized.[20]
What is beyond doubt is that large sections of the economy, for
large parts of the interwar period, were in recession. Many
long-term forces were at work; but the war had been the critical
period of disruption to basic British exports, when countries
which had formerly been customers for British goods turned to
developing their own industries instead; the industries on which
Britain concentrated (coal and heavy engineering) were ones
whose products faced greatly diminished demand after the war.
Everywhere newly emergent nations were endeavouring to foster
their own economic development behind customs barriers; America
withdrew into a baleful isolation. The old financial system had
been based on confidence, with London operating as an international financial centre on remarkably small holdings of gold.

That confidence was shattered by the war and London found it impossible to continue to operate in the old way. Socially the main implications of all this were high unemployment and the determination of employers to reduce wages.

At the personal level the destruction of life was tragic, but not really critical within the long-term trend of declining birth rates. Much was made at the time, and since, of the notion of a 'lost generation'. It can reasonably be argued that there was a shortage of dedicated middle-generation figures in the 30s; but probably more important was the more general sense of revulsion against war and old-style power politics. The survivors of the war were the men of the generation of Harold Macmillan, a leader of 'Middle Opinion' in the 1930s, Anthony Eden (one of the few actually to attain high government office before the next war), and Clement Attlee (already leader of the Labour party in the 1930s, but not, of course, Prime Minister till after the next war); Neville Chamberlain, like many others, was undoubtedly strongly affected by a tragic awareness of the loss of colleagues and friends in the war.

My fundamental general point is that the horrific destructive costs of war must always be the first to be considered; it is only when they have been taken into account that one may proceed to assess changes of a rather different sort.

2. Labour, 'Revolution', and Class

Before the war, the two important political parties were the Conservatives and the Liberals; the Labour party was really little more than an adjunct to the Liberal party. The British electoral system is not kind to third parties. If the Labour party in 1914 were ever to supplant the Liberals, it faced a long and daunting process. The war experience gravely weakened the Liberals, cruelly *testing* their unwillingness to adopt collectivist remedies in the national emergency, and their faith in traditional liberal values, while it greatly strengthened Labour, through the *partici-pation* of its leaders in the successful wartime coalition, and through the greater confidence and cohesion the working class as a whole derived from its *participation* in the war effort. This line of argument has been hotly contested by Dr Ross McKibbin, who has argued that any changes in the status of the Labour party were entirely due to the expansion of the franchise in 1918.[21] However, as I shall suggest in sub-sections three and four, it really does seem impossible to separate the expansion of the franchise from the processes of change instigated by war. The 1922 general election clearly established Labour's position as the second of the major political parties, and by the end of 1923 it was actually in a position to form a minority government. More critical, from the point of view of the lives of ordinary people, was the strong position that Labour developed on local authorities in urban areas. Of course, the origins and early development of the British Labour party lay well outside the war period: but war circumstances were critical to the precise way in which the party developed in the 1920s, more particularly since the manner in which the war *tested* older *laissez-faire* ideas gave appeal and credibility to Labour's socialist ones.

Dr Jay Winter has shown conclusively that standards of civilian health and nutrition rose significantly, and permanently, over the war period, thanks to high living standards due to labour's strengthened position in the market place and to the government's concern for maintaining civilian morale and cooperation through fair distribution of available foodstuffs.[22] At the end of the war most trade unions were able to ratify enhanced wage levels (which still left a margin above inflation) and to establish shorter working hours. The industrial conflicts of the 1920s were very largely fought over the attempts of employers to remove wartime gains. In fact, as price levels fell in the recession, workers in employment continued to be measurably better-off than they had been in pre-war times. The gigantic constraint was the existence of mass unemployment.

To historians strongly influenced by the conflict models of society established by the Marxist and the Weberian traditions, the complex, and often ambiguous, interaction between war and society has little significance compared with 'The Crisis Of Class Society' (the title of Chapter 5 of Harold Perkin's *The Rise of Professional Society*, 1989), said to have occurred in the period 1910–20. A number of books have been written explaining why the revolution which ought to have been brought to fruition by the extreme stresses of war did not in fact materialize: the usual suspects in this lamentable matter of history's failure to do its duty are unified national sentiment fostered by the war and the supreme skill and adaptability of the ruling class, the latter, according to one theory, sponsoring a corporatism which brought into collusion business, Labour leaders, and government.[23] In fact, there was no 'crisis' (Perkin scrupulously admits that almost all recent research demonstrates this): what the British response to the call to arms in 1914 shows is a remarkably unified society.[24] Where there can be general agreement is over the fact that the overall *shape* of the class structure was not greatly changed, though, as I suggest in *The Deluge*, and as has been substantiated by more recent writers, there were important changes *within* classes, and in *relationships* between classes.[25] The working class was more consolidated and coherent than ever before. General income levels for both the working class and lower sections of the middle class had risen; there were now more salaried workers. While there were many new sources of profit for industrial and financial entrepreneurs, the landed elements within the upper class had suffered from war's vicious potion of duty, death and death duty. The balance within the upper class was further swinging towards those whose wealth came from finance and industry (Stanley Baldwin is a good example, despite the rustic image which he sought to project); yet the landowners, still enjoying great prestige, consolidated their holdings and continued to diversify their portfolios.

3. Democracy and the Position of Women
It must be remembered that Britain in 1914 certainly was not a democracy, even in the purely political sense: the franchise was not based on any universalist principle, but on certain property or residential qualifications, with the result that two-fifths of all men, apart from all women, did not have the vote; some men had several votes.[26] In the last year of the First World War an act was passed giving all men over 21 the vote and recognizing the principle of female suffrage, though in fact confining it to women over 30 who fulfilled a small property qualification. Now it has been argued that regular extensions of the franchise were part of a firmly established long-term process (involving the Reform Acts of 1832, 1867 and 1884) whereby Britain took its own particular route towards the liberal parliamentary democracy to which all

industrialized societies approached. No doubt further reforms in the franchise would have come at some stage. However, if we look at the arguments which were actually advanced in the press and by politicians for bringing about this major change while the country was still engaged in a desperate war, we can see that, as far as men were concerned, three arguments, which in themselves demonstrate the interaction of the different processes touched off by war, were paramount: first of all, through the disruptions of war, men previously entitled to vote had, through the very action of serving their country, lost their residence qualification (twelve months of continuous occupation) and thus could no longer vote – for that reason alone the basis of the franchise required alteration; second, many men who had never previously had the vote, had, in the most horrific conditions, played a vital part in the war effort and thus, few could disagree, had fully earned the vote; and, thirdly, it was widely held that immediately the catastrophic experience of war, in which, for instance, old party allegiances had been broken, was over, an election to determine the country's future course must be held, and in this vital decision-making those who had participated in the nation's efforts must have a full say.[27]

With regard to the political enfranchisement of women the argument has been made that the movement for votes for women, supported by men as well as women, was already strong before the war and that on several occasions there had been majorities in parliament in favour of votes for women. On this basis, Dr Martin Pugh has argued that women now actually got less than what they would have done had there been no war. This seems to me a very difficult argument to sustain. While most feminist writers have preferred to stress the significance of the women's suffrage movement, they do usually recognize that women's participation in the war effort did play a part in changing the opinions of influential men who had hitherto been opposed to votes for women. In a recent book on *Feminism and Democracy*, Sandra Holton contradicts Pugh, and recognizes that the agreement by the women's suffrage leader, Mrs Fawcett, to the limitation of voting rights to women over 30 was a carefully worked out tactical move to appease those men (many in the Labour party) who feared women becoming a majority in the electorate. Doubtless, once more, women would have got the vote eventually, but they got it at this precise time, and in this particular way, first of all because of the need to change the franchise for men. Immediately it became clear that change was being contemplated, Mrs Fawcett's National Union of Women's Suffrage Societies, which had taken the initiative in encouraging women to seize the different types of employment opportunities offered by the war, now skilfully exploited the strengthened situation which this participation in the war effort had given them. Mrs Fawcett was entirely correct in believing her tactical concession to be a purely temporary one: without any fuss whatsoever, all women, on equal terms with men, got the vote in 1928. [28]

Generally, however, feminist writers have resisted the notion that the war experience brought anything in the way of longer-term economic and social freedoms for women. It is perfectly true that, despite the substantial expansion in women's employment during the war, by the early 1920s the situation was much as it had been before the war. For myself, I believe that the permanent gains women made in certain of the higher professions from which they had previously been excluded (for example law and accountancy) were of critical importance, but it must be accepted that for the vast mass of women there was no immediate and substantial change. [29] There is evidence that within marriage, and within traditional occupations such as domestic service, women's attitudes and aspirations had changed in the direction of increased self-confidence and willingness to stand up for themselves: I believe this to be important (and some feminists have agreed with me), but it is a point easily missed if one sticks within the confines of traditional political sources. What we have to do is to consider the way in which the different aspects of the war's interaction with society created a general mood critical of old authorities and conventions and favourable to new freedoms for young people in general, as well as for young women. Much nonsense used to be talked about an alleged Victorian belief that respectable women had no sexual desires; nevertheless both the double standard in sexual morality, and the crippling constraints of what was considered proper decorum were very much realities. How much changed in the upheavals and dislocations of war must be a matter for some debate (Penny Summerfield and Gail Braybon have recently made some sensible comments on this[30]) due to the intractability of the source material: *The Deluge* contains some of the evidence for change.

Whatever weight one puts on such developments the basic framework of the traditional family certainly had not changed.

4. Collectivism and Social Reform

Given the suppression of initiative and discouragement of small business by British governments after 1945, 'collectivism' can scarcely be represented as synonymous with desirable progress; but it must be remembered that many aspects of state inter-ference which even a Thatcherite polity takes for granted were scarcely dreamt of in Edwardian Britain. Central to the analysis presented in *The Deluge* is the notion that there was an expansion in the powers of the state and in a willingness to use these powers on behalf not just of the ruling minority, but of the people as a whole, the people who had carried the burdens of the war effort. It has rightly been pointed out that most of the new powers assumed by the state were dismantled at the end of the war. An important collection of specialist essays edited by Kathleen Burke has shown how economic innovations were invariably responses to specific wartime problems and the editor herself has shown that the leading practitioner of increased control was the Treasury itself: a strengthened Treasury, paradoxically, meant restraint upon the power of individual departments to spend money on progressive social reform.[31] Still, one simply cannot ignore the list of major acts passed in the period 1918 to 1920: whatever arguments may be advanced about continuity with pre-war initiatives on social reform it simply was not usual for so many measures to be concentrated into such a short space of time. The *timing* clearly owed much to the processes I have discussed, the desire, to repair the disruptions of war to reward participation in the war effort, and to acknowledge the widespread sense that so cataclysmic a war must be succeeded by a better world. The forces released by war ensured that the legislation was of a different character from anything contemplated before the war – the Housing Act, for example, for the first time brought in central government subsidies, the new unemployment insurance system was comprehensive in a way in which the pre-war one, limited to a few specified trades, was not. The Maternity and Child Welfare Act may have reinforced the traditional role of women but at least, through local authority action, it did much to improve their lot within that role. Acts of parliament do not in themselves create paradise, and many of these ones were weakened as government economies began to take effect. To me, their significance lies in the ways in which they set new standards of expectation in social welfare (a point missed by those who have spoken of 'The Failure of Social Reform')[32]: as the Labour party grew in strength on local authorities it was often able to maintain welfare provision despite central government attempts at retrenchment.

In the world of science, collectivism manifested itself in the establishment of the Department of Scientific and Industrial Research, and the total reorganization of the Medical Research Committee (set up by the 1911 National Insurance Act) as the Medical Research Council. In *The Deluge* I note some of the scientific and technological developments fostered by the test of war. Recently Guy Hartcup has published *The War of Invention*, confessing however that his title is snappier than it is accurate: there was precious little invention, but instead 'the extension of the boundaries of science for specific applications'.[33]

5. High and Popular Culture, Customs and Behaviour, Mentalities
The major movement in the arts in the twentieth century is that of 'modernism' which, quite indisputably, was well established long before the First World War. What can be said with equal assurance is that the trauma (i.e. *psychological* shock) of war gave a new currency and relevance to non-representational, introverted, and sometimes cacophonous and irrational modes: the language of modernism became acceptable where previously it had been rejected. The self-confidence and faith in progress of intellectuals, never as monolithic as textbook accounts suggest, was cracking before 1914: but the great disaster, the ultimate in the mockery of man's pretentions to civilization, hastened the plunge into doubt and isolation; in a famous book Paul Fussell has suggested that with the war, the ironic became the dominant mode in English literature.[34] We must be careful, however, not

to confuse the intellectual and the poet with the ordinary British soldier. Careful recent research has brought out that the Tommie was more phlegmatic than his sensitive social superiors.[35] Life for him had always been unfair, as belief in the inherent superiority of his nation and rightness of its causes had always been strong. For changes in popular culture we must look more to the rise of new media, mass-circulation newspapers, film, and after the war, radio broadcasting. All had their origins before the war, but film, a marvellous tool of propaganda, received a considerable boost during the war, spreading in popularity from the working to the middle classes; wartime exploitation of radio for communications purposes, and the development of a considerable capacity in radio components, had their effects on the development of a considerable pressure for civilian broadcasting in the post-war years. Many lower working-class people before the war had not been at all religious: ordinary people as a whole shared in the general sense of disenchantment with organized religion which was a natural response to the slaughter of war, and the seeming complicity of the churches in it. In its scale and destructiveness the First World War was very much a product of industrialized mass society; but in itself it marked an important stage towards a developed mass society with its characteristic nationwide, increasingly homogenized, leisure and cultural pursuits.

[V] BRITAIN AND THE SECOND WORLD WAR

This time I identify seven areas of change: two bring together the major negative effects, the other five serve to highlight some of the more positive effects.

1. World Position and Economic Plight

Britain's undignified pre-war posture in face of Nazi aggression has been explained by the weakening, in the previous war, of her position as a world power.[36] Yet if, in the 1930s, a 'troubled giant', she was still a 'giant', in the sense of being a worldwide, colonial power, one of several 'great powers'. However, there was already a strong element of, as it were, artificiality in this. Waging a second world war subjected the already stretched framework to the final *test*, driving home geopolitical realities;

overseas assets, and export-producing resources, had to be thrown into the bonfire of war; dire straits for Britain was opportunity for colonial peoples to assert themselves, to *participate* in the manner which offered most gains for themselves. By the end of the war many colonial peoples were well on their way to freedom; Britain no longer had the resources to claw them back. Politicians recognized the serious economic problem, but fooled themselves that Britain was still a great power with an empire. Corelli Barnett has mounted a withering attack on arguments that the Second World War did force Britain to make some salutary changes in economic structures and industrial practices, arguing that the war simply exposed, and hastened, Britain's dependency on American technology. Certainly, in watching the famous Second World War film, *Millions Like Us*, one cannot help noticing that the machine tools in the factory, whose women workers are the focus of the film, are all labelled 'Cincinnati', but Barnett almost certainly overstates his case; the distinguished economic historian, Sidney Pollard, has persuasively argued that, within the general context of destruction and economic loss (which after all affected the mainland European countries in greater degree) Britain did have many assets in 1945, particularly in the form of technologies developed during the war.[37]

However, the main point I want to make here is that whatever might be done with respect to improving life for ordinary Britons would be circumscribed by the very heavy material losses occasioned through waging war.

2. Complacency

Myth, in one of several usages of that word, means a version of past events which has some foundation in fact, but which alters, or exaggerates, circumstances in order to favour a particular country or group. Britain had fought alone after the fall of France; although the aerial bombing suffered by many British cities was less devastating than what eventually happened in other countries, it was at the time almost unprecedented, and no one knew if, and when, it would end. The myths, then, which sustained British society in the post-war years were of having 'fought alone' and having 'won the war'; that, as *The Economist* put it, 'in moral terms we are creditors'.[38] Britain had faced the test of war, and her institutions and ways of doing things had responded magnificently to the challenge, so that society was organized and controlled to a degree exceeded only by the Soviet Union: the wartime system worked, why make further changes? At the same time, the sense that, the war won, there must be major changes in social conditions and social provision was a much more confident, a much more informed one, and appeared much earlier than the analogous sentiment in the previous war.[39] While in mainland European countries, devastated by war, expectations were lower, so that resources could be withheld from wages and welfare in order to invest in modern infrastructures, all parties in Britain were committed to immediate social improvements. The incoming Labour government had many achievements, but put too much faith in a superficial notion of 'planning' without really addressing the problems of an outdated infrastructure. In short, complacency, over-reliance on mythic achievement, formed an important component of the war's negative legacy.

3. Material Conditions

Rationing and austerity were inescapable features of post-war life; yet in the wider view, the single most salient feature of life after 1945 is an upward shift in the disposable income available to the vast majority of families, based on the maintenance (this is the fundamental contrast with pre-war years) of high levels of employment. Deliberate government policies may have played a relatively small part here. It was the war itself, as an international economic phenomenon, destroying capital and creating unsatisfied needs, which brought about the high levels of demand upon which full employment was based; in addition, the international community was determined to avoid the nationalistic excesses which in the aftermath of Versailles had contributed to the interwar depression.[40] Penny Summerfield has shown in detail how many families made no gains, or actually 'suffered losses, *during* the war:[41] but longer term calculations have to take into account the global figures for real wages after the war, which indisputably moved up: soldiers' families may well have been extremely hard-pressed during the war, but the soldiers returned to a buoyant full-employment society. Dr Paul Addison has suggested that the period affected by war-inspired change was a short one.[42] I do not agree with this judgement: I believe that new levels of expectation were established in the war which could never be gone back upon.

4. The Welfare State

The term 'welfare state' should not, in the apocalyptic manner of certain social scientists, be taken as describing a whole society, an analogue say of 'totalitarian state', but as connoting the totality of schemes and services through which the central government, together with the local authorities, assumes a major responsibility for dealing with the different types of social need which beset individual citizens, principally: income or *'social' security, health, housing,* and *education.* Between 1944 and 1948 there was a cluster of legislation dealing with these matters. A number of questions arise. Was this burst of interrelated legislation simply the culmination of a trend going back at least to Lloyd George, or was there now a welfare state qualitatively different from what was available before the war? Two points stand out: the new legislation substituted the principle of universality (covering all classes) for the old one of selectivity (covering only the working class); and the national health service, above all, amounted to a total reform of the utterly inadequate pre-war provisions with, in particular, its damaging divide between 'voluntary' and 'local authority' hospitals. It may be noted, in any case, that 'trends' do not produce legislation: that requires political will. Did this will come from wartime changes affecting all shades of opinion, or was it specifically due to the Labour election victory in 1945?

The answers, once again, illustrate the complex, interconnecting effects of war. In the 1930s Labour policies on welfare had been extremely hesitant; it was only in the war period that the party developed a strong and coherent programme.[43] The trade unions, feeling their new power, had taken the lead in pressing for reform of social insurance; hence the famous 1942 Beveridge Report on *Social Insurance and Allied Services.* At the same time there was, across the political spectrum, a shift towards the left, with a widespread acceptance of the welfare policies implied in this Report.[44] To cope with the expected high level of civilian casualties, an Emergency Hospital Scheme had already been established by the government; this could readily form the basis of a unified national hospital service. Whatever party had won the 1945 election, there would have been some form of welfare state, though aspects of the national health service were hotly contested. But the very Labour victory itself was integrally related to the circumstances of the war. As matters had stood in 1939 Labour looked very unlike winning any forthcoming general election: but from its *participation* in the wartime coalition it gained prestige, while ordinary members of the working class themselves gained in determination and confidence, voting Labour in greater numbers than ever before; meantime sufficient numbers of middle-class people were affected by the leftward shift to ensure Labour a clear victory.[45]

5. Equality and Class
It could be argued that Britain's rather carefully delineated class structure had helped to provide unity in time of war. The main framework remained unchanged after the war. However, the working class as a whole did now have a security and standard of living it did not have in the pre-war years, and attitudes towards it were much less authoritarian and patronising. Incomes within the middle class were compressed, with the old upper middle class coming off worst. The upper class remained remarkably unchanged, though individuals within it were now happy to move into jobs in less-traditional areas, such as advertising and mass communications generally.[46]

6. High and Popular Culture
The composer Benjamin Britten was not alone in detecting a 'cultural renaissance' in the middle years of the war. The disruptions of the blitz dispersed both performers and cultural audiences around the country; at the same time there was a feeling that the whole heritage of western culture was one of the things being fought for. At the end of the war the Sadlers Wells Ballet became the Royal Ballet, and a Royal Opera was for the first time established; there were new provincial theatres; the wartime Council for the Encouragement of Music and the Arts became the Arts Council, dispensing state patronage. On cultural production itself the war experience had slightly paradoxical

effects: or to put it plainly, some creative artists reacted one way, some another, some first one way and then the other. The most profound immediate influence was that of reasserting a special Britishness, as in, say, neo-romantic painting, and the films of Ealing Studios. But, in the context of international exchange at the end of the war, there was also a new opening to international influences: specifically the 1946 Picasso–Matisse exhibition, and the arrival of American Abstract Expressionism profoundly affected certain British artists. In the realm of mass communications the most important single circumstance was the almost universal dependence of British families during the war upon radio: here, it seems to me, was the turning point in the arrival of the concept of news and entertainment in the home at the touch of a button – something that was eventually to develop into television and video.

7. Women

I have put this topic last simply because it is the one over which most controversy continues to rage.[47] Once again it can be fully recognized that the traditional family structure was not seriously disrupted by the war: indeed what many, many people longed to do, soldiers overseas, young women in the munitions factories, was to set up home and family as quickly as possible once the war ended. In the mildly patronising feature film of 1943, *The Gentle Sex*, young women in uniform are rather surprised to find that an older woman had served as an ambulance driver under fire in the First World War: her message is that the women of her generation did not fully exploit the opportunities opened by that war, but that the new generation would do so. Elsewhere I have used the Diary of Nella Last to present an example of an older woman who, both managing a family and playing a managerial role in the Women's Volunteer Service, discovers that she is in fact a much more competent person than her husband, and have suggested that increased self-confidence and self-assertion went outside the family circle.[48] A good example is the National Housewives League which, after the war, campaigned vigorously against Labour government restrictions which bore down heavily on ordinary housewives.[49] Both this line of argument and my other one that the key change in the war period was the growth in the employment of married women and indeed their acceptability as employees have been strongly contested by Harold L. Smith.[50] There is certainly much scope of differences of opinion over the interpretation of the evidence, but most recently Penny Summerfield, in a remarkably tenacious pursuit of what might be called 'the statistics within the statistics' has shown that there was a growth in the employment of married women, particularly on a part-time basis.[51] Now this, of course, marks no revolutionary break in the family structure, but it did bring much satisfaction and a certain amount of freedom to the women themselves.

Compared with the possibilities of a feminist, or of a socialist, or a classless, society, the various changes, as with those associated with the First World War, may seem rather minor. Yet it is surely beyond doubt that neither the interwar years, nor the years since 1945, can be understood without examining closely the complicated legacy left by both world wars.

[VI] WHERE NOW?

Research, therefore, will continue. What areas will the coming generation be investigating? Before offering some hesitant and tentative suggestions (confining myself to the First World War), I want to refer to two books which, though rather far from the immediate concerns of *The Deluge*, are of such breadth and daring, and demonstrate so vigorously the excitement and relevance of history, grandly conceived, that they each created a stir unusual for works of serious scholarship. Both offer large-scale generalizations and theoretical constructs, both lay a primary stress on the significance of economic factors; yet – is this a portent? – each mentions Marx only once, and then simply in passing.

The first book is the massive *The Rise and Fall of the Great Powers: Economic Change and Military Conflict from 1500 to 2000*, by the already celebrated and well-established historian Paul Kennedy. Kennedy's theme is 'the crucial influences of productive economic forces – both during the struggle itself, and during those periods *between* wars when differentiated growth rates caused the various Powers to become relatively stronger or weaker'; 'the differentiated pace of economic growth among the Great Powers ensures that they will go on, rising and falling, relative to each other'.[52] Human volition and human achievement are allowed for throughout so that 'it would be quite wrong . . . to claim that the outcome of the First World War was predetermined'; nevertheless 'the overall course of that conflict . . . correlates closely with the economic and industrial production and effectively mobilized forces available to each alliance during the different phrases of the struggle'.[53]

Avner Offer, author of the second book, had already received some renown for his highly original deployment of the concepts of property associated with Rousseau, Adam Smith, Bentham and Ricardo (*not* Marx) in his *Property and Politics 1870–1914: Landownership, Law, Ideology and Urban Development in England* (Cambridge, 1981). His *The First World War: An Agrarian Interpretation* is a model both in setting down what it is proper for a single historical work to seek to achieve, and for setting out how historical processes actually work. In analysing the origins and outcome of the struggle between Britain and Germany (other countries are excluded) his analysis is fundamentally economic – the keys are the search for, and the availability of, basic resources, and are, therefore, ultimately agrarian: Germany,

suffered badly from shortages of food. Likewise the Allies: their agrarian resources decided the war. So not only a war of steel and gold, but a war of bread and potatoes.[54]

But Offer also draws effectively upon social psychology: men do not simply make rational economic calculations. Our mental equipment is imperfect – hence the concept Offer employs of 'bounded rationality'. Too often politicians (and others) are prone to (highly fallible) 'intuitive reasoning'. Too often, also, the motivation is not rational advantage, but 'approbation'. These are 'concepts, not a vigorous theory. They can help us to form a realistic conception of how people actually perceived and pursued their interests.'[55] Offer makes no totalizing claims for his thesis: 'this book does not exclude other interpretations. It explores a dimension, a decisive one, which has not received the attention it deserves.'[56]

The structure of the book – into four parts – is original, and places the unfolding of argument well above chronology. The first part deals with the role of food shortages in Germany's defeat. Part two goes back into the nineteenth century to show the way in which Britain ceased to be a food-producing nation, instead developing a vital 'Agrarian Bond' with the United States, Canada and Australia. The third and fourth parts deal with the origins of the war: Britain, Offer argues, developing a strategy which looked to supply from the Atlantic, while imposing blockade on Germany; on 'The Other Side of the North Sea' German strategists planned a quick war to beat the likely blockade and, once involved in a slow war, resorted to 'A Second Decision for War' – the U-Boat Campaign.

The ordinary PhD researcher will not be thinking in such wide-ranging terms, yet I do feel that initiatives towards comparative study must be accelerated. By, for example, examining movements during the war in real incomes in three industrial towns, one in Britain, one in Germany, and one within a designated 'military zone' in Italy, my contention about the participation effect and the way in which it is circumscribed in dictatorial regimes could be tested. Or social welfare developments in two or three countries could be examined in the light of Kennedy's stress on 'productive economic forces' or of Offer's on primary needs: do we here have reliable predictors of differential rates of social change in the war period, or does war itself bring in other factors as well?

It does seem to be pretty clear that those serving under army discipline are less likely to make direct gains than those working in the relatively more relaxed conditions of the home front: but how exactly, in this respect, do returning soldiers integrate with (a changed) civilian society? Such critics of my work as Ross McKibben have made much of the lack of evidence for change in such important indicators as population statistics. Detailed study of rural villages is required if the thesis about the disruption of traditional life is to be firmly underpinned (or refuted!) There is also a discrepancy between popular accounts and popular memory of the war as some kind of 'watershed', and the more cautious interpretations (particularly with regard to the role and status of women) which historians have been producing in the last twenty years. Women's studies is perhaps now an overcrowded area; nonetheless the sort of work Penny Summerfield has been doing on the Second World War (assessing the accounts given by women themselves) could be applied to the First World War and all sectors of the population: can 'the historians' and 'the people' *both* be right?

Excellent work on the British working class has been done by such historians as Alastair Reid and Bernard Waites: but what was *really* happening to the upper sections of society? The notion of 'class crisis' in the period 1910–20 has become increasingly hard to sustain: but there may still be value in studying labour relations in two or three industrial areas before, and then right through, the war. Is there anything at all to be said in support of the thesis that 'corporatism' was the saviour of bourgeois society, threatened by the 'crisis of war', as argued (with respect to Germany, Italy and France) by Charles Maier in a famous book.[57] There is, I flatter myself, some logic in the notions of working-class, or female participation in war, but what about children? Can one talk of children's 'participation' in the war effort? – most children, some children? What exactly does happen to them? What, with respect to children, would constitute 'gains'?

I started those sketchy paragraphs with comparative history: the other stock catching the eye of the shrewd speculator is that of interdisciplinary studies. Good work on the popular culture of the trenches is already appearing: it may be that reorientation towards élite culture (whose relations with society, and with war, are much more complex and intangible) is now required. Were anti-German and anti-Austrian sentiments, particularly in music, simply of unregenerate jingoism, or did they perhaps conceal a deeper hostility to modernism? Can we relate cultural development to the extremes of war, or were artists and intellectuals reacting to a general 'catastrophe of the twentieth century' of which the First World War was merely a specific incident? Is it true that while the war influenced particular artists and particular works, it had no significant effect on broader cultural trends? There is still, I believe, much more to be discovered about the cross-relationships between science, technology, society, and war (though I flatter myself that *The Deluge* makes not a bad start).

It is well known that sometime between the opening of the Edwardian era and the 1920s great changes took place in clothing and the use of cosmetics. It is a fraught subject, perhaps now ready for truly dispassionate analysis. It is well known, also, that the Second World War was accompanied by the founding of a number of important new theatres. We are beginning to know something of 'the culture of the trenches'. We know, too, that where women were brought together (in munitions areas, or in the auxiliary services) amateur dramatics flourished. What exactly did the First World War do for British theatre?

To get themselves started, historians have to identify problems (though the nature of the problems will change as their work advances). They have to work out a strategy related to the sources they know to exist, the ones they hope to find, and to imaginative new ways of interrogating apparently irrelevant or intractable evidence. Despite the ill-informed jibes of the 'postmodernists', history is neither a mere 'set of narratives',[58] nor 'an endless poking in the potentially infinite archive of the "past"'.[59] History is a systematic subject which responds to the need human societies have for as truthful an account of their past as is possible.

NOTES TO INTRODUCTION

1. Simone de Beauvoir, *The Second Sex*, first English edn 1953, 1988 paperback, p. 155.

2. Robert Roberts, *The Classic Slum*, 1971, p. 174.

3. Helen Zenna Smith (Evadne Price), *Not So Quiet . . . Stepdaughters of War*, 1930, p. 165. The novel was intended as a female *All Quiet on the Western Front*.

4. A. L. Bowley and A. R. Burnett-Hurst, *Livelihood and Poverty*, 1915, p. 5; A. L. Bowley and M. Hogg, *Has Poverty Diminished?* 1925, p. 3.

5. Arthur Marwick, 'The Impact of the First World War on British Society', *Journal of Contemporary History*, III, January 1968, p. 57; referring to Stanislav Andreski, *Military Organisation and Society*, 1954, pp. 33–8.

6. Arthur Marwick, *Britain in the Century of Total War: War, Peace and Social Change, 1900–1967*, 1968, p. 12.

7. Ian F. W. Beckett, 'Total War', in Colin MacInnes and G. D. Sheffield (eds), *Warfare in the Twentieth Century: Theory and Practice*, 1987, p. 2. They are also discussed in friendly spirit by Alan S. Milward, *The Economic Effects of Two World Wars on Britain*, revised edn, 1984, p. 26, and John Stevenson, 'More light on World War One', *Historical Journal*, 33, no 1, 1990, pp. 195–210, a very helpful bibliographical essay. Stevenson notes that what I call the 'test'

effect has been referred to as the 'inspection effect' by some economic historians. For a more discursive application of the basic ideas to another country, see Neil A. Wynn, *From Progressivism to Prosperity: World War I and American Society*, 1986.

8. Reinard Sieder, 'Behind the lines: working-class life in wartime Vienna', in Richard Wall and Jay Winter (eds), *The Upheaval of War: Family, Work and Welfare in Europe 1914–1918*, 1988, pp. 109–38.

9. Norman Davies, *God's Playground: A History of Poland*, 1981, vol II, pp. 435–91.

10. A. J. Toynbee, *A Study of History*, 10 vols, 1934–54, esp. vol II, p. 260; See also Karl Marx, *The Eastern Question*, 1897: 'The redeeming feature of war is that it puts a nation to the test'.

11. David Englander and James Osborne, 'Jack, Tommy and Henry Dubb: the armed forces and the working class', *Historical Journal*, XXI, 3, 1978, pp. 593–621; Ian F. W. Beckett and Keith Simpson (eds), *A Nation in Arms: a Social Study of the British Army in the First World War*, 1985. And see the excellent *Trench Warfare 1914–1918: The Live and Let Live System*, 1980, by Tony Ashworth.

12. See: P. A. Sorokin, *Man and Society in Calamity*, 1943; G. W. Barker and D. D. Chapman (eds), *Man and Society in Disaster*, 1962; A. H. Barton, *Social Organisation under Stress*, 1963; and F. C. Ikle, *The Social Impact of Bomb Destruction*, 1958.

13. Angus Calder, *The People's War*, 1969; Henry Pelling, *Britain and the Second World War*, 1970.

14. A classic, but far from isolated instance, is John Macnicol, *The Movement for Family Allowances, 1918–1945*, 1980, pp. 178, 195–6.

15. Harold L. Smith (ed.), *War and Social Change: British Society in the Second World War*, 1986. John Macnicol (p. 24) says that wartime evacuation helped 'to construct an ideological climate favourable to welfare legislation'; Daniel Fox (p. 42) stresses how a national hospital system emerged from wartime needs; Rory MacLeod (p. 96) writes that the 'war changed national life and individual ways of living'; Deborah Thom (p. 109) recognizes that 'war focussed attention on schooling'.

16. J. M. Winter, *The Great War and the British People*, 1985.

17. John Turner (ed.), *Britain and the First World War*, 1988, pp. 2–3, 91, 97–8, 139; Wall and Winter, pp. 221–1; J. M. Bourne, *Britain and the Great War 1914–1918*, 1989, pp. 177, 191–2, 199, 225. Trevor Wilson, *The Myriad Faces of War: Britain and the Great War, 1914–1918*, 1986, pp. 669, 705; Gerry R. Rubin, *War, Law, and Labour: The Munitions Acts, State Regulation and the Unions, 1915–1921*, 1987, p. 262. A rather similar monograph, P. E. Dewey, *British Agriculture in the First World War*, 1989, does recognize that war brought a change in the structure of land-holding, to the advantage of farmers (pp. 236–7).

18. By his chosen periodization, Keith Robbins in his *Eclipse of a Great Power: Modern Britain 1870–1975*, 1983, deliberately plays down the influence of war.

19. Gerd Hardach, *The First World War, 1914–18*, 1977, paperback 1987,

pp. 293–4; Richard Sieder, in Winter and Wall, pp. 109–38, Peter Scholliers and Frank Dallemans, 'Standards of living and standards of health in wartime Belgium' in ibid, pp. 139–58; Alan S. Milward, *The Reconstruction of Western Europe 1945–51*, 1984.

20. J. A. Dowie, '1919–20 is in Need of Attention', *English Historical Review*, 1975; Derek Aldcroft, *The Interwar Economy: Britain 1919–1939*, 1970; S. Glyn and J. Oxborrow, *Interwar Britain: A Social and Economic History*, 1976.

21. Ross McKibbin, *The Evolution of the Labour Party 1910–1924*, 1974, p. 239. See also H. C. G. Mathew, R. McKibbin, J. A. Kay, 'The franchise factor in the rise of the Labour Party', *English Historical Review*, XCI, 1976.

22. J. M. Winter, *Great War*, pp. 103–244.

23. Harold Perkin, *The Rise of Professional Society: England Since 1880*, 1989; Keith Middlemass, *Politics in Industrial Society*, 1979.

24. The point has most recently been made in Peter Simkins, *Kitchener's Army: The Raising of the New Armies, 1914–1916*, 1988.

25. See especially, Bernard Waites, *A Class Society at War: England 1914–1918*, 1987; see also Julia Bush, *Behind The Lines: East London Labour 1914–1919*, 1982.

26. Neal Blewett, *The Peers, the Parties and the People: the general election of 1910*, 1972, pp. 357–64.

27. See David H. Close, 'The Collapse of Resistance to Democracy: Conservatives, Adult Suffrage, and Second Chamber Reform, 1911–1928', *Historical Journal*, XX, 4, 1977.

28. Martin D. Pugh, *Electoral Reform in War and Peace, 1906–1918*, 1978; David Morgan, *Suffragists and Liberals*, 1975; Sandra Stanley Holton, *Feminism and Democracy: Woman's Suffrage and Reform Politics in Britain, 1900–1918*, 1986.

29. Gail Braybon, *Women Workers in the First World War*, 1981; Arthur Marwick, *Women at War 1914–1918*, 1977. See also Jenny Gould, 'Women's Military Services in First World War Britain' in *Behind the Lines: Gender and the Two World Wars*, 1987, ed. M. R. Higonnet, Jane Jenson, Sonya Michel and M. C. Weitz, a variable collection with a pretentious introductory section.

30. Gail Braybon and Penny Summerfield, *Out of the Cage: women's experiences in two world wars*, 1987, pp. 107–13; 205–18.

31. Kathleen Burke (ed.), *War and the State: the Transformation of British Government, 1914–1919*, 1984.

32. Philip Abrams, 'The Failure of Social Reform 1918–1920,' *Past and Present*, no. 24, April 1963.

33. Guy Hartcup, *The War of Invention: Scientific Developments, 1914–1918*, 1988, p. 189.

34. Paul Fussell, *The Great War and Modern Memory*, 1975, esp. p. 35. More generally, see Modris Eksteins, *Rites of Spring: The Great War and the Birth of the Modern Age*, 1989. On related matters, see Stuart Wallace, *War and the Image of Germany: British Academics 1914–1918, 1984*; and Peter Parker, *The Old Lie: The Great War and the Public School Ethos*, 1987. Useful recent

books are: Samuel Hynes, *A War Imagined: the First World War and English Culture*, 1990; Dominic Hibberd, *Context and Commentary: The First World War*, 1990; John Onions, *English Fiction and Drama of the Great War 1916–39*, 1990; Brian Murdoch, *Fighting Songs and Warring Words: Popular Lyrics of two World Wars*, 1990; Claire M. Tylee, *The Great War and Women's Consciousness: Images of Militarism and Womanhood in Women's Writings, 1914–64*, 1990.

35. Bourne, pp. 225–7; John Fuller, *Popular Culture and Group Morale in the British Army*, 1991.

36. F. S. Northedge, *The Troubled Giant: Britain Among the Great Powers 1916–1939*, 1966.

37. Correlli Barnett, *The Audit of War: The Illusion and Reality of Britain as a Great Nation*, 1986; Sidney Pollard, *The Waning of the British Economy*, 1976.

38. *Economist*, 8 December 1945.

39. Arthur Marwick, *The Home Front: The British and the Second World War*, 1976.

40. Alan S. Milward, *The Reconstruction of Western Europe 1945–51*, 1984, esp. p. 464. Another important book by Milward is *War, Economy and Society 1939–1945*, 1977.

41. Penny Summerfield, 'The "leveling of class" ', in Smith, pp. 179–207.

42. Paul Addison, *Now the War is Over*, 1985, pp. 197–206.

43. Arthur Marwick, 'The Labour Party and the Welfare State in Britain 1900–1948', *American Historical Review*, LXXIII, December 1967.

44. Paul Addison, *The Road to 1945: British Politics and the Second World War*, 1975.

45. Marwick, *Home Front*, pp. 116–69.

46. I have provided fuller accounts in *Class: Image and Reality in Britain, France and the USA Since 1930*, 1980, chap. 11, and *British Society Since 1945*, 1982, chap. 2.

47. The new, 1988, edition of *Women Workers in the Second World War*, 1984, by Penny Summerfield suggests a softening of attitudes.

48. Arthur Marwick, *Britain in Our Century*, 1984, pp. 121–2; R. Broad and S. Fleming (eds) *Nella Last's War: a mother's diary*, 1981.

49. Addison, *Now the War*, pp. 41–4, 205.

50. Smith, 'The effect of the war on the status of women' in Smith, pp. 211, 218–25.

51. Penny Summerfield, 'Women, War and Social Change: Women in Britain in World War II' in Arthur Marwick (ed.), *Total War and Social Change*, 1988, pp. 95–118.

52. Paul Kennedy, *The Rise and Fall of the Great Powers: Economic Change and Military Conflict from 1500 to 2000*, New York, 1988, p. 537.

53. Ibid, p. 274.

54. Avner Offer, *The First World War: An Agrarian Interpretation*, Oxford, 1989, p. 1.

55. Ibid, p. 20.

56. Ibid, p. 7.

57. Charles S. Maier, *Recasting Bourgeois Europe: Stabilization in France, Germany and Italy in the Decade after World War I*, Princetown, 1975.

58. See David Harvey, *The Condition of Postmodernity: An Enquiry into the Origins of Cultural Change*, Oxford, 1989, esp. p. 9.

59. Paul Q. Hirst, *Marxism and Historical Writing*, 1985, p. ix.

Preface

TWO YEARS ago I published a small book called *The Explosion of British Society, 1914–62*. 'What explosion can he possibly have in mind?' a Cambridge historian demanded querulously. An Edinburgh scientist perceptively pointed out to me that what I really meant was *The Explosion of Society as it Affected Britain*, his point being that the main social and technological changes which I sought to examine were common to all Western industrialized countries. That there have been mighty and spectacular changes since 1914 must be apparent to all save the inhabitants of those antiquated institutions which still persist in believing that history came to a halt in that year, if not actually with the death of our late Queen Victoria. Yet aside from the broad highway of change, the historian is concerned with the limited, the specific and the unique; he has at times a sacred duty to be parochial.

The present study narrows the focus. There are several excellent accounts of Britain in the years after 1918, but all of them seem to me to be weakened by the feeling one has of joining the feast after the first course is over. Here we content ourselves with the *hors d'œuvres*: sharing the lettuce of social upheaval, pecking at the olives of endless age, consuming the salami of welfare legislation slice by slice. It is a meal in itself; but it is also prescribed eating for what comes after.

Of course, when people talked of 'the Deluge', as I do in the title of this book, they were thinking of the shattering effects of the war on an existing, and on the whole happy, state of life. But in destroying the old, the war helped the rise of the new: out went gold sovereigns, chaperons, muffin men, and the divine right of private enterprise; in came State control, summer time, a new prosperity and a new self-confidence for families long submerged below the poverty line, and, in the aftermath, a biting scepticism and challenge to established authorities. The laments for the dead world of 1914 were essentially products of the sick world of 1921.

49

Britain in the nineteen-twenties, after the terrible bleeding of the war, had every right to be sick; but we, fifty years after, without denying the validity of the bitterness, or forgetting the futile horror which gave rise to it, are in a better position to assess the true value of the deeper social changes occasioned by the war.

The condition of Britain in the four years before 1914 was not really such a happy one – a whirlpool of industrial strife and suffragette agitation, of Ulstermen openly preparing for civil war in Ireland and last-ditch Tories misbehaving themselves in the House of Commons. Similar waves and eddies of violence afflicted other European countries. Indeed the war can be seen as an irresistible flooding-over of tensions too great to be contained in the existing social and world setting: philosophers and poets had glorified it in advance, futurist painters had elevated it to an aesthetic canon, even peoples had seemed eager for it. But the war also had more precise economic and political causes. From the point of view of British participation, four sets of circumstances are critical: the rivalries and conflicts in the Balkans between the several minor nations and the two major powers – Austria–Hungary and Russia – seemingly remote but productive of the immediate cause of the war; the growing awareness in Britain that her world economic position was steadily being challenged by Germany; the conviction that any German aggrandizement on the European continent would fatally upset the balance of power; and, fourthly, the manner in which pre-war diplomacy had resolved the manifold cross-conflicts and jealousies of many nations into the rigid and highly dangerous line-up of two armed camps. In the end, the decisions and the miscalculations that brought war as a definite fact were those of diplomatists and statesmen – with one qualification: behind the statesmen stood the general staffs and strategic planners; or rather, the military, believing that the modern technology of war had made speedy action and the perfect interlocking of alliances essential, had jumped in front of the statesmen. Once the first hesitant moves to war had been made, the military authorities ensured that there could be no turning back.

If we accept, as we must, that the war was partly the result of forces and tensions developing in early twentieth-century European society, including Britain, then this must certainly serve as a qualification upon any attempt to analyse the consequences of

the war for British society. But to make too much of this would
give an inexact quality of inevitability to the war. Although in this
study I shall largely be concerned with the processes of material
change, with social behaviour and attitudes, this is not a history
without heroes: the wider forces and the accidental collisions of
circumstance are there, but the responses are the responses of
individual men, sometimes wise, sometimes foolish, often un-
comprehending, but seldom completely blind. To study the
development of British society during the First World War and
to leave out Lloyd George would be as absurd as to claim that his
accession to power in December 1916 brought a revolutionary
change in domestic social policy, and as narrow as, at the other
extreme, the exclusion of Sir Thomas Beecham, who exploited
wartime conditions for the permanent enrichment of British music,
Arthur Burrows, the first man in Britain to foresee the possibilities
of wireless broadcasting, Holt Thomas, a pioneer of civil aviation,
John Wheatley, the brains behind 'Red Clydeside', E. M. H.
Lloyd, one of the civil servants who formulated the food policy
which took Britain safely through the war, or Lord Rhondda, an
architect of the Ministry of Health.

The first aim of this book is to describe what it was like to live
in Britain while the first total war in history was being waged.
The second, and major, aim is to examine the sequence and causation of the social changes which took place during that war,
indicating their long-term importance in the evolution of contemporary British society. The battles and bloodshed of the
military war have been discussed, are being discussed, and no
doubt ought to go on being discussed in library upon library of
books; here they are dealt with only as the massive and convoluted
frame round the picture which I wish to paint. Politics, in the conventional sense, cannot be left out altogether, but they are stressed
only at points of crisis when their relation to social trends is
clearly exposed. Ireland, where great and moving events took
place, has been the subject of many exciting monographs; it
figures here only when it cuts across the domestic social narrative.
In the main, the treatment is chronological, for, if history without
analysis is meaningless, without chronology it does not exist. The
domestic history of the war falls fairly readily into three parts:
the first eight months, after a brief spell of panic and excitement,

were dominated by the slogan 'Business as Usual'; thereafter, from the spring of 1915, right through 1915 and 1916, came the beginnings of the big changes associated with the war – new freedoms for women, new status for the labour movement, the first fumbling measures of State intervention; 1917 and 1918 were years of much more rigid State control, and, for the people as a whole, the time when serious shortages began to be felt for the first time.

On the whole Britain in the inter-war years was a better place to live in than it had been in 1914, which does not, of course, in any way imply that the war was 'a good thing'. At the same time there were many things wrong with Britain in the twenties and thirties, mass unemployment and an ineffectual foreign policy being the two most obvious examples. It is the final task of this book to explore and explain the paradoxical influences of the war on British society.

Many of the matters discussed in the course of the book, attitudes to sexual morality, to the arts, to patriotism even, are in their very nature tenuous and problematical. Some of the judgements may be deplored by historians, or rejected by sociologists and psychologists. Where there seem to me to be meaningful statistics, I have cited them; but I have relied to a great degree on written sources, the traditional material of the historian. There are many direct quotations in the text, for, although such quotations may show no more than what one single person thought at one single moment in time, that at least is concrete.

Acknowledgements are due to George Allen and Unwin Ltd for excerpts from F. H. Keeling, *Keeling Letters and Reminiscences*; to Ernest Benn Ltd for excerpts from R. D. Blumenfeld, *All In A Lifetime*; to the Bodley Head Ltd for excerpts from I. Clephane, *Towards Sex Freedom* and C. S. Peel, *How We Lived Then*; to Jonathan Cape Ltd for excerpts from Robert Graves, *Goodbye to All That*; to Cassell and Co. Ltd for excerpts from Arnold Bennett, *Journals*; to Chatto and Windus Ltd for excerpts from C. E. Montague, *Disenchantment* and Lytton Strachey, *Eminent Victorians* and to Mr Harold Owen and Chatto and Windus Ltd for a quotation from the *Collected Poems* of Wilfred Owen; to Constable and Co. Ltd for excerpts from C. à C. Repington, *The First World War*; to Eyre and Spottiswoode Ltd for excerpts from M. McDonagh,

In London During the Great War; to Faber and Faber Ltd for excerpts from E. L. Woodward, *Short Journey*, Paul Nash, *Outline, an Autobiography and other Writings*; to Faber and Faber Ltd and British Book Service (Canada) for excerpts from Lord Salter, *Memoirs of a Public Servant*; to Hodder and Stoughton Ltd for excerpts from C. L. Warr, *The Glimmering Landscape*; to The Hogarth Press Ltd for excerpts from Ray Strachey (ed.), *Our Freedom and Its Results*; to Hutchinson and Co. Ltd for excerpts from C. Addison, *Four and a Half Years*; to Hutchinson and Co. Ltd and G. P. Putnam's Sons, New York, for excerpts from *A Mingled Chime* by Sir Thomas Beecham; to Herbert Jenkins Ltd for excerpts from C. Addison, *Politics from Within*; to Macmillan and Co. Ltd for excerpts from S. Gwynn (ed.), *The Anvil of War*; to Methuen and Co. Ltd for excerpts from C. F. G. Masterman, *The Condition of England*; to Putnam and Co. Ltd and McClelland and Stewart Ltd for excerpts from R. Bruce Lockhart, *Your England*; to Sidgwick and Jackson Ltd for excerpts from M. G. Fawcett, *The Women's Victory and After*; to Weidenfeld and Nicholson Ltd for excerpts from Lucy Masterman, *C. F. G. Masterman*; and to the Controller of H. M. Stationery Office for excerpts from British Government Publications.

Among the many librarians in various libraries who have helped me in my researches I should like to mention Mr Ian Thomson of the University Library, Edinburgh, and I should like to thank my colleague, Mr Esmond Robertson, for his helpful criticisms of my text.

CHAPTER ONE

Early Days: August 1914 – March 1915

GEOGRAPHY IS an important influence on history. Britain, an island power, in 1914 possessed a vast overseas empire. Much of her wealth came from trade carried on freely with other parts of the world, both inside and outside the Empire. The island was small, but packed with coal and criss-crossed with good natural communications; geographical advantages, a relatively untroubled domestic history, and a certain native inventiveness, had combined to make her the first industrial power in the world: her lead was only now being overhauled, principally by Germany and the United States of America. For the maintenance of her happy condition *vis-à-vis* the rest of the world Britain relied on the might of her Navy; the Army was primarily thought of as a force for manning the outposts of the Empire.[1] Although R. B. Haldane, Secretary for War in the Liberal Government in power after 1905, assisted by Sir Douglas Haig, had carried out some valuable Army reforms, establishing a general staff, and preparing an expeditionary force ready for immediate continental service, the Regular Army in January 1914 numbered less than a quarter of a million men, scattered about the four corners of the globe. There was an Army reserve of about 150,000, a special reserve of 63,000 and a Territorial force of 63,000. Expenditure on the Army ran at less than £29 millions a year, comparing with £51½ millions on the Navy.

Here was one feature which marked Britain off from the European continent, familiar with vast armies and the idea of compulsory military service. In most other respects, Britain shared in a common West European tradition of a franchise fairly widely diffused and a representative assembly with some influence at least on the executive government of the State. But while continental countries could see that interference by the State in the activities of society might well be in the best interests of the

55

members of society, in Britain there was a stronger individualism, a stronger resistance to too much action by the State. Since 1906 the pace of social reform had been accelerating, but the Liberal Government and its Chancellor of the Exchequer, David Lloyd George, full of Welsh radical fire though he was, did not go beyond the limits so brilliantly defined by the late Professor Tawney:

Minimum wage acts were added to factory acts; old age pensions and insurance to the poor law; the limitation of hours in mines to regulations as to safety; supertax to income-tax; but the Government, apart from the Post Office and a few naval and military establishments, did not own or administer business undertakings, did not concern itself with the organization of industry or the marketing of its products, did not attempt directly to influence the course of trade, and rarely intervened, except as a borrower, in the money or capital markets. Thus, while barriers were erected against the downward thrust of economic pressure, the upper ranges of business enjoyed almost complete freedom. It was assumed that the unrestricted initiative of profit-making entrepreneurs would secure the most effective utilization of national resources, and that the consumer would be protected against exploitation by competition.[2]

With Western Europe and North America, Britain shared in the growing benefits accruing from the scientific revolution of the seventeenth century and its application, since the late eighteenth century, to the problems of industry and society; but as a country which set greatest store by the individualist graces of politics, it accepted and exploited less readily the boons of science than did, say, Germany. The effervescent Liberal back-bencher, Sir Leo Chiozza Money, whose enthusiasm for German state-sponsored efficiency was rivalled only by his fears of her aggressive aggrandizement, lamented that

An ex-Prime Minister is not ashamed to state publicly that he is ignorant of science, and the majority of those who have received what is known as a 'liberal' education could not intelligently explain the ringing of an electric bell or the action of their own hearts. This deplorable neglect of science is sadly handicapping us as a nation in every department, and it is a notable fact that the majority of recent scientific discoveries have been made in other lands.[3]

Through her scientific ignorance, Britain was going a long way towards nullifying her geographical advantage: zinc concentrates and wolfram ores, produced in Australia, had to be smelted in Germany; Australian lead and the bulk of the Indian mica mines were controlled by German financial interests. The attempts made to remedy these deficiencies were modest ones. Opening the National Physical Laboratory in 1902, the Prince of Wales described it as 'almost the first instance of the State taking part in scientific research'. In the same year the Government took over the Imperial Institute, which sponsored some scientific research related to industry, and in 1907 the Imperial College of Science and Technology was founded. By 1914 the National Physical Laboratory was getting the distinctly un-mammoth grant of £7,000 per annum, with an additional grant for aeronautical research. A little-noticed subsection of the 1911 National Insurance Act made provision for a medical research fund, and it was out of this that, just before the war, the Medical Research Committee began to take shape.[4]

Great Britain, comprising England, Wales and Scotland, governed since 1707 by the same Parliament, was one island. Ireland was another. Together, in 1914, they formed the United Kingdom of Great Britain and Ireland, governed since 1800 by this same Parliament at Westminster. Britain was prosperous and heavily industrialized; Ireland, lacking the mineral bounty with which Britain was blessed, was poverty-stricken and, save for the Belfast area, almost entirely agrarian. Her population was in decline, and stood, in 1911, at just over four millions; the population of Britain, 40·8 millions, that is to say about ten million families, was still increasing, though the rate was less healthy-looking than it had been in the nineteenth century. Britain's two strongest commercial rivals, Germany and the United States, had populations of 64·9 millions and 91·7 millions respectively.

Forty million people crammed into a small island meant that Britain was markedly an urban country. The location of coal had determined the direction of the population flow provoked by the industrial developments of the eighteenth and nineteenth centuries: thus in Lancashire, Northumberland, Yorkshire, the Midlands, South Wales and the Scottish lowlands, big towns had erupted like boils, surrounded by an unsightly rash of smaller towns and villages. Birmingham, like a number of other towns, expanded its boundaries shortly after the 1911 Census, giving administrative recognition to the growing urban sprawl: it then comprised a total of 840,202 inhabitants. Glasgow had 784,496, Liverpool 746,421, Manchester 714,333, Leeds 445,550, Newcastle 266,603. In 1914 the basic industries associated with these areas – iron and steel, textiles and coal – were prospering, though in every case Britain's position was being strongly challenged. It was as futile to lament over this as it was to believe that by some magic incantation Britain could somehow freeze other countries at a level of development which left her supreme. None the less, there was a disquieting lack of flexibility and amenity to new ideas in British industry; and for a country which had called herself the workshop of the world the growing dependence of her export market on a primary raw material, coal, was ominous.

Only 21·9 per cent of the population of England and Wales lived in what the Census, somewhat inprecisely, termed 'rural districts', and since the depression of the 1870s farming had become a rather neglected craft. The slight revival of the Edwardian era could not stand comparison with the conscious German policy of creating farm out of forest, marsh and sand dune.[5] On the eve of the war Britain was dependent on imports for four-fifths of her wheat and 40 per cent of her meat.

The country's ballast, then, was in the north, southern towns like Bristol (population in 1911, 357,048) and Bath having lost much of their former importance. But there was one tremendous make-weight. Irrespective of all other population trends, London, since Roman times, had advanced steadily and far ahead of its nearest population rivals and it now mustered in what was officially termed the Greater London area 7¼ million inhabitants. London was the centre of the far-flung Empire, the seat of government, and the control point for business and the professions. As such it had already been invaded by the germs of one of the major afflictions of twentieth-century urban society, the special care of the London Traffic Branch of the Board of Trade, which reported of the year 1913:

Among the various phases of the London traffic problem, one most important feature is the daily movement of a very large section of the population from their residences within an area of 30 miles round London to places of business in Central London and back again. . . .

There can be no longer any doubt about the gradual withdrawal of a large amount of traffic of all sorts from the railways to the roads, owing to the development of the motor vehicle. The convenience of the mechanically propelled vehicle for passenger purposes very rapidly asserted itself, and today it accounts for fully 94 per cent of the passenger vehicles met with on the roads round London. . . . Street accidents are an unfortunate phase of the traffic problem and there is no hope that they can ever be entirely eliminated. . . .[6]

London was the geographical focal point for the élite of British society. That Edwardian and early Georgian Britain was a very rigid class society is abundantly clear from a wealth of contemporary material, even if the same material does not furnish evidence for any very precise analysis of the class structure. In his highly perceptive *The Condition of England*, published in 1909, C. F. G. Masterman distinguished three major classes, the 'conquerors', the 'suburbans', and the 'multitude', with a fourth depressed class, the submerged proletariat, whom he called the 'prisoners' tacked on to the underside of the 'multitude', or working class.[7] Leo Chiozza Money, concerned more with inequalities of wealth and income, limited himself to three classes, which he preferred to call rich, comfortable and poor, rather than upper, middle and lower.[8] There were forces at work which were blurring the more rigid and more complicated hierarchy which had obtained in mid-Victorian times: a rise in money incomes had brought classes and gradations within classes closer together; direct progressive taxation, which got steeper and steeper on higher incomes, had 'compressed the whole scale of disposable incomes'; and, most important, technological advance had brought to the less well-off material circumstances not in character far different from those of the better off.[9] The main consequence was not so much a mixing of classes as the creation of a greater homogeneity within the working class, a tendency assisted by the expansion of trade unionism among the unskilled workers. At the same time it was still true in 1914 that a skilled artisan earned double the wages of the unskilled labourer.

Yet within the same historical period the growth of a suburban white-collar lower-middle class, associated with the rise of large-scale industry and its ancillary developments in insurance and accountancy, had added a new subtlety to the class structure. It is almost entirely from this class that Masterman drew his picture of the 'suburbans', who lead

> a life of Security; a life of Sedentary occupation; a life of Respectability; and these three qualities give the key to its special characteristics. Its male population is engaged in all its working hours in small, crowded offices, under artificial light, doing immense sums, adding up other men's accounts, writing other men's letters. It is sucked into the City at daybreak, and scattered again as darkness falls. It finds itself towards evening in its own territory in the miles and miles of little red houses in little silent streets, in number defying imagination. Each boasts its pleasant drawing-room, its bow-window, its little front garden, its high-sounding title – 'Acacia Villa' or 'Camperdown Lodge' – attesting unconquered human aspiration.[10]

'The rich,' says Masterman, 'despise the Working People; the Middle Classes fear them.'[11]

The major social fact of the day remained the great and accepted gulf which existed between the working class and the whole of the rest of society, a gulf very apparent in the attitudes of the Schlegel sisters towards the self-improving artisan, Leonard Bast, portrayed by E. M. Forster in *Howards End*. So certain are people of the existence of this separate working class that it is rather difficult to find a definition of it, the implication being that to meet a member of the working class was to recognize him at once, by his smell if not by his garb. Bowley, in introducing the valuable surveys he conducted in 1913, did make the attempt:

> The definition of 'the working class' cannot be exactly drawn on preconceived lines. Of course, in the great majority of cases included in our Tables the principal occupant of the house was working for weekly or hourly wages, and in the great majority of houses in our samples treated as non-working class the occupier was professional, commercial or living on income from property. The necessity for less obvious discrimination arose in houses rented at from 7/6 to 12/- a week. If the principal occupants were clerks, travellers, teachers, shop managers or employers in a small way they were excluded from the working class Tables. Shop assistants were included in the working class if working for butchers or grocers. The great majority of shop assistants are, of course, not householders but living with their parents. The working class householders include among their supplementary

earners a not very large number of persons who would, if principal occupants, have been excluded.[12]

In effect he is really doing little more than elaborating upon what might be called definition by instinct; an instinct at its most sensitive in its appreciation of the special proletarian attributes of butchers and grocers. In the last sentence Bowley reveals, incidentally, that there is little in the way of social mobility out of the working class.

There is one administrative line of division in society which is worth a little attention, the income-tax line. It is a striking fact that on the eve of the war there were less than 1¼ million income-tax payers, that is less than seven per cent of the occupied population. Payment of income-tax is scarcely a highly sought-after social privilege, yet it is a measure of a man's respectability as a financial pillar of society, and an indication of his positive stake in the community. The figure of £160 per annum, the lowest upon which income-tax was assessed, is too high to be taken as the upper boundary of the working class, but it is a useful pivotal point to bear in mind. The actual size of the pre-war working class can only be estimated very roughly, though it is at once evident that it is very large. The grand total of wage-earners, men, women, boys and girls, as revealed by the 1911 figures, was 15·6 millions, or three-quarters of the occupied population; this is the main core of the working class as understood by contemporaries. However, to this we should, almost certainly, add the 1·2 million men and women employed as small shopkeepers, hawkers, dressmakers, etc., whose earnings were not more than those of most wage-earners, and, less certainly, a proportion of the 1·2 million salaried men and women earning less than our pivotal £160 per annum;[13] following Leo Chiozza Money, we would call these last, at least, the lower-middle classes rather than part of the working class. Included in this debatable group we have the elementary school-teachers, almost all working-class in origin and outlook.

Moving into the middle class proper, we have 400,000 salaried men earning over £160 per annum[14] (the number of women in this elevated station was negligible), a professional group of 330,000 (this includes clergymen, doctors, lawyers, engineers, writers, artists, entertainers, law clerks, but not teachers, who go under the salaried classification), and a proportion of the 580,000 farmers (some of whom might more properly be accounted lower-middle, or even working-class owing to their lowly earnings). Finally, among the occupied classes there are 620,000 employers, ranging from the shopkeeper with one assistant, the small provincial businessman who is quite definitely middle-class, to the owner of a large national concern who might be regarded as belonging to the uppermost class in society, the London-based élite. Among the unoccupied in 1911, 60,000 stated that they had 'independent means'. Class lines at the top of the social scale are rather harder to define than at the bottom, unless one unjustifiably restricts the uppermost class to the old landed aristocracy. There is a self-evident difference in status between John Dewar, the Perth whisky manufacturer, elevated to the peerage as Lord Forteviot, and a small Lancashire businessman like Elijah Sandham, whose only political outlet was in the local organization of the Independent Labour Party.

The uppermost class, characterized by its wealth, status, and, above all, political power, was an amalgam of top business and professional men and the landed aristocracy, who still enjoyed a social and political primacy in town, and a feudal dominance in the countryside.[15] The way to the heights for the man not born with aristocratic connexions was through an apprenticeship in politics; the looser conventions of the Edwardian era had made great wealth itself a possible passport to high society, but not to high politics. Masterman and Money seem to have a large rather than a small group in mind for their uppermost class of 'conquerors' or 'rich'. Bowley in a more recent study[16] has given various random figures relevant to 1913–14 upon which a computation of the total upper class might be based – 13,850 people with incomes over £5,000, 47,000 with over £2,000, 75,000 private dwelling-houses with an annual value of over £150 per annum in London or £100 per annum in the provinces, 151,000 motor-cars on the roads. Or one could limit the upper class to that 2·5 per cent of the population which, according to Bowley, held two-thirds of the country's wealth.

Before attempting a complete proportional picture we must turn again to Bowley's 1913 survey: before giving his attention to his sample of 2,150 working-class households, Bowley creamed off 480, which he described as middle and upper class[17] – just over 20 per cent of the total. This accords fairly well with the occupational figures given above: very roughly, then, we could divide the country on the outbreak of war into 80 per cent working class, anything from 10 to 18 per cent middle class depending on definition, and the remainder upper class. However, we can see again where the really important divide lay, when we reflect that the average wage for the adult male industrial worker on the eve of war was about £75 per annum, whereas the average annual income of the salaried class was £340.[18] In terms of human relations the class divide was most clearly expressed in the enjoyment by every middle-class household of the amenity of one or more servants. It was most obviously buttressed by the educational system: though some secondary schools had as many as 25 per cent free places, few working-class children ever progressed beyond the rudimentary disciplines acquired in the free elementary schools. All in all, there were only 200,000 secondary-school pupils in 1914. Political equality was much more widely diffused than social or economic equality. Every adult male householder had the Parliamentary franchise – that is, out of about 25 million adults, 8 million had the vote. Attempts to rationalize local government – where some women did have the vote – had been made in the nineteenth century; but before the formation of borough councils and urban and rural district councils there had been a great proliferation of *ad hoc* bodies which gave the middle classes opportunities both for service and for a demonstration of their social status. Since 1902 the trend had been towards the elimination of these bodies, but the Boards of Guardians for administration of the Poor Law and a number of minor educational authorities still existed.

Poverty among the working class was the main theme of the various social surveys. Leo Chiozza Money put it dramatically when he pointed out that the five-million-odd people whose principal bread-winners (or caviare-winners, Money implied) were above the £160 line had half of the total national income at their disposal, whereas the remaining 39 million had to make do with the other half. Bowley, using the very bare definition of the 'poverty line' adopted by Seebohm Rowntree in 1901, found 16 per cent living in what he called 'primary' poverty, as distinct from the 'secondary' poverty brought about by unwise disposition of available income. His vigorous conclusion was that 'to raise the wages of the worst-paid workers is the most pressing social task with which the country is confronted today'.[19] Poor dieting gave many members of the lower orders yet another characteristic which distinguished them from the rest of society: their small stature. In 1914 the Board of Trade's 'average family' – reckoned as equivalent to 3·84 adult males in calorific requirements (4·57 units would actually have been a more realistic figure) – spent about 23s per week on food (the larger, and more usual, family, taken as including 1·2 supplementary earners, would spend about 25s), including 7 lb of meat at from around 6d to 8d a pound, 1 lb of bacon at 1s a pound, 6 four-lb loaves at 5d each, 9–10 pints of milk at 2d a pint, 10 eggs at 1d each or more, and less than 2 lb of butter and 1 lb of margarine.[20]

Bad housing came second to malnutrition as a social evil. Asquith, the Prime Minister, estimated the shortage of houses in 1913 at between 100,000 and 120,000. Bowley described conditions in the Northumberland mining village of Stanley as 'horrifying'. In Carmarthen, the Medical Officer of Health reported that there were houses 'that may aptly be described as squalid hovels and hot-beds of diseases'.[21] Industrial Scotland had an especially notorious reputation for bad housing; a Royal Commission on Housing in Scotland had already been appointed and its report was to explode with maximum effect bang in the middle of the war. The provision of working-class housing was, and was expected to be, very largely the job of private enterprise,[22] though there were in existence a number of modest local-authority schemes. The 1913 plans of the Invergordon burgh council reveal the limits expected of working-class domiciliary ambition, and take account of the existence of an upper- and lower-working class:

The houses, which are built of stone and slated, have gardens in front and behind, and are of two sizes. The larger house is rented at £19 per annum without taxes, and consists of parlour, kitchen, scullery with sink and tub, coal place, and press on the ground floor, with two bedrooms, bathroom and napery press on the upper floor. Only one block of four houses of this type is being built. Four blocks – each containing four houses – will be built of the smaller house. Each house on the

ground floor contains a kitchen, parlour, bedroom, scullery with sink
and tub, water-closet, press and coal place; each house on the upper
floor contains a kitchen, parlour, two small bedrooms, scullery with
sink and tub, water-closet and coal place. The rents for these houses are
£11.10 without taxes.[23]

Being in Scotland, these proposed rents are rather on the low
side for the United Kingdom as a whole; existing working-class
housing in England varied in rent from about 4s to 7s or more a
week.[24] Some large companies built housing estates for their
workers, the Coltness Iron Company building to the following
specification: 'one room, kitchen, scullery, water-closet and coal
cellar.' Only 19 per cent of working-class houses in York,
Rowntree had reported in 1901, had a separate water supply, let
alone baths, which, throughout the Edwardian period, were not
considered a necessary adjunct to working-class housing. A
miners' village in Dumfriesshire was so far in advance of its age
that the Local Government Board officials noted 'with pleasure . . .
the provision of baths in the later houses.'[25]

While housing was on the whole bad, there were elsewhere
continuous signs of improvement in social welfare and the
amenities of living. Out of the previous eight years of Liberal rule
had come free school meals and free school medical services, old
age pensions at five shillings a week, and the National Insurance
Act of 1911, of which the Health provisions, covering practically everyone (unless self-employed) earning under £250 per
annum, were the more important; the Unemployment Insurance
was much more restricted in scope and, in particular, applied only
to the 2¼ million members of the building, shipbuilding, and iron
and steel trades, the ones most affected by fluctuations in employment. Over the whole span since the turn of the century public health
had shown a steady improvement: to compare the figures for
1912 with the average experience in the last decade of the nineteenth century, infant mortality had declined 38 per cent, the
death-rate from measles 16 per cent, from scarlet fever 66 per cent,
from whooping cough 40 per cent, from diphtheria and croup 57
per cent, from enteric fever (a special affliction of those among
the poor who ate quantities of cheap and suspect shellfish) 75
per cent, from tuberculosis (all forms) 32 per cent, and from pul-
monary tuberculosis 25 per cent. Up to 1911 the decline in the

death-rate from puerperal diseases was 28 per cent, from pneumonia 15 per cent, and from bronchitis 45 per cent. The death-rate from all causes declined 27 per cent between 1891–1900 and 1912.[26] There were, none the less, in the latter year more than ninety deaths from starvation or privation due to destitution.[27]

It was not, however, the issues of social reform which disturbed British society in the years immediately prior to the outbreak of war: attention rather was concentrated on Ireland, where civil war between Ulstermen and Irish nationalists seemed imminent, on the repeated outbreak of serious strikes, often accompanied by bloodshed, and on the arson and disorder created by the suffragettes. Before the passing of the 1911 Parliament Act, which curbed the powers of the House of Lords, there had also been the unedifying last-ditch demonstrations of the peers. These issues had their separate roots, but they were covered by a common hot-house blossom of violence. British society in 1914, having enjoyed since 1898 a long golden cycle of rising prices which yet opened no escape from the insistent industrial challenge of foreign powers, which cosseted the wealthy in their lust after conspicuous consumption but left the real wages of the working classes at a standstill and bypassed the many pools of misery and depression, was demonstrating an unmistakable urge towards bellicosity. 'Beneath an outward prosperity so brilliant', there was, said Sir Michael Sadler, the famous Civil Servant and educationist, 'a deeply felt unrest of heart and mind'.[28] Britain, said another commentator, was in a condition of 'moral chaos' in which her 'inner state' was 'marked by profound unrest'.[29]

War had been talked of as a possibility all through the early years of the century. The most-used argument to confute suffragette claims had been that women were incapacitated from voting by their inability to participate in the military defence of the community, a curious line of thought when few men really expected that they would be called upon to handle a rifle, but symptomatic of the orientation towards the prospect of war. One of the most popular of all socialist agitators, Robert Blatchford, was an open and vigorous Germanophobe. That the British, given any sort of a lead, were a belligerent and jingoistic lot was apparent in music-hall songs,[30] in the doggerel cry for more battleships, 'We want eight and we won't wait', and in the hysteria which had accom-

panied the Boer War, when one particular outburst of patriotic
jubilation had brought a new word, 'Mafficking', into the language. There was a school of thought which saw a new war as a
necessity if the Empire were to prove that in the bloated years of
peace lasting from the Crimean War, and interrupted all too
briefly by the Boer War, it had not forfeited its honour. Idealists
like William Archer in his *The Great Analysis*, published in 1911,
reckoned that some 'great catastrophe' might be the prerequisite
of the establishment of a happier world order. To say that the
country as a whole consciously looked forward to war would be to
say too much; but there can be no doubt that there was abroad in
the land a spirit which made war, when it came, intensely welcome.

Turning our attention to the more articulate expressions of the
wish for war, we can distinguish two strands of thought, frequently in practice intertwined. What we might call the realists
felt that in a world in which 'war is a fact of life that cannot be
ignored',[31] and, more specifically, a world in which Germany was
challenging British commercial and naval supremacy at every turn,
a great trial of strength, regrettably or otherwise, was inevitable.
But there was also a strong strand of idealism, going no further in
many cases than the conventional calls of patriotism, love of
country, service of King, service of God, but stemming too from
young radicals and reformers, out of sorts with panting Georgian
Britain and anxious to take a new broom to Britain and to the
world. Both strands are to be found in a tract of 1906 advocating
national military service. Conscription, the writer says, is necessary 'if England is to be saved from the grave dangers which now
threaten her'. The writer of a separate introduction declares that
'there is a very real need for some new note, for some clarion call,
as it were, which shall inspire us to march forward under new
auspices to a new destiny.'[32] Moving forward to 1909, we hear
the older generation, in the person of Lord Rosebery, speaking
directly to the younger, as represented by the boys of Wellington
College, whose responses we can also detect:

The stress that patriotism will have to bear in days not distant, and
perhaps imminent, will be greater than has yet been known in the
history of this country (*Hear, hear*). There never was a time when men
were more needed to speak and act up to their faith (*Cheers*). I think
that men will have to be more universally armed in the future than they

are now (*Hear, hear*). . . . There are encroaching opinions which threaten patriotism, menace our love of country, and imply the relaxation, if not the destruction, of all the bonds which hold our empire together (*Hear, hear*). I would urge that so far as possible the study of patriotism should be promoted (*Cheers*).[33]

There is an even clearer response in a school prize-winning poem of 1911 or 1912 which ran:

> England, narrow seas divide thee
> From the foe.
> Guard the waves lest ill betide thee;
> Lest the foe that lurks beside thee
> Lay thee low.[34]

After 1910 and up till the summer of 1914 there was less open hostility towards Germany. Events then plumbed the currents flowing just below the surface. As *The Times* journalist, Michael McDonagh, wrote in his diary on 3 August:

Germany has always been disliked and distrusted for her bullying policy of sabre-rattling, the mailed fist, the goose-step, and the spiked helmet – symbols of violence and brute force. Indeed she has been suspected for years of looking forward to a war with Great Britain.[35]

The source for the patriotic poem quoted above is a disapproving pamphlet by Arthur Ponsonby, who is representative of another important section of articulate British opinion, those who, strongly aware of the militaristic currents of the age, were as strongly determined to resist them. From 1911 such Liberals as Ponsonby and C. P. Trevelyan were increasingly critical of a Liberal Government which appeared to be swinging the wheel of policy further and further round on collision course, and they had powerful support from two daily papers, the *Daily News* (edited by A. G. Gardiner) and the *Manchester Guardian* (edited by C. P. Scott), and from the weekly *Nation* (edited by H. W. Massingham). Pacific liberal opinion veered between a belief in internationalism and a simple desire for isolation. The City of London and many businessmen believed that war would be an unmitigated disaster.[36] They had the intellectual reinforcement of Norman Angell's *The Great Illusion* (1910), which sought to show that not even the victor could profit economically from war.

Apart from one or two individual, but highly popular, figures, the Labour movement was strongly pacifist in inclination. Formally it was committed to the resolution passed at the 1907 International Socialist Conference:

> If war threatens to break out it is the duty of the working class in the countries concerned and of their Parliamentary representatives, with the help of the International Socialist Bureau as a means of coordinating their action, to use every effort to prevent war by all the means which seem to them most appropriate, having regard to the sharpness of the class war and to the general political situation.
>
> Should war none the less break out, their duty is to intervene to bring it promptly to an end, and with all their energies to use the political and economic crisis created by the war to rouse the populace from its slumbers, and to hasten the fall of capitalist domination.[17]

The class-war emphasis of this resolution was rather out of keeping with the atmosphere of the British Labour movement, but the anti-war sentiments which are at its centre were reinforced in Britain by the strong moralistic flavour of the native movement. As we move to the actual outbreak of war we shall see that anti-war sentiment was momentarily almost as demonstrative as pro-war sentiment.

[II] EXCITEMENT AND EMERGENCY

Summarizing what has been said in the final part of the previous section, we might say of British opinion, both militant and pacifist, prior to August 1914, that war was widely expected as an eventual probability, but it was scarcely visualized at all as an immediate contingency. This explains why the breaking of war brought both a sense of long-sought release and an atmosphere of panic and untempered emergency. The immediate excitement and panic evaporated pretty quickly; the emergency legislation of the last days of peace and the first days of hostilities endured throughout the war, being constantly added to and consolidated.

Although the alarms and excursions of world politics from the assassination of the Archduke Franz Ferdinand on 28 June onwards were reported in the British newspapers, they scarcely succeeded in driving the impending civil war in Ireland from the main headlines. On the whole, Conservative newspapers showed a greater awareness of the implications of the international situation than did their Liberal counterparts.[38] But by the end of July it was common knowledge that Britain might be involved in a European war. On the last day of the month *The Times,* repository of worldly wisdom about national security and the balance of power, produced a very prosaic appeal for an immediate British declaration of war on Germany:

A German advance through Belgium to the north of France might enable Germany to acquire possession of Antwerp, Flushing, and even of Dunkirk and Calais, which might then become German naval bases against England. That is a contingency which no Englishman can look upon with indifference. But if it is merely a contingency why should England not wait until it is realized before acting or preparing to act? Because in these days of swift decision and swifter action, it would be too late for England to act with any degree of success after France had been defeated in the North. . . . Even should the German Navy remain inactive, the occupation of Belgium and northern France by German troops would strike a crushing blow at British security. We should then be obliged alone and without Allies to bear the burden of keeping up a Fleet superior to that of Germany and of an Army proportionately strong. The burden would be ruinous.[39]

The appreciation that the technology of modern war had put a premium on speed was shared by the military commands in the various European countries, and helps to explain the inexorable massing of the forces of doom once the first fatal hesitant steps had been made. After that, decisions were fudged, and action, to the confusion of all military experts, was the opposite of swift.

As Bank Holiday Monday (3 August) approached, greater folk prepared for the worst and lesser for the best, the wealthy concerned for the security of their savings, the less wealthy concerned to make their annual spree go with a swing: together they created a run on the banks and a great strain on the Bank of England.[40] Bank Rate, which stood at four per cent on Thursday, 30 July, was doubled the following day, and pushed up to ten per cent on Saturday, 1 August. The Government further girded up its loins for battle with a series of Royal Proclamations. On 1 August the use of wireless telegraphy by merchant ships within the harbours or territorial waters of the United Kingdom was prohibited, as was the flying of aircraft over the United Kingdom (2 August), and the export of a certain specified list of warlike materials (3 August). Putting into force an Act of 1871, the Government took over control of the railways. To give the Bank of England the breathing space which was its greatest need, the payment of certain bills of exchange was postponed for a month, the Bank Holiday was extended right up to Thursday, 6 August, and postal orders were made legal tender. The excitable and unpatriotic rushed off to lay in stores of food and on 3 August there was a sharply marked rise in food prices. While railway stations and coastal resorts were besieged over the week-end, crowds also gathered in central London, where there was shouting of 'Down with Germany.'[41]

Germany declared war on Russia on 1 August, and on France on 3 August. The British Cabinet had to give consideration to two immediate issues, apart from the broader threat which a possible German conquest of France would present: her ties of friendship and moral obligation to France, and the likelihood of a German violation of Belgian neutrality, which Britain had a *right* rather than an *obligation* to defend. Grey, the Foreign Secretary, persuasively expounded these points to the House of Commons on the afternoon of the Bank Holiday. The following day news came through of a definite German invasion of Belgian territory, and the Prime Minister, Asquith, announced that an ultimatum expiring at 11 p.m. (midnight in Berlin) had been served upon the Germans calling upon them to withdraw from Belgium. As the time-limit approached, a great concourse of people gathered in Trafalgar Square and Whitehall waving Union Jacks, singing patriotic songs and displaying 'marked tendencies towards Mafficking'; when the British declaration of war upon Germany was issued at the Foreign Office it was greeted with 'round after round of cheers'.[42]

The patriots did not have things all their own way. On Sunday, 2 August, there had been a Labour demonstration against war addressed by Keir Hardie, H. M. Hyndman, George Lansbury and Arthur Henderson, Secretary of the Labour Party. On Monday, 3 August, pleas for neutrality from a group of distinguished Cambridge Fellows and from a couple of bishops were published and a Neutrality Committee, which included Lord Courtney of Penwith, Gilbert Murray, the classical scholar and advocate of international arbitration, Basil Williams, the Oxford historian, Ramsay MacDonald, the Chairman of the Parliamentary Labour Party, and a number of prominent Liberal publicists, announced itself.[43] In Trafalgar Square on the fateful 4 August anti-German demonstrators had competition from an organized anti-war demonstration.[44] That evening a women's protest against war in the Kingsway Hall had as principal speaker Mrs Fawcett of the National Union of Women's Suffrage Societies. A body calling itself the Neutrality League was wealthy enough to take out, too late, a full-page exhortation against war in the *Daily News* of 5 August. In the daily press the lead to the opposition to British involvement was given by the *Manchester Guardian* and the *Daily News*, the latter being little moved by the Belgian issue: war, it said, commenting on Sir Edward Grey's Bank Holiday speech, would quite probably lead to the absorption of Belgium by France, while at the same time opening the way to the creation of 'a dominant Russia' – something which Liberals constantly feared.[45]

This opposition to the war was striking, but no more striking than the speed with which the bulk of it dissolved. On the morrow of the war the *Daily News* still felt bound to record its conviction 'that a mistaken course of foreign policy, the departure from our traditional policy of splendid isolation, has led us to the terrible conflict in which we are now engaged', but it agreed that the major task now was 'to win'. After Asquith's speech of 5 August, declaring that Britain was fighting 'for the principles whose maintenance is vital to the civilized world', and the publication of the Blue Book showing the avenues the Government had explored and the stones it had turned in the pursuit of peace,[46] this grudging acceptance of war gave way to wholehearted enthusiasm for it. There were many other thirteenth-hour conversions. The Labour Party and the trade unions swung their weight behind the war effort so that Ramsay MacDonald, who maintained his anti-war views, had to resign from the chairmanship of the Parliamentary Labour Party. Mrs Fawcett invited the members of the National Union of Women's Suffrage Societies to put their organization at the disposal of the nation in its hour of need.[47] The prophet of Edwardian nonconformism, the Reverend Dr John Clifford, a bearded Old Testament figure, former President of the National Free Church Council and leader of the pacifist opposition to the Boer War, returning in the last days of peace from a conference of the Churches' Peace Alliance, held in Germany, had drawn up a statement 'in favour of a rigorous abstention from joining in the war'; but becoming convinced 'that our Government had done everything that could be done to allay the storm and preserve the peace of the world . . . that Prussia had launched an ultimatum to Russia . . . had violated Luxemburg', and then, 'deliberately and of express purpose and according to long prepared plans, had broken into Belgium, flung to the winds as veriest chaff her solemn treaty obligations, flouted public law, and trampled under foot with ineffable scorn the rights of small nationalities as not even the small dust of the balance', he held support for this war to be as much a religious duty as ever opposition to the Boer War had been:

> The path of duty shone out in clearest light, and wherever it might lead us we had to go. It was the pillar of cloud by day and the pillar of fire by night. We must follow.[48]

These conversions, we shall discover, were not achieved without mental suffering. There remained an important cluster of socialists, Liberals, philosophical pacifists, unflinchingly committed against the war. But by and large the country, on the surface at least, was united and enthusiastic: F. S. Oliver, businessman, social-imperialist, and political *éminence grise*, sent a number of reports to his brother in Canada: 'England is already a different place than it has been for years past.' . . . 'I had not conceived it possible that a nation could be born again so quickly. This war even now has undone the evils of a generation.'

> The ordinary man's belief is – even Radicals and Socialists, for the opposition to the war is more nearly 'nil' than I have ever known it to be to anything – that Germany has made this war to impose a military supremacy over the whole of Western Europe, including Britain, and that it is better to be beaten than to submit. Also there is a feeling that since the Kruger telegram, eighteen years ago, things have been working up to this issue, and a sense of relief is experienced by the ending of it.[49]

Less exhilarating was the rise in prices of ordinary food-stuffs: imported meat rose by one penny a pound; bread rose more

drastically from 5½d for the 4-lb loaf to 8d or more.[50] Greater
increases in the cost of imported goods were contained by the
Government's introduction of a State insurance scheme to cover
war risks. After consultation between Government and shopkeepers, a scale of maximum retail prices was drawn up but never
properly operated.[51] High prices, unemployment, general distress,
that was what serious observers expected. On 4 August a Cabinet
Committee on the Prevention and Relief of Distress had been
established and the Local Government Board, in a circular to the
local authorities, had warned:

> The outbreak of war upon the Continent of Europe may involve a
> considerable dislocation of trade in this country, and in consequence,
> there may be a serious lack of employment in certain industries.[52]

An appeal for a National Relief Fund was issued by the Prince of
Wales on 6 August, and the administration of this was at once
taken over by an Executive Committee which contained three
members of the Cabinet.

The Labour movement made its own preparations. On the
initiative of Arthur Henderson a special conference of all organizations affiliated to the Labour Party was held on 5 August and a
Workers' National Committee set up to watch over the special
interests of the working classes during the War Emergency.[53]
Where there was distress in the first months it was very acute: in
patriotically turning their minds from dress to higher things,
women of the middle and upper classes helped to throw more
than 40 per cent. of their labouring sisters out of work or on to
short time.[54] Yet it was one of the lesser ironies of the war that,
after all the preparations for unemployment, it was in the end to
furnish an unprecedented demand for labour.

Shortly before war broke out, the Liberal Secretary of State for
War, Colonel Seely, had resigned, and his duties, pending a fresh
appointment, had been taken over by the Prime Minister. The
military colossus of the age was Lord Kitchener, Commander-in-
Chief of the British forces in the latter two years of the Boer War,
presently British Representative in Egypt, and described by the
Observer as 'Cromwellian':[55] a strong campaign was waged in the
press calling for Kitchener, who was on leave in Britain, to be
seconded to the War Office. The Government vacillated, but

finally, when Kitchener was on the point of re-embarking, he was summoned back to have the secretaryship thrust upon him. A non-political figure, Kitchener added the right quality of national solidarity to the Ministry; large in stature as in military reputation, he was undoubtedly a hero in the eyes of the public, concentrating upon himself the imperial longings of the little man, which had now burst out in joyous flood; but at sixty-four, he was past his best; much had changed in the dozen years since the South African War; he was ignorant of politics and caused laughter upon his first appearance in the Lords as War Secretary by seating himself upon the episcopal bench.[56]

Kitchener's appointment was taken as an earnest of the Government's good intentions in regard to the prosecution of the war. On 6 August Parliament authorized an increase in the Army of 500,000 men; the first recruiting appeal appeared the following day:

YOUR KING AND COUNTRY NEED YOU

A CALL TO ARMS

An addition of 100,000 men to His Majesty's Regular Army is immediately necessary in the present grave National Emergency. Lord Kitchener is confident that this appeal will be at once responded to by all who have the safety of our Empire at heart.

TERMS OF SERVICE

General service for a period of three years, or until the war is concluded.

Age of enlistment, between 19 and 30.[57]

The terms of service show that Kitchener at least did not share the widely held belief that the war would be over within six months. Because of the confusion and ineptitude of the authorities, the first 100,000 was not obtained till 25 August,[58] though recruiting offices were thronged with eager volunteers. A call for a further 100,000 was issued on 28 August; the age-limit was raised to thirty-five, and a special appeal was made to married men. By 15 September, after a further increase of 500,000 had been authorized there were already more than 500,000 recruits – half a million of the country's bravest and most idealistic young men, heroically committed to a cause greater than themselves. Rupert Brooke, poet, former President of the Cambridge Fabian Society, to whom 'Honour has come back, as a King, to earth', spoke for all of them; many came from respectable Evangelical backgrounds, and to them duty to God and duty to King and Country were sufficient call; others were atheistic or pantheistic social reformers, like F. H. Keeling, who wrote, 'I may possibly live to think differently; but at the present moment, assuming that this war had to come, I feel nothing but gratitude to the gods for sending it in my time;'[59] miners from South Wales were as much in evidence as the sons of the prosperous middle and upper classes. These men were first crammed into inadequate, overcrowded camps, so short of basic amenities that recruits were told to bring their own blankets and toilet articles. Soon they would be required across the Channel, for the professional British Expeditionary Force, after helping to bring the German advance to a halt on the Marne (6 to 9 September), was shortly wiped out at Ypres. An increase in the Army of another million was authorized in November, and by 21 December 1915, a third and then a fourth million had been sanctioned.[60]

The culmination of the first burst of emergency legislation was the Defence of the Realm Act of 8 August. 'D.O.R.A' – the widely used name conjured up in the public mind the image of a cruel and capricious maiden who at the snap of her fingers could close down a newspaper, requisition a ship, or prohibit whistling for cabs – will be so often referred to in the course of this book, that it is worth quoting the original act in full:

An Act to confer on His Majesty in Council power to make Regulations during the present War for the Defence of the Realm.

Be it enacted by the King's most Excellent Majesty by and with the advice and consent of the Lords Spiritual and Temporal, and Commons, in this present Parliament assembled, and by the authority of the same, as follows:

1. His Majesty in Council has power during the continuance of the present war to issue regulations as to the powers and duties of the Admiralty and Army Council, and of the members of His Majesty's forces, and other persons acting on His behalf, for securing the public safety and the defence of the realm; and may by such regulations authorize the trial by courts martial and punishment of persons contravening any of the provisions of such regulations designed –

(*a*) to prevent persons communicating with the enemy or obtaining information for that purpose or any purpose calculated to jeopardize the success of the operations of any of His Majesty's forces or to assist the enemy; or

(*b*) to secure the safety of any means of communication, or of railways, docks or harbours;

in a like manner as if such persons were subject to military law and had on active service committed an offence under section five of the Army Act.[61]

Additions were made by a second D.O.R.A. of 28 August, and there were amendments and revisions in the Defence of the Realm Consolidation Act of 27 November, further modified by Acts of 1915 and 1916. Trial by court-martial for civilians was possible under the original D.O.R.A.; the Consolidation Act of November went so far as to authorize the death penalty in the case of offences 'committed with the intention of assisting the enemy'. Protests in the House of Lords produced the amending Act of 16 March 1915, which largely restored the right of trial by jury, though this could still be suspended in case of invasion or other military emergency: it was under this dispensation that the executions after the Irish Easter Rising of 1916 were carried out. In the later stages of the war there would be a constant stream of orders and regulations from many different ministries, covering lighting, early closing, food control, and so on, all issued under the umbrella of D.O.R.A. The lights of London – a vulnerable target for German air attack, the authorities feared – were lowered for the first time on 11 September, and as a further precaution the distinctively shaped lake in St James's Park was drained.

During the Napoleonic Wars the British scientist Humphry Davy had been able to leave the country to collect a medal in France from 'the enemy'. In this war there could be no charity, let alone enthusiasm, on either side, for aliens. Anti-German sentiment was pretty spontaneous, though helped along by the popular press; attacks on people with German-sounding names were at first probably motivated as much by fear of espionage as by hatred. Many people with German names made haste to change them; *sauerkraut* and liver sausage appeared in shop windows labelled simply 'good English viands'.[62] The first Aliens Restriction Act was introduced on 5 August and subsequent legislation required that enemy aliens of military age should be interned and others repatriated. From 28 November it was decreed that everyone, British or foreign, must register with the police when moving into hotels or boarding-houses.

Nor could the press be left untrammelled. To begin with, a clumsy double censorship of war news was carried out by the Admiralty and the War Office acting independently, with the result that newspapers had practically no war news at all. An Official Press Bureau was therefore set up which itself doled out highly uninformative official communications to the newspapers, and to which editors were supposed to submit all controversial news items; it was still possible for the press to circumvent the Bureau, but it would then, of course, invite prosecution under D.O.R.A.[63]

Young men flocked to the colours, but not fast enough for the old men, often, like the novelist Arnold Bennett, stirred out of the pacifism of a lifetime:

When one sees young men idling in the lanes on Sunday, one thinks: 'Why are they not at war?' All one's pacific ideas have been rudely disturbed. One is becoming militarist.[64]

Women were not behind in their enthusiasm, which showed itself in two traditional responses: bandaging and knitting. 'I spend my time . . .' a schoolboy reported to his mother, 'being bandaged and unbandaged by the girls who want to be V.A.D.s'. If some of them ever manage to get into a hospital, Heaven help their patients.'[65] Mrs C. S. Peel recollected that:

We knitted socks (some of them of unusual shape), waistcoats, helmets, comforters, mitts, body belts. We knitted at theatres, in trains and trams, in parks and parlours, in the intervals of eating in restaurants, of serving in canteens. . . . It was said that such a stock of knitted goods flooded into the trenches that men cleaned their rifles and wiped their cups and plates with their surplus socks and comforters.

Arnold Bennett, at least was gratified: 'This instinct to do something on the part of idle young women or half-idle is satisfactory to behold.'[66]

Excitement and enthusiasm for the war bordered upon derangement, as is seen most strikingly in the story which began to circulate at the end of August, that Russian reinforcements 'with snow on their boots' were passing through Britain on their way to the Western Front. Even the hard-bitten McDonagh fell for the story and played his part in circulating it; the *Daily News*, anxious still for an easy ending for a war it had swung behind so late and so unhappily, was highly credulous; the *Daily Mail*, which was already taking a lead in insisting on the seriousness of the war, on the other hand, was highly satirical about the whole affair. The rumours were not formally denied till 16 September. Whether they originated from a misunderstood report that a consignment of Russian *eggs* was on the way, or from the bearded soldier who declared from the window of a train that he came from *Ross-shire*, is immaterial; they are the heady froth upon the first bubbling month of war.[67]

[III] BUSINESS AS USUAL

While the legislation for war continued to be extended and refined, the panic and excitement subsided, though it was never completely subdued. Businessmen were well aware that their best interests would be served by a continuance of normal trading habits. As early as 11 August, H. E. Morgan of W. H. Smith and Son, in a letter to the *Daily Chronicle* suggested that the country would do well to follow a policy of 'Business as Usual'. Harrods, the top department store of Edwardian England, took up the phrase in a display advertisement which, two days later, announced their policy for the war. Later in the month a crowded meeting of advertisers and traders resolved that, together in unity, they would fight the war on the slogan 'Business as Usual'.[68] Tom Bruce Jones, a Scottish economist of erratic views, published a tract on *The Danger of Britain's Invasion, And How It May Be Met Whilst Carrying On 'Business as Usual'*. The phrase, then, was not, as has been said, coined by Winston Churchill, but by the big shopkeepers, anxious to unite duty with profit; once coined, however, its velocity of circulation was enthusiastically boosted by the Government.

Official endorsement of Business as Usual was shown most obviously in the first war budget, introduced by the Chancellor of the Exchequer, David Lloyd George, on 16 November.

Income-tax was already calculated on an elaborate graduated scale: at the outbreak of war the ordinary wage-earner was, as we have seen, totally exempt; salaries between £160 and £500 paid at the rate of 9d in the pound, above £500 the rate was 1s 3d, and incomes above £3,000 paid an additional supertax. In doubling the ninepenny rate to one and six, Lloyd George cast before him the faintest shade of things to come. The tea duty was raised from 3d per pound to 8d, and the tax on beer put up by the equivalent of a penny a pint, raising the price to 4d. And that was about it – no new taxation of any sort. If *The Economist* praised the Government for having boldly faced an 'unprecedented emergency by calling upon the nation to make an unprecedented sacrifice',[69] that just showed how far orthodox opinion was out of touch with the needs of the hour.

Politics were much as usual as well. Asquith, treading warily as ever, decided to enact his Irish Home Rule Bill, but with the proviso that it would not become law till the end of the war, when there would be an amending act to make possible the exclusion of the six Ulster counties where Protestant sentiment was strongest. None the less, the Conservatives were deeply angered, and after a bitter speech Bonar Law led his followers out of the House of Commons, giving the Prime Minister the opportunity to mock them as 'middle-aged gentlemen trying to look like early French revolutionaries in the tennis court'. Party government, therefore, continued, qualified only by the presence in the Cabinet of Lord Kitchener, by the loyal restraint which Conservatives put on their criticisms of the conduct of the war, and by such smaller instances of collaboration as the consultation between Lloyd George and Austen Chamberlain over the preparation of the first war budget.[70]

One slight change there was in the technique of government. On 5 August there came into existence a War Council, in effect a development of the pre-war Committee of Imperial Defence. In November the former Conservative Prime Minister, A. J. Balfour, was invited to its meetings, but the body had an advisory function only.[71] Executive power stayed in the Cabinet, where the three leading figures were Asquith, intellectually powerful but not readily given to speedy decision-making, Winston Churchill, impetuous and full of daring schemes, and Kitchener, a god in the eyes of the public, but already shown to be out-of-date in his strategic thinking and utterly lacking in the organizational gifts required in a war of the new scale. The military aspects of the war were turning out to be altogether different from what had been expected. As Sir John French, the Commander-in-Chief of the British forces, plaintively put it:

No previous experience, no conclusion I had been able to draw from campaigns in which I had taken part, or from a close study of the new conditions in which the war of today is waged, had led me to anticipate a war of positions. All my thoughts, all my prospective plans, all my possible alternatives of action, were concentrated upon a war of movement and manœuvre.[72]

So, too, not unnaturally, had the war been misunderstood by the younger generation:

War to my generation implied campaigns on the Indian frontier, in Egypt or in South Africa. My ideas of European war were derived from panoramas of the Franco–Prussian conflict to be seen in continental cities. It was the war of tradition. Cavalry charged at the foe. When death came, it was a heroic death brought about by heroes on the other side.[73]

Instead, the same writer continues, there came 'war atrocities' and 'frightfulness'. Worse, wholesale slaughter became a commonplace. As early as 24 October the editor of the *Daily Express*, R. D. Blumenfeld, was noting in his diary:

One would have thought, before the war began, that the single report of the killing or disablement of any friend or acquaintance would be terribly disconcerting. So it was, at the beginning. The first eight or ten casualties had as much publicity as all the rest put together. People discussed deaths of young second lieutenants with bated breath. Gradually the familiarity of the thing became apparent. You receive the news of the death of your friends as a matter of fact.[74]

The fighting was still being waged as of yore by a Regular Army augmented, admittedly on an unprecedented scale, by volunteers, not in any real sense by a nation in arms. Where industrial distress and disruptions of trade had been expected, stay-at-homes found that trade was booming. These two facts, added to this warty defensiveness in face of news of death, account for the widening rounds of giddy social pleasures found among the upper classes in the last months of the old year and the first months of the new. Described as 'desolate and dreary wastes' shortly after the outbreak of war,[75] theatres were in January said by a prominent actor-manager to be 'booming'.[76] Two months later, according to Blumenfeld, social activity had not abated in the least.[77] There were exaggerated tales of the working classes 'warming themselves in the sun of affluence', buying pianos, 'that coveted proof of respectability', gramophones, and motor-bikes.[78] More in evidence than affluence was the further privation caused to the lower-paid workers and their families by the sharp price rises. Labour members forced the issue in debate early in February 1915, when it was claimed that many labourers were getting only one good meal a week. The Prime Minister admitted that, compared with February 1914, prices of flour had risen 75 per cent, home meat 6 per cent, imported meat 12 per cent, sugar 72 per cent, coal 15 per cent, but he justified Government inaction on the grounds that these rises were no worse than the ones brought by the aftermath of the Franco-Prussian war of 1870.[79] 'Business as Usual' could hardly be taken to more absurd lengths.

Ruling opinion was still strongly against Government interference in the free play of the market, and, indeed, against too much Government action in any direction once the necessary emergency measures of national self-defence had been taken. The period of 'business as usual' was marked by a last great flowering of grand-scale private charity of a type more suited to the world of Blandings Castle than to the waging of modern war. Allowances and pensions for the dependants of men on active service were an obvious first charge upon the nation, but the only official organization at the outbreak of war for administering such benefits was the Commissioners of the Royal Hospital for Soldiers at Chelsea, and the actual rates paid had not changed since the Boer War. Any supplementation had to come from charitable funds channelled through the Soldiers' and Sailors' Families Association or from the National Relief Fund. It was the Executive Committee of the latter body which took the decision to raise allowances from 11s 1d per week, with

1s 9d for each child, to 12s 6d with 2s for each child; these rates, with a further slight increase in the child's allowance, were officially adopted by the Government on 1 October. As it was discovered that in a large number of cases soldiers were not in fact married to the women they were living with, the Executive Committee decided that 'where there was evidence that a real home had been maintained allowances should be made to unmarried mothers and their children'.[80] In this way there was, despite many earnest protests about the licensing of sin, admitted into the well-defended regions of nineteenth-century middle-class morality a first spy from the earthier realms of working-class *mores*.

Even when allowances were established as due there were often outrageously long delays before payment was made. So great was the outcry against the muddle and mismanagement that the voluntary societies concerned were forced to conduct an investigation into their own affairs; confusion, if anything, was worse confounded, and eventually the Government had to appoint its own Select Committee.[81] From the deliberations of this Committee came, in November 1915, the Naval and Military War Pensions Act, still, in essence, an attempt to integrate private charity and public appeal into Government action.

The readiest opportunity for private philanthropy was provided from the very beginning of the war by the Belgian refugee problem. As the Germans marched into Belgium a full million of the rightful inhabitants sought refuge outside the borders of their country, over a hundred thousand embarking at once for Britain.[82] To cope with this influx, three august and public-spirited personages, Lady Lugard, the Hon. Mrs Alfred Lyttelton, and Viscount Gladstone, formed on 24 August a War Refugees' Committee; Lord Hugh Cecil became Chairman. From the public at large there came at once offers of hospitality for a hundred thousand refugees. From 9 September the whole business was taken over by the Local Government Board, but the treatment received by individual Belgians continued, naturally, to depend very much on the reactions of individual Britishers. On the whole it can be said that, in the early stages at least, the British people rallied magnificently to those felt to have suffered unjustly in a common cause, giving a sign both of timeless human generosity and of the moral idealism of the first part of the war. But as the months wore on many an unfortunate Belgian found himself in the position of the much-adored kitten which has grown into an unwanted cat.

The first rude shaking of domestic complacency into a new sort of awareness that war was no longer just something that other people fought came when on 16 December a German cruiser force shelled the Hartlepools, Whitby and Scarborough on the east coast. As the censorship had not yet quite grasped the idea of suppressing all news which might affect civilian morale, the episode, with its 110 dead (more careful counting brought the total to 137 killed and 592 injured),[83] was given a large spread in the press, pointed up by graphic photographs of the destruction wrought to buildings on the sea-front. Actually the censorship should perhaps be credited with wisdom as well as restraint, since the British sense of outrage expressed itself palpably in the next few days in the first marked rush to the recruiting stations since the palmy days of August.[84] So lacking in Christian feelings were the Germans that on Christmas Eve they sent an aeroplane over Dover and the following day another one over Sheerness. These incidents, however, merely became a further matter for complacent self-congratulation, since the one bomb unloaded on Dover had done no hurt to anyone, and the inhabitants of Sheerness had had their Christmas celebrations enlivened by the exciting spectacle of British planes in hot pursuit of the raider.[85] After these pioneer efforts by aeroplane, the Germans devoted themselves in the New Year to aerial attack by Zeppelin, a raid of 19 January over Yarmouth and Sheringham killing four. Further raids caused much damage, but little loss of life: business could still continue much as usual.

[IV] EMOTIONAL ATTITUDES

Propaganda, as a facet of war, was well understood by the military authorities. In the British Expeditionary Force routine orders for 24 September 1914, mention was made of the Kaiser's alleged description of the force as 'the contemptible little army'. Though without factual foundation, the phrase was exploited to the full and had fantastic success in encouraging recruiting.[86] Yet it was through private enterprise that the first body devoted to the dissemination of propaganda for domestic consumption was established – the Central Committee for National Patriotic Organizations, of which the Prime Minister became Honorary President with Lord Rosebery and A. J. Balfour as Vice-Presidents. From its headquarters at 8 Carlton House Terrace, the Committee invited prominent individuals to lecture or write upon the causes of the war with a view to justifying 'both historically and morally England's position in the struggle'.[87] The approach was almost Victorian in the weight it placed on men of intellectual and academic standing, and in the way in which their efforts were directed, not towards the ignorant masses, but to educated doubters. From six members of the Oxford Faculty of Modern History the Committee secured *Why We Are at War, Great Britain's Case,* which was followed by the 'Oxford Pamphlets', which, while never descending into downright mendacity, did not, of a set purpose, maintain the highest standards of objective scholarship.

Among the reams of distressful special pleading, the distressed *How Can War Ever be Right?* by Gilbert Murray, signatory to the plea for British neutrality published on the first day of war, stands out. For him, as for Dr Clifford, the Belgian issue was the immediate occasion for his change of heart. Aware as ever that 'as far as the rights and wrongs of war go, you are simply condemning innocent men, by thousands and thousands, to death, or even to mutilation and torture', he none the less proceeded now to argue that war could not be judged as 'a profit-and-loss' account, leaving 'out of sight the cardinal fact that in some causes it is better to fight and be broken than to yield peacefully'.[88] The causes Gilbert Murray had in mind were those of 'honour';[89] in elaborating this, the argument veers towards the quaint, the path being all the sadder for the writer's tortured awareness that for a high intellectual he is on dangerous ground:

A deal of nonsense, no doubt, is talked about 'honour' and 'dishonour'. They are feelings based on sentiment, not on reason; the standards by which they are judged are often conventional or shallow, and sometimes utterly false. Yet honour and dishonour are real things. I will not try to define them; but will only notice that, like Religion, their characteristic is that they admit of no bargaining. Indeed we can almost think of honour as being simply that which a free man values more

than life, and dishonour as that which he avoids more than suffering
or death. And the important point for us is that there are such things.[90]

Moving from the abstract to the present European situation,
Murray continues:

Great Britain had, by a solemn treaty more than once renewed, pledged
herself to maintain the neutrality of Belgium. Belgium is a little state
lying between two very strong states, France and Germany, and in
danger of being overrun or maltreated by one of them unless the Great
Powers guarantee her safety. . . . Germany suddenly and without excuse
invaded Belgium. . . . Our answer was: 'Evacuate Belgium within
twelve hours or we fight you.'
I think that answer was right. . . . For my own part, weighing the
whole question soberly and without undue passion, I feel that in this
case I would rather die than submit; and I believe that the Government, in deciding to keep its word at the cost of war, has rightly interpreted the feelings of the average British citizen.[91]

'So much,' then says Murray, 'for the questions of honour, pure
and simple.'[92] He now argues with great cogency that even without the Belgian issue, national security would probably have
demanded British intervention to prevent an all-powerful Germany dominating the European continent, concluding triumphantly with what he admits is 'one of the old optimistic beliefs of
nineteenth-century liberalism': 'our interest coincides with our
honour'.[93]
    Most illuminating of all, both for its perceptive analysis of the
war enthusiasm shown by the first volunteers and for its revelation of the way in which this enthusiasm has affected an academic
opinion-former like Murray, is his final answer to his agonizing
question, 'How can war ever be right?' Again Murray's scrupulous personal honesty permits points of doubt to penetrate through
the glossy surface of the page:

War is not all evil. It is a true tragedy, which must have nobleness and
triumph in it as well as disaster. . . . This is dangerous ground. The
subject lends itself to foolish bombast, especially when accompanied
by a lack of true imagination. We must not begin to praise war without
stopping to reflect on the hundreds of thousands of human beings
involved in such horrors of pain and indignity that, if here in our ordin-

ary hours we saw one man so treated, the memory would sicken us to the end of our lives. . . . But when we have realized that, we may venture to see in this wilderness of evil some cases of extraordinary good.

These men who are engaged in what seems like a vast public crime ought, one would think, to fall to something below their average selves, below the ordinary standard of common folk. But do they? Day after day come streams of letters from the front, odd stories, fragments of diaries, and the like; full of the small intimate facts which reveal character, and almost with one accord they show that these men have not fallen, but risen. . . . I think again of the expressions on faces that I have seen or read about, something alert and glad and self-respecting in the eyes of those who are going to the front, and even of the wounded who are returning. 'Never once', writes one correspondent, 'not once since I came to France have I seen among the soldiers an angry face or heard an angry word. . . . They are always quiet, orderly and wonderfully cheerful.' And no one who has followed the war need be told of their heroism. I do not forget the thousands left on the battlefield to die, or the groaning of the wounded sounding all day between the crashes of the guns. But there is a strange deep gladness as well. . . .

Human nature is a mysterious thing, and man finds his weal and his woe not in the obvious places. To have something before you, clearly seen, which you know you must do, and can do, and will spend your utmost strength and perhaps your life in doing, is one form at least of very high happiness, and one that appeals – the facts prove it – not only to saints and heroes but to average men. Doubtless the few who are wise enough and have enough imagination may find opportunity for that same happiness in everyday life, but in war ordinary men find it. This is the inward triumph which lies at the heart of the great tragedy.[94]

Once this sort of idea had been enunciated by men of intellect, it was easily perpetuated by countless mushy stories in book and newspaper; long after the first enthusiasm of the early volunteers had evaporated, their decimated ranks replenished with less enthusiastic conscripts, people at home went on believing in the 'happiness' of the men in the trenches.

In admitting that once war had broken out Britain's task was 'to win', the Liberal *Daily News* had added the flat proviso that in so doing she should try to *avoid* ruining 'European civilization and European liberty'; but soon the pulse quickened – Britain was fighting *for* European civilization, *for* 'the emancipation of

Germany' as well as *for* the 'liberties of Europe'; the war was seen
as 'the last supreme struggle of the old dispensation against the
new'.[95] In arguing thus the Liberals contributed to the concept of
the war as a high crusade; but in justifying their abandonment of
the anti-war position they were also placing a heavy emotional
mortgage upon the future world dispensation. Nor could they
forget their existing commitment to European civilization: news
of German atrocities might strengthen their belief in Britain's
holy cause, but what would ultimately affect them most, unless the
outcome of the war proved all to be supremely worth while, would
be the blows rained by civilized man upon civilized man. The
reality of the doubt behind the enthusiasm for the war is revealed
in a reference to German atrocities made by Dr Clifford in a
speech of January 1916:

The effect of this revelation of the German mind on ourselves is many-
sided, deep, disturbing and yet strengthening. In its presence the last
shred of doubt as to the righteousness of our cause has gone. We were
sure of our ground in 1914; we are a thousand times more sure to-day.
Doubts that haunted us a year ago have been swept to the ends of the
earth; and questions we discussed with seriousness then are no longer
put.[96]

Conservatives, on the whole, felt less need to garb their patriotic
sentiments in the flowing robes of ideal objectives, though it was
J. L. Garvin, editor of the Conservative *Observer*, who on the day
war was declared coined the words which eventually were to
become wounds:

We have to do our part in killing a creed of war. Then at last, after a
rain of blood, there may be set the greater rainbow in the Heavens
before the vision of the souls of men. And after Armageddon war,
indeed, may be no more.[97]

H. G. Wells took the idea up and became the great phrasemaker of
Liberal pro-war idealism, writing of 'The War that Will End War'
and of how 'in the hour of victory' Britain would 'save the liber-
ated Germans from vindictive treatment'.[98] For his contribution
to the Oxford pamphlets, A. D. Lindsay, the great educationist
and political philosopher, chose the title, *The War to End War*.
Although Wells, through his articles and his novels, particularly

Mr Britling Sees it Through, reached a wide audience, few to begin
with paid much attention to such notions as fair treatment for the
German people; it was enough that he and other eminent authorities should confirm that this above all wars was a war on behalf of
righteousness.

'Duty' and 'honour' were the emotional moulds within which
British attitudes set. Each class, each group, each individual then
added the trimming of whatever precise ideal he had most at heart.
In explanation of the attitude of the Parliamentary Labour Party,
the joint spokesmen of the Trades Union Congress, the General
Federation of Trade Unions, and the Labour Party, declared that
the Party 'recognized that Great Britain, having exhausted the
resources of peaceful diplomacy, was bound in honour, as well as
by treaty, to resist by arms the aggression of Germany'; they
then added their conviction that the war was being fought for 'the
preservation and maintenance of free and unfettered democratic
government'.⁹⁹

Of the mood of the inarticulate public it is difficult to say more
than that its most obvious features were an intense hatred of the
German Kaiser and people, and a mighty sense of righteous exaltation, the one clearly reinforcing the other. It must be stressed that
the exaltation was based on a deeply felt sense of moral purpose:
it is this which, despite the unexpected grimness of the test, held
aloft British enthusiasm till nearly the end of the war, then plunged
it into a well of emptiness. Lloyd George, the supreme demagogue,
put this sense of moral purpose into words of fire and velvet in his
first speech on 'the Great War' (the title was already universally
recognized), delivered at the Queen's Hall on 19 September 1914:

There is something infinitely greater and more enduring which is
emerging already out of this great conflict – a new patriotism, richer,
nobler, and more exalted than the old. (*Applause*). I see amongst all
classes, high and low, shedding themselves of selfishness, a new recognition that the honour of the country does not depend merely on the
maintenance of its glory in the stricken field, but also in protecting its
homes from distress. (*Hear, hear*). It is bringing a new outlook to all
classes. The great flood of luxury and sloth which had submerged the land
is receding, and a new Britain is appearing. We can see for the first time
the fundamental things that matter in life, and that have been obscured
from our vision by the tropical growth of prosperity. (*Hear, hear.*)¹⁰⁰

'He personifies our War aims and emotions', McDonagh wrote in his diary, seeing Lloyd George now as second only to Kitchener as a 'War Minister'.[101]

There were other types of response, some overtly sexual or sadistic in origin. A girl in Dumfriesshire began an atrocity story by forging a letter which purported to describe how her sister, a nurse in Belgium, had had her breasts cut off by the Germans.[102] Before August was out young women in Folkestone were handing out white feathers to young men still to be found skulking in civilian clothes (the instigator of the original scheme, however, was said to have been a certain Admiral Penrose-Fitzgerald).[103] For puritanical zealots the war came as a token of heavenly encouragement to renewed endeavours. Drink, gambling, professional football – here in the extreme was the conspicuous consumption of the energies of young men eminently eligible for the trenches – came under very heavy fire. Posters and sandwich boards outside football grounds which once had read 'Are you prepared to meet your God?' or 'Repent, for the time is at hand' were replaced by 'Are you forgetting that there's a war on?' 'Your country needs you', or 'Be ready to defend your home and women from the German Huns'.[104] For all that, despite the evangelical thunderbolts of the leader of the campaign, Frederick Charrington, football, like other activities, continued as usual and before large crowds. The Reverend Spencer H. Elliott thundered against football pools:

The war found us with forty thousand bookmakers in our country, with an annual turnover of at least eighty millions. The law did not touch them. Football coupons flooded the country, offering odds that were utterly unfair, and working men, women, lads, and even girls, emptied their pockets into those of anonymous scoundrels.[105]

Racial hatred, which went far beyond anything that the Government can have possibly desired or welcomed, was kept going by a number of charming messages, all prominently boxed and heavily leaded, carried by the *Daily Mail*. One declared:

REFUSE TO BE SERVED BY AN AUSTRIAN
OR GERMAN WAITER.
IF YOUR WAITER SAYS HE IS SWISS
ASK TO SEE HIS PASSPORT.

At the end of October the First Sea Lord, Prince Louis of Battenberg, was forced out of office because of his German origins. In accepting the resignation, Churchill as First Lord of the Admiralty placed the situation perfectly:

This is no ordinary war, but a struggle between nations for life and death. It raises passions between nations of the most terrible kind. It effaces the old landmarks and frontiers of our civilization.[106]

The first Government venture into the world of propaganda was the secret War Propaganda Bureau established in Wellington House, the offices of the National Health Insurance Company, under the direction of C. F. G. Masterman, the social commentator and Liberal politician.[107] Given the attitudes of the various voluntary agencies we have already discussed, there was no need for complete control of opinion. The popular press, though subject, as were all newspapers, to a strict censorship of overseas news and to the provisions of the Defence of the Realm Acts, otherwise approached the issues of wartime in much the same way as it had been in the habit of approaching the issues of peacetime, following current attitudes rather than leading them, going in for stunts and sensationalism rather than calculated brainwashing. Headlines got bigger and bolder, effecting a permanent change in newspaper presentation, but the patriotic rubbish printed remained the invention of proprietors and editors rather than of governments.

Where the Government did have to engage itself from the start was in such mundane problems as the promotion of enlistment in the Army and in the war industries, the launching of relief work, and the encouragement of economy in the purchase of food and extravagance in the purchase of Government bonds. Towards the end of 1914 the Parliamentary Recruiting Committee, also something of a do-it-yourself propaganda body, gave commissions for more than a hundred posters, all of them of rather low quality save for Alfred Leete's distinguished 'Kitchener', which has secured immortality for the War Minister and whose accusing finger must have directed many a wavering young man towards the nearest recruiting office. Acting on its own account, the London Electric Railways Company began to commission posters of greater aesthetic distinction, as, indeed, in its various guises, the

Company has continued to do ever since.[108] In January there appeared a number of posters aimed directly at women, inciting them to send their menfolk to the trenches. Among the most famous of all was the one picturing a little girl asking her father in the post-war years, 'Daddy, what did you do in the Great War?' ('I tried to stop the bloody thing, my child,' is what Bob Smillie, the Scottish miners' leader, said his reply would be.) Local recruiting committees throughout the country kept up the pressure.

On 18 February 1915, Germany imposed a submarine blockade on the British Isles; this was widely accounted a further piece of German 'frightfulness', and it enabled the Liberal press to overcome the qualms aroused by Britain's own naval blockade of Germany.[109] Ultimately the domestic repercussions of the submarine threat were to be enormous, though for the time being the tendency in high places was to take the threat rather lightly. A recruiting notice published on 17 February and addressing 'Five Questions to Patriotic Customers', did ask, 'Have you realized that we cannot have "Business as Usual" whilst the war continues?' But 'Business as Usual' ended, not with the whimper of a recruiting poster, but amid the bangs of the Battle of Neuve Chapelle. Neuve Chapelle was fought to the same basic plan as practically all the other offensives on the Western Front throughout the war. First of all a heavy bombardment was launched to smother the enemy's artillery, cut his barbed wire, and kill the inmates of his front trenches; then the guns lifted to targets farther back, and the infantry leapt out of their own trenches and into the fire of his machine-guns. This simple two-point strategy lost lives in thousands but gained ground only in yards.

First dispatches from Sir John French, however, were couched in glowingly optimistic terms. But by late March news of enormous losses was seeping through, elaborated by horrifying tales of men hung up like washing on German barbed wire which faulty British shells had failed to cut. Sir John French's final dispatch[110] was markedly less ebullient than earlier reports had been, and was the signal for a prolonged bout of heart-searching in the British press. It was Neuve Chapelle which jerked society to an awareness of what was involved in this most beastly of wars. The politicians continued to be happily insulated from the changing currents of opinion for another month, but already, well before the first Ministerial reconstruction, a new phase of the domestic war had begun.

NOTES TO CHAPTER ONE

1. *Hist[ory of the] Min[istry of] Mun[itions]*, Vol. I, 1922, p. 7.

2. R. H. Tawney, 'The Abolition of Economic Controls, 1918-21,' in *Economic History Review*, 1943, p. 1.

3. L. C. Money, *Riches and Poverty*, 1905; 1913 edn., p. 202.

4. *Report of Committee of Privy Council for Scientific and Industrial Research for 1915-16;* P.P., 1916, VIII, Cd. 8336, pp. 3-8. *1st Annual Report of Medical Research Committee, 1914-15;* P.P., 1914-16, XXXI, Cd. 8101, pp. 3-5.

5. B. H. Hibbard, *Effects of the Great War upon Agriculture, in the United States and Great Britain*, New York, 1919, p. 173.

6. P.P., 1914, XLI, Cd. 7190, pp. 6-8.

7. C. F. G. Masterman, *The Condition of England,* 1909, *passim.*

8. *Riches and Poverty*, p. 49.

9. T. C. Marshall, *Citizenship and Social Class,* 1950, pp. 46-7.

10. *Condition of England*, pp. 57-8.

11. ibid, p. 58.

12. A. L. Bowley and A. R. Burnett-Hurst, *Livelihood and Poverty*, 1915, p. 176.

13. A. L. Bowley, *The Division of the Product of Industry*, 1919, pp. 8-13.

14. ibid, on which the next sentences are based.

15. See F. M. L. Thompson, *English Landed Society in the Nineteenth Century*, 1963, pp. 292-326.

16. A. L. Bowley, *Studies in the National Income*, 1942.

17. *Livelihood and Poverty*, p. 46.

18. *Division of the Product of Industry*, p. 18.

19. *Livelihood and Poverty*, pp. 46, 42.

20. A. L. Bowley, *Prices and Wages in the United Kingdom, 1914-20,* 1921, p. 34. *Report of Working Classes Cost of Living Committee, 1918*; P.P., 1918, VIII, Cd. 8980.

21. *Annual Report of Local Government Board, 1913-14;* P.P., 1914 XXXVIII, Cd. 7610, p. xii.

22. ibid, pp. xxxvi-xxxvii.

23. *Annual Report of Local Government Board for Scotland, 1913;* P.P., 1914, XXXVIII, Cd. 7327, p. lxxviii.

24. *Livelihood and Poverty*, p. 18.

25. Cd. 7327, pp. lxxxi, lxxxii. B. S. Rowntree, *Poverty, a study of town life*, 1901, p. 187.

26. *Annual Report of Local Government Board, 1912-13 – Report of Medical Officer;* P.P., 1914, XXXVII, Cd. 7181, p. v.

27. *Annual Report of Local Government Board, 1913-14;* P.P., 1914, XXXVIII, Cd. 7444, p. liv.

28. In A. P. Newton (ed.), *The Empire and the Future,* 1916, p. 3.

29. *New Republic*, 11 September 1915.

30. See e.g. C. Booth, *Life and Labour of the People in London*, Final Vol., 1902, p. 53.

31. Quoted in R. B. McDowall, *British Conservatism, 1832–1914*, 1959, p. 95.

32. T. C. Horsfall, *National Service and the Welfare of the Community*, 1906, pp. 71, v.

33. Quoted in D. Newsome, *Godliness and Good Learning*, 1961, p. 202.

34. Quoted in A. Ponsonby, *Social Reform versus War*, 1912, pp. 4–5.

35. M. McDonagh, *In London during the Great War*, 1935, p. 5.

36. R. C. K. Ensor, *England 1870–1914*, 1936, pp. 492–3.

37. *Labour Year Book 1916*, p. 15.

38. I. Cooper Willis, *England's Holy War*, New York, 1928, pp. 16–42.

39. *The Times*, 31 July 1914.

40. F. L. McVey, *The Financial History of Great Britain, 1914–18*, New York, 1918, p. 10.

41. *Annual Register 1914*, p. 184. *Labour Gazette 1914*, p. 323. *The Times*, 4 August. 1914.

42. *Daily News*, 5 August 1914. *Daily Mail*, 5 August 1914.

43. *Daily News*, 3 August, 4 August 1914.

44. McDonagh, p. 5.

45. *The Times*, 5 August 1914. *Daily News*, 4 August, 5 August 1914.

46. H.M.S.O., *Great Britain and the European Crisis*, 1914.

47. *Common Cause*, 7 August 1914.

48. J. Clifford, *Our Fight for Belgium and What It Means*, 1917, p. 7.

49. S. Gwynn (ed.), *The Anvil of War: letters from F. S. Oliver to his brother*, 1936, pp. 30 (12 August), 42 (6 September), 37 (19 August).

50. *Labour Gazette 1914*, p. 323.

51. E. V. Morgan, *Studies in British Financial Policy 1914–25*, 1952, p. 36.

52. *Memorandum on Steps taken for the Prevention and Relief of Distress;* P.P., 1914, LXXI, Cd. 7603, pp. 3, 29–32.

53. War Emergency: Workers' National Committee, *Report, August 1914–March 1916*, p. 3.

54. I. Andrews and M. Hobbs, *Economic Effects of the War upon Women and Children in Great Britain*, New York, 1918, p. 23.

55. *Observer*, 16 August 1914.

56. McDonagh, p. 18 (25 August 1914).

57. *The Times*, 7 August 1914.

58. J. A. Fairlie, *British War Administration*, New York, 1919, p. 84.

59. F. H. Keeling, *Keeling Letters and Reminiscences*, 1918, p. 209.

60. Fairlie, pp. 18, 84.

61. *Public General Statutes* (4 & 5 Geo. 5), Ch. 29.

62. McDonagh, p. 11.

63. *Memorandum on the Censorship;* P.P., 1914–16, XXXIX, Cd. 7679. *Memorandum on the Official Press Bureau;* P.P., 1914–16, XXXIX, Cd. 7680.

64. A. Bennett, *Journal 1896–1926*, 1932, p. 98 (10 August 1914).

65. C. S. Peel, *How We Lived Then*, 1929, p. 27.

66. Bennett, p. 95 (6 August 1914).

67. See esp. A. Ponsonby, *Falsehood in War Time*, 1926, pp. 63–66. For other examples see C. E. Playne, *Society at War 1914–15*, 1931, pp. 255–81.

68. *The Times*, 26 August 1914.
69. *Economist*, 21 November 1914.
70. F. W. Hirst and H. Allen, *British War Budgets*, 1926, p. 15.
71. J. P. Mackintosh, *The British Cabinet*, 1962, pp. 329 ff. Lord Hankey, *The Supreme Command, 1914–1918*, 1961.
72. Lord French, *1914*, 1919, p. 11.
73. E. Wrench, *Struggle 1914–20*, 1935, pp. 112–3.
74. R. D. Blumenfeld, *All in a Lifetime*, 1935, p. 17.
75. ibid, p. 7 (22 August 1914).
76. *Daily Mail*, 13 January 1915.
77. Blumenfeld, p. 20 (9 March 1915).
78. See esp. *Daily Mail*, 1 February 1915.
79. *House of Commons Debates*, 11 February 1915.
80. P.P., 1914–16, XXI, Cd. 7756, pp. 4–5.
81. Fairlie, p. 158.
82. P.P., 1914–16, VII, Cd. 7750, p. 4, XXV, Cd. 7763, on which the remainder of this paragraph is based.
83. *The Times*, 17, 18 December 1914.
84. *The Times*, 30 December 1914.
85. *The Times*, 26 December 1914.
86. See Ponsonby, *Falsehood in War Time*, pp. 84–7.
87. *Report of the Central Committee for National Patriotic Organisations*, 1914, p. 3.
88. G. Murray, *How Can War Ever Be Right?*, 1914, pp. 5–6.
89. p. 7.
90. pp. 7–8.
91. pp. 13–15.
92. p. 15.
93. p. 22.
94. pp. 24–7.
95. *Daily News*, 5 August, 8 August 1914.
96. J. Marchant, *Dr John Clifford, Life, Letters and Reminiscences*, 1922, p. 100.
97. Quoted D. Thomson, *England in the Nineteenth Century*, 1950, p. 219.
98. *Daily News*, 14 August 1914. *Daily Chronicle*, 8 August 1914.
99. *British Labour and the War*, 1915.
100. D. Lloyd George, *The Great War*, 1914, p. 14.
101. McDonagh, pp. 28–9 (19 September 1914).
102. Ponsonby, *Falsehood in War Time*, pp. 67–70.
103. *Daily Mail*, 31 August 1914.
104. McDonagh, p. 44 (16 December).
105. Society for the Propagation of Christian Knowledge, *The Enemy Within*, 1915.
106. *The Times*, 1 November 1914.
107. J. D. Squires, *British Propaganda at Home and in the United States from 1914–1917*, Cambridge, Mass., 1935, pp. 26–7.
108. M. Hardie and A. K. Sabin, *War Posters*, 1920, pp. 9–10.
109. Willis, *England's Holy War*, pp. 201–2.
110. *The Times*, 15 April 1915.

CHAPTER TWO
Changed Men: 1915–1916

[1] LABOUR

IF THE weaknesses now revealed in the British armoury were to be remedied, the first problem to be dealt with must be that of manpower; in a 'war of machines' it was at least as necessary to look to the supply of machine-makers at home as to the supply of machine-users on the fields of battle. It is this problem of labour which is the flash-point for many of the major changes in social status, relationship, and environment which are apparent from early 1915 onwards. The process was a fairly simple one. To get the most out of the existing labour force the Government had to cajole and bargain with trade union leaders, giving them a status they had never possessed before; to combat the inefficiency allegedly caused by alcoholism they remodelled the country's liquor licensing system; to surmount labour shortages they upgraded unskilled labour and encouraged women to take on new tasks; as women flexed their muscles on behalf of their country they found that they were at the same time winning the battle for emancipation so long fought by their pioneers; all in themselves of outstanding importance, these developments reacted and interacted to create an immense range of ramifications and side effects.

The first great hindrance to the war industries was the indiscriminate recruiting of the early days of the war. Statistics compiled after a year of war showed that almost a quarter of the employees in the chemicals and explosives industry had enlisted, as had a similar proportion from electrical engineering; over a fifth had gone from coal-mining and almost as many from the metal trades.[1] The private armaments firm of Vickers was the first to sense the danger of too much patriotism and, in September 1914, suggested a system of badges which could be worn by men on vital production and thus protect them from the attentions of the recruiting sergeant and the young women with their white feathers.[2]

The idea of badging as a defence against badgering was taken up by the Admiralty in December and, finally, in March the War Office, with great show of reluctance, introduced a similar scheme into its own ordnance establishments. By May the War Office had become aware of the need to look beyond the walls of its own factories and it issued a circular to recruiting officers telling them to keep their hands off men in certain specified occupations. At the same time efforts were made to bring back some of the skilled men already enlisted. Thus, after a sharp drive at the beginning of the war to get men into the trenches, there followed a more spasmodic movement to keep certain men out of the trenches. Later in the war, as military strategy continued to demand that men must be hurled against machines, it was necessary to start debadging some of these men, to conduct a 'comb out', as the charming phrase had it, of the reserved occupations.

There were other obstacles to the maximizing of labour power. The most important of these was the elaborate structure of trade union rules and restrictions built up over the years of struggle with the employing classes. Immediately after the outbreak of war a number of private firms, acting independently of the Government, entered into negotiations with the unions in the hope of securing the abandonment of restrictive practices; conferences were held on Clydeside and on Tyneside and a rather vague 'industrial truce' was offered on behalf of labour.[3] A more positive step was the meeting in November between the Engineering Employers' Federation and the unions, which produced the so-called Crayford Agreement whereby it was established that, though female labour was not to be employed in place of skilled men, such labour could be employed on purely automatic machines, these machines being set up by fully skilled mechanics.[4] This was no great advance from the aspect of increasing productivity and the little the agreement did achieve was vitiated by a series of disputes in the engineering industry throughout the winter. It was this state of affairs, together with the unfavourable military situation, which made Government intervention necessary.[5]

The crying need was to secure trade union approval for 'dilution', the introduction of semi-skilled, unskilled, or female labour into jobs, or parts of jobs, hitherto reserved for skilled craftsmen. This was the main problem considered by a special Government committee (shortly called the Committee on Production) set up in February 1915; but for the time being the Government confined itself to a policy of exhortation. The first big agreement on dilution was again a private one, the Shells and Fuses Agreement of early March 1915 between the engineering unions and the Employers' Federation. Confined to the duration of the war, the agreement laid down that in return for the acceptance of some dilution the employers would avoid any permanent restriction of employment in favour of semi-skilled or female labour, and that at the end of the war, or before, the 'dilutees' would be the first to be dismissed.[6]

It was at this stage that the Chancellor of the Exchequer, Lloyd George, depressed by the set-backs of the war, and already feeling himself to be the strong man at his leader's elbow if not yet the eager man breathing down his leader's neck, stepped in. Upon his initiative a conference was held at the Treasury from 17 to 19 March between Arthur Henderson and a number of other trade union leaders on the one side and Lloyd George and Walter Runciman, President of the Board of Trade, on the other. Henderson and his colleagues gave an undertaking that unions engaged on war-work would forgo the right to strike, that disputes would go to arbitration, and that there would be a relaxation of 'present trade practices'; it was understood that these concessions were for the duration of the war only, and that the Government for its part would see to it that the permanent standards of trade unionists were not endangered.

The miners were the only major grouping to stand aside from this agreement, for, although the representatives of the Amalgamated Society of Engineers declared that they had no authority to sign the first agreement, a further special agreement was concluded with them on 25 March.[7] On the surface the outcome of these negotiations was scarcely favourable to the labour movement; but already the point had been made that if the war were to be fought to a successful conclusion the co-operation of labour leaders must be enlisted. This point was driven home by the appointment of the labour representatives at the Treasury conference as a standing National Labour Advisory Committee to the Government, though in the event this body was to prove of symbolic rather than practical importance.

The Treasury conference showed Government awareness of the

problem of manpower; but awareness was no substitute for
firmness. Without legal sanction, the agreements soon proved
themselves inadequate. While this was becoming apparent the
Government itself was rocked by two separate crises: a sharp conflict at the Admiralty between Winston Churchill and Lord
Fisher, which resulted in the latter's resignation, and a scandal
over the shortage of shells on the Western Front. Either alone
would probably have been sufficient to force a change of Gover-
ment. Historians have tended to follow too uncritically Lord
Beaverbrook's insistence that the Admiralty crisis alone brought
the downfall of the Government:[8] it certainly made a Ministerial
reshuffle an immediate inevitability, but without either crisis the
general disparity between social and military needs and Government action would have brought change before very long.

In the present context greater interest attaches to the shell shor-
tage, which became a crying public issue with the publication in
The Times of a dispatch from its military correspondent, Colonel
Repington, which read in part:

We had not sufficient high explosives to lower the enemy's parapets to
the ground, after the French practice. The infantry did splendidly, but
the conditions were too hard. The want of an unlimited supply of high
explosives was a fatal bar to our success.

This article appeared on 14 May; that same day Lord Fisher resigned. Five days later Asquith announced that he was proposing
to reconstruct his Ministry and on 21 May there was a debate in
the House of Commons on the munitions crisis. In the new
Ministry established a few days later the Conservatives took their
places as partners in a war coalition. Even more significant was
the inclusion in the Cabinet, as President of the Board of Education, of the Secretary of the Labour Party, Arthur Henderson;
this was the first time a member of the Labour Party had held
Government office. Two other Labour M.P.s attained minor
office: William Brace, a South Wales miner, became Under-
Secretary at the Home Office, and G. H. Roberts, a printer, became a Government Whip.

One of the first major acts of the new Government was the creation of a Ministry of Munitions, with a Minister in the person of
David Lloyd George. Almost at once, a Munitions of War Bill,

which sought to put the Treasury Agreement on a legal footing, was presented to the House. Its first part was concerned with the avoidance of industrial stoppages: strikes and lock-outs in all industries covered by the Munitions Act were prohibited, and all labour differences were, if the Board of Trade so decided, to be resolved by compulsory arbitration. In the second part of the Act provision was made for the Ministry of Munitions to take over direct control of certain factories concerned in war production. In these factories all trade union practices were to be suspended, though, as in the Treasury Agreement, it was made clear that this was for the duration of the war only, and that wage rates would be safeguarded; any changes in wage rates, however, had to be vetted by the Ministry. As a sop to the workers it was at the same time enacted that there would be a limitation of profits within the controlled establishments.

That Government control, in the sense of a constant watchfulness over discipline, time-keeping, and the achievement of a reasonable level of output, was intended to be a reality is demonstrated by the following clause:

The employer and every person employed in the establishment shall comply with any regulations made applicable to that establishment with a view to attaining and maintaining a proper standard of efficiency with respect to the due observance of the rules of the establishment.

There was at least a rough justice in this, even if it did carry overtones of *1984*. The one clause which was manifestly unjust was the following:

A person shall not give employment to a workman who has within the previous six weeks . . . been employed on or in connexion with munitions work . . . unless he holds a certificate from the employer by whom he was last so employed that he left with the consent of the employer.

The evil this clause was intended to deal with was that of employers bidding against each other for the limited supply of skilled labour; but in binding the employee hand and foot to his employer it substituted a worse one, for there was no equal restriction upon the employer's right to dismiss the employee. The 'leaving certificate' was a standing grievance for the next twelve months. The second part of the Munitions of War Act also dealt with another labour problem which we have not so far touched on – the problem of mobility. In the early stages of the war it had been left to the employment exchanges to exhort men to move to the jobs where they were most needed. At the end of the year the town of Middlesbrough took the initiative in forming what was called the 'King's Squad', a volunteer group of skilled workmen who undertook to go wherever their work was required. By May 1915 this had developed into an official War Munitions Volunteer Scheme and by June it had taken the shape typical of the transition stage of the war: men all over the country were invited to volunteer, but once they had done so they were expected to go unquestioningly wheresoever the Government sent them. Legal sanction for this was provided by Clause 4(6) of the Munitions Act. This amalgam of initial voluntaryism and final compulsion, the traditional basis of the armed forces, was not in the result very successful in increasing the mobility of labour. The third part of the Munitions of War Act, as it finally passed into law, was an addendum brought in by the Government to meet criticism in Parliament that the ordinary courts should not be left to deal with the offences created by the Act: it was now enacted that these offences should be dealt with by specially created Munitions Tribunals.[9]

It is in the months following the creation of the Ministry of Munitions that the movement to keep useful men out of the forces by giving them badges reaches its apogee and is overtaken by the contrary movement to get as many men as possible into the forces by depriving men of their badges. To cut through the entanglement of the many schemes then in force and to resolve the opposing needs of the home front and war front, the Government hit upon the bold stroke of compiling a National Register of all persons, male or female, between the ages of fifteen and sixty-five. The necessary Act of Parliament received the Royal Assent on 15 July 1915, and Sunday, 15 August, was the day set aside for the populace to provide particulars of age and occupation. Left-wingers and liberals stirred uneasily as they felt the cold chill of conscription in the air,[10] but it would seem reasonable in view of the economic and industrial difficulties we have been discussing to take at its face value Lord Lansdowne's explanation of the Government's intention:

that every member of the community should bear not merely a part in the national task but the part which he is best qualified to take.[11]

If there was anything sinister to be read between the lines of this, it was not simply military conscription, but conscription for all aspects of the war effort. For the time being, however, the Prime Minister denied that there was any intention of introducing military conscription.

As the National Registration forms came in, those of men of military age were copied on to pink forms (the Civil Service having a most inept sense of colour values), and a star was placed against the names of those in essential occupations. But attention had by this time turned from the shell shortage, now being handled with unquiet confidence by Lloyd George, to the shortage of men on the Western Front. The first stage in the new recruiting drive which was, in the end, to culminate in the imposition of conscription, came with a conference on 28 September between the Government and the unions. In face of the inflexible opposition to conscription expressed by the latter it was agreed that one further great voluntary effort should be made. This was followed by the appointment on 11 October of Lord Derby in the new office of Director-General of Recruiting.[12]

[II] LIQUOR

Describing the England in which he lived for a time in the mid-eighteenth century, Benjamin Franklin tells of a printer who 'drank every day a pint before breakfast, a pint at breakfast ... a pint between breakfast and dinner, a pint in the afternoon about 6 o'clock, and another pint when he had done his day's work'.[13] Alternative amusements certainly were scarce in the eighteenth century, but what is perhaps most significant is that the beer was clearly regarded as a necessary adjunct to work. In Edwardian times heavy drinking of an evening was still an important leisure activity of a big section of the people, and for many heavy manual workers it was felt to be an essential support to the earning of their daily bread by the sweat of their brows.

That alcoholic liquors stood on a slightly different footing from other food and drink had long been recognized by British Governments: Acts regulating the drink traffic had been passed in 1495, 1551, at the height of the Gin Age in the eighteenth century, and during the burst of Gladstonian piety in the nine-teenth century. The total effect was that all premises selling alcoholic liquors had to seek a licence year by year from the local magistrates, and that, in 1914, there was in all areas a legally imposed closing time: in London this was half an hour after midnight (the pubs opened again at 5 am); in other towns the opening hours were 6 am to 11 pm and in country districts 6 am to 10 pm. Scotland suffered a harsher régime, the open hours being from 10 am to as early as 9 pm in some areas, 11 pm in others; on Sundays pubs in both Scotland and Wales were closed. England treated her Sabbath in the more complicated fashion which has now become standard for every day of the week: the pubs were open for a couple of hours in the middle of the day, then were closed in the afternoon, to open again at six for a further four or five hours.[14]

When war broke out, therefore, there was ample scope for the indulgence of patriotic feeling. The civilian, perhaps, could harm no one by himself; but the War Office and the Admiralty perceived at once the undesirability of recruits coming on parade, or on board ship, suffering from heavy hang-overs. Thus one of the earliest regulations under the Defence of the Realm Act[15] declared:

The competent naval or military authority may by order require all premises licensed for the sale of intoxicating liquor within or in the neighbourhood of any defended harbour to be closed except during such hours as may be specified in the order.

The regulation itself is of no great importance: it was purely military in purpose, and it was soon superseded. But as the indulgence of patriotic feeling hardened into a pattern of 'ribald songs, dancing and quarrelling'[16] each evening at closing time, the Government opened its massive onslaught upon traditional British drinking habits. By the terms of the Intoxicating Liquor (Temporary Restriction) Act of 31 August, the Chief Officer of Police in any licensing district or the licensing justices for any licensing district, acting upon the recommendation of the Chief

Officer of Police, were empowered to impose such restriction upon the hours of sale of alcohol as might seem desirable for the maintenance of order or the suppression of drunkenness. The Act was to be valid till a month after the end of the war.

By the end of 1914 nearly one half of the one thousand licensing authorities in England and Wales had made use of the Act to stipulate an opening time of 8 or 9 am. In London a new closing hour of 11 pm was introduced on 4 September; it became 10 pm on 19 October. Many good consequences flowed immediately, so that even the ranks of the brewing trade could scarce forbear to cheer:

A transformation of the night scenes of London has followed from the closing of the public-houses at 11. Great traffic centres, like the Elephant and Castle, at which immense crowds usually lounge about until 1 o'clock in the morning, have suddenly become peaceful and respectable. The police, instead of having to 'move on' numbers of people who have been dislodged from the bars at 12.30 at night, found very little intoxication to deal with, the last hour and a half being responsible for much of the excess of which complaint is made. Many of the public-houses were half empty some time before closing time.[17]

This, however, was not enough for the sanctimonious watchdogs of manners and morals, for whom the war provided a glorious field-day in which they paraded, fangs bared and tails wagging. Led by Lord Kitchener at the top and fuelled by the various abstinence societies, there was a powerful campaign against drinking generally and against, in particular, 'treating' – the traditional custom of buying drinks in rounds, aggravated into a clear nuisance when many a man saw an easy way to doing his duty vicariously by buying drinks for his fellows in uniform. Kitchener, in a 'Message to the Nation' of 24 October 1914, issued through the Press Bureau, appealed

to the public, both men and women, to help the soldiers in their task. He begs everyone to avoid treating the men to drink, and to give them every assistance in resisting the temptations which are often placed before them.[18]

All that happened, however, was that the 'business as usual' budget put the price of beer up from 3d to 4d a pint.

Lloyd George had once been the great rabble-rouser of Welsh nonconformity; he was now in process of developing into one of the greatest war statesmen in British history. The merging of the one into the other can be seen in two speeches of 28 February and 29 March 1915. In the first he concluded a blistering attack on the 'small minority of workmen' given to drunkenness with the cry: 'Drink is doing us more damage in the war than all the German submarines put together.'[19] A month later the threat had assumed even more serious proportions: 'We are fighting Germany, Austria and Drink, and, as far as I can see, the greatest of these deadly foes is Drink.'[20]

One man who was clearly impressed was the King, who on 15 April 'took the pledge', and was rather hurt by the failure of other public figures to follow his lead despite the efforts of a teetotal organization specially founded to canvass businessmen and politicians.[21] But the Government took the drastic action which has left permanent scars, first preparing the ground with an investigation into bad time-keeping in shipbuilding, munitions and transport areas. The main conclusion of the Report, presented on 29 April 1915, was that, although there were no doubt many reasons for loss of time, the most important was the ease with which men now enjoying high rates of wages and abundance of employment could obtain beer and spirits. From the Clyde, however, it was reported that no noticeable increase in drinking had taken place since the war began; whether this was because the men of the Clyde were a particularly sober breed, or whether it was because no increase upon the amount consumed before the war was humanly possible, the Report does not make clear; elsewhere it is stated that the influx of Scotsmen into Barrow 'has led to the greater sale of spirits'.[22] Taken along with what has already been said about drinking habits in 1914, the Report is substantial evidence of the prevalence of heavy drinking, given the opportunity, among the working classes. But its conclusions were too sweeping, and in many cases unconvincing. It failed to bring out prominently that the basic evil really was that a very tiny minority of drunkards could hold up the labours of entirely sober mates. It said nothing of other classes in the community, who, to judge from the lack of response to the King's pledge and from the widespread stories about London night-clubs and drinking dens, were no less fond of their liquor. By the activist section of the working classes the Report, rightly, was regarded as an unjustifiable slight.

But the Government had secured its verdict. The Defence of the Realm (Amendment No. 3) Act was passed on 19 May 1915; by an Order in Council which followed on 10 June the Defence of the Realm (Liquor Control) Regulations were promulgated, and these in turn led to the establishment of the Central Control Board (Liquor Traffic).²³ The Central Control Board was not intended to impose its rule on the entire country indiscriminately, but rather to take over control of liquor-licensing in those areas where excessive drinking could be held, in some way or another, to be impeding the war effort. By 1 October control had been taken of fourteen such areas, and, among other limitations, an important general order restricting sale, whether for consumption on or off the premises, to two and a half hours in the middle of the day and to three (or, in some cases, two) hours in the evening was put into force. The sale of alcohol, that is, was prohibited before midday and throughout the afternoon after 2.30 pm.

The Board's other main measure was the prohibition of the controversial 'treating'. The police were enthusiastic: from Bootle the Chief of Police expressed the hope that the prohibition had come to stay:

It has in my opinion been largely instrumental in almost entirely wiping out what is locally known as the public-house 'bummer'.²⁴

Everywhere reductions in the incidence of drunkenness were reported. This, however, was the negative side of the Board's work. More positively it made itself responsible for the provision of canteen facilities in the new munitions areas, and its attempts to foster 'model pubs' did much to eradicate the sordid image of the British pub as a mere drinking den.

From early 1916 the Board was in a particularly strong position to carry out these reforms in three areas, for in them it was decided that the State should itself acquire all licensed premises. The areas concerned were Enfield Lock in London, where there was an important munitions factory; the march lands embracing Carlisle in England and Gretna in Scotland, where the enormous influx of munitions workers had created a state of drink-sodden chaos; and Invergordon and Cromarty, where there were important naval establishments. These experiments in State control have endured, but although there were many pressing recommendations, particularly from the Board itself,[25] for total nationalization, this was never accomplished. Rather, the Board proceeded by piecemeal extension of control: by March 1916 its regulations applied to twenty-seven areas and 30 million people; by March 1917 to 38 million people out of a total population of 41 millions.[26] At no stage in the war was the entire country under control: when the Armistice came it was still possible in the more desolate, rustic parts, far from the madding crowds of war workers and military personnel, to drink without a break from dawn till dusk. It was left to the Licensing Act of 1921 to remove this dire anomaly.

The other main lines of attack on heavy drinking lay through increasing prices, decreasing potency, and introducing special restrictions on the sale of spirits. In its first series of orders the Board laid down a maximum of seventy degrees proof for all spirits, the figure which still obtains widely today; it forbade spirit sales by the bottle on Saturdays and Sundays, and otherwise limited such sales to the midday opening hours – even then, by a curious process of reasoning, it was stipulated that sales must be made only in quart bottles, the working men being more regularly in the habit of purchasing smaller quantities for speedy consumption.[27] In some areas where the favourite tipple had been a glass of spirits followed immediately by a 'chaser' of beer, the rather difficult task of preventing such simultaneous purchases was imposed upon publicans.[28] Successive budgets throughout the war placed punitive taxation on spirits: from being, at 3d a glass, on a par with beer in 1914, spirits now soared into the luxury class and were being sold at four or five times that price by 1920.

Reductions in output and strength of beer, which were enforced in 1916 when the acreage under hops was reduced by more than half and supplies of grainstuffs were severely curtailed, were as much designed to conserve essential food supplies as to combat drunkenness.[29] Scarcity conditions brought sharp price rises up to, in some areas, as much as 10d a pint. Weak beer – 'Government Ale' – and high prices became a standing grievance – one member of the drinking classes was heard to remark darkly as news filtered in from Russia in March 1917, 'Russia was never troubled by revolution till she went teetotal.'[30] In October 1917 the Government were forced to introduce price-control, at 4d and 5d a pint, for beer. In April 1918 the gravity of beer was again reduced and by 1919 the permitted price – depending on strength – was anything up to 9d a pint: from $\frac{1}{4}$d on the average pint costing 3d, taxation had risen to $3\frac{1}{2}$d on the average pint costing 7d.

Whatever criticisms may be made of certain of the utterances of rhetorical bigots there can be no question that the liquor restrictions of the First World War brought about a salutary change in one of the most important social habits of the people of Britain. From being a melancholy but inescapable feature of the British scene, drunkenness became a limited and manageable problem: in 1914 average weekly convictions for drunkenness were 3,388 in England and Wales; by the end of 1918 they had fallen to 449. In Scotland the weekly average fell from 1,485 immediately before October 1915 to 355 in 1918. As female drunkenness was affected too, the figures could not just be written off as due to the absence of men at war.[31] Drink was no longer, from morning to evening, an indispensable adjunct to the work of many; money was conserved for the more essential commodities of a healthy life. One Scottish Chief Constable reported:

Non-licensed grocers and other shopkeepers say that they have never done so good business amongst the working classes on Saturdays. This they believe to be due to the fact that working men get home with their wages, which they hand over to their wives, and partake of a proper meal prior to the opening of licensed premises.[32]

All of this is directly traceable to the regulation and reduced supply brought about by the necessities of war; but that is not to say that controls which were highly desirable in Edwardian conditions are necessarily desirable today.

[III] RED CLYDESIDE AND OTHER PLACES

When we talk of the labour movement, we can mean either or

both of two things. Speaking generally, we are referring to all attempts, however haphazard, whatever the philosophical motivation, of the working classes to better their lot politically and economically; to anything in fact where there are both labour and movement, whether that movement be forward, backward, or circular. Speaking more specifically, we mean the broad advance under organized leadership of the working classes towards the present high slopes occupied, on the one side, by the Labour Party, and, on the other, by the trade unions. The period of the First World War is distinctive in recent labour history for the way in which, despite superficial appearances, the disorganized sporadic outbursts of labour protest meshed with the formal organized movement to the great advantage of the working class as a whole. In entering into industrial bargains and political coalitions the official leadership in some degree put themselves out of commission as frontline defenders of the local interests of working men: the defence of these interests now fell to unofficial agitators or to those minor union officers, the shop stewards, whose one main function before 1914 was to supervise the piece-work arrangements in their own shops.[33]

That these interests were often in need of defence is an obvious concomitant of the stringent labour regulations we have already discussed. But the first outbreaks of discontent after August 1914 must not be attributed entirely to the new situation created by the war. All of them owed something to the ideas of syndicalism and industrial unionism which had been disseminated in previous years. Syndicalism presented the doctrine that through a universal strike the workers could create for themselves the opportunity to seize power. Industrial unionism concentrated on the proposition that the workers could greatly strengthen their position by organizing themselves in large unions based on whole industries, rather than in small, sectional, craft unions: ultimately the objective was the creation of one vast industrial union which would be a centre of political as well as industrial power. Accepted in whole or in part, these theories fostered a definite militance in the trade union world and created a current favourable to 'workers' control' – a thesis most persuasively argued by the exponents of guild socialism, itself in part an offshoot of syndicalism. For a few double-dyed syndicalists and neo-Marxists,

the war was at once a final demonstration of the follies of capitalism, to be resisted at all costs, and a glorious opportunity for
the workers to press home their advantage. All this apart, the
first open industrial troubles are directly attributable to the
normal expiration of various trade agreements towards the end
of 1914.

War-time events in the Clydeside area of the west of Scotland
are of especial interest both because the informal labour movement
here was at its most colourful and cohesive, and because 'Red
Clydeside', possessing an enduring quality of its own, wrote
itself into history long after the noise of wartime struggles had
died away. The Clyde movement can, as it were, be examined
both horizontally and vertically: horizontally in the sense that,
for a comparatively limited period of time, it was part of a wider
phase of working-class discontent which affected all parts of
Britain; vertically in the sense that it had a specific local quality
which made it an influence long after the wider movement had
died away.

Much of what is distinctive about the labour history of Glasgow can be explained by the way in which over the half-century
before 1914 the city, like a vast dirty blotting paper, had sopped
up the flow of immigrants from the Scottish highlands and from
Ireland; Celtic fire and spirit, and, be it said, Celtic parochialism,
coexisted with lowland Scottish caution and rationality. Here there
had been sympathetic ears enough for the industrial unionism
propagated by the Irish republican, James Connolly, whose
party, the Socialist Labour Party, though numerically tiny, had
important leaders in the Clyde engineering shops, men like
Arthur McManus, J. W. Muir, and David Kirkwood, the last-
named the prototype of the hard-headed lowland Scot.[34] The
Socialist Labour Party was the twin child of Britain's first
Marxist political party, the Social Democratic Federation (founded 1884). The other twin was the British Socialist Party, whose
most active members in the Glasgow area were William Gallacher
(son of a highland father and an Irish mother) and John McLean,
a schoolmaster who did more than any other single person to
spread the fundamental doctrines of Marxism throughout the
west of Scotland. At the same time there was a strong tradition
of democratic socialism stemming from Keir Hardie's Scottish

Labour Party of the 1880s, merged in 1893 into the Independent Labour Party (I.L.P.). The I.L.P., itself the most important component part of the ramshackle structure which the Labour Party then was ('the Labour Party is a jelly-fish, the I.L.P. its backbone' was a later and less kind metaphor), was also the most important Labour political organization on Clydeside, despite the fact that it drew most of its membership from the craftsmen, small tradesmen, schoolteachers and white-collar workers rather than from the engineers and more characteristic industrial workers.[35] The most important figure in the Glasgow I.L.P. was an Irish-born Catholic, John Wheatley, a chubby owl behind his pebble-lens spectacles, who, after working in the Lanarkshire coal-pits as a boy, had built up a small publishing business of his own. Although the different sects slanged each other in public, there was a deeper inter-dependence. One of John McLean's pupils, James Maxton, spent a lifetime in the I.L.P.; Kirkwood, shortly after the outbreak of war, was persuaded by Wheatley to leave the B.S.P. for the I.L.P.[36] Coherence was given to a movement which might otherwise have been fragmented among the different factories and workshops by the existence of vigilance committees whose prime function was to maintain a high level of trade union membership, but which tended to be staffed by the more politically conscious figures.[37]

On the first Sunday after the outbreak of hostilities there were, in the Glasgow area, big demonstrations against the war as a purely capitalist venture. But what really affected the main body of working men was the demand made in June by the local committee of the Amalgamated Society of Engineers for an advance of twopence per hour to take effect in January 1915, when the three-year agreement then in force was due to terminate. Negotiations took place from November onwards, but the most the employers would offer was an hourly increase of three farthings. A disputed wage claim combined with syndicalist agitation against the war created a likely situation for a rank-and-file revolt against the executive of the Amalgamated Society of Engineers, which was in favour of acceptance of the three farthings.[38] But there was one new, almost fortuitous circumstance, which reveals much about the working class on Clydeside, always in the final analysis touched by a near and real issue rather than any hypothesis about the final collapse of capitalism: in February the firm of Weir's of Cathcart, on the outskirts of Glasgow, engaged, at higher pay, a number of Americans. Within days 5,000 engineers were out on strike.[39]

It was a spontaneous strike, but it was also very efficiently organized. From being minor cogs in the official trade union machinery the shop stewards in the various factories affected became the major wheels of unofficial discontent; joined together, they became a mighty conveyor-belt of working-class action, the Central Withdrawal of Labour Committee, which demanded that it, and not the A.S.E., should be responsible for negotiations with the employers. The strike ended, however, when, on a ballot vote, the men decided by a small majority in favour of arbitration and were finally awarded a penny an hour increase, with 10 per cent on piece rates.

These increases, half of what had been asked for, left a sense of injury; insult was added when there appeared on 1 May the report, referred to in the previous section, which blamed bad time-keeping on heavy drinking, a slight which men like Gallacher and Kirkwood, who were life-long teetotallers, must have found hard to bear. The waters, then, were already pretty troubled when the Munitions of War Act, with its leaving certificates and provisions for dilution and the total abolition of strikes, was launched. The members of the Withdrawal of Labour Committee determined upon full-scale resistance to the Act and 'for the purpose of concentrating the whole force of the Clyde area against it' formed itself, along with others interested, into the Clyde Workers' Committee.[40] President of the Committee was Gallacher, secretary an engineer, James Messer, treasurer Tom Clark, shortly succeeded by Kirkwood, who acted as a channel of communication with the political genius in the background, John Wheatley.[41] Its first manifesto declared:

The support given to the Munitions Act by the officials was an act of treachery to the working classes. Those of us who have refused to be sold have organized the above Committee. . . .[42]

It is only towards the end of this manifesto that anything is said about the theory of industrial unionism. A later article in the weekly paper which the Committee established, *The Worker*, brings out the same point: the main purpose of the Committee was the limited and practical one of dealing with the infringement of traditional rights felt to be involved in Government policy; the question of establishing 'one big industrial union' is relegated to the end of the article and defined as 'an ultimate aim', the words being heavily leaded.[43]

A wider objective, which the Committee did put in the forefront of its demands, was that of 'Workers' Control' – that, as it was put in the first issue of *The Worker*, 'organized labour' should have 'a direct share in the management down through all departments'; again there was a certain stern practicality in that the proposals for the reorganization of industry were all extremely carefully elaborated. Two incidents in the months following the passing of the Munitions Act revealed to the Government the seriousness of the Clyde movement. Resistance at the firm of Lang's of Johnstone forced the withdrawal of the Ministry's dilution circular of August 1915, and a strike at another firm resulted in three strikers who refused to pay the fines imposed by the Munitions Tribunal being sent to prison. A general Clydeside strike seemed a possibility until the unions of the men concerned solved the problem by paying their fines for them.[44]

Meanwhile there were rumblings of discontent throughout the trade union movement over the working of the Munitions of War Act. The Government appointed a two-man Commission of Investigation, which took a special interest in Clydeside.[45] Hard on its heels came the great prince of industrial peace, Lloyd George. The Minister of Munitions first addressed a mass meeting in the St Andrew's Hall on Christmas Day, but in that chill un-Christian assembly Lloyd George's Welsh wizardry for once fell completely flat – so flat, indeed, that the press was prohibited from publishing any report of the meeting save a small official hand-out. For printing a full and circumstantial account, the Glasgow socialist weekly, *Forward*, was suppressed. The report began:

The best paid munitions worker in Britain, Mr Lloyd George (almost £100 a week), visited the Clyde last week in search of adventure. He got it. . . .[46]

Never a man to be deflected from his set purpose, Lloyd George now insisted upon meeting the shop stewards from the whole area at the Parkhead Forge, where Kirkwood was chief shop steward. Dull egoist though Kirkwood in many ways was, he managed, in introducing the Minister to his fellows, to hit upon words which deservedly became famous:

I can assure him that every word he says will be carefully weighed. We regard him with suspicion, because every action with which he is associated has the taint of slavery about it.[47]

Considering the series of slaps in the face to which Lloyd George was subjected, he comported himself very ably. Kirkwood informed him that he and his fellow shop stewards were not opposed to dilution as such, but that 'dilution must be carried out under the control of the workers'.[48] Responding with great sensitivity, the Government dispatched three further commissioners to Glasgow to work out with the shop stewards a mutually acceptable scheme of dilution. The man who drafted the scheme which in the later stages of the war worked to the satisfaction of both sides was John Wheatley.[49]

Before the *via media* was established, there was another big strike, whose causes appear remarkably similar to those of the strike of February 1915. While unskilled workers and women were being steadily brought in, the management at the Parkhead Forge, in a strange and ill-considered reversal of tactics, suddenly banned Kirkwood from checking on the conditions under which the dilutees were employed. Of the strike which broke out on 17 March and lasted till 4 April the careful official Labour Party inquiry reported:

We do not think that the Clyde Workers' Committee as a collective body was responsible for the strike which occurred. . . . In our opinion, that strike was a *spontaneous outbreak* of the general body of workmen employed there, and was intended as a protest against what they regarded as the unfair restriction of facilities which had previously been allowed to the chief shop steward.[50]

Drastic Governmental action followed, ten of the leaders, including Kirkwood, being deported to other parts of the country. Ironically this helped to speed up something which was taking place already, the spread of the Clydeside pattern of industrial action to other areas.[51] At the same time it brought to an end the first and most important phase of Clydeside activity. For the next two years the various leading figures, Gallacher and the shop stewards as well as Wheatley, the lawyer dandy Rosslyn Mitchell, and the members of the I.L.P., devoted themselves to precise, practical campaigns, of which the one against increased rents was the most important. While men from the industrial side of the movement turned towards non-industrial social objectives, such an eminently political figure as James Maxton, schoolteacher and member of the National Administrative Council of the I.L.P., showed his sense of identity with the industrial side of the movement by having himself arrested and imprisoned for a speech advocating further strike action.[52] Bound thus tightly together, the threads of industrial action and of political agitation made a strong rope.

Before examining the way in which the Clydeside pattern spread we must look at another troubled area where extreme discontent, canalized in pre-war days by the South Wales Miners' Unofficial Reform Committee,[53] arose concurrently with, and independently of, the first disturbances on Clydeside. Just as the engineers on Clydeside had had a three-year agreement with the employers which was due to expire six months after the outbreak of war, so the South Wales Miners' Federation had a five-year agreement with the mine operators which was due to expire on 1 April 1915. Before April came round, however, the miners throughout the country had successfully pressed their claim for a war bonus, and through the arbitration of the Prime Minister a national agreement involving definite increases had been arrived at.[54] In Wales the coal-owners insisted that this national agreement should take the place of the new local agreement due to be concluded in April. This was not acceptable to the miners in Wales, who were anxious to secure a permanent rise rather than a war bonus which might well terminate with the conclusion of hostilities.

When negotiations between the miners and the South Wales coal-owners appeared to have reached an impasse, the Government, aware of the serious effects a coal strike would have on the war effort, took a hand; in this case its attempts at mediation were unsuccessful, and it was announced on behalf of the miners that the strike would begin on 14 July. Before that date the Government found itself armed with the provisions of the Munitions of War Act, and on the day before the strike took place it issued a proclamation threatening the miners with the pains and penalties provided in the Act. This merely heightened the sense of grievance of the miners, for they claimed that in the previous negotiations with the Government Lloyd George had given an undertaking that no such coercion was contemplated. Thus, despite the opposition of the Miners' Federation itself, the strike began on the appointed day. Five days later, so serious was the cessation of coal supplies from South Wales that Lloyd George, in company with Runciman and Arthur Henderson, Labour's first Cabinet Minister, had to scuttle down to Cardiff and there agree that the miners' demands should be met in full. Work began again on 20 July; a further brief interruption in August merely emphasized that the workers in this industry had the Government at their mercy, so that it was better to accept their demands rather than risk a prolonged coal stoppage.[55] The successes of the South Wales miners provided the encouragement for rebel movements in other areas, but it was Glasgow which provided the method.

The big organizational change which emerged from the Clydeside struggles was the conversion of the shop stewards from minor trade union officials into major spokesmen of rank-and-file discontent who derived their strength from the fact that they served with and were elected by the men on the shop floor. In some cases the change was an immediate one; in others there grew up first of all unofficial shop stewards alongside the official ones, till eventually the unofficial ones got *de facto* recognition as the true powers in the workshop.[55] This new machinery was to furnish a valuable outlet for working-class action in the later stages of the war when the official leadership, suffocated in the Governmental embrace, was unable to function properly, especially when the workings of the Conscription Acts brought new grievances.

[IV] CONSCRIPTION

Lord Derby was Lord Kitchener's answer to the shortage of manpower in the trenches. Lord Derby's answer to Lord Kitchener was the Scheme for which his name will always be celebrated, one of those shot-gun weddings between the fair maid of Liberal idealism and the ogre of Tory militarism of which recent British history has not been entirely innocent and for which Asquith's last ministry provided peculiarly efficient brokerage. At the base of the scheme was the continental practice of dividing the adult males of the country into annual classes, each class in turn to become available for military service with the changing of the calendar.[57] The one refinement was the pledge that no married men were to be considered until there were no longer any unmarried men available. For this curious theory that, although all men are eligible, bachelors are more eligible than others, there was no moral or legal sanction, save perhaps loyalty to the ideal of the family unit; the suspicion that the main intention was to set the one group of men against the other seems well founded.

The Derby Scheme, then, provided some of the groundwork of conscription on the continental plan, but there was no compulsion – liberal principle was still strong enough to see to that. Instead, by a mixture of suasion and blandishment, men were pressured into 'attesting', that is to say undertaking to serve if and when called upon to do so. Every man was to attest, but those who were found to have good national (skilled work in a munitions factory, say) or personal (single-handedly running a sweet-shop and supporting an aged mother and five maiden aunts on the proceeds, say) reasons were to be given exemptions. It was for the purpose of determining these exemptions that a Local Government Board circular of 19 November 1915 announced the establishment of tribunals throughout the country, with a central tribunal under Lord Sydenham in London.[58]

As it affected society the Derby Scheme was a gigantic engine of fraud and moral blackmail, but, given that the Government had to find soldiers somehow, it was a very astute piece of political tactics. If it succeeded, well and good – the sanctity of voluntaryism had been maintained; if it failed, the case for conscription would be well-nigh irresistible. Opinion on conscription was still very divided in the autumn of 1915. In the years before, it had been advocated by a small group of right-wing imperialists, and it had had an able supporter in J. L. Garvin, editor of the influential Sunday newspaper, the *Observer*. Realizing that the bulk of the country still disliked the very notion of

conscription and believing national unity to be of greater importance than the principle of universal military service, Garvin, very
laudably, had donned velvet gloves to restrain the iron hand of
Lord Northcliffe, whose pro-conscription campaign had begun
in August 1914, and the other extreme conscriptionists. Liberal
newspapers like the *Daily News* and the *Manchester Guardian*
carried strongly worded editorials against conscription and, in
order to lay the dreaded shadow, were forced to praise the substance in the Derby Scheme. The Labour movement, partly
because of the industrial implications, maintained its opposition.

The Derby Scheme had been in operation for only just over a
fortnight when Asquith put his finger up to the wind. 'If', he said

> there should still be found a substantial number of men of military age
> not required for other purposes, and who, without excuse, hold back
> from the service of their country, I believe that the very same con-
> ditions which make compulsion impossible now – namely the absence
> of general consent – would force the country to a view that they must
> consent to supplement, by some form of legal obligation, the failure
> of the voluntary system.[59]

Another six weeks elapsed before the results of the Scheme were
put to statistical test: in his *Report on Recruiting*, published as a
White Paper at the beginning of the following year, Lord Derby
announced that of 2,179,231 single men shown by the National
Register to be of military age only 1,150,000 had attested; the
proportion of married men was not greatly different – 1,152,947
out of 2,832,210. His conclusion was that, in view of the pledge to
take single men first,

> it will not be possible to hold married men to their attestation unless
> and until the services of single men have been obtained by other means,
> the present system having failed to bring them to the colours.[60]

The 'other means' appeared within days in the Military Service
Bill introduced on 5 January 1916, by the Prime Minister. Its
main clause declared that all single men (including widowers
without children) would be deemed to have enlisted and to have
been transferred to the Reserve, whence they could be called up
as required. The Liberal newspapers were most unhappy about
this, even if it could be simply represented as the necessary

redemption of the pledge to the married men, but only one Liberal Cabinet Minister resigned – Sir John Simon, who thereafter made no further attempt to fight the issue. While Sir John Simon resigned because of his opposition to the Bill, the Labour representatives in the Government, who believed its provisions to be necessary, were expected to resign in order to be free to support it; the T.U.C. had just voted against the Bill by over two million votes to less than half a million. But in the end the Labour members withdrew their resignations, and criticism from the Party outside was stayed until a formal conference could meet and thrash out the problem.[61]

Semi-conscription was inadequate to the ever-mounting demands of the trenches and on 25 April a second Conscription Bill was presented to a secret session of the House of Commons: so fumblingly did the measure try to reconcile present needs with past promises, however, that the Government found itself faced with a storm of opposition which blew the Bill back into their own faces. At the beginning of May a new universal conscription Bill, which soon became law, was introduced. Again the resignations of the Labour Ministers were announced; again, after a more seemly interval had elapsed, they were withdrawn. The real hub of the hostility of the Labour movement to military conscription had been the fear that it would be followed by industrial conscription, that conscript labour would be set to work in the home factories and workshops at army pay and under army discipline; the seeming inconsistency of Arthur Henderson and his colleagues can be justified on the grounds that, for the time being, there was no hint of this.

The imposition of universal conscription was an event of central importance in the social history of the war. It implied a definite swing in Government policy from the careful hoarding of its skilled labour to a prodigal casting of copper, silver and gold into the lottery of the trenches; it meant that the highly controversial 'dilution' which had been designed to maximize the domestic labour force now became 'substitution', the attempt to release the able-bodied by the employment of the less able-bodied. By greatly exacerbating the labour shortage, it marked the lowering of the remaining barriers of prejudice to the full-scale employment of women. Above all it brought first-hand

'Importance of Conscription

experience of the horrors of war, not just to a couple of million volunteers and horny-handed professionals, but willy-nilly to twice as many ordinary unadventurous civilians – one in three of the adult male population. Of the experience in wait for them we have already said a little, and there are whole libraries of books which say the rest. Life in the trenches was a life lived in a new dimension of foulness, a tunnel life lived in a troll kingdom in which immobility never brought peace, and activity scarcely ever brought mobility. Once upon a time the putrefaction of war could be concealed in the salt of glory and conquest. Now conquest seldom extended beyond a few hundred yards of mud or the desolate stones of a shattered village: the salt had lost its savour.

The imposition of conscription did not silence opposition to the war. A group of Liberals and Socialists in December 1914 had founded the Union of Democratic Control (U.D.C.) dedicated, in the immediate view, to the securing of an early negotiated peace, and ultimately to the adoption by British Governments of an open, democratically-controlled foreign policy which would avoid the errors which had led to war.[61] In the same month, Fenner Brockway, Clifford Allen and C. H. Norman founded the No Conscription Fellowship (N.C.F.) for young men of military age:[62] this body fixed careful eyes on the various manoeuvres of the Government which seemed to presage conscription. From November 1915 the N.C.F. was in a full state of preparedness, with a complicated mesh of communications holding together the branches which spread throughout the country. Modelling itself partly on the Irish Sinn Fein movement and partly on the suffragettes, it provided each of its officers with a 'shadow' to carry on his duties if he himself were arrested. It was ready to act as an open pressure group upon Parliament, as a semi-legal organization disseminating its propaganda under the shadow of D.O.R.A., and as a clandestine conspiracy maintaining contact among its members as they disappeared into prison.

It was partly due to the pressure of the N.C.F., which could count on the good offices of a handful of friendly M.P.s, that the first Conscription Act directed that the tribunals, set up by the Derby Scheme, under which they considered appeals for exemption on economic and personal grounds, were now also to hear appeals based on 'a conscientious objection to the under-

· objectors.

taking of combatant service'. A new term (usually of abuse), 'conscientious objector', had entered the English language. But the N.C.F. was not satisfied: 'it is not fighting in particular which revolts us', it declared; 'it is war itself that we will not assist'. Again it had some success in that in the Second Conscription Act it was made clear that in certain cases absolute exemption from all duties connected with the national effort could be granted to conscientious objectors.

Made up of solid local worthies, the tribunals could scarcely be expected to treat the claims of conscientious objectors with sympathy: hatred, fear and horror at the mounting slaughter on the Western Front could be vented vicariously on such 'shirkers', the exposure of whom seemed a patriotic duty. A few tribunals did comport themselves with scrupulous attention to the letter and spirit of the conscience clauses of the Military Service Acts, but all found great difficulty in comprehending the attitude of the young man who declared he could play no part at all in the national effort and demanded absolute exemption. To begin with, as conscientious objectors had their applications rejected by the tribunals, they were passed on to the military authorities. Three groups, deemed to have enlisted in the Non-combatant Corps, were smuggled out to France: there sentence of death was read out to thirty-four men, commuted (after a pause) to ten years' penal servitude.

The information service of the N.C.F. had already got wind of this and at once alerted its friends in Parliament, who secured from Asquith, who was undoubtedly appalled by the action of the military, a statement that no executions would be carried out. A further triumph for the anti-conscription movement was the issue on 25 May 1916, of Army Order X, which laid it down that after being court-martialled conscientious objectors should be handed back to the civilian authorities for incarceration in one of His Majesty's prisons. In June the Government, to its credit seriously disturbed by the problem of the conscientious objector, set up the Pelham Committee, which was charged with finding alternative national work for men who were prepared to take it. A Central Appeals Tribunal was to consider all cases of men already in prison held to be 'genuine' and to direct them towards the Pelham Committee. Those who were willing were released from prison and employed under what was called the Home Office Scheme.[64] Altogether there were about 16,000 conscientious objectors: about 3,300 accepted service in the Noncombatant Corps, somewhat under 3,000 did various forms of ambulance work or work under the direct supervision of their tribunals, around 4,000 accepted work forthwith from the Pelham Committee, and rather more than 6,000 went to prison at least once. Of these, 3,750 were subsequently employed under the Home Office Scheme, leaving 1,500 intractable absolutists whose challenge to the authority of the State the Government simply could not comprehend.[65] Shortly after his translation from the War Office to the Ministry of Munitions, Lloyd George delivered himself of a resounding denunciation of the absolutists:

I do not think they deserve the slightest consideration. With regard to those who object to the shedding of blood it is the traditional policy of this country to respect that view, and we do not propose to depart from it: but in the other case I shall only consider the best means of making the lot of that class a very hard one.[66]

That these sentiments in regard to all types of conscientious objectors were shared by most members of the community, there can be little doubt. There are many reports of I.L.P. or U.D.C. peace demonstrations being broken up, of Quaker meetings being disturbed, and of conscientious objectors serving the national interest in such innocuous occupations as felling trees being molested by local inhabitants.[67] For the absolutists the Government provided only a dismal treadmill of arrest, courtmartial, imprisonment, release, arrest, court-martial, and so on. Clifford Allen, Chairman of the No Conscription Fellowship, was imprisoned thrice before becoming so seriously ill that the Government, reluctant to have him die on their hands, gave him a conditional – that is, conditional upon his remaining seriously ill – release. Allen's case was typical of many; about seventy men actually died from their prison treatment.[68]

The organized resistance to military conscription of the First World War is of importance because it added a draught of physical action to the internationalist theorizing of the U.D.C. As more and more people, in the years after 1918, began to see the whole war as a ghastly mistake, the men who at the time had suffered persecution for that same belief emerged as leaders of public opinion. More important than that, the 16,000 conscientious objectors and, above all, the 1,500 unshakable absolutists were standing for the right of individual protest against the demands of the State and of the majority. Whether they were right or wrong – wrong, obviously, in their underestimation of the war-lust of the Prussian military caste, right, perhaps, in their realization that war would not remove militarism but only harden its yoke upon the peoples of the world – they were helping to safeguard that most precious of man's possessions, his right of individual judgement. Mention must be made of the many Liberals, so out of touch in many ways with the needs of the hour, who did defend this right: F. W. Hirst, Gladstonian editor of the *Economist*, Philip Morrell, husband of the great Edwardian society hostess, Lady Ottoline Morrell, Dr John Clifford, whose abandonment of a former pacificism has already been noted. Though a whole-hearted supporter of Britain's cause against Germany, Clifford was a wholehearted opponent of conscription, as is shown in his address to the second national convention of the No Conscription Fellowship:

The Military Act has imposed Conscription upon this country. Let us remember how it came upon us. It was a fraud. It does not express the matured judgement of the people. . . . I know something about the Tribunals. I am ashamed of my country. These Tribunals are a disgrace to our name. . . . Let us go forward; we are fighting for human wellbeing; we are fighting for the most precious possession of the British people. Conscience is the best asset a nation can possess.[69]

Lord Hugh Cecil, in pre-war days more often found inhabiting last ditches than leading the humanitarian vanguard, strongly denounced the bad treatment of conscientious objectors, and even *The Times* 'confessed' to 'considerable sympathy' with them, though it thought, using the same argument upon which it has always based its opposition to votes for women, that they ought to be disfranchised.[70] The war showed British mass hysteria at its worst; in flashes it showed British individualism at its best.

Leaving the philosophical and political opponents of the war, we must turn again to the attempts of the Government to 'comb out' skilled labour for service in the trenches. This too, of course, made good rabble-rousing material for the popular press. 'Probably there are very few of our readers who do not know at least one case of men who should be serving but have escaped,' declared the *Daily Mail* in the black lead it reserved for its frequent spasms of patrio-sadism.[71] There had been, in connexion with the Derby Scheme, a Reserved Occupations Committee in existence since October 1915; its functions were taken over in March 1916 by a Central Cabinet Committee, which, by an administrative development typical of the war, was replaced later in the year by the Manpower Board.

A proposal of this board to nullify the exemptions of all men under twenty-six brought to straining point the tensions which had been developing between the unions and the War Office in the latter part of 1916. The wrongful enlistment of a Sheffield engineer, called Hargreaves, an incident analogous in its personal quality to the banning of Kirkwood from the workshops at Parkhead, brought an unofficial strike organized by the shop stewards, among whom there was in J. T. Murphy a leading proponent of 'workers' control'. So serious was the strike, which lasted from 9 to 17 November, that the Amalgamated Society of Engineers had to take the matter up formally with the Government. The outcome was a signal victory for labour, the conclusion of the Trade Card Agreement, by which decisions in the matter of exemptions from military service were to be left in the hands of the union itself.[72] For all that the individual workman might still feel his disabilities and grievances, this victory must be accounted a powerful symbol of the power and status enjoyed by labour at the end of 1916. This was confirmed by the Cabinet changes of December. Arthur Henderson held down a seat in the new small War Cabinet over which Lloyd George now presided, John Hodge of the Steel-smelters became Minister of Labour, G. N. Barnes of the Engineers became Minister of Pensions, and three other Labour M.P.s, William Brace, G. H. Roberts and James Parker, all got minor posts. One of the first acts of the new Government was to appoint a sub-committee under J. H. Whitley, M.P., on the 'relations between employers and employed'. Reporting early the following year, it recommended the appointment throughout industry of councils representative of both employers and trade unionists.[73] The 'Whitley Councils' never amounted to much, but the mooting of them at this stage in the war is again symbolic of the Government's desire to recognize and meet the claims of labour.

NOTES TO CHAPTER TWO

1. *Board of Trade Report on State of Employment in United Kingdom, July 1915.*

2. H. Wolfe, *Labour Supply and Regulation,* Oxford, 1923, p. 19.

3. N. Dearle, *Economic Chronicle of the War,* Oxford, 1929, pp. 5-15.

4. G. D. H. Cole, *Trade Unionism and Munitions,* Oxford, 1923, pp. 53-4.

5. *12th Report of Proceedings under the Conciliation Acts;* P.P., 1919, XIII, 185, p. 5.

6. *Hist. Min. Mun.,* Vol. I, pt. 2, p. 110.

7. P.P., 1919, 185, pp. 11-12.

8. Lord Beaverbrook, *Politicians and the War,* I, 1928, pp. 100-3.

9. Wolfe, pp. 107, 196, 110.

10. J. W. Graham, *Conscription and Conscience,* 1922, p. 52.

11. *House of Lords Debates,* Vol. XIX, Col. 336.

12. P.P., 1914-16, XXXIX, Cd. 8149.

13. Quoted by E. N. Williams, *Life in Georgian England,* 1962, pp. 115-16.

14. A. Shadwell, *Drink in 1914-22, A Lesson in Control,* 1923, p. 1.

15. Regulation No. 7 of 12 August 1914.

16. *Brewers' Gazette,* 26 September 1914, quoted by Shadwell.

17. ibid.

18. H. Carter, *The Control of the Drink Trade,* 1918, p. 24.

19. *The Times,* 1 March 1915.

20. *The Times,* 30 March 1915.

21. C. Addison, *Politics from Within,* I, 1925, p. 80. *Observer,* 11 April 1915.

22. *Report of the Committee on Bad Time-Keeping;* P.P., 1914-16, LV, 220, pp. 3, 24.

23. *1st Report of Central Control Board;* P.P., 1914-16, XXV, Cd. 8117, p. 4.

24. *2nd Report of Central Control Board;* P.P., 1916, XII, Cd. 8243, p. 29.

25. *Memorandum of Central Control Board;* P.P., 1917-18, XXVI, Cd. 8613.

26. *2nd Report of Central Control Board,* pp. 15-17. *3rd Report,* p. 5.

27. Shadwell, pp. 41-2.

28. P.P., 1916, XII, Cd. 8243.

29. Shadwell, pp. 83-4. W. Beveridge, *British Food Control,* Oxford, 1925, pp. 101-2.

30. *Daily Mail,* 2, 3 April 1917.

31. *Report of War Cabinet for 1918;* P.P., 1919, XXX, Cmd. 325, p. 293.

32. Quoted by Carter, p. 264.

33. G. D. H. Cole, *Workshop Organization,* 1923, pp. 1-25.

34. W. Gallacher, *Revolt on the Clyde,* 1936, pp. 26-7. D. Kirkwood, *My Life of Revolt,* 1935, pp. 1-32.

35. A. Marwick, 'The Independent Labour Party, 1918-32', unpublished Oxford B.Litt. Thesis, 1960.

36. Kirkwood, p. 87.

37. Labour Party, *Report on Clydeside Deportations,* 1917.

38. W. R. Scott and J. Cunnison, *The Industries of the Clyde Valley during the War,* Oxford, 1924, pp. 139–41.

39. Gallacher, pp. 38–9. Kirkwood, pp. 88–9. Scott and Cunnison, p. 141.

40. *The Worker,* 29 January 1916.

41. Kirkwood, pp. 84, 87, 128.

42. Quoted in Labour Party, *Report on Clyde Deportations.*

43. *The Worker,* 29 January 1916.

44. Scott and Cunnison, pp. 144, 150.

45. G. D. H. Cole, *Trade Unions and Munitions,* p. 117. P.P., 1914–16, XXIX, Cd. 8136.

46. *Forward,* 1 January 1916.

47. Scott and Cunnison, p. 144.

48. *The Worker,* 8 January 1916.

49. Kirkwood, pp. 117–18.

50. Labour Party, *Report on Clyde Deportations.* My italics.

51. Cole, *Workshop Organization,* p. 33. Scott and Cunnison, p. 151.

52. A Marwick, 'James Maxton', in *Scottish Historical Review,* April 1964.

53. Cole, *Workshop Organization,* pp. 107–8.

54. M. B. Hammond, *British Labour Conditions and Legislation During the War,* New York, 1919, pp. 231–4.

55. ibid.

56. Cole, *Workshop Organization,* pp. 38–47, 76–84. B. Pribicevik, *The Shop Stewards' Movement and Workers' Control 1910–1922,* 1959, p. 35.

57. *Report on Recruiting;* P.P., 1914–16, XXXIX, Cd. 8149, p. 3.

58. *Annual Report of Local Government Board,* 1915–16; P.P., 1916, XX, Cd. 8331, p. 21.

59. *House of Commons Debates,* 2 November 1915.

60. Cd. 8149, pp. 5, 7.

61. Labour Party, *Report of Annual Conference 1916,* p. 8.

62. See H. H. Hanak, 'The Union of Democratic Control in the First World War,' in *Bulletin of Institute of Historical Research,* November 1963.

63. See Graham, *Conscription and Conscience,* pp. 171–204, and A. Marwick, *Clifford Allen: the Open Conspirator,* 1964, pp. 20–45, on which the next paragraphs are based.

64. *Annual Report of the Local Government Board 1915–16;* P.P., 1916, XX, Cd. 8331, p. 24. *Ibid 1916–17;* P.P., 1917–18, XVI, Cd. 8697.

65. Graham, pp. 344–52.

66. *House of Commons Debates,* 26 July 1916.

67. B. Russell, *Portraits from Memory,* 1956, pp. 32–3. McDonagh, p. 91. *Manchester Guardian,* 16 February 1916. *Daily Mail,* 27 April 1917. *Observer,* 29 April 1917.

68. Graham, pp. 312 ff.

69. J. Marchant, *Dr John Clifford,* p. 154.

70. *The Times,* 17 October 1916, 6 July 1916.

71. *Daily Mail,* 30 March 1917.

72. Wolfe, *Labour Supply and Regulation,* pp. 38–40, 44–5.

73. P.P., 1917–18, XVIII, Cd. 8606.

CHAPTER THREE
New Women: 1915–1916

[I] WINNING THE WAR

BEFORE THE War, women of the lower classes were the industrial drudges of the community, earning an average wage of 11s 7d per week, about one third of the male average. For women of the upper classes it is true that professional opportunities were beginning to open, but by and large it could with equal literalness be said that these women were good for nothing – educated only sufficiently to grace a leisurely life. The first effects of the war were disastrous for the women in the 'sweated' and dressmaking trades. But before the end of the year the first attempts at dilution in munitions and ordnance factories had brought an expansion and change in the work done by female factory workers. It is easy to exaggerate the importance of this and forget that hard industrial work had been a commonplace in the lives of very many women since before the industrial revolution; however, while for some only a very slight change in job was involved, there were other cases where large numbers of girls and women had been drawn in who had never previously worked in a factory or workshop, including girls hitherto entirely engaged in their parents' homes, waitresses, shop assistants, clerks and domestic servants, as well as unemployed women from miscellaneous women's industries.[1] These developments were confined to munitions and ordnance factories and were on such a small scale that a mere restoration of the pre-war level of employment was not achieved till April 1915.[2]

Many women of the middle and upper classes showed from the start great anxiety to contribute to the patriotic cause. Indeed one of the most interesting psychological phenomena of the war is the way in which the suffragettes, who for ten years had been waging war on the Government and the community, now outshone everyone in their patriotic fervour and stirring appeals for national unity and endeavour. The moderates of the National

Union of Women's Suffrage Societies (led by Mrs Fawcett, who had been opposed to war till the very last) were prepared for the time being entirely to submerge their campaign for women's suffrage. As Mrs Fawcett expressed it in the suffragist paper, *Common Cause*, two days after the outbreak of war:

In the midst of this time of terrible anxiety and grief, it is some little comfort to think that our large organization, which has been completely built up during past years to promote women's suffrage, can be used now to help our country through the period of strain and sorrow.[3]

Mrs Emmeline Pankhurst, matriarchal head of the famous suffragette family, swung the extremist Women's Social and Political Union sharp right into fervid nationalism, to the disgust of her radical daughter, Sylvia, who turned left, establishing her own Workers' Suffrage Federation, which maintained a resolute opposition to the war. It must also be recorded that the No Conscription Fellowship was only kept in being through the devoted resourcefulness of the young women who took over as the male members disappeared into prison. In a famous trial held in March 1917, an anarchistic second-hand-clothes dealer from Derby, Mrs Alice Wheeldon, whose real crimes were the sheltering of deserters and conscientious objectors and a vociferous general hostility to the Government, was accused of plotting with her daughters and son-in-law to kill Lloyd George and Arthur Henderson by means of poison darts. It is clear from reports of the case that the police had made use of *agents provocateurs*, and it was on the most dubious evidence that Mrs Wheeldon was sentenced to ten years' penal servitude, her married daughter to five years, and her son-in-law to seven years; the other daughter, Harriet, was discharged.[4]

Upper-class Amazons, who, for months prior to the war, had gasped in admiration at photographs of the women Volunteers of Ulster preparing to defend the integrity of British Ireland, in February 1915 established the Women's Volunteer Reserve.[5] Women who sought a more constructive part in the war effort found that, while the knitting of garments and comforts for the troops was welcomed, more ambitious efforts were treated with extreme reserve: when, for instance, the distinguished Scottish

medical woman, Dr Elsie Inglis, offered to form a women's
ambulance unit, she was rebuffed at the War Office with the
words, 'My good lady, go home and sit still.'[6] In March, coinci-
dent with the general abandonment of 'business as usual', the
Government announced that it was compiling a register of women
willing to do industrial, agricultural or clerical work.[7] Although
there was an immediate and enthusiastic response, little work
was in fact found for the applicants;[8] as with so many other
pieces of early Asquithian war legislation, the motivation seemed
to be no more than some sort of vague desire to do the right
thing. There was no sense of the intrinsic value of the possible
contribution women might make.

In Glasgow, where dilution was already being successfully
applied in the engineering shops, the municipal tramways, with
Scottish intrepidity, took on two women conductresses on a
week's trial; the experiment was soon extended, the women being
fitted out with natty uniforms in Black Watch tartan.[9] The opening of a new Tube station at Maida Vale in July gave the London
Electric Railway Company the opportunity to bring in from the
outset an all-female staff.[10] For the convenience of its middle-class
readership, the *Daily Mail* in June listed 'some of the new occupations for women': they were, tramway conductors, lift attendants,
shopwalkers, bookstall clerks, ticket-collectors, motor-van
drivers, van guards, milk-deliverers, railway-carriage cleaners,
window-cleaners, dairy workers, shell-makers. The implication
that these were jobs for middle-class women with time on their
hands and not suggestions for the working-class housewife was
borne out by the placing of the most proletarian job last, and
reinforced by an article two days later describing the Women's
Police Force as an occupation for 'gentlewomen'.[11] But the overall
picture was one of willing women finding no outlet for their
desire to serve. This was more than could be borne by the flesh
and blood of Mrs Emmeline Pankhurst and the W.S.P.U., who,
on Saturday 17 July, organized in the centre of London a procession and demonstration of 30,000 women on behalf of women's
'right to serve'.[12]

But the first large-scale exploitation of the services of women
and the revelation of the adaptability of female labour to tasks
long believed to be beyond their powers, which came in the late

summer and autumn of 1915, owed far more to economic
necessity and the dilution clauses of the Munitions of War Act
than to feminist agitation. Already in August we find a trade
magazine commenting a little incredulously that by no means all
of the work being done by women

has been of the repetition type, demanding little or no manipulative
ability, but much of it ... taxed the intelligence of the operatives to a
high degree. Yet the work turned out has reached a high pitch of
excellence ... It may safely be said that women can satisfactorily
handle much heavier pieces of metal than had previously been dreamt
of.[13]

Before the year was out the new use of female labour was being
extended to industries other than those directly involved in the
manufacture of munitions, and the Board of Trade had increased
its strength of women factory inspectors by 50 per cent. These
developments in the main were limited to working-class women,
although when the Ministry of Munitions' recruitment of
'munitions girls' got under way many of the delicate products of
middle- and upper-class homes were found to possess a remarkable
toughness and resilience.[14]

Society, like a pub full of bachelors, was from the start very
conscious of the feminine intrusion, and contemporary accounts
tended greatly to exaggerate it; for the press, starved by the
censorship of most hard news, articles on the new role of women
were highly marketable and served the patriotic purpose of
encouraging women as yet without employment to follow the
example of their sisters. It was, furthermore, easy to argue from
the odd encounter with a female shop-assistant or ticket-collector
that a whole liberating army of women was on the march when in
fact only a few outposts had been established. The London
General Omnibus Company was not converted to the use of
employing women as conductresses until February 1916;[15] in
March there were still only one hundred bus conductresses in
London, though training schemes were by then on hand to
provide another five hundred within a month. As late as July
1916 *Women's Industrial News* commented sharply on popular
misconceptions as to the extent of the employment of women
in agriculture:

Most of the press paragraphs referring to the replacement of men by women upon farms have been calculated to give an erroneous impression to the unknowing public. The demand for female labour in agriculture during 1915 was not very great and large numbers of girls who offered to take up such work failed to find employment.[16]

The fact was that quite apart from their innate conservatism, farmers preferred to hire the cheap labour of school children rather than pay an adult wage to women workers.

The event which began the second and definitive growth in women's employment and determined that the changes involved should go far beyond a limited expansion and upgrading of industrial labour, made a trifle more dramatic by the entry for the first time into hard physical work of a few adventurous members of the upper classes, was the introduction of universal military conscription. On 8 June, two weeks after the passing of the Act, the Government launched its first concerted national drive to fill the places vacated or about to be vacated by men. Only now did the war-time pattern of women's employment begin to assume its final shape.

In July 1914 there had been 212,000 women employed in what were to become the munitions industries. The figure for July 1915, 256,000, shows only a relatively small increase; but the great expansion of later 1915, combined with the impact of compulsory military service in early 1916, is seen in the next July figure, 520,000, an increase of over one hundred per cent. There was still a great deal of slack, so that by July 1917, when the National Service scheme introduced by the Lloyd George Ministry had had six months to bear fruit, the figure was 819,000;[17] in the last year of the war there was a further increase of well over 100,000.

In industry as a whole the total employment of women and girls over ten as between 1914 and 1918 increased by about 800,000, from 2,179,000 to 2,971,000.[18] Narrowing our range again to a field we glanced at before, we find that by February 1917 the total number of bus conductresses leapt from the timorous handful of the previous year to about 2,500, some half of whom, it was said, were former domestic servants. Over the whole war it is transport which shows the biggest proportionate increase in women's employment – from 18,000 in 1914 to 117,000 in 1918. And it is domestic service which is the one industry which shows a decline – from 1,658,000 in 1914 to 1,258,000 in 1918:[19] the decline is substantial (400,000) but, as can be seen, domestic service was far from being wiped out, as is sometimes suggested. Contemporaries were well aware of what was happening. Describing to a correspondent the way in which housemaids were flocking into the munitions factories, R. D. Blumenfeld added his conviction that they would never come back.[20]

After transport the biggest proportional increases were in clerical, commercial, administrative and educational activities. In banking and finance there was a fantastic rate of growth – from a mere 9,500 female employees in 1914 to 63,700 in 1917. Taking the entire span of the war, the number of women and girls employed in the whole of commerce and its allied occupations rose from 505,000 to 934,000. In national and local government, in which education is included, numbers rose from 262,000 to 460,000.[21] It is in these arid statistics that we traverse a central theme in the sociology of women's employment in the twentieth century, the rise of the business girl, taking the term to cover the whole range from executive secretary to shorthand typist. The growth of large-scale industry and bureaucracy would undoubtedly have brought this development eventually, but it was the war, in creating simultaneously a proliferation of Government committees and departments *and* a shortage of men, which brought a sudden and irreversible advance in the economic and social power of a category of women employees which extended from sprigs of the aristocracy to daughters of the proletariat.

The new economic power was noted as early as mid-September 1915. 'No woman worker is in greater demand than the shorthand typist,' reported the *Daily Mail*, adding that wages had in a year risen from £1 to 35s per week. The social development was described under the heading 'Dining Out Girls':

The wartime business girl is to be seen any night dining out alone or with a friend in the moderate-priced restaurants in London. Formerly she would never have had her evening meal in town unless in the company of a man friend. But now with money and without men she is more and more beginning to dine out.[22]

The writer further noted the public smoking of 'the customary cigarette'.

More than half a century before the Great War, Florence Nightingale had established the right of the respectable young lady to the role of ministering angel, and it was to nursing that young ladies had most readily turned in the early stages of the war. By July 1917 there were 45,000 of them thus occupied.[23] For all that the nursing of wounded heroes was accepted as a reasonably natural task for girls of the middle and upper classes, the figure does none the less represent the fact that these girls were for the first time doing hard and rewarding work, and were in many cases doing it under conditions of unprecedented freedom. Despite the rebuff administered to the more ambitious project of Dr Elsie Inglis, this intrepid lady, in fact, proceeded on her own initiative to establish her Scottish Women's Hospitals in France and in the Balkans, so becoming a legend of the courage and resourcefulness of women all the more potent since she herself died in harness. Shortage of male doctors at home very quickly opened new opportunities for the few women who possessed the necessary qualifications: there was the rub – there were so few that already in November 1915 the demand for women doctors was greater than the supply.[24] By the end of 1916 a fair variety of women's paramilitary organizations had sprung up, consolidated by the Government at the beginning of the following year into the Women's Auxiliary Army Corps (WAACS); there followed the WRENS and the WRAFS, all providing for adventurous women an opportunity for overseas travel and service hitherto denied them.

Given the rigidities of the Edwardian class structure, there are difficulties in the way of summing up the consequences of the war for women as an entire sex. In the business, medical and military functions which have been mentioned, the women concerned were very largely women of the middle and upper classes. Yet the major section of these women had been in pre-war years a depressed class, tied to the apron-strings of their mothers or chaperons, or to the purse-strings of their fathers or husbands. Now that they were earning on their own account, they had economic independence; now that they were working away from home, in some cases far from home, they had social independence. Above all, in their awareness that they were performing arduous and worthwhile tasks, were living through experiences once confined only to the most adventurous males, they gained a new self-consciousness and a new sense of status.

Upper- and middle-class women learned that they could perform hard physical work, if only in their own deserted kitchens. This was no news to women of the lower classes; yet the ultimate experience for working-class women was remarkably similar to that of upper-class women, save that the former were less well placed to defend the gains of the war period than were those of the classes above. Most important for women of the lower classes was the escape from ill-paid life-diminishing drudgery as dressmakers and domestic servants or low-grade industrial labour into work which gave both economic status and a confidence in the performance of tasks once the preserve of skilled men. Even those women who were unable to free themselves from the swamps of the worst-paid trades were able to command at least £1 a week as opposed to the 9s of pre-war days. By the last year of the war the female munitions workers were pulling in well over £2 per week, and other women factory workers could count on about 25s a week.[25]

For the consequences of this upon the social character of working women we have the thoroughly reliable evidence of the Chief Factory Inspector in his report for 1916, in which he refers to 'the new self-confidence engendered in women' by the new conditions of work.[26] The *New Statesman*, too, reported:

They appear more alert, more critical of the conditions under which they work, more ready to make a stand against injustice than their pre-war selves or their prototypes. They have a keener appetite for experience and pleasure and a tendency quite new to their class to protest against wrongs even before they become 'intolerable'.[27]

Obviously, then, women of all classes shared in a similar kind of emancipation. The suffragette movement before the war had, for whatever sophisticated motives (the main one being that 'votes for women' must come on its own merits, not as a part of a general extension of the franchise), aimed simply at the same limited franchise for some women as was enjoyed by some men. The Women's Movement from 1915 onwards is a more unified movement than ever it had been previously.

[II] WINNING THE VOTE

Upper-class women in the eighteenth century enjoyed a certain rough equality with their men-folk, though in politics they were limited to the right to own the property on which all political power was based. One bemused foreigner said of them:

They do whatsoever they please and do so generally wear the breeches ... that it is now become a proverb that England is the hell of horses and the paradise of women; and if there were a bridge from the island to the continent, all the women in Europe would run thither.[28]

The middle-class society at the end of the century, however, very firmly thrust women into a subordinate position; almost at once the Women's Movement came into being, and over the ninety years from the 1820s to the outbreak of the Great War a great deal was achieved in the way of social and political emancipation: married women's property acts were secured; the local government franchise was won; medical degrees were wrested from the guardians of hallowed privilege; at discreet distances from the ancient universities women's colleges were founded. The preliminary question one must ask before discussing how votes for women were achieved in the war period is not what had women so far achieved, but why had they not achieved more. On several occasions favourable majorities had been secured in the House of Commons for private members' bills to give women the franchise, but the feminists never managed to get up the head of steam which automatically forms itself behind a measure sponsored by a government firmly established in power, or which can be directed behind a measure if there is an organized public opinion strong enough and intense enough.

For all their valiant propagandist work, the feminists still had against them two fortresses of prejudice: the prejudice of men, and the prejudice of women, who feared to be thrust out from cloistered femininity into the harsh male world of politics. Within Parliament the feminists, who had influential supporters in both Liberal and Conservative parties, fell victims to the party structure. As Mrs Fawcett neatly put it: 'The Liberals were an army without generals, the Conservatives generals without an army.'[29]

In this particular impasse the women were especially helpless – excluded from Parliament, it was impossible for them to argue a parliamentary case. As *Punch* made a suffragette explain, 'We could not get the vote because we had not got the franchise.'

In the first light of the social and economic advances made by women in the war years, it would hardly seem necessary to explain in detail how each obstacle to women's suffrage was overcome. There are, it can be argued, great subterranean currents in history of which political changes (the winning of the vote, say) are simply surface manifestations; but, more often than not, the time and the form of these manifestations depend on individual whim, accidents of circumstance, or confluence with another separate movement of change: these, singly or together, are some-times powerful enough to distort or submerge. So it was with the Women's Movement. Before considering how the suffrage ques-tion, to the surprise of the women as much as anyone else, sud-denly became a pressing issue half-way through the war, the precise manner in which the two great fortresses of prejudice were reduced must be examined. Before the war the feminists had had to contend with the apathetic indifference of the vast mass of British womankind, and with the active hostility of one or two leading women, such as Miss Violet Markham or the novelist Mrs Humphry Ward. The war brought unity in the higher ranks and a dissipation of apathy in the lower: men were quick to heap praises on the women's war effort, but scarcely any quicker than the women themselves. Inflated by the wind of patriotic romanticism purveyed by the press, the women of Britain became a gigantic mutual-admiration circle; now that they knew their worth, they knew that they were worthy of the vote. Having leapt on the band-wagon of adulation for women's contribution to the common effort, Miss Markham and the others could not suddenly jump down again when the question of the suffrage came up. By 1916 the female anti-suffragist was a negligible figure.

Behind the weakening of male bigotry lay a number of con-siderations. On the margin of importance was the disappearance of suffragette militance, which had certainly been an irritant in pre-war years, but which had probably served to confirm masculine prejudice rather than to create it. Mrs Fawcett, who was herself biased against the militants, quotes one humble member of the Liberal Party as referring in the middle stages of the war to the way in which 'the women had made good their cause by their services where they had formerly spoilt it by their threats'.[10] More important is the relationship of the theme of post-war reconstruction – a phrase which was on all articulate lips from 1916 onwards – to the woman question. In demonstrating their talents, women also demonstrated the gross national wastage implied in not exploiting these talents to the full, politically as well as economically. As early as October 1915 the National Union of Women Workers held a conference to stress the importance of the role women would have to play in reconstruction after the war.[11] This concept of not wasting women's talents merges into the larger one of women's place in the national defence, which most men had by 1916 and 1917 to accept as clearly established; some even went further and declared that in courage and martial valour women had shown themselves capable of equalling men. One way or another the foundations beneath the old premise about the non-military role of women being sufficient reason to debar them from the vote were thoroughly mined. Lloyd George, as in so many other topics, opened the floodgates of rhetorical affirmation of this truth when he greeted Christabel Pankhurst's procession of July 1915 with the words: 'Without women victory will tarry and the victory which tarries means a victory whose footprints are footprints of blood.'[12]

When that confirmed opponent of women's suffrage, Walter Long, President of the Local Government Board and a man who concealed a fine brain and a humane heart behind the externals of an old-world country squire, introduced National Registration he explained that any exclusion of women would be taken by them 'as a serious rebuff wholly unjustifiable in face of the splendid services which they had rendered already to the prosecution of the war.'[13] Speaking to the Women Workers' Reconstruction Conference, a noted feminist, Mrs Henry Morgan, exposed the naked heart of the male argument:

There is the much-discussed question as to whether women are able to take any part in the defence of their country and thus prove themselves worthy to have a voice in its reconstruction. This oft-debated question has at last been settled by actions rather than words.[14]

The national defence idea was clearly apparent in Churchill's remark that without the women it would have been impossible to
win the war, and also in the maiden speech of Lloyd George's
successor at the Munitions Ministry, E. S. Montagu, who declared that 'our armies have been saved and victory assured by the
women in the munition factories'.[35]

Fatuous as were most of the statements about women's martial
valour, they were not more fatuous than the military theory of
men's supremacy which they helped to destroy. One of the most
senseless of all the senseless acts of German militarism was the
execution of Nurse Edith Cavell. Working with the Red Cross in
German-occupied Belgium, Edith Cavell had nursed British, Belgian and German soldiers, but because she had helped Allied
soldiers to escape, she was court-martialled by the German authorities, and, despite the valiant endeavours of the American Embassy,
hastily shot. Technically the Germans no doubt had a case, but
it was a case which signally failed to commend itself to world
opinion. Asquith, again with an enforced glance at the suffrage
issue, expressed British civilian opinion when he declared:

She has taught the bravest man amongst us a supreme lesson of courage;
and in this United Kingdom and throughout the Dominions of the
Crown there are thousands of such women, but a year ago we did not
know it.[36]

Great prominence was given in the press to the work of Dr Elsie
Inglis and the Scottish Women's Hospitals, now combating the
military and climatic rigours of Serbia with quite fabulous courage
and resourcefulness. One remark by the Prefect of Constanza was
very widely quoted:

It is extraordinary how these women endure hardships; they refuse
help, and carry the wounded themselves. They work like navvies. No
wonder England is a great country if the women are like that.

No one was churlish enough to point out that the women were
Scots. Heroism was to be found nearer home. In one nasty shell
factory explosion in the North of England the behaviour of the
women employees was considered so exemplary that it was announced that Sir Douglas Haig was to be asked to let the men at

the front know of the courage and discipline of their womenfolk.[37]

Thus the last philosophical argument against giving women political rights was destroyed. Journals such as the *Morning Post* remained firmly unconvinced; politicians like Asquith (till the end of 1916, at least) remained not entirely convinced; other politicians, such as Lord Curzon and the last-ditch elements in the House of Lords, never would be convinced. But on the whole late 1916 and early 1917 were marked by a number of prominent conversions. Sir Arthur Stanley, Chairman of the British Red Cross, could scarcely resist the evidence of women's contribution to his own organization; his brother, Lord Derby, agreed with him; so did Winston Churchill; so did Sir Arthur Conan Doyle. In the newspaper world, *The Times,* the *Observer* and the *Daily Mail* swung round. J. L. Garvin pronounced a formal recantation:

Time was when I thought that men alone maintained the State. Now I know that men alone never could have maintained it, and that henceforth the modern State must be dependent on men and women alike for the progressive strength and vitality of its whole organization.[38]

In 1916 a similar tide of conversions swept through the North American continent, and many states in both Canada and the U.S.A. extended the franchise to women. There is, however, little evidence to warrant any suggestion that Britain was fired by the transatlantic example.[39] More worthy of study is the experience of France. France with its tradition of conscript national service had from the outbreak of war extended welcoming arms to the women participants in the nation's business, and full political emancipation for women was being freely predicted as early as 1915.[40] In fact French women had to wait another generation and endure another world war before they secured the vote. In Britain the women benefited from a rather fortuitous concatenation of political circumstances. Among the minor points, the establishment of two coalition Governments created a parliamentary situation in which there were no longer hard-and-fast party alignments inimical to the interests of the suffragists: Mrs Fawcett's pre-war armies now had generals, the generals now had armies. Personal changes, too, were important. The formation of the first coalition meant the disappearance of one or two bigoted anti-suffrage Liberals, and the entry of well-disposed politicians like Arthur Henderson and open-minded ones like A. J. Balfour, Bonar Law, Lord Robert Cecil and Lord Lytton.

Balfour, indeed, in 1892 had made a pregnant utterance:

> If any further alteration of the franchise is brought forward as a practical measure, this question will again arise, menacing and ripe for solution, and it will not be possible for this House to set it aside as a mere speculative plan advocated by a group of faddists. Then you will have to deal with the problem of women's suffrage, and deal with it in a complete fashion.[41]

The British electoral franchise was at that stage, and was still in 1916, governed by the Reform and Redistribution Acts of 1884 and 1885. The Reform Act of 1884 had extended to the country householder the right to vote which, since 1867, had applied to his counterpart in the towns. To qualify as a householder it was necessary to prove unbroken occupation of the house in question for twelve months prior to the previous 15 July; that is to say, qualification was essentially one of physical occupation rather than of mere residence. In 1914 about seven million men were entitled to vote by virtue of the householder occupation qualification: additionally there were about a further million voters based on various qualifications, of which the most important were the historic forty-shilling freehold franchise and the lodger franchise.

By the terms of the Parliament Act of 1911 the normal life of any one Parliament was limited to five years; there should, therefore, at the very latest have been an election in January 1916. Quite apart, however, from the question of the wisdom of holding a general election in time of war, there was the problem that by going overseas to fight, or to other parts of the country to make munitions, several million men had lost their occupation qualification, and hence disfranchised themselves; moreover, there was a strong current of feeling that, purely as it affected men, the old register was insufficiently democratic, and that men in the forces, whether householders or not, had a strong claim to enfranchisement. In November 1915 there were a number of rumours that the Government was proposing to clean up the franchise muddle with a new Registration Bill. The N.U.W.S.S. at once threatened that if the political truce, which the suffragists took to imply an embargo on all political innovations, were thus broken, suffragist activity would be resumed.[42] What the Government did finally do in December was to produce a Bill which would prolong the existing Parliament beyond the date when a general election was legally due, but which left the existing register in force.[43]

Once aroused again, however, suffragist suspicions did not die easily. The following May, Mrs Fawcett felt impelled to send a letter to Asquith on the implications of the obsolescence of the present register and the necessity for a revised one:

When the Government deals with the franchise, an opportunity will present itself of dealing with it on wider lines than by the simple removal of what may be called the accidental disqualification of a large body of the best men in the country, and we trust that you may include in your Bill clauses which would remove the disabilities under which women now labour. An Agreed Bill on these lines would, we are confident, receive a very wide measure of support throughout the country. Our movement has received very great accessions of strength during recent months, former opponents now declaring themselves on our side, or at any rate withdrawing their opposition. The change of tone in the press is most marked ... The view has been widely expressed in a great variety of organs of public opinion that the continued exclusion of women from representation will ... be an impossibility after the war.[44]

In reply, Asquith denied that alteration of the register was being contemplated by the Government, but added that if such an alteration should become necessary Mrs Fawcett's points would be 'fully and impartially weighed without any prejudgement from the controversies of the past'.[44]

Whatever Asquith's intentions may or may not have been at this stage, his elbow was given a sharp jog in the House of Commons by a back-bench M.P. who raised the question of the compilation of a new electoral register.[45] Four weeks later the Government produced its proposals, or rather, for what it was worth, its one proposal. In the course of a long meandering speech, characterized by the Ulster Unionist leader, Sir Edward Carson, as a piece of opera bouffe, the Home Secretary, Sir Herbert Samuel, indicated that, the old register being now useless, something would have to be done, but that to draw up a new register on the old basis, still leaving many fighting men without the franchise, would be nearly as bad; thus all sorts of other complicated problems such as redistribution, plural voting, adult suffrage, and votes for women would have to be faced. The Home Secretary therefore proposed that, the matter being too complicated for the Government, it should be thrashed out by a Select Committee of the House of Commons. Falling like stale tea into a choked sink the proposal was at once withdrawn, though not before Sir Edward Carson had given a thorough airing to his own proposal for a franchise based on national military service.[46] The curious fact that the suffragists at this stage themselves believed that emancipation was still a long way off is brought out by an article in *Common Cause* which admitted that the question of franchise reform was, as Charles James Fox had put it in the analogous circumstance of parliamentary reform at the height of the Napoleonic Wars over a hundred years before, 'a sleeping question'. An almost unbelievably quaint footnote added, 'This article was written before the answers about a possible Redistribution Bill *threatened* to bring the question of the Suffrage into the sphere of immediate practical politics.'[47] Two N.U.W.S.S. deputations followed: one received by Asquith on 25 July, the other by Bonar Law and Robert Cecil on 3 August 1916. The main point made by the women, illustrating well their own diffidence about plunging boldly into a suffrage struggle at this stage, was that, provided there were no proposal to alter the basis of the old register (as opposed to the modifications necessary to enable voters who had enlisted to maintain their qualification) and no intention of holding a general election, they would not press their own claims: they would, however, force the suffrage issue if the male vote was to be democratized, or if it was proposed to consult the electorate on the vital topic of reconstruction.[48]

Since the House of Commons had refused the Government's invitation to grasp the problem of franchise reform it was essential that the Government should produce definite proposals of its own. Accordingly on 14 August 1916 Asquith introduced his Special Register Bill, designed to prolong once again the length of Parliament, and, furthermore, to make it possible for householders who had lost their occupational qualification to retain the vote. Clearly, however, this was intended only as a basis upon which more drastic amendments might be built, as indeed the Prime Minister implied when introducing the Bill:

Have not the women a special claim to be heard on the many questions which will arise directly affecting their interests ... ? I cannot think that this House will deny that, and I say quite frankly that I cannot deny that claim.[49]

With this piece of ponderous Asquithian thinking-aloud booming in their ears, the N.U.W.S.S. leaders gathered at the House of Commons to concert tactics with sympathetic M.P.s,[50] of whom the most prominent was the same Sir John Simon who had been a bit of a broken reed in the anti-conscription movement, but who was to be the stoutest of oaks in the final stages of the suffrage struggle. For the student of the political pressure group there is an obvious similarity between the parliamentary activities of the N.C.F. and the moves now made by the N.U.W.S.S.

But any jubilation was premature, for the following day the Speaker, Mr J. Lowther, ruled out all amendments designed to extend the franchise, whether to soldiers or to women, to abolish plural voting or to introduce proportional representation. Above the ensuing clamour there floated the rational suggestion of Walter Long that all of these delicate problems should be referred to a committee drawn from all parties and from both Houses of Parliament, to sit under the chairmanship of the Speaker. The idea was enthusiastically accepted; for many politicians with axes of their own to grind, the inclusion of the topic of women's suffrage was a rather minor detail.

The Speaker's Conference held its first meeting on 12 October. All of its deliberations were secret, and the request made by the N.U.W.S.S. to be allowed to give evidence was declined. Instead, a memorandum putting the women's case was circulated among members of the Conference, and a series of feminist resolutions from political associations, town councils, trade unions, and women's societies was forwarded to the Speaker, himself believed to be an anti-suffragist.[51] Now there began, in a manner familiar in recent British experience, a period of waiting upon the pronouncements of the oracle; the Government tacitly recognized this by dropping, in early November, the idea of a Special Register Bill.[52]

The accession to power of Lloyd George a month later augured well for the women and it is during his period of office that the story is completed. Reporting on 30 January 1917, the Speaker's

Conference unanimously supported three basic propositions and a host of lesser ones. The three proposals were that the unsatisfactory occupational basis of the existing franchise should be replaced by a simple residential qualification, that proportional representation should be introduced, and that there should be a simplification of the local government register. Unanimity was lacking on Section VIII of the Report, the one which dealt with women's suffrage. It read as follows:

The conference decided by a majority that some measure of woman suffrage should be conferred. A majority of the conference was also of opinion that, if Parliament should decide to accept the principle, the most practical form would be to confer the vote in the terms of the following resolution:
'Any woman on the Local Government Register who has attained a specified age, and the wife of any man who is on that register, if she has attained that age, shall be entitled to be registered and to vote as a parliamentary elector.'[53]

For the 'specified age' the report suggested thirty or thirty-five. The theory behind this projected age-bar was that the country could not risk having an electorate in which women were in a majority; absurd vestige of prejudice though this was, the moderate suffragists were prepared for the time being to let it pass in the belief that once women had been exercising the vote for some years the prejudice would die – as indeed it did.[54]

The next move was a highly astonishing one. Asquith, ousted Prime Minister, bastion of the resistance to the women's claims in pre-war days, reluctant conceder of women's value in time of war, now moved a resolution calling for an early Bill to implement the recommendations of the Speaker's Conference. 'Some of my friends may think,' he said contritely, 'that . . . my eyes, which for years in this matter have been clouded by fallacies and sealed by illusions, at last have been opened to the truth.'[55] It was a graceful retraction; the motion was passed by 341 votes to sixty-two. The following day Lloyd George played host to a deputation of women war workers organized by the N.U.W.S.S. The women successfully insisted that the promised Bill must embody women's suffrage from the start, avoiding the pre-war device of a general Bill to which women's suffrage could be tacked on as an amendment. The Bill, which settled upon thirty as the minimum voting age for women and gave the vote to all adult males but ignored proportional representation, had a fairly easy passage through the Commons, the largest minority against the women's suffrage clause being fifty-five.[56] The House of Lords, which still had the power of delay, seemed likely to be a tougher proposition. A full-dress debate on the final reading, which contained some unconscious humour, as when Lord Chaplin declared that the whole country looked to the Lords in such times of peril, culminated on 11 January 1918. Much interest attached to the line Lord Curzon would take in winding up the debate. The word was passed on to a group of suffragists by a policeman, who is recorded as saying, 'Lord Curzon is up, ladies. But 'e won't do you ladies no 'arm.'[57] The policeman was right. Curzon recommended abstention, to avoid an open clash with the Commons. The Bill anyway secured a clear majority of 136–71, and passed into law on 6 February 1918.

[III] MANNERS AND MORALS

The historian of sexual *mores* faces difficult, though intriguing, problems, and in paying attention to surface changes, to the clamour of bigots or the calculated indiscretions of fops, almost inevitably underestimates the basic constancy of human behaviour. Shakespeare describes youth as a time of 'getting wench with child'; the close-knit rural society of pre-industrial revolution England seems to have had a humane and tolerant attitude towards the illegitimate child born within its midst; to the eighteenth-century aristocrat 'gallantry' was one of the most important of the do-it-yourself pastimes of that age; and as a corrective to taking the sanctimonious protestations of the Victorians at face value one need only glance at the institution of child prostitution which catered especially for the Victorian businessman.[58] But if behaviour does not essentially change, attitudes do; and in a patriarchal society such as that of the Victorians the received attitude will also be the actual reality for the female members of that society.

In middle- and upper-class Britain in Victorian times, therefore, a double standard obtained: the male, ashamed of his sexual desires, for which he might find outlet outside the pale of respectable society, enforced his ideal standard upon his women-folk.

Most feminists in the nineteenth century had no desire to free themselves from this ideal standard; what, for example, Josephine Butler, who conducted a courageous and successful campaign against licensed prostitution in garrison towns, was aiming at was rather a raising of the secret male standard up to the feminine ideal.

Ironically, it was already becoming clear before 1914 that, if anything, the opposite process was taking place. One important factor was the spread among the upper classes after about 1880 of efficient methods of mechanical contraception. In his evidence before the National Council of Public Morals in 1925, Sir William Beveridge declared that:

1. The revolutionary fall of human fertility in Europe since 1880 is due mainly, if not wholly, to deliberate prevention.
2. The sudden spread of the practice of prevention after 1880 cannot be connected with any change of economic conditions, including the need for restricting families, and must be attributed to the invention of more effective means of prevention.[59]

An earlier report, published in 1916 and based on what was admitted to be rather bare evidence drawn from the immediate pre-war years, found grounds for 'a strong presumption that, among the middle and upper classes, conscious limitation of fertility is widely attempted.'[60] This growth in the use of contraceptives was almost entirely within the framework of normal family life, but obviously for women of *avant-garde* inclinations it did provide for the first time the opportunity for secure extra-marital relationships. Stimulus to such experimentation was provided, within the limited circle familiar with his works, by the theories of Sigmund Freud, loosely interpreted. The Edwardian chapters of Richard Aldington's *Death of a Hero* give a good picture of the puzzled growth of the 'New Woman', of whom H. G. Wells's Ann Veronica is the prototype.

There is no need to look for parallel developments in the lower orders of society. As Mary Agnes Hamilton perceptively put it:

Of necessity, female 'delicacy', in any of its forms, was the prerogative of the relatively well-to-do, as was the ignorance that was part and parcel of it. The village girl and boy, and the girl and boy who grew up in dense industrial areas, of necessity knew a good deal more than was once thought proper in their better-off sisters.[61]

The problem of dependants' allowances, we have seen, was to reveal a whole underworld of irregular conjugal relationships. The best way of summarizing the position on the outbreak of war would be to say that, for the upper and middle classes, Victorian conventions still stood (Aldington brings this out beautifully when his 'hero's' mistress collapses back into all the nineteenth-century formulae at the first hint of pregnancy), but that effective methods of birth-control – the euphemism was coined by an American, Mrs Margaret Sanger, just in time for the outbreak of war[62] – were available; for the lower classes there had never been any such conventions, but they did not have easy access to contraceptives. What the war did was to spread promiscuity upwards and birth-control downwards.

'When I left England in 1911,' commented Sir Robert Bruce Lockhart, 'contraceptives were hard to buy outside London or other large cities. By 1919 every village chemist was selling them.'[63] In the last year of the war Marie Stopes, the great propagandist for the use of contraception, published her classic, *Married Love*.

First *frisson* of the storm was the discovery in April 1915 of 'War Babies' (contraception obviously had not got very far yet). In a letter to the *Morning Post*, which was extensively quoted and added to in the rest of the press,[64] a Conservative M.P., Mr Ronald McNeill, announced that throughout the country, in districts where large numbers of troops had been quartered, 'a great number of girls' were about to become unmarried mothers. The topic was a godsend for journalists and for the letter-writing public. Mrs Wannop, the literary woman in Ford Madox Ford's war tetralogy, keeps pestering the hero, Tietjens, for material for an article on War Babies. For two weeks even the *Observer* devoted a great deal of space to it, but on the third week the editor peevishly snapped that the 'whole matter had been grossly exaggerated' and that despite the masses of letters still pouring in the correspondence must be discontinued.[65] There was justification for the *Observer*'s embarrassment: the year 1915 actually presented the highly moral combination of an exceptionally low illegitimate birth rate and a phenomenally high marriage rate. Next year the illegitimate rate did go up and by the end of the war it was about thirty per cent up on pre-war.[66]

The 'War Babies' episode is important, not for an exact estimate of increased promiscuity, but for the illumination it throws on public attitudes. Although one young woman of breeding (she read the *Observer*) felt strongly that young men should have been sent to the trenches with 'something more noble and helpful than lowering the whole standard of womanhood',[67] McNeill's thesis, which was widely upheld, was that no shame should attach to 'the mothers of our soldiers' children', nor to the children themselves. 'Suffer the little children to come unto me' was the *Sunday Pictorial*'s proud quotation.[68] In time the war was to destroy the conventional belief in the sanctity of private enterprise and free trade; already it was loosening the belief in conventional purity. There was a charming naïvety about McNeill and his fellow enthusiasts. Later in the war a more sophisticated argument was raised against a too rigid maintenance of conventional canons: by hook or by crook, as it were, the country needed births to mitigate the slaughter of the war.[69] The rise and fall of newspaper campaigns, or interest in the wider trend in sexual behaviour, should not, as Sylvia Pankhurst pointed out, be allowed to obscure the misery and misfortune which fell upon many girls of the poorer classes deserted by their soldier lovers.[70]

The exact reality behind the stories and the statistics is difficult to determine, but obviously it sprang from two related circumstances: changed conditions at home, especially for women, and the new awareness, in face of the slaughter on the battlefields, of the transience of human life. Something has already been said of the new economic and social freedoms women derived from their war-work, of the way in which young girls travelled daily long hours from home, or, in many cases, left home to live in hostels or lodgings of their own. Explaining the 1916 upsurge in the illegitimacy rate, the Registrar-General referred to 'the exceptional circumstances of the year, including the freedom from home restraints of large numbers of young persons of both sexes'.[71] Concerning the second circumstance the words of two women historians who themselves lived through the war cannot be improved upon:

Life was less than cheap; it was thrown away. The religious teaching that the body was the temple of the Holy Ghost could mean little or nothing to those who saw it mutilated and destroyed in millions by Christian nations engaged in war. All moral standards were held for a short moment and irretrievably lost. Little wonder that the old ideals of chastity and self-control in sex were, for many, also lost ... The great destroyer of the old ideal of female chastity, as accepted by women themselves, was here. How and why refuse appeals, backed up by the hot beating of your own heart, or what at the moment you thought to be your heart, which were put with passion and even pathos by a hero here today and gone tomorrow.[72]

If these young men, alive today and dead tomorrow, if these young women who, as they read the casualty lists, felt fear in their hearts, did not seize experience at once, they knew that for many of them it would elude them for ever. Sex became both precious and unimportant: precious as a desired personal experience; unimportant because it had no implications – except to mothers of 'war' babies.[73]

Gone too were those pillars of Edwardian upper-class virtue, the chaperons. They were, as one young lady explained in a letter to Mrs C. S. Peel, 'hard at work canteening and so on, and people who gave parties didn't want to feed and water them. And if they were elderly they didn't feel like having to walk home after late nights'.[74]

Allied to all this, the horror and austerity of war produced a hedonism more powerful than that denounced in Edwardian times by C. F. G. Masterman and other social critics. Degraded cinema pictures, immoral night-clubs and theatres purveying 'exhibitions of scantily dressed girls and songs of doubtful character' were denounced by clerics, magistrates and generals.[75] More relevant to our present theme:

'Give the boys on leave a good time' was the universal sentiment at home, and the good time consisted to a very large extent in consuming alcohol and enjoying sex. As a popular song of the period had it, 'There's a girl for every soldier'.[76]

Just as the Victorians had concealed the suggestive legs of their tables behind elegant draperies, the Edwardians still wrapped the question of venereal diseases in a web of guilt and ignorance. Victims who could afford it avoided their respectable family doctor by going to expensive quacks, and the poor often found that evidence of one of the diseases could be sufficient excuse for the Poor Law Guardians to refuse outdoor relief, or, more cruelly absurd, to debar them from receipt of Health Insurance benefits.[77]

It was a great tribute to governmental and administrative concern with a serious problem rendered more intractable by evasions and secrecy that in 1913 a Royal Commission on Venereal Diseases was established.

The Battle of the Somme was at its height, the moral climate in Britain was warm and mild, when the Commission published its final report, which, in calling for wider public knowledge and education and for 'a franker attitude towards these diseases',[78] set the keynote for subsequent discussion. When Sir Malcolm Morris declared, 'Before the war it would have been practically impossible to have held a Commission on Venereal Diseases, on which there had hitherto been a conspiracy of silence',[79] he was wrong on a point of actual fact (the Commission having been established in 1913), but right in contrasting the present roar of frankness with the previous silence.

Much of the work of the Commission had been taken up with the evidence and examination of prostitutes. Many a sex-starved Edwardian youth had had a romantic image of the prostitute as the emblem of glorious femininity scornfully shaking her buttocks in the face of social conventions by which he, apart from one or two guilty escapades, felt himself to have been rigidly confined. Further acquaintanceship during the war must have done much to weaken this image in any case, but it was the Commission on Venereal Diseases which most convincingly stripped away the romantic aura of the fallen woman, leaving a stark picture of a pox-ridden, money-grubbing harridan. Now, just when sweethearts who had formerly been cherished and guarded until the wedding-night were beginning to show a readiness to anticipate that ceremony, men began to find resort to a prostitute definitely unsatisfactory. However one interprets matters which are by their very nature insubstantial and conjectural, it is certainly true that there has been a decline in the number of prostitutes in Britain since the years before the First World War;[80] better economic standards for women and for the lowest strata of society as a whole are obviously also an extremely important cause of this.

Human behaviour, we have said, does not change much. There seem, as between men and women, to be certain ingrained differences of approach towards sexual questions. Kingsley Amis's Patrick Standish, in *Take a Girl Like You*, written fifty years later,

is still fighting a very hard battle over the virginity of Miss
Jennie Bunn, and he is reduced to the taunt that the kind of man
she craves for died out in the early months of the First World
War, a statement which many of Mr Amis's male readers may well
have resented. All the historian can do is to note the more obvious
changes. The safest generalization about the First World War
would be that it was a time of powerfully heightened emotional
activity and responses. Often this just meant earlier and hastier
marriage, reflected in the fantastic 1915 figure of 19·5 marriages
per thousand inhabitants.[81] But even this, in an earlier age, would
have smacked of a lubricious disregard of the requirements of
social security. Marriage in haste often meant divorce at leisure:
there was nearly a threefold increase in the number of divorces
'made absolute' between 1910 (596) and 1920 (1,629).[82] Whatever
the subtle differences in sexual standards among individuals, this
did represent a fundamental cracking in the cement of conventional society as the Victorians understood it. Women who were
deserted by their 'war husbands', or who were unable to obtain a
divorce, helped to swell the scrap-heap of unemployed in the
1920s.[83]

In considering the other ways in which the new-found freedoms
of women showed themselves, we move away a little from what, in
the limited usage of today, we call 'morals', towards what can best,
perhaps, be described as 'manners'. The unabashed ordering of
restaurant meals, the public smoking of cigarettes, the much publicized invasion of the public-houses, made light of by Shadwell as
merely a return to the Middle Ages, when public-houses were not
only frequented by women but were generally kept by them[84] –
these features were all part of the new manners. Most striking of
all was the change in women's dress; for, however far politicians
were to put the clocks back in other steeples in the years after the
war, no one ever put the lost inches back on the hems of women's
skirts. The shortened dress-length is usually attributed to the
obvious need while engaged on war-work for a garment unham-
pered by trailing skirts. Actually the first fashion changes anticipated any wide use of women's desire to serve: the *Observer*'s
Woman's Page is talking of 'short full skirts' with 'more than a
suspicion of ankle visible' in the first December of the war,[85] of the
'extravagantly short skirt' at the beginning of January, and of

'skirts six inches off the ground' in February. The very desire itself, however, combined, one would think, with a shortage of
luxury dress materials, may well have been the crucial motivation
in the adoption of a style of dress readily adapted to active service.
The growth of women's employment certainly consolidated the
development.

The Northcliffe press fought a bitter rearguard action against
the new fashions. 'Just now our young and pretty girls are pushing
the craze for short skirts to the utmost limit,' the *Daily Mail*, three
months behind the times, declared in May 1915. 'But even now,' it
added snidely, 'these ultra-remarkable models are regarded with
suspicion by women of good taste.' A day or two later it returned
again to 'the walking skirt that is absurdly short' and which 'is not
worn by the best-habited woman'. In June it was still sounding
off against the 'extraordinarily short skirt' . . . 'revealing, as it does,
the feet and ankles and even more of the stockings.'[86] But shorter
skirts were not the whole of it. Girls engaged on farm-work took
naturally to the wearing of trousers during their labours, and by
an easy stage to the wearing of trousers even while off duty. In at
least one case the County Women's Field Labour Committee, one
of the *ad hoc, noblesse oblige* committees typical of the early stages of
the war, attempted to insist upon the resumption after work of
'ordinary feminine dress', but was overruled by the Government-
sponsored Country Agricultural Committee.[87] The growth of the
women's para-military organizations with their 'trim short ser-
viceable skirt' gave a further impetus to the shortening of skirt-
lengths.[88] *Punch*, as so often, summed it all up neatly in a post-war
cartoon in which a little girl looking at an Edwardian beauty asks,
'Mummy, hasn't she got any legs?'

Towards the end of the war Arnold Bennett noted in his diary,
more as a piece of social reportage than as a hostile criticism, the
prevalence of 'painted women .[89] Self-adornment in all its forms
was an age-old custom of women, but in prim Victorian Britain
the use of powder and paint had died away.[90] In the Edwardian
era the foundations of the modern beauty trade were laid but it
needed the stress and excitement of war, the affluence among the
lower classes and the greater spending money available to middle-
class girls, to bring a return to the heavy use of cosmetics. This
was deplored by the older generation, though Joyce Cary's ageing

Sally in *Herself Surprised* readily went with the fashion, and it was too readily assumed (mainly by men) that the basic object of the exercise was sexual. Mary Agnes Hamilton made a good point when she suggested that the new preoccupation with 'Beauty' was 'self-absorption' rather than 'sex-absorption'.[91] The new pride in personal appearance, especially among a class of women who had formerly become ill-kempt sluts by their mid-twenties, if indeed they had ever been anything else, was one of the pleasantest by-products of the new female self-confidence remarked upon by the Chief Factory Inspector. Small wonder if women performing long arduous tasks, covering long journeys in crowded trains and trams, facing the unremitting stares of their fellow human beings for whole days on end with scarcely the briefest interlude of privacy, felt the need of rouges and creams.

One other beauty aid whose boisterous career really begins with the war is the brassière. Advertisements for this garment, it is true, are to be found in pre-war papers, but it is only from about 1916 that they seem to be successfully ousting what their manufacturers contemptuously refer to as 'the old-fashioned camisole'.

[IV] WOMEN, WELFARE AND CHILDREN

One by-product of the entry of women into factories and industries where they had not previously been employed was the development of what the Chief Inspector of Factories and Workshops described as 'a striking degree of solicitude on the part of the managers for their welfare and comfort'.[92] Welfare facilities were by no means completely lacking in British factories before the war. An enthusiastic young research student from Australia, drawing her evidence from the last year of peace and the first year of war, before the influx of women had had time to make itself felt, was able to compile a three-hundred-page tome on British welfare work. In a preface to the book, which was published in 1916 when the topic was becoming one of pressing interest, Lloyd George stressed that great and important changes had taken place since the completion of the text; in particular the modest private initiatives in the matter had been bolstered by the inception of a Special Welfare Department at the Ministry of Munitions.[93]

Before the war, factory inspectors had for many years been

pressing upon employers the advisability of the provision of qualified medical services, of the setting aside of canteens and rest-rooms, of the supervision of women factory workers by women welfare officers, and of the need for hygienic lavatory and washroom facilities, expecially where there were employees of both sexes in the same workshops.[94] It was on the last point that complaints were most prevalent. The lady Inspector for the North-west reported in 1913:

It is impossible to describe in a public paper how low the standard has been and still is in many places, where in other respects the conditions are not only not noticeably bad, but are quite good.[95]

The more intelligent factory-owners were becoming dimly aware of the correlation between output and the physical condi-tion of their workers, so that 'dining-rooms and restaurants' were 'slowly becoming more general, more especially in the modern and most up-to-date factories, and in those so situated that the wor-kers cannot return home readily for their meals'. But it was in 1915 that a 'great advance in welfare work' was noted, with arrange-ments for dealing with sickness and injury appearing, as well as canteens and mess-rooms.[96] The reasons were various. The employment of women where no women had been employed be-fore, and the employment especially of the delicate flower of the middle and upper classes, were definitely the starting point at the personal level of individual employer-employee relationships,[97] though its importance must not be over-stressed. Britain had a long tradition of factory acts designed to protect women and children, but qualified by the persisting belief that to attempt to legislate for the adult male was to reflect upon his manhood.

The hectic conditions of the home front created new needs. The concentration of labour in a munitions centre brought a heavy pressure on available accommodation, so that it became not unusual for the same bed to be in use day and night, first for a night-shift worker, then for a day-shift worker. In other cases the worker, man or woman, might have long distances to travel each day, which, when added to the overtime hours frequently worked, might leave barely six hours available for sleep.[98] Attention was therefore directed to problems of fatigue, sickness and nutrition;

in the case of girls living, or daily travelling, far from home, there was felt to be an especially strong case for the establishment of welfare supervisors. Women working on T.N.T. ran grave health risks and were nicknamed 'canaries' as they developed a yellow discoloration of the skin: for them a free daily pint of milk was provided.[99]

It was perhaps something of a natural reaction on the part of the wealthy Briton, steeped in the Victorian ideal of the charitable soup-kitchen, to reach, in time of stress, for the soup-ladle. 'Canteening' was an activity of elderly chaperons in the first stages of the war. There was a touch of the same austere charity in the anti-drink campaign and the establishment of the Liquor Traffic Central Control Board, one of whose most valuable achievements was to foster the growth of restaurants and canteens as an alternative calorific source to unadulterated alcohol. At the same time the dim stirrings of a few advanced factory-owners became merged in a 'new general awakening to the dependence of efficient output on the welfare of the human agent'.[100] Where private employers remained asleep the Government was prepared to act as knocker-up.

Some innovations were less well received than others by the factory workers. Canteens, in time of food difficulty, performed a welcome task in providing cheap, if not exciting, food. A typical menu is as follows:

Sausage and Mash, 2½d. Mince and Mash, 2d. Patties, 1d. Beans, 1d. Stewed Fruit, 1d. Milk Pudding, 1d.[101]

But rebellious working-class spirits of Clydeside calibre and independent-minded women were frequently resentful of welfare supervision, which with shrewd cynicism they saw as merely a paternalistic attempt to maintain their efficiency as so many units of labour in the total sum of production.[102] Nevertheless, when the Chief Factory Inspector, in his report for 1915, suggested that the war-time welfare schemes would be 'likely to be felt and to spread long after the war has ended, and to leave behind a permanent improvement in factory life',[103] he was making an eminently sound prediction which subsequent industrial history has more than vindicated.

Concern for the welfare of working women soon broadened into concern for the welfare of working men. But, important for immediate survival as was the maintenance of the morale and efficiency of the domestic labour force, there was a yet more serious long-term problem to be faced:

In no direction are the ravages of war more serious or more difficult to replace than in the loss of human lives. Whatever degree of success may attend the nation in the present European war, the cost in life must inevitably be heavy.

'Consequently,' the Chief Medical Officer of the Board of Education argued, 'the question of the preservation of the rising generation, and care for its physical fitness and equipment, is of more than ordinary importance.'[104] School meals and school medical services in some areas dated back to the turn of the century: as national institutions they were products of the first burst of social reform legislation of the 1906 Liberal Government. The Chief Medical Officer's Reports for the pre-war years are a sorrowful indictment of the community's manifest failure to interest itself in the preservation of the generation rising in the working-class, elementary-school background. All reports are agreed that children were better fed, better clothed, and in better health during the war years than ever before. But this had nothing to do with the calculated piety of the Board of Education's desire to make good the loss of life in the war; it was a consequence of high wages and the heavy demand for labour. After 1916 the school medical services were in fact very drastically curtailed, and the number of children medically examined dropped by 28 per cent.[105]

The plans for the development of a national education system drawn up by the Liberal Government in 1914 were stifled by the outbreak of war. Even the total amount of the bare and inadequate instruction which was the main business of the existing elementary structure was allowed to fall away in face of demands that the national cause required the physical services of children rather than the development of their minds. The laws governing school attendance and child employment in 1914 had the appearance of wishing to be all things to all men, a strange medley of firm and laudable principles vitiated by exceptions and qualifications. Children were required to attend school until the age of fourteen,

with the exception of those who at thirteen had secured a certificate of 'proficiency' or of regular attendance. Children could not
work in factories until their school attendance was completed, unless they were 'half-timers', girls and boys of twelve or over who
might work not more than thirty-three hours a week and were
compelled to go to school half the time. Children under eleven
might not sell articles in the street and boys under fourteen might
not work in coal-mines. Local authorities might if they liked (not
many did) forbid all work by children under the age of fourteen.
Working conditions for children over fourteen were governed by
laws similar to, but more stringent than, those applicable to the
employment of women. Well intentioned in their various ways as
these provisions no doubt were, they were already becoming pav-
ing stones for the road to a hell of national ignorance and educational deficiency.

Before the first year of war was out the Board of Education
found itself under heavy pressure from local authorities desirous
of suspending the school attendance by-laws. County magistrates
were especially anxious that children should be released to undertake 'national work' (i.e. work on the farms of the county magistrates). A sad letter from the secretary of one County Education
Committee to the Board of Education explained the importance of
paying heed to 'influential persons, including magistrates, chair-
men of district councils, and so on' and the danger of alienating the
'sympathies of magistrates and employers of labour'.[106] More
humane motives played a part too. For all that wages and living
standards began to rise during the war, some families were placed
in a serious plight when the one wage-earner was on active service
overseas; pleas for the release of school-children based on strai-
tened family circumstances were not easy to resist. Over all the
wastage was enormous. In August 1917 H. A. L. Fisher, the
responsible minister, admitted in the House of Commons that
during the first three years of war 600,000 children had been put
'prematurely' to work;[107] this figure did not include the hundreds
of other children set to work in total violation of the law.

Juveniles over the age of fourteen did very well out of the war
boom; it was possible for both boys and girls to earn from £1 to
£2 a week in the munitions factories. In fact it was among boys
and girls under eighteen that the wartime rise in wages was most

marked. As with the trend towards economic status for the female secretarial worker, this was a socio-economic movement which has never been reversed. The war as a whole brought a revolution in the age-sex earning pattern in Britain, and marked the beginning of the trend leading to the affluent teenager of the 1960s.

Affluence, disruptions in the educational structure, and the social upheaval and flux of wartime Britain, brought a serious increase in juvenile delinquency,[108] especially among children between eleven and thirteen. Referring to the attitudes and policies of the war period, the Secretary of the Howard Association of London, Cecil Leeson, asked bluntly and rhetorically, 'Had we set out with the deliberate intention of manufacturing juvenile delinquents, could we have done so in any more certain way?'[109]

But among magistrates and local dignitaries the most favoured scapegoat for delinquency was the cinema. Certain incidents, such as the appearance in court of nine boys calling themselves the Black Hand Gang of St Luke's, seemed to lend justification to this. In its investigation of the cinema, the National Council of Public Morals recorded:

It is very strongly alleged and widely believed that the picture house is responsible for the increase in juvenile crime, and that boys are often led to imitate crimes (larceny and burglary) which they have seen in the pictures, or to steal money that they may pay for admission.

The evidence, the committee reckoned, was largely against these two theories, overwhelmingly so in the case of the latter. Increased crime by young offenders, they declared, must be considered in relation to wider social and economic questions; statements as to the extent of this increase in crime were probably inflated, for, as a Westminster probation officer pointed out:

There has been a tendency in recent years to increase the variety of offences with which children may be charged. For instance, children are now charged with wandering, with being without proper guardianship, with being 'beyond control'. Our streets are now more rigidly supervised than ever before. There is a large and increasing army of officials whose duty it is to watch over child life. In many cases it has seemed to me that the zeal of those officers was not always tempered by humanity and expediency.[110]

These qualifications were less valid for the latter stages of the war when the manpower shortage began to affect policing and officialdom.

Youth, being central to every discussion of post-war developments, was a topic which received in full measure its wartime quota of extrovert bombast and sentimental fustian. One turns with relief to the Final Report of the 1917 Departmental Committee on Juvenile Education.[111] After a model exposition of the deplorable situation obtaining at the outbreak of war, it proceeds, eyes unclouded by romantic optimism, throat unchoked by patriotic fervour:

Upon this educational and industrial chaos has come the war to aggravate conditions that could hardly be made graver, and to emphasize a problem that needed no emphasis. Many children have been withdrawn at an even earlier age than usual from day schools, and the attendances at those evening schools which have not been closed show a lamentable shrinkage. We are not prepared to say that much of the work which is now being done by juveniles in munition factories and elsewhere is in itself inferior to the work which most of them would have been doing in normal times, but there can be no doubt that many of the tendencies adversely affecting the development of character and efficiency have incidentally been accentuated . . . Parental control, so far as it formerly existed, has been relaxed, largely through the absence of families from their homes. Wages have been exceptionally high, and although this has led to an improved standard of living, it has also in ill-regulated households induced habits of foolish and mischievous extravagance. Even the ordinary discipline of the workshop has in varying degrees given way; while the withdrawal of influences making for the social improvement of boys and girls has in many districts been followed by noticeable deterioration in behaviour and morality. Gambling has increased. Excessive hours of strenuous labour have overtaxed the powers of young people; while many have taken advantage of the extraordinary demand for juvenile labour to change even more rapidly than usual from one blind alley employment to another.[112]

NOTES TO CHAPTER THREE

1. *Report of Chief Inspector of Factories and Workshops, 1914;* P.P., 1914-16, XXI, Cd. 8051, pp. 32–3.

2. I. O. Andrews and M. A. Hobbs, *Economic Effects of the War upon Women and Children in Great Britain,* New York, 1918, p. 24.

3. *Common Cause,* 7 August 1914.

4. Marwick, *Clifford Allen,* p. 34. McDonagh, *In London During the Great War,* pp. 180–1. *The Times,* 9, 10, 12 March 1917.

5. *The Times,* 10 February 1915.

6. F. Balfour, *Dr Elsie Inglis,* 1918, p. 144.

7. *Manchester Guardian,* 18 March 1915.

8. *Suffragette,* 14 May 1915. *Common Cause,* 24 September 1915.

9. *Daily Mail,* 30 March 1915. *Suffragette,* 16 April 1915. Scott and Cunnison, *Industries of the Clyde Valley during the Great War,* p. 65.

10. *Observer,* 6 June 1915.

11. *Daily Mail,* 4 June 1915.

12. *The Times,* 19 July 1915.

13. *Engineer,* 20 August 1915. Quoted by Andrews and Hobbs, p. 33.

14. *Report of Chief Inspector of Factories and Workshops, 1915;* P.P., 1916, IX, Cd. 8276, p. 14. M. Cosens, *Lloyd George's Munitions Girls,* 1916. L. Yates, *The Women's Part,* 1918.

15. *Manchester Guardian,* 16 February 1916.

16. Quoted by Andrews and Hobbs, p. 35.

17. *Report of the War Cabinet for 1917;* P.P., 1918, XIV, Cd. 9005, p. 69.

18. *Report of Committee on Women in Industry, 1919;* P.P., 1919, XXXI, Cmd. 135.

19. *Daily Mail,* 24 February 1917. Cmd. 135.

20. Blumenfeld, *All in a Lifetime,* p. 61 (8 May 1916).

21. Cmd. 135.

22. *Daily Mail,* 14 September 1915, 17 April 1916.

23. Cmd. 135.

24. *Observer,* 14 November 1916.

25. Bowley, *Wages and Incomes,* p. 192.

26. P.P., 1917–18, XIV, Cd. 8570, p. 7.

27. *New Statesman,* 23 June 1917.

28. Quoted by E. N. Williams, *Life in Georgian England,* 1962, p. 52.

29. M. Fawcett, *The Women's Victory and After,* 1920, p. 125.

30. Ibid, p. 118.

31. National Union of Women Workers, *Report of Reconstruction Conference, October 1915,* 1915.

32. *Suffragette,* 23 July 1915.

33. *House of Commons Debates,* 5 July 1915.

34. National Union of Women Workers, *Report of Reconstruction Conference,* 1915, pp. 15–16.

35. *House of Commons Debates,* 15 August 1916.

36. *The Times,* 3 November 1915.
37. Fawcett, *Women's Victory,* p. 116.
38. *Observer,* 13 August 1916.
39. Fawcett, pp. 118–19.
40. *Suffragette,* 15 April 1915.
41. *House of Commons Debates,* 27 April 1892.
42. *Common Cause,* 20 October 1915.
43. *House of Commons Debates,* 9 December 1915.
44. *Common Cause,* 19 May 1916.
45. *House of Commons Debates,* 22 May 1916.
46. Ibid, 16 August 1916.
47. *Common Cause,* 30 June 1916. My italics.
48. Ibid, 4, 11 August 1916.
49. *House of Commons Debates,* 14 August 1916.
50. *Common Cause,* 18 August 1916.
51. Fawcett, p. 138.
52. *House of Commons Debates,* 12 November 1916.
53. *The Times,* 30 January 1917.
54. Fawcett, p. 142.
55. *House of Commons Debates,* 28 March 1917.
56. Ibid, 19 June 1917 (col. 1751).
57. Fawcett, p. 149.
58. See generally, I. Clephane, *Towards Sex Freedom,* 1936.
59. National Council of Public Morals, *The Ethics of Birth Control,* 1925, p. 168.
60. National Council of Public Morals, *The Declining Birth Rate,* 1916, p. 21.
61. In R. Strachey (ed.), *Our Freedom and its Results,* 1936.
62. Clephane, p. 209.
63. R. Bruce Lockhart, *Your England,* 1955, p. 79.
64. *Morning Post,* 17 April 1915. *Daily Mail,* 17 April 1915. *Observer,* 18 April 1915, 25 April 1915. *Sunday Pictorial,* 18 April 1915.
65. *Observer,* 2 May 1915.
66. *Annual Report of Registrar-General for 1916;* P.P., 1917–18, V, Cd. 8869, p. xix. *Annual Report of Registrar-General for 1915;* P.P. 1917–18, V, Cd. 8484, p. vii.
67. *Observer,* 25 April 1915.
68. *Sunday Pictorial,* 18 April 1915.
69. See e.g. Sir A. Conan Doyle in *Observer,* 14 October 1917.
70. S. Pankhurst, *The Home Front,* 1932, pp. 182–3.
71. Cd. 8869, p. xix.
72. M. A. Hamilton, in *Our Freedom,* p. 251.
73. Clephane, p. 196.
74. C. S. Peel, *How We Lived Then,* p. 70.
75. *Observer,* 27 August 1916, 17 September 1916.
76. Clephane, p. 197.
77. *Final Report of the Royal Commission on Venereal Diseases;* P.P., 1916, Cd. 8189, pp. 62, 2, 43.
78. Ibid, p. 62.
79. *The Times,* 10 March 1917.

80. *Our Freedom*, p. 223.
81. Cd. 8484, p. vii.
82. G. Heard, *Morals Since 1900*, 1955, p. 113.
83. Scott and Cunnison, *Industries of the Clyde Valley during the Great War*, p. 171.
84. Shadwell, *Drink in 1914–22*, p. 108.
85. *Observer*, 13 December 1914.
86. *Daily Mail*, 25 May 1915, 31 May 1915, 2 June 1915.
87. Ibid, 30 August 1916.
88. T. Meech, *This Generation*, 1928, Vol. II, p. 77.
89. Bennett, *Journal*, p. 229 (28 April 1918).
90. V. Ogilvie, *Our Times*, 1950, p. 91.
91. *Our Freedom*, p. 273.
92. P.P., 1916, IX, Cd. 8276, p. 14.
93. E. D. Proud, *Welfare Work*, 1916, pp. ix–xiii.
94. Cd. 8276, p. 15.
95. P.P., 1914, XXIX, Cd. 7491, pp. 9–10.
96. Ibid, p. 8. Cd. 8276, p. 10.
97. See esp. M. Cosens, *Lloyd George's Munitions Girls*.
98. P.P., 1914–16, LV, Cd. 8151, p. 3.
99. Andrews and Hobbs, *Economic Effects of the War upon Women and Children*, p. 133.
100. Cd. 8276, p. 15.
101. Cosens, p. 78.
102. Andrews and Hobbs, pp. 138–9.
103. Cd. 8276, p. 10.
104. *Annual Report of Chief Medical Officer of Board of Education;* P.P., 1914–16, XVIII, Cd. 7730, p. v.
105. *Report of Board of Education for 1916–17;* P.P., 1918, IX, Cd. 9045, p. 5.
106. Board of Education, *Correspondence relating to School Attendance 1915;* P.P., 1914–16, L, Cd. 7803, p. 9. See also Cd. 7881 and Cd. 7932.
107. *House of Commons Debates*, 10 August 1917.
108. *Report of Board of Education for 1916–17*, Cd. 9045, p. 4.
109. Andrews and Hobbs, p. 159. See C. Leeson, *The Child and the War*, 1917.
110. National Council of Public Morals, *The Cinema*, 1917, pp. xxxiv–xxxvii, 204–5.
111. P.P., 1917–18, XI, Cd. 8512.
112. Ibid, p. 5.

CHAPTER FOUR

Gentlemen in England Now Abed: 1915–1916

---

[1] AN AFFLUENT SOCIETY?

SURVEYING SOCIETY as a whole in 1915 and 1916, Government inspectors and newspaper reporters were agreed that there was a widespread diffusion of affluence. Most obvious in the case of war profiteers, it touched all classes. 'Profiteering' was one of the emotional corrosives of the war period, eventually in compound with other acids of discontent to eat away at social ideals till many people could see only the bitter contrast between those who had fought and suffered and those who had stayed at home and waxed fat. Working-class leaders, labour politicians, and a sizeable section of the press kept up a constant denunciation of high profit margins and luxury spending. It is a topic worth lingering on for a moment.

In August 1917 the *Spectator* took it upon itself to deplore the popular denunciations, insisting that high prices were not due to profiteering.[1] But the *Spectator* protested too much: although there was little evidence of new monopolistic rings being set up, there was no doubt at all that industrialists and traders were using their existing economic power to exact the highest possible terms from the community. The not untypical case of the South Wales millers, Spillers and Bakers, was one of the first to attract attention. According to *The Times* report of 3 May 1915, the company, after paying dividends on preference and ordinary shares (preferred and common stock), disbursed extra dividends to the tune of £80,165, or 17½ per cent on the ordinary shares: there then remained from the year's earnings the sum of £248,419, which represented an added return of 54 per cent on the ordinary shares. The big profiteering debate in Parliament on 17 October 1916 brought out many other examples and instances.

The industries which were completely indispensable to the nation's survival in time of war were shipping and coal-mining, and they took care that the nation knew it. In his evidence before the Sankey Coal Commission at the end of the war, A. Lowes Dickinson, Financial Adviser to the Coal Controller, produced evidence to show that coal profits in 1916 were 'just treble those of the average of the five pre-war years'.[2] For the high ransom exacted by the shipping firms we need look no farther than the budget statement of 2 May 1917 made by Bonar Law, then Chancellor of the Exchequer and a shareholder in the shipping industry. A man of rigid principle, Bonar Law described his own sense of shock at the high returns that his own investments were yielding willy-nilly.[3] A later parliamentary statement put shipping profits at 33⅓ per cent *after* payment of excess profits duty[4] (introduced for the first time in September 1915, and in itself a good indication of the high profit level).

For the wage-earning classes constant employment, longer hours, and war bonuses meant an upward movement in earnings, clearly noticeable from February and March 1915. Over the whole year there was an average rise of 3s 10d per week.[5] A year later the *Labour Gazette* was commenting:

No complete account can be given at this time of all the changes in rates of wages which have been made since the beginning of the war, as amongst unorganized work people many changes escape attention, but so far as reported it appears that up to the end of December 1916, nearly six million work people had received some advance. The amount varied, but on average the weekly increase to these work people was about six shillings per head, and in some of the industries directly concerned with the supply of war requirements ranged from ten shillings to twelve shillings per week.[6]

Relatively the gains were most marked among the submerged workers of pre-war days (Masterman's 'prisoners'), those in casual or sweated employment, and those who had been pretty well constantly out of employment. In 1915 and 1916 there was a very sharp decline in the incidence of pauperism, and in the autumn of the latter year it was confidently reported that there was 'less total distress in the country than in an ordinary year of peace'.[7] The Glasgow figures for underfed and ill-clad school-children are instructive: there were 209 such children in the last year of peace; the number rose to 264 in the first year of war, before rising employment had made itself felt; in 1915–16 it had dropped to 150, and it was down to 68 in 1916–17.[8]

Till the end of 1915 the popular press was full of stories of lavish spending both on the part of the working classes and the profiteers. 'There are no poor in Newcastle-upon-Tyne,' reported the *Daily Mail* in one of a series of articles on working-class affluence.[9] Reliable evidence as to working-class purchases of what Mr Wemmick called 'portable property' and what we would call status symbols is not lacking; sale-rooms in the first months of post-war depression were to be tragically saturated with fur coats and less portable, but more status-giving, cottage pianos.[10] At the other end of the social scale the *Draper's Record* noted increasing expenditure on women's clothing. Whether this was entirely due to the *nouveau riche* is less certain. One West End shop manager was reported as describing 'our luxury women' as

Rather a different clientele than before the war . . . and hardly so discriminating, but certainly more free with money. Many of our regular West End clients are economizing, but evidently there is a new and prosperous section of the community taking their places. This new section is so well-off that no article is approved unless it is costly.[11]

From the beginning of 1916 newspaper references to the condition of the working classes concentrated on the high cost of living rather than affluence. Actually, apart from a brief plateau immediately after the first excitement and emergency had subsided, prices had been showing a constant upward movement, so that in June 1915 food prices were about 32 per cent up on those prevailing in July 1914. Butter was up by 2½d, bacon by 3d or 4d, cheese by 3d, pork sausages by 2½d and cooked meat by 4d to 6d (all per pound). If the standard working-class budget in 1914 is taken as 25s 8d per week, the equivalent figure was now 33s or over. By September 1916 the increase (weighted by the Board of Trade in order to reflect actual spending habits) was 65 per cent. Price increases in towns with more than 50,000 inhabitants were noticeably greater (68 per cent) than those in small towns and villages (62 per cent). The highest increase of all was in the price of sugar, 163 per cent up. Otherwise increases were highest in the case of imported meat, as high as 123 per cent in the case of breast of mutton in town shops. Alternative sources of protein also rose steeply in price; fish, only 70 per cent up in country areas, was 103 per cent up in towns; eggs, on average, were 82 per cent up.[12]

High earnings, the British *penchant* for sweetstuffs, and the failure of the Government to channel the short supplies of sugar away from the sweet manufacturers, combined to produce a situation in the early months of 1916 in which the ordinary Britisher was eating more sweetmeats than ever before.[13] However, it was clear that it was only through the working of longer and more regular hours by more of its members that the ordinary family managed to keep a seat on the unbroken bronco of price inflation. The 1915 Government report, whose phrase about 'less total distress than in an ordinary year of peace' was widely quoted, actually went on to point out:

Certain classes normally in regular employment, whose earnings have not risen in the same proportion as the cost of living – for example, the cotton operatives and certain classes of day-wage workers and labourers – are hard pressed by the rise in prices, and actually have to curtail their consumption, even though the pressure of high prices may have been mitigated, in some cases, by the employment of members of a family in munition works, and by the opening of better-paid occupations to women. Many people in receipt of small fixed incomes necessarily also feel the pressure; and it is obvious that while the total receipts of families past school age may have greatly increased, a family of the same class in which children are within school age may suffer exceptionally.[14]

In the summer of 1916 there were several important protests and demonstrations against the high cost of living, including one organized by the National Union of Railwaymen and held in Hyde Park on 27 August.[15]

One of the most resented facets of war-time domestic economy was the rise in house rents. Bad and inadequate housing was a serious cancer in 1914: the war brought a general cessation in house-building and a slackening in the activities of Local Government Board inspectors. A number of measures early in the war, adapting to military exigencies the ideas of the great 1909 Act and foreshadowing the definitely collectivist approach of the post-war years, did little in practice to remedy the overall deficiencies. An Act of 10 August 1914 authorized local authority assistance to building societies prepared to limit their own profits to five per cent, and gave the Commissioners of Works power to acquire and dispose of land and buildings, and to build dwellings for Government employees. On 16 March 1915, the Government took powers under D.O.R.A. to take possession of land for housing, and later on the Ministry of Munitions assisted directly in the building of working-class housing.[16]

Essentially the problem remained one of an expanding and, more important, a moving population being crammed into houses whose condition was steadily deteriorating, of munitions workers crowding into small towns like Carlisle, workers of all types bumping up the already appalling density of large towns like Glasgow, and office workers for the new bureaucracy pouring into the centre of London. Landlords naturally took advantage of heavy pressure on limited space to put their rents up. Resistance was so strong on Red Clydeside that the Government was forced in 1915 to appoint a special Departmental Committee on Rent Increases in Scotland. Once again John Wheatley was the chief spokesman on behalf of the Clyde working man, and the upshot was the passing of the Rent and Mortgage Interest (Rent Restriction) Act of 1915. Pressure from all classes of society upon space in the centres of the great towns, London especially, combined with heavier taxation and shortage of servants, meant that small houses and flats were at a premium, whereas large houses were often empty.[17] The First World War was the master interior builder which turned the rambling town houses of a more spacious age into the cramped flats and bed-sitters of the contemporary world.

Working-class advances in the years 1915 and 1916, taking the rising cost of living into consideration, owed as much to longer hours and increased employment as to war-time bonuses and higher wage rates. In truth the working classes did, in the long view, make very real gains in their material standards; but for the ordinary working man the long-term reality tended to become lost in the welter of immediate hard-felt grievances. What of the middle-class man who did not enjoy a war bonus and was neither one of the charmed élite for whom 'social activity had not abated in the least'[18] nor a profiteer? The statistics are tenuous and hard to interpret. By the end of the war the class portrait of Edwardian Britain had changed to comprise a rather smaller working class and a slightly larger middle class. This could imply that over the war years the old middle class had done badly in that it was being threatened by newcomers to its ranks. At the same time, after the war, sections of the middle classes, professional people in particular, were taking a bigger share of the national income than they had done before it; this could again in part be attributed to new recruitment. Lawyers did well from the confusion of D.O.R.A. regulations, and were kept happy disentangling the exact legal status of British firms which were offshoots of larger German companies. In so far as some members of the middle classes, being on fixed salaries, were not as readily able to secure rises as, for instance, the Welsh miners, they clearly suffered from rising prices. On the other hand, growing bureaucracy opened new opportunities of social and material advancement to the salaried classes, and small businessmen were often the ones to cash in most obviously on the war boom.

In October 1915 a middle-class reader in the £400 per annum bracket, stung by loose talk of extravagance and tight talk of economy, submitted his own budget[19] which showed no obvious evidence of extravagance and no apparent margin for economy:

Food, laundry, cleaning, etc.	£130
Rent	40
Servant	18
Education (2)	12
Rates	14
Coal	12
Light	7
Water	4
Clothes (4)	50
Season ticket	12
Holiday	None
Insurance	14
City expenses, lunch and tobacco	40
Income-tax	25
Others (doctor, repairs, etc.)	10

The first war budget had made little difference to the relative economic positions of the different social classes. The second war budget, still the responsibility of Lloyd George, did little that was new, save impose greatly increased duties on alcoholic drinks: the ample warning provided by the Chancellor's own bombastic pronouncements and the King's pledge had enabled the wealthy to lay down extensive cellars in good time.[20] The great buoyancy shown by existing taxes is indicative of the prosperity being enjoyed by the middle and upper classes. Whatever else Lloyd George was, he was not a great wartime Chancellor of the Exchequer, and it was necessary for his successor, Reginald McKenna, to bring in a supplementary budget in September. McKenna raised the income-tax by 40 per cent, and increased the supertax on incomes above £8,000 per annum. The first was of greatest importance socially in its effects on the middle classes; both measures, together with the new excess profits duty, accelerated the equalization of incomes. More significant, the great engine of income-tax was for the first time directed towards working men who were earning more than £2 10s per week. On the obvious level this added to working-class grievances; on a more subtle level it meant the beginning of a new process destructive of the rigid line between the Edwardian classes and masses. Other measures, such as the 50 per cent increase in the tea and tobacco duties, and the abolition of the halfpenny postage stamp and the sixpenny telegram, fell on the poorer rather than the wealthier elements in society.

McKenna's next budget continued the movement towards a progressive, equalizing tax structure: at the same time, among the handful of new or increased indirect duties the imposition for the first time of an amusements tax added a new element to the rising cost of living, already blatant in the case of the necessities of life. Thereafter there were no striking alterations in the tax system, for the burden of the war, in fact, was financed out of borrowing. This traditional method of war finance had in the past had the effect of fostering inequalities of wealth, since it was only the rich who could afford to lend, and it was these same rich who had in succeeding years become richer as they raked in their interest payments. For the middle years of the war the traditional practice was largely maintained: two long-term loans were floated with suitable éclat in November 1914 and June 1915, and the last of the same type was launched in January 1917. Immediate needs were met by various expensive short-term devices which were very much to the liking and profit of the financial and banking world. But the 1915 loan did represent a nod in the direction of democracy, for it made it possible for the humble to subscribe through five-shilling, ten-shilling, and one-pound vouchers, obtainable at post offices.[21] The Montagu Committee, appointed in November 1915, further examined this aspect, and as a result of its deliberations there appeared early in 1916 the eminently democratic War Savings Certificate, holdings of which were limited to a total of five hundred; there had been some idea of enforcing a means test on would-be purchasers, but the War Savings Committee decided that to do so would be to introduce undesirable class distinctions.[22] There was no one-way trend in the economic developments of 1915 and 1916 as they affected the different social classes, but on the whole sentiment and fact were combining to weaken the sturdy barriers of Edwardian days.

[II] RIPPLES FROM THE WAR

A journalist's description of the first Easter of the war shows how far away 'business as usual' now was:

Twelve months ago lamps blazed in the London streets at night. Theatres were full. The West End was glittering and full until midnight . . . And now! Although Brighton is reported to be nearly full for Easter, although some of the South coast hotels are booked up, although passenger boats are running to the Continent and Ireland, and although one hears of excursions into Wales by motor char-à-bancs, the general atmosphere of the seaside resorts is one of reconciliation to their lot. We see khaki everywhere. Military searchlights send staggering gleams across the sky, taking the place of the flickering advertisements which did so much to make London look gay by night.

Hundreds of thousands of men – colliers, shipwrights, munition makers, and the like – will be at work who in normal times would be at play. There will be few visitors to Scotland and the north, for on these long journeys the ordinary fares are more than double the excursion fares. For the normal holiday traffic to the Continent, all brightness and new frocks and motor-cars and golf-clubs, is substituted an exodus of a different kind. True the Folkestone boats are full; but there is very little joviality and holiday tackle. People go quietly, with grave faces, to visit wounded friends in hospital.[23]

Almost at once there followed an incident which severely shook public sentiment still inclined to underplay the German submarine menace. Early in April, the Cunard liner *Lusitania* was sunk off the West Coast of Ireland by a German torpedo. Two thousand passengers were drowned, many of them children, who were later pathetically washed up on the beaches of Shannon where, looking like a McTaggart seascape gone horrifically out of control, they were photographed for the gratification of righteous British war-lust. The immediate reaction was an outburst of rioting and pillaging on the night of 12 April; in the East End of London many a harmless shopkeeper who had the misfortune to have a German name had his property wrecked. This was the most serious test yet for the Special Constables: insufficiently distinguishable by their armlets, many were inadvertently coshed by the Regulars, with the consequence that the Specials were henceforth given a proper uniform of their own.[24]

The *Lusitania* incident shows well the relationship between popular hysteria and official propaganda. The riots, following so quickly upon the news of the disaster, have every appearance of a spontaneous outburst of hatred which grew on a diet of harrowing sensationalism and righteous indignation. However, Lord Newton, head of Foreign Office propaganda, improved the shining hour by having large quantities of the medal said to have been issued by the German Government to commemorate the occasion reproduced for circulation in Britain and abroad; actually the medal (one of a series struck by a Munich craftsman) was intended as a satire on the Anglo-American cupidity which had allowed the *Lusitania* to sail despite German warnings that she would be sunk. Within weeks quantities of leaflets illustrating the medal and featuring the phrase, 'another triumph for our glorious Navy', torn from context so as to appear to apply to the *Lusitania* incident, were distributed.[25]

So far the secret propaganda department at Wellington House, concentrating its energies on enemy and neutral countries, had not done much to influence domestic opinion. Its most brilliant stroke was the choice of Lord Bryce, who had for many years been a well-loved and much-respected ambassador in Washington, to chair a committee appointed in December 1914 to investigate alleged German outrages. With access to the flimsiest of uncorroborated evidence the Committee none the less reported unhesitatingly that the Germans were guilty of deliberate and systematic massacres of civilians, violation of women, the use of civilians as a shield for advancing armed forces, and calculated looting, incendiarism and destruction of property as part of a policy of general terrorization. 'Murder, lust and pillage,' the Committee declared, 'prevailed over many parts of Belgium on a scale unparalleled in any war between civilized nations during the last three centuries.'[26] As hoped, the Report had a powerful effect on American opinion.[27] Masterman also showed a touch of genius in his awareness that the cinema could be exploited for propaganda purposes. At first he encountered great opposition from the War Office and the Admiralty, where it was believed that there was something vulgar and disreputable about this new-fangled contraption, but eventually the first British propaganda film, *Britain Prepared*, was completed and given its première at the Empire Theatre on 27 December 1915;[28] in retrospect this occasion can be seen as a pointer towards the metamorphosis of the great music hall of the naughty nineties into the luxury cinema of today. Again the target was American and other neutral opinion rather than the British cinema-goer. The effect was spoiled in certain parts of the United States where exhibitors of German sympathies exhibited the film as *How Britain Prepared*.[29]

While distinguished ambassadors and Oxford dons as well as barons of the press were giving a lead to anti-German sentiment, the voice of organized religion was not silent. In *On Forgiving our Enemies,* one of a series of 'Wartime Tracts for the Workers' published by the Society for the Propagation of Christian Knowledge, the Reverend Prebendary Burn touched the central moral dilemma:

The challenge is flung at us. Can I forgive the unforgivable? To the question thus expressed a Christian can answer 'No' with a clear conscience. Divine Love is revealed as wrath against all unrighteousness. Our Lord Jesus Christ showed at times the most terrible wrath which can be imagined against foul injury to the weak and helpless, against that lie in the soul which betrays a man into calling evil good and good evil. What the Bible calls the wrath of the Lamb is the righteous anger of the meek and gentle flaming into fury for the sake of others.[30]

Even science added its mite. Addressing the British Association meeting at Manchester in September 1915, Professor Arthur Schuster, moved by 'the shadow of a great catastrophe' to talk on 'the Common Aims of Science and Humanity', concluded with the following words:

Happy were the times when it could be said with truth that the strife of politics counted as nothing before the silent display of the heavens [Professor Schuster was an astronomer]. Mightier issues are at stake today; in the struggle which convulses the world, all intellectual pursuits are vitally affected, and Science gladly gives the power she wields to the service of the State. Sorrowfully she covers her face because that power, acquired through the peaceful efforts of the sons of all nations, was never meant for death and destruction; gladly she helps, because a war wantonly provoked threatens civilization, and only through victory shall we achieve a peace in which once more Science can hold up her head, proud of her strength to preserve the intellectual freedom which is worth more than material prosperity, to defeat the spirit of evil that destroys the sense of brotherhood among nations, and to spread the love of truth.[31]

Popular fury flamed again at the execution of Nurse Edith Cavell and later at that of Captain Fryatt, a British merchant seaman who had turned defence into attack by ramming a German submarine. In July 1916, the Secretary for War, Lord Kitchener, set off on a mission to Russia, but got no farther than Scapa Flow, where his ship was sunk. To Kitchener's colleagues, long aware of his gross deficiencies as a war minister, this was a blessed release, but for the country as a whole it was the tragic loss of a beloved hero. To everyone capable of adding two and two (but little beyond that) it was obvious that Kitchener was the victim of a dastardly spy-plot, and there was a spasm of spy-scares and hunt-the-alien campaigns more intense than at any time since the first months of the war. The death of Lord Kitchener was an occasion for national grief, but by the end of 1916 there were few families untouched by personal grief. Each day at Charing Cross station a double line, mostly of women, waited patiently for disembarking troop trains; each day the newspapers carried a list of about 4,000 casualties. Yet the universal numbness and the patriotic fervour kept private grief from becoming national outcry. One diarist echoes the sentiments expressed eleven months before by R. D. Blumenfeld:

The very multitude of names of killed, wounded or missing does something to blunt the sharpness of sympathy. Death on the battlefield has become so much a matter of course as to deprive it of some of its terrors.[32]

On the evidence of letters to the press and of the continued breaking up not just of pacifist but of internationalist meetings, enthusiasm for the war, for all the slaughter it entailed, had not abated by the end of 1916. Most famous of all demonstrations of this is the 'Letter of "a little mother"' quoted by Robert Graves in *Goodbye to All That*:

To the man who pathetically calls himself a 'common soldier', may I say that we women, who demand to be heard, will tolerate no such cry as 'Peace! Peace!' where there is no peace. The corn that will wave over land watered by the blood of our brave lads shall testify to the future that their blood was not spilt in vain. We need no marble monuments to remind us. We only need that force of character behind all motives to see this monstrous world tragedy brought to a victorious ending. The blood of the dead and the dying, the blood of the 'common soldier' from his 'slight wounds' will not cry to us in vain. They have all done their share, and we, as women, will do ours without murmuring and without complaint. Send the Pacifists to us and we shall very soon show them, and show the world, that in our homes at least there shall be no 'sitting at home warm and cosy in the winter, cool and comfy in the summer'. There is only one temperature for the women of the British race, and that is white heat. With those who disgrace their sacred trust of motherhood we have nothing in common. Our ears are not deaf to the cry that is ever ascending from the battlefield from men of flesh and blood whose indomitable courage is borne to us, so to speak, on every blast of the wind. We women pass on the human ammunition of 'only sons' to fill up the gaps, so that when the 'common soldier' looks back before going 'over the top' he may see the women of the British race on his heels, reliable, dependent, uncomplaining.[33]

There was one potent intoxicant which helped even intelligent men to accept 'the indescribable suffering and sorrow which have been imposed upon millions of our fellow creatures'[34] long after the sentiments of honour and duty were becoming tarnished. This was the feeling that here indeed was *the* Great War, a time of historical intensity such as had never been lived through before, a time when what was old and bad must inevitably be consumed, and what was good and new triumph. In part this was merely a development of the wishful thinking of the idealist reformers who had hailed the outbreak of war so enthusiastically; in part it was a mistaking of the first swallows, women conductresses, say, for the whole summer; in part it was a perceptive appreciation of the deeper implications of the social changes that were in truth taking place. Writing in August 1916, Sir Michael Sadler saw the war as a time of 'gestation of a new social ideal'.[35] Blumenfeld had already noted, 'The war has simply turned the whole world topsy-turvy';[36] in October 1917 he was writing, 'That horrible ogre, Tradition, lies in the dust.'[37] McDonagh was most struck by the effect of the war on poverty; by December 1917 he had concluded that 'there is now no such word as "poor" in our social vocabulary'.[38] For Professor G. C. Henderson, whose description of the war is quoted at the beginning of this paragraph, the 'silver lining' was that 'the upheaval of existing habits and traditions' caused by the war had aroused the British nation from 'its state of apathy towards science' to a realization that its future prosperity was 'ultimately dependent on the progress of science'.[39] Official reports and commissions nearly all have somewhere a touch of optimism: change *is* taking place. The historian W. H. Dawson, writing in late 1916, expressed the whole mood very well:

We are living at a time when days and weeks have the fulness and significance of years and decades. Who does not feel that since August 1914 England has in many ways broken with her past and entered an entirely new epoch in her history, marked by transformations of every kind, so that when the day of peace arrives, be it soon or late, we shall be confronted at home by an altogether altered situation?[40]

What people at home heard of the fighting man's war was only a confused murmur. They knew the statistics of death – nearly 20,000 killed on 1 July, the first day of the Battle of the Somme[41] – but not the foul horror of it; they saw the glory, but not the sordid filth of trench life. Fighting men, appalled at the nature of the war in which they found themselves, were unable to convey the unbelievable substance (any success in this line that they did achieve was doubtless frustrated by the censorship). 'There are some things better left undescribed . . . Perhaps in the afterwards when time has deadened matters, you will hear of them,' wrote one young soldier.[42] 'Everyone out here,' wrote another, 'considers it only fair to one's womenkind to hush up the worst side of the war.'[43] Wellington House sponsored films of the Somme fighting, which played to packed houses, but the horror was carefully left out; occasional flashes of truth and terror, as the *Manchester Guardian* film critic remarked, were completely subordinated to the spectacular.[44]

Government attitudes towards British soldiers imprisoned in Germany, of whom there were 37,000 by the end of March 1917, caused much heart-searching and bitterness. The first British schemes, resulting in the establishment of the Prisoners of War Help Committee, were entirely voluntary, and the War Office, though invited to do so in June 1915, refused to take over responsibility for this body. From September of that year the Committee did have the co-operation of the Home Office but it was only in September 1916 that the War Office established an official Central Prisoners of War Committee; by this time better treatment had been secured for some prisoners by the agreement of May 1916 that British and German wounded and invalided prisoners should be transferred to Switzerland. Finally the War Office Committee did decide to undertake the provision of all British and Indian prisoners of war with a supply of food and clothing, causing much resentment among voluntary workers and private donors, who wanted to earmark their gifts for specific recipients.[45]

By the summer of 1915 people at home were beginning to feel that in the German air threat they had a considerable problem of their own. Small and rather ineffective night-attacks took place throughout the spring; on 1 June the press presented a most uninformative account of a Zeppelin raid on 'outlying London', no details being given for reasons of 'public safety'; in fact ninety bombs, mostly incendiary, had been dropped, causing much damage and twenty-four fatalities.[46] Another raid on 7 June rubbed in the seriousness of the situation, so much so that on the 18th the police, for the first time, published a list of suggestions as to the appropriate behaviour during an air-attack. Raids continued on all parts of the country (the south-east took most punishment) at a rate of roughly two a month, with occasional lulls and periods of intensive raiding. Under regulation 12 of the Defence of the Realm Regulations it was open to the local military authorities to impose some form of black-out. Early in April 1915, the Chief Constable of Middlesbrough took the initiative in bringing together the Garrison Commander, Tees and Hartlepools Garrison, and the local ironmasters to discuss the best means of obscuring ordinary lighting, and, more particularly, the glare from the blast furnaces, in the event of an air-raid. There was as yet no question of a perpetual black-out. The scheme eventually perfected allowed for the dowsing of all light and glare within twelve minutes of receiving a code warning of the approach of the enemy.[47]

During the sleeping hours between 12 October and 13 October 1915 there came the most severe raid of the middle period of the war, when Zeppelins over Norfolk, Suffolk, and the Home Counties and London, inflicted a casualty list of 199. A crescendo of protests over the absence of an advance-warning system followed. It was at the same time pointed out that the introduction of lighting regulations had led to an increase in street accidents. Early in 1916 clocks, believed to be a gratuitous navigational gift to the night-fliers, ceased to chime, and the comprehensive London lighting orders were extended to the Midlands and the West. In Middlesbrough the Chief Constable encountered strong resistance from the public and from the Watch Committee when he attempted to introduce a more general black-out. Yet resistance to the lighting regulations existed side by side with criticism of their ineffectiveness, which the *Manchester Guardian* attributed to the lack of a common policy among the various local authorities charged with enforcing them;[48] the Government even lost a by-election to an independent candidate campaigning for a more vigorous air policy against the raiders. By late 1916 it was coming to be believed again that inconvenience rather than danger was to be expected from air-raids. Travellers into Waterloo after nightfall might find that their train suddenly stopped, the lights went out, and a wait of several hours in cold and darkness ensued, enlivened only by distant flashings and rumblings.[49]

Even without the attentions of airships and aeroplanes, nighttime was the distinctive time in war: total darkness (after mid-1916) where once there had been a constellation of light; sounds of steam-hammers and factory machinery where once there had been silence; rumbling convoys of armoured vehicles where once there had been only the occasional errant drunk; long ominous trains packed with munitions or carrying the shattered bodies of soldiers direct to the sidings at military hospitals. Day and night were stood upon their heads: where once the forenoon streets had been filled with breathless bustle, now they were deserted, for all had work to do, be it in a munitions factory or at the local forces' canteen. Unmitigated darkness at sunset brought an awareness of the good daylight going to waste in the hours before many families rose from their beds. In the autumn of 1915 a few small businesses tried to wring the last ounces of light out of the shortening days by starting work earlier in the morning. The idea of organizing this sensible husbanding of the natural bounty of light on a national scale through the simple device of putting all clocks forward by an hour had been advanced in 1908 by a Mr William Willett, F.R.A.S. The first Bill embodying his idea had been introduced into Parliament in February of that year, and a subsequent Select Committee reported favourably; but despite a further series of similar Bills, all of which got considerable support, nothing was done at Government level.[50] As the days lengthened into the summer of 1916 the matter came up again in Parliament, and a motion in favour of the institution of Summer Time, introduced by Sir Henry Norman, was passed on 8 May by 170 votes to two. On 21 May the Summer Time Act became law, so that from 21 May till 30 September 1916 all British clocks ran one hour in advance of Greenwich mean time, giving longer and lighter evenings. A committee appointed to investigate the effects spoke enthusiastically of increased efficiency and more healthful recreation, and, although it admitted the parental problem caused by children staying up later at night, it wholeheartedly recommended Summer Time as a 'permanent insititution'.[51] It was in fact introduced again in 1917, and has been every year since, save for the 'Double Summer Time' of the Second World War.

One of the reasons for the ignorance of people at home of the true nature of life in the trenches was the censorship; it also served to keep people unaware of the extent of German air-attacks. The official attitude was explained in the following censorship order issued by the Press Bureau:

It is undesirable that too much space should be given to describing Zeppelin raids.

The actual military damage that has been done is slight, but at the same time so long as the Germans think that the raids have great effect they will be continued, and long accounts tend to produce an impression both in England and Germany that they are of greater importance than they are in reality.[52]

The temporary suppression of journals like *Forward*, the *Labour Leader,* organ of the I.L.P., and *Tribunal,* the organ of the No Conscription Fellowship, need cause no surprise, but the Conservative *Globe,* too, fell under the censor's interdiction in November 1915, and the Liberal *Nation* was not allowed to travel beyond the confines of the British Isles. Even *The Times*, revealing under the ownership of Lord Northcliffe some of the old nineteenth-century thunder, incurred a D.O.R.A. prosecution.

D.O.R.A. could impinge upon people in all walks of life: negligent citizens could find themselves facing stiff fines for showing lights at night; from August 1916 the Londoner was deprived of the normal liberty of whistling for a cab; the Government could requisition private land and property for military purposes. That such requisitioning was, to begin with, done under the prerogative power of the Crown is sometimes cited as illustration of the tremendous control over the liberties and property of the subject exercised by the State, in this case by reference to its figurehead, the monarch; actually the resort to forms more appropriate to the Tudor age, and the absence of any machinery of control adapted to the requirements of the twentieth-century constitution, show rather how exceptional this control was, and how little the State was expected in normal times to interfere with the individual. In the spring of 1915 the Government appointed a permanent commission to adjudicate upon claims for compensation made by individuals who felt they had suffered loss from Government action under D.O.R.A. In its decisions the Commission showed a consistent lack of generosity, though it must be said that many of the cases brought before it showed great triviality and lack of public spirit on the part of the claimants.[53]

In financial transactions of a lesser sort the distant presence of the war made itself felt: gold sovereigns continued to circulate side by side with paper money till the autumn of 1915; thereafter they rapidly disappeared.[54] The implacable casualty lists apart, these intimations that the nation was at war were far from calamitous. But preparations were on hand in case of calamity. A hand-book for civilians described among other things the correct behaviour should the country be occupied by the Germans. In various areas arrangements were elaborated to be put into practice in the event of the Germans attempting to land an invading force: they involved the dismantling of all machinery and rolling stock, the collection of all tools likely to be of use to the enemy, the immobilizing of motor vehicles and carts, the slaughter of animals, and the evacuation of the population and preparation of food supplies.[55] No invasion came, but, as 1916 passed away, the community began to savour more sharply the realities of modern total war.

[III]   LIFE AND LEISURE

More people at work, and each person working longer hours, meant less total time available for leisure pursuits. The balance was restored by the greater spending money accumulated by many of those in domestic employment, and by the presence of soldiers on leave with little to do but sample the pleasures of civilian life. The type of entertainment for which there was the highest demand was of the lowest quality: everyone desired to escape from present reality.

The Edwardian era had been a great age of the theatre. But since the time when Queen Victoria set her personal seal of respectability on the drama, theatres had been largely the preserve of the middle classes, a fact which Charles Booth confirmed in his researches at the end of the century. Certainly suburban and provincial music-halls had derived much of their support from the lower classes, but for the poor anything more than the very occasional visit was out of the question. It was the advent of the cinema, of which there were 3,000 in 1914, which did most to bring dramatic or musical entertainment of a sort within the reach of the poorer members of the community. As the chairman of the London branch of the Cinematograph Exhibitors Association pointed out:

The cheapness of this form of amusement has created what is really a new type of audience. Over half of the visitors to the picture theatres occupy seats to the value of threepence or less. In the main, the vast majority of picture house patrons were not in the habit of attending any other places of amusement. The picture house is emphatically the poor man's theatre.[56]

The picture palace, also, was the theatre of the young, 'being attended by a larger number of children than any other form of public amusement'. If the cinema did nothing else, it at least provided a strong counter-attraction to street hooliganism and to the public house. In the years of war-time liquor legislation it was almost an enforced alternative and so played its part in the enduring modification of the alcoholic basis of working-class leisure.

As early as 1911 objections raised against the moral tone of certain imported films had opened up the question of a film censorship. In October 1912, with the approval of the then Home Secretary, Reginald McKenna, a Board of Censors was established, with a Mr Redford as president. He, in collaboration with four censors, began work on 1 January 1913, dishing out 'U' certificates to films suitable for viewing by all types of audience including children, and 'A' certificates to those suitable for adult audiences. It was at first intended that the Board of Censors should deal direct with the cinema-owners, but it soon became clear that the latter felt no strong inclination to adhere to the Board's rulings; accordingly the local authorities were brought in as middlemen. Redford was regarded, even by his own colleagues, as being rather too lenient, about 97 per cent of all films submitted being allotted certificates. When T. P. O'Connor succeeded him, there was a perceptible tightening up.[57]

Puritans and busybodies were very sensitive to the moral danger of a form of entertainment, freely attended by members of both sexes, which took place in the dark. Pre-war cinemas had employed specially trained supervisors to watch for offences against public pudency, but they were withdrawn during the wartime labour shortage. The National Council of Public Morals was very concerned that there should continue to be 'adequate supervision' and, if possible, 'sufficient light'. In dismissing the many complaints of the prurient, a Mr Goodwin, representing the London Cinema Exhibitors, coined a fine phrase. 'When investigation is made,' he said, 'it is usually found that the alleged misconduct is nothing more than the privileged manifestation of affection between the sexes.'[58] More to the point were complaints, despite the best attentions of the censor, about suggestive films which portrayed desperate struggles between members of the opposite sexes and scenes of rape which were only faded at the very last instant. Most of the press agreed with the National Council of Public Morals that a stricter censorship was required, and the *Daily Mail* expressed its horror of 'objectionable, unwholesome films'.[59] Good wines need no bush, but bad films have always needed their bare bosoms:

The posters advertising the films are often much more objectionable than the films themselves, when they emphasize the sensational or sensual aspects.[60]

That films could join the ranks of creative art, and could produce entertainment of high quality, was recognized by intelligent critics;[61] Charlie Chaplin and the American film-maker D. W. Griffith were showing in their various ways what could be done with the medium. But on the whole the emphasis during the period of the First World War was on escapism, whether sensual or spectacular. In referring to this the National Council of Public Morals remarked:

It has been insisted again and again by representatives of the trade that exhibitors can only provide profitably what the public will take. They state, for instance, that the public does not to any extent want the educational film. This contention cannot be allowed absolutely; the danger of the position of the purveyor of public amusements is that it inclines him to rate both the intelligence and the conscience of his patrons lower than they actually are, or at least can possibly be made.[62]

Nine-tenths of the films shown in British picture houses were American. This situation was partly caused by Britain's technological backwardness, but it was exacerbated in the days when films were still made out of doors by her execrable climate. The film is a mass medium, designed to sell to a mass audience and financed out of a budget to match. America with her large population had the mass audience ready made; British film-makers were less agreeably placed financially. While Britain was only a fraction of the American film-maker's market, the British producer found the greatest difficulty in selling his films in America. The final twist to the American stranglehold was provided by the fact that in time of war national energies and scarce resources had to be directed away from the non-essentials such as films. The growing demand, which had been given a certain respectability by the exploitation of the cinema for national purposes, could only be met by more and more American imports.[63]

The empty leisure pursuits of the 1920s are often seen as part of a reaction against the war. Yet just as the basic pattern of a Hollywood-dominated cinema was consolidated in the war, so, too, many of the other features associated with the high life of the twenties were born in the fevered atmosphere of 1915 and 1916. There was, said Mrs C. S. Peel, reporting on the upper-class life with which she was familiar, a great craze for dancing[64] – with chaperons absent on other business. The syncopated rhythms of ragtime and jazz had filtered into Britain in pre-war years; now sophisticated and complicated dances, such as the fox-trot, were fabricated upon them. It was due to the difficulties of the new dances, a dancing master declared, that couples spent entire evenings together rather than hazard their toes to an untutored outsider;[65] the older convention that one should never dance twice successively with the same partner was broken, though a more potent reason was the brevity of civilian reunions when dances were held on the brink of a departure for the front.

Dancing was still essentially the recreation of the wealthier set; as was the much-discussed new growth from the fertilizations of war, the night-club. Wartime hedonism, wartime darkness and dullness and wartime liquor restrictions created the appetite; young officers on leave provided the material upon which it could feed and multiply. By all accounts they were unconscionably dull places, these wartime night-clubs. Their main function was the provision of alcohol, sold as 'ginger ale' or 'tea' and astronomically priced; the one other main activity practised within the precincts was gambling, and the press was full of harrowing stories of young officers ruined through being tempted into uttering cheques they could not honour. One way or another the First World War put that quaint and dingy area of London known as Soho on the map; mainly in fact as a conveniently central shopping area with the added attraction of exotic foods unobtainable in the bigger West End shops.[66]

Theatres, after a few bare first days, prospered throughout the war. Visiting Edinburgh in the summer of 1918, Clifford Allen, the pacifist leader, noted in his diary the difficulties of getting a seat at any of the city's several theatres.[67] Further comments of his suggest that the audience was drawn from a wide cross-section of the community. Undoubtedly the intellectual content of almost all the theatrical productions of the period was minimal: there was a plethora of musical revues, garnished with the scantily-dressed dancers to whom angry old men took such exception, but grounded on a witless patriotism which could incorporate into songs phrases like 'Your king and country need you'. An enterprising management did cash in on the interest aroused by the Royal Commission on Venereal Diseases to revive the French play *Damaged Goods*, which in feeble and cumbersome manner dealt with this problem. Ibsen enjoyed a revival, and the Old Vic, a theatre still almost as genuinely proletarian as its geographical setting, had crowded houses at its Shakespearian productions.[68]

Most people, it might be said, wanted frivolity and *ersatz* excitement, but there were stirrings of seriousness. Ernest Newman, the distinguished music critic, expressed his amazement at the popularity of serious music:

Taking the country as a whole, audiences have been larger than they were in pre-war days; and it is all the more amazing when we remember that every town has been denuded of many hundreds of the men who used to be the most regular attendants at concerts.[69]

In part, Newman thought, 'the demand not merely for plenty of music but for plenty of good music' could be attributed to what he called 'the keener psychosis of the nation'. But he was prepared to give most credit to the personal efforts of Sir Thomas Beecham, the daring young conductor, whose supply of good music created a new demand: 'had there been no war, Sir Thomas Beecham's activities would have had practically the same results.' Ernest Newman's opinions are ones which the historian must treat with the utmost respect, as he must treat Sir Thomas Beecham's labours with the admiration he would, in another sphere, accord to Lloyd George. Without Beecham, as without Wood, Elgar, Bax, Vaughan Williams and Elgar, there would have been no British musical renaissance; none the less, with the experience of the 'keener psychosis' of the Second World War to refer to, the conclusion that a deeper interest in good music was a side-product of the emotional upset of the war is inescapable. Beecham offered the following explanation of the success of his English Opera, which performed extensively in the provinces as well as in London:

The combination of a high mood of idealism in the public and of economic stringency in the musical profession was effective in enabling me to create and develop the finest English singing Company yet heard amongst us. In wartime the temper of a section of the people for a while becomes graver, simpler, and more concentrated. The opportunities for recreation and amusement are more restricted, transport is limited, and the thoughtful intelligence craves and seeks these antidotes to a troubled conscience of which great music is perhaps the most potent.[70]

Through the Hallé Orchestra Beecham was able to introduce concert works by French, Russian, Italian and, above all, English composers to audiences prepared on patriotic grounds to lend an ear where once they would have turned and fled. There were strong pressures in favour of the banning of all German music, but these, fortunately, were successfully resisted.[71]

Visiting art galleries was not the ordinary Briton's distinctive leisure pursuit. But the statistics of admissions at the principal London museums and galleries, though clearly useless as absolutes, do seem to suggest a trend for the early twentieth century: a growth in the appeal of the two major art galleries, the National and the Tate, and a decline in the appeal of the two major museums, the British Museum and the Victoria and Albert;[72] a growth, to push generalization to its most dangerous limits, in aesthetic interest, if not appreciation, at the expense of mere antiquarian curiosity. The excitements of war brought a slight drop in attendances in 1914 as against 1913. The Director of the National Gallery, however, found 'healthy' and 'gratifying' signs in

the growing interest on the part of the British public in the National Collections, as demonstrated by attendance at the galleries, the interest shown by the Press and Parliament in the acquisition or presentation of important pictures, the increasing sensitiveness at the loss of national treasures, and the formation of a powerful and representative society to resist the prevailing exodus.[73]

Attendances further declined during 1915. In 1916 the Government took the incredibly obscurantist decision to close for reasons of economy the London art galleries and museums. There were such strong protests from the *Observer*, the *Nation*, the *New Statesman*, and the *Manchester Guardian*[74] that the decision was at once partially rescinded. Later in the war, so great was the crush of visitors to the National Gallery that on certain days the turnstiles had to be put out of commission.[75] If visiting art galleries is a minority pursuit, patronage and purchase of works of art are very much more so. Something of that war psychosis which called for satisfactions of the mind and spirit, apparent in the world of music, seems to have shown itself in the British art market. Certainly there was a boom in works of art, as in many other commodities,[76] though doubtless this can in part be written down as a reflection of the increased affluence of the wealthy, of the bid of the profiteer for social acceptability, or of general price inflation.

When we turn to sport, and, in particular, the great spectator sports which originated in Victorian Britain, we come to the very marrow of working-class and lower-middle-class leisure activity. After a winter of failure Frederick Charrington secured total success for his campaign for the abandonment of professional football in the spring of 1915. Everything else went by the board: 'no cricket, no boat race, no racing', Blumenfeld lamented in August of the same year.[77]

With the lights of simple pleasure going out all around him, the ordinary man had as consolations home and reading. The war coincided with some important developments in the newspaper press. The Canadian businessman, Sir Max Aitken (shortly to become Lord Beaverbrook), had taken over the *Daily Express* and launched it on a colourful and successful career. Rudimentary forms of the tabloid already existed in the *Daily Mirror* and the *Daily Graphic*; on 14 March 1915, the *Sunday Pictorial* appeared for the first time, aimed rather at the lower middle class than the working class, to judge from the pseudo-intelligent nature of its features. In fact it is clear that the working classes were not yet a powerful enough advertisers' market for it to be worth while designing newspapers specifically for them. At a time when much of the colour was diluted out of the news by the censorship, pictorial features were at a premium, and the war gave a boost to those papers which orientated themselves in this direction. The war also brought new freedoms in the use of banner headlines and cross headings: with glorious advances (or retreats) taking place every day it became essential to have some means of distinguishing the occasional really important headline from the routine ones. The majority of papers, including the *Daily Mail*, continued, however, to print their news inside, leaving the front page for advertisements.

The two most popular novelists of the war period, Nat Gould and Victoria Cross, were without pretensions to literary quality. Even so, the lower classes probably sought such creative writing as they desired from the *feuilletons*, the serial sob-stories of romantic love printed in the popular newspapers. Gramophone sales were booming, and records were extensively advertised in the press. Popular patriotic songs, or songs like the nostalgic 'Tipperary', which was written just before the war, seized upon by the first British troops, and praised for its aesthetic qualities by the distinguished composer Ethel Smythe,[78] accounted for the bulk of the records pressed during the war.

For members of the upper classes, especially those with religious affiliations, the opportunities for canteening as a genteel leisure activity increased as the war progressed. There was a healthy rivalry between the nonconformist churches and that of the establishment. In Middlesbrough the former got off their mark first, establishing Free Church Canteens for Soldiers and Sailors in 1916: the Church of England Canteen for Sailors and Soldiers appeared early in 1917.[79] The quaint period quality of canteening can be gathered from a contemporary account of the work of the Free Church organization:

The Refreshment Room in the Park was put at the disposal of a special Committee by the Lessee (Mr Dent), and, with the hearty co-operation of the Colonel, the Secretary organized a group of lady workers under the general management of Mrs Gaines, and every parade morning during a long and bitter winter supplied the men with a mug of hot coffee and a cake or biscuit. The Officers of the Battalion cordially assisted by so arranging the drilling of the companies that in turn the men fell in for refreshments.

The cost, which was heavy, was borne by voluntary subscriptions. Frequently over a thousand men daily partook of the Town's hospitality in this way.

Both Officers and men expressed the deepest gratitude and shared equally in the fare provided. The R.S.M. said, 'I believe you have saved lots of these lads' lives.'

Another branch of work largely organized by the Secretary was the securing of homes to which men were invited on Sunday afternoons and evenings. This spread through most of the Churches and hundreds of men in this way found homes and friends which helped to make their stay in the Town pleasanter and safer than it could otherwise have been. The Troops at Maron Hall were included in this hospitality in the homes. Each Christmas and New Year the men were entertained to parties and suppers free of charge and many scores of concerts were given.[80]

Soldiers were not the only lonely people in Britain during the war. Organizations were formed, too, to bring together the wives, mothers and sisters of soldiers. The ladies of the Tipperary Rooms in Middlesbrough furnished their own description of their activities:

The rooms provide for our comfort in every way. There is a book-lending library and savings bank. There is also a nursery for our children to play in. For the small sum of $1\frac{1}{2}$d we can get the eatables with the cup that cheers but does not inebriate. On Wednesday evenings we are entertained with a splendid musical programme. We do not feel that we are wasting our time, as we have already knitted and sent socks to our soldiers and sailors, also made sandbags, and we are now knitting mufflers. The materials are supplied by the ladies who so kindly try to make our lives brighter while our men are doing their duty.[81]

The war brought a re-knitting of community life, even in the intractable territories of rural Scotland, where prior to the war 'the greatest defect ... considered from the standpoint of the working population, has been the almost complete absence of community and social life'. The war years, the same writer continues, 'brought to rural Scotland a welcome increase in associated effort ... building up the much needed ... social interest' and giving 'confidence and a sense of value to the community'.[82]

NOTES TO CHAPTER FOUR

1. *Spectator*, 4 August 1917.
2. *Report of Coal Industry Commission*, Vol. I; P.P., 1919, XII, Cmd. 359, p. 4.
3. *House of Commons Debates*, 2 May 1917.

4. ibid, 24 May 1917.
5. *Labour Gazette*, 1915, pp. 67, 105, 142, 354-5.
6. ibid, 1916, pp. 4-5.
7. Board of Trade, *Report of Departmental Committee on Prices;* P.P. 1916, XIV, Cd. 8358, p. 5.
8. Scott and Cunnison, *Industries of the Clyde Valley during the Great War*, p. 172.
9. *Daily Mail*, 27 December 1915.
10. Scott and Cunnison, p. 184.
11. C. S. Peel, *How We Lived Then*, p. 68. *Daily Mail*, 8 December 1916.
12. *Labour Year Book 1916*, p. 212. *Daily Mail*, 24 May 1915. Cd. 8358, p. 4.
13. *Board of Trade Journal 1916*, pp. 388, 457.
14. Cd. 8358, p. 5.
15. *The Times*, 28 August 1916.
16. Hammond, *British Labour Conditions and Legislation During the War*, pp. 221-2.
17. *The Times*, 29 September 1915.
18. Blumenfeld, *All in a Lifetime*, p. 20 (9 March 1915).
19. *Daily Mail*, 19 October 1915.
20. Blumenfeld, p. 23 (17 April 1915).
21. *National War Savings Committee 1st Annual Report;* P.P., 1917-18, XVIII, Cd. 8516, p. 1.
22. ibid, p. 7.
23. *Daily Mail*, 2 April 1915.
22. ibid, p. 7.
24. Peel, pp. 34-5.
25. Lord Newton, *Retrospection*, 1929, p. 50. Ponsonby, *Falsehood in Wartime*, pp. 121-5. L. Masterman, *C. F. G. Masterman*, 1939, p. 280.
26. *Report of Committee on Alleged German Outrages*, 1915, p. 48.
27. J. D. Squires, *British Propaganda at Home and in the United States*, Cambridge, Mass., 1935, pp. 27 ff.
28. L. Masterman, p. 284.
29. D. Brownrigg, *Indiscretions of the Naval Censor*, 1920, p. 37.
30. S.P.C.K., *Tract No. 15*, 1915.
31. *Report of British Association for the Advancement of Science 1916*, p. 23.
32. H. Lucy, *Diary of a Journalist*, 1922, p. 218 (24 September 1915).
33. R. Graves, *Goodbye to All That*, 1929, pp. 283-6.
34. Professor G. C. Henderson addressing Chemistry Section of British Association, 8 September 1916. *Report of the British Association 1916*, p. 366.
35. In A. P. Newton (ed.), *The Empire and the Future*, 1916, p. 4.
36. Blumenfeld, p. 51 (18 April 1916).
37. ibid, p. 95 (14 October 1917).
38. McDonagh, *In London during the Great War*, p. 237 (16 December 1917).
39. *Report of British Association 1916*, p. 366.
40. W. H. Dawson (ed.), *After War Problems*, 1917, p. 7.
41. J. E. Edmonds, *Short History of World War I*, 1952, p. 182.
42. J. Hendrie, *Letters of a Durisdeer Soldier*, n.d., p. 84.
43. Quoted in L. Housman (ed.), *War Letters of Fallen Englishmen*, 1929, p. 30.
44. *Manchester Guardian*, 29 August 1916. L. Masterman, p. 286.

45. *The Organization and Methods of the Central Prisoners of War Committee;* P.P., 1917–18, XVIII, Cd. 8615, pp. 2–6.

46. *The Times,* 1, 2, 24 June 1915.

47. W. Robertson (ed.), *Middlesbrough's Effort in the Great War,* n.d., p. 126.

48. *Observer,* 17 October 1915. *Daily Mail,* 1 February 1916. *Manchester Guardian,* 9 February 1916. *Middlesbrough's Effort,* p. 126.

49. Blumenfeld, p. 70.

50. *Report of Summer Time Committee;* P.P., 1917–18, X, Cd. 8471, p. 3.

51. ibid., p. 18.

52. Quoted by Blumenfeld, p. 130.

53. *Defence of the Realm Losses Commission 1st Report;* P.P., 1916, VII, Cd. 8359.

54. Blumenfeld, p. 67 (18 November 1916).

55. Robertson (ed.), *Middlesbrough's Effort,* p. 127.

56. National Council on Public Morals, *The Cinema,* 1917, pp. 5–6.

57. ibid, pp. lxxx–lxxxi, 114–15, 216.

58. ibid, pp. 267, xxv, 83.

59. ibid, pp. 134, 143, 240, xxx. *Daily Mail,* 26 January 1916.

60. National Council on Public Morals, *The Cinema,* p. xxxi. See also pp. 18, 24, 26, 85, 135, 208.

61. *Manchester Guardian,* 28 March 1916.

62. *The Cinema,* p. xxi.

63. Commission on Educational and Cultural Films, *The Film in National Life,* 1932, p. 46.

64. Peel, *How We Lived Then,* p. 68.

65. *Daily Mail,* 4 September 1918.

66. Peel, p. 67.

67. Marwick, *Clifford Allen,* pp. 50–1.

68. Meech, *This Generation,* II, p. 176.

69. *Observer,* 12 December 1918.

70. T. Beecham, *A Mingled Chime,* 1944, p. 152.

71. ibid, pp. 133, 156–7, 161–2.

72. *Report of the Director of the National Gallery for 1913;* P.P., 1914–16, XXIX, 116, p. 60.

73. ibid, pp. 4–5.

74. *Manchester Guardian,* 22 January, 23 January 1916. *Observer,* 30 January 1916. *New Statesman,* 28 January 1916. *Nation,* 28 January 1916.

75. *Report of Director of National Gallery for 1919;* P.P., 1919, XXI, 21, p. 6.

76. *Manchester Guardian,* 18 August 1918.

77. Blumenfeld, p. 27 (20 August 1915).

78. *Observer,* 25 October 1915.

79. Robertson (ed.), *Middlesbrough's Effort,* p. 169.

80. ibid, p. 170.

81. ibid, pp. 184–5.

82. J. S. Duncan, in W. R. Scott *et. al.,* *Rural Scotland During the War,* Oxford, 1922, pp. 218–19.

The declaration of war: crowds gather outside the House of Commons. *Radio Times Hulton Picture Library*

The aftermath of anti-German riots in the East End of London, June 1915. *Radio Times Hulton Picture Library*

Taking the Oath: recruits at the White City, June 1915.
Radio Times Hulton Picture Library

Damage from a Zeppelin raid on London, September 1915.
Imperial War Museum

Replacing men: a woman worker in an engineering shop.
Radio Times Hulton Picture Library

Recruiting fervor: Miss Olga Nethersole addresses a meeting in

'Patriotic' women raise the white-feather flag. White feathers were presented to men in civilian clothes.

Radio Times Hulton Picture Library

In March 1915 Glasgow municipal tramways boldly took on two conductresses on a week's trial. Here, later, are a driver and a conductor wearing their natty Black Watch uniforms.
Imperial War Museum

A grocer's shop run by women, Bedford Park, London, August 1915. *Radio Times Hulton Picture Library*

'High' society supports the war effort by patronizing a Russian exhibition at Hampstead, January 1917.

Radio Times Hulton Picture Library

Scouts help with the harvest: pulling flax, August 1918. Children's war work helped the economy, but not their education.

Radio Times Hulton Picture Library

The art of disenchantment: 'La Mitrailleuse' by C. R. W. Nevinson. *Reproduced by permission of the Trustees of the Tate Gallery, London*

Handing in rifles and equipment at Wimbledon, December 1918.
Only the fortunate were demobilized as early as this: delays
caused much discontent.   *Radio Times Hulton Picture Library*

CHAPTER FIVE

The Challenge to Laissez-Faire

[1] SACRED PRINCIPLES

LAISSEZ-FAIRE as a complete and coherent economic and political philosophy was evolved in the early stages of the Industrial Revolution. It was born at a time when ancient limitations and restrictions and the current belief in the necessity of tariffs and bounties seemed to be holding back the natural progress of industrial growth; its proponents, of whom the earliest one of importance was Adam Smith, author of *The Wealth of Nations*, published in 1776, argued that ideally there should be no state interference in economic and social matters, that individual initiative and unfettered private enterprise were the keystones of prosperity, and, by logical extensions made by the followers of Smith rather than by Smith himself, that if it resulted in the grinding of the faces of the poor, this, though no doubt regrettable, was unavoidable. Overseas trade, said the classical political economists (often justly described by their opponents as 'the dismal scientists') should be freed of all tariffs, restrictions and bounties. Their third point of substance was that the Government should not meddle with the country's currency, which should be securely based on the actual amount of its gold reserves.

These theories were most nearly (but never completely) put into full practice in the middle decades of the nineteenth century, but were very shortly challenged by a countervailing philosophy, that of collectivism. The advocate of laissez-faire (or individualist) argues that by leaving the individual to his own devices the best interests of the community will be served. The collectivist argues that such a system, in stimulating excessive competition, is often inefficient and that, under its sway, many of the weaker members of the community will go to the wall: he therefore favours collective action, which, in effect, usually means State action, on behalf of the interests of the community as a whole, or of major sections of it. Up to a point economic theories are the product of prevailing economic conditions: the early and mid-nineteenth century was a time of small business enterprises competing with each other in the unsullied conditions of the free market; the later nineteenth century saw the beginnings of large-scale industrial combination with the element of free competition sensibly diminished. Even so, there was still a basic philosophical divergence between the individualist who was prepared to allow amalgamations on the part of individual businessmen on the grounds that they were thereby increasing economic efficiency, and the collectivist who saw such amalgamations as possible threats to the community as a whole. Industrial combination, then, could be a stimulus to developing the theory of collectivism, but was not itself a part of collectivism.

In any event it is too easy a temptation to talk of individualism, collectivism, progress, reaction, as broad impersonal, ineluctable forces, forgetting that the theories behind them are the theories of particular men, the measures that implement them the measures of particular men, and that these men, as often as not, are struggling with the events of fortuitous circumstance. The hard-boiled Marxist has an elegant circular argument to deal with this, but the greatest Marxist playwright, Bertold Brecht, gets nearest to the point. His Galileo, ageing, conscious that he has betrayed his great scientific discoveries, is being comforted by one of his former pupils, who tells him that the forces of reason are none the less steadily triumphing: 'the triumph of reason,' Galileo breaks out bitterly, 'is the triumph of reasonable men.' Leaving aside the meaningless question of whether, in the abstract, the collectivist or the individualist solution is the more reasonable, I hope here, and in a later chapter, to bring out from the shadows of historical inevitability some of the individuals who participated in the challenge to laissez-faire which is one of the salient and enduring features of the domestic history of the First World War.

In 1914 the three principles of free trade, free currency, and free enterprise, were still sacrosanct to the vast majority of politicians, businessmen, and civil servants; though a small group of Conservatives, led at the turn of the century by Joseph Chamberlain, had attempted to controvert the first. The existence of a highly elaborate system of direct taxation was a modest infringement of the second, and the collectivist social reforms

enacted since the 1870s a qualification of the third. Almost
everyone accepted these reforms, which were aimed, not at the
reorganization of society, but at filling in the more glaring gaps
where the existing system failed to provide the barest necessities
of social well-being.

Among the tiny minority who were prepared to go far beyond
this in the direction of collectivist intervention it is possible to
distinguish five groupings. At the centre stands the Fabian
Society, founded in 1884 and committed to seek by propaganda
and political activity the progressive socialization of Britain. Here
we rub against another word which presents problems of definition: in the nineteenth century and later, people often used
'socialism' as a synonym for collectivism, perfectly correctly since
the emphasis in the word itself is on putting the interests of
society as a collective unity before the ambitions of the individual;
it is in this sense that the Liberal Chancellor of the Exchequer, Sir
William Harcourt, could in the 1890s make the famous declaration, 'We are all socialists now.' However, it is a good rule in the
use of language that where two distinct words exist they should
be used according to the separate nuances which they have attached to them, rather than as loose synonyms. There can be
no precise definition of socialism, a word which is highly emotionally charged, and which is used by the body of its adherents
rather as the adolescent girl uses the word 'nice', but, as distinguished from collectivism, it connotes a more positive egalitarianism; being the philosophy of the have-nots, it is associated with
the conscious working-class movement, and it implies that in the
desired reorganization of industry and society the worker will
have managerial and political power, whereas collectivism alone
could result in former employers continuing in exactly the same
jobs, only as highly-salaried employees of the State. All socialists,
then, are collectivists (though some, for example the guild
socialists, would desire the collective unit to be very small);
but not all collectivists are socialists. None the less, throughout
our period of study we shall find people using the terms as pretty
well interchangeable.

The Fabians, among whom the most consistently important
was Sidney Webb, the small, egg-headed author of weighty
treatises, were a society of intellectuals, and tended to stress the

collectivist rather than the egalitarian or working-class aspects of their beliefs. Although formally affiliated to the Labour Representation Committee (which took the title Labour Party after 1906), the society continued to believe in the possibility of 'permeating' the major parties with its ideas. By 1914 the commitment to the Labour Party, partly because of the agitation of the younger generation of Fabians, was becoming more pronounced, and most Conservative and Liberal sympathizers had flown from the Fabian aviary to their own political cages, often, however, taking Fabian ideas with them. Just before the war the Fabians founded a new organ of intellectual and political opinion, the *New Statesman*, edited by Clifford Sharp, which in February 1914 published the first part of a meticulous report on the problems of nationalization, compiled by the Fabian Research Department; the second and third parts followed in May 1914 and May 1915 respectively.[1]

The Labour Party in 1914 was scarcely a party at all: rather was it a loose alliance between confirmed socialists who demonstrated their socialism through being members of the I.L.P. or Fabian Society, and hard-headed working men whose main interest was in the immediate bettering of their industrial lot, and whose first thoughts centred on their trade union. Only one side of this alliance was necessarily socialist, for many trade unionists had little interest in the philosophy of socialism and saw the Labour Party merely as a means to limited ends. The Labour Party as an entity, therefore, had not committed itself to a complete socialistic programme. Most of its most active members, however, were convinced socialists, and they make up the second of our five groupings.

At Labour Party conferences resolutions calling for the nationalization of basic industries had already become something of a formality, though there was an awareness that nationalization (or collectivization) would not itself bring Utopia. This is apparent in a resolution carried at the 1913 conference of the T.U.C. and repeated in 1915:

This Congress expresses the opinion that nationalization of public services, such as the Post Office, is not necessarily advantageous to the employees and the working classes unless accompanied by a steadily increasing democratic control, both by the employees and the representatives of the working classes in the House of Commons. It, therefore, pledges itself to work steadily to develop public opinion in both these directions.[2]

During the war there was a sharp divergence between the trade union side of the Labour alliance, which was firmly behind the war effort, and the political and socialist side as represented by the I.L.P., most of whose important figures were against the war (Fabians, however, on the whole supported the war); yet the two sides could unite at the 1916 Labour Party conference in calling for the nationalization of railways, mines, shipping, banking and insurance.[3]

A third group of collectivists was to be found on the radical wing of the Liberal party, where the most vociferous personality was Sir Leo Chiozza Money, a former Fabian (this illustrates the central position of the society), and author of *Riches and Poverty*. In May 1908 a number of radicals had formed themselves into the Railway Nationalization Society, of which the president was the barrister and Liberal M.P., Clement Edwards.[4] Money himself had brought in a Bill for the nationalization of the railways in the last months before the outbreak of war.

The Conservative Party is not readily thought of in connexion with collectivist social reform, yet in the later nineteenth century it was often more progressive in this respect than the Liberal Party, which was wedded to Gladstonian ideas of private enterprise and free trade. If the Conservatives hankered after a static, paternalistic society with the rich man in his castle and the poor man at his gate, it was part of the paternalism that the poor man at the gate should not die of starvation. Ideas of imperial grandeur fostered by Benjamin Disraeli went hand in hand with a desire to make the British a strong and healthy people. At the domestic end of the rope labelled 'constructive imperialism' and thrown to the underdeveloped colonies by Joseph Chamberlain was 'Tory radicalism'. The collectivist process is often taken as beginning with the Artisans' Dwelling Act of 1875, passed by a Conservative ministry under Disraeli. Although, on the whole, Edwardian Conservatives went no further than the filling-the-gaps type of social reform, there were a number of extreme right-wing Conservatives whose interest was primarily in war and empire, who were favourable to State action in the form of military conscription, and who were not unaware that German military potential owed much to her social welfare schemes.

Here we come up against another of the complications of the problem: members of the Conservative élite were prepared to talk in terms which sounded favourable to the idea of State interference, but there was always the unvoiced reservation that the interference should always be with other people, never with the élite. In other words, when Conservatives said 'the State', they often simply meant themselves, an attitude which Bernard Shaw had pinned down with one of his barbs in 1884 when he remarked that the Government had no more right to call itself the State than the smoke above London had the right to call itself the weather. Yet historians have rightly stressed the 'social imperialism' – that is to say, the buying of working-class support for imperial and militaristic policies with social welfare legislation – of both Conservative and Liberal ministries at the beginning of the twentieth century.[5] Although historically ends are more important than means, so that one can draw a distinction between the militarist who desires happy and healthy cannon-fodder, and the collectivist who desires a better and more humane society, it is necessary in discussing collectivism to keep the 'social imperialist' element in view. The strength of Conservatism as a political philosophy, furthermore, is its empiricism and adaptability, and Conservatives, presented with the unique circumstances of the war, were often far more ready than their political opponents to adopt the collectivist solution.

The fifth grouping included various administrators and technically non-political figures, many of whom had at one time or another been influenced by the Fabians. The overwhelming mass of the permanent Civil Service, especially at the Treasury, the War Office and the Local Government Board, was strongly laissez-faire in outlook, but in pushing through their social insurance legislation in 1911 Lloyd George and Winston Churchill had made use of a small storm corps of civil servants led by Sir Hubert Llewellyn Smith and W. J. Braithwaite,[6] and Churchill had, at the suggestion of Beatrice Webb, the female half of the great Fabian partnership, brought in a young journalist, William Beveridge, who was thereafter to lead a brilliant career in the public service.[7] With the growth of factory and public health legislation there had, too, grown up a tradition of enlightened bureaucracy, many of whose servants, on grounds of efficiency alone, were not averse to seeing it farther extended. The Board of Trade had become quite a hot-bed of eager young bureaucrats, of whom U. F. Wintour, shortly to take himself and a new broom to the Contracts Department of the War Office, was one. However, there can be no doubt that to the Liberal Government, to the Conservative opposition, and to right-thinking people everywhere, the three sacred principles stood unshaken when war broke out.

[11] MEASURES OF SELF-DEFENCE

In the interests of national self-defence even the most confirmed Liberal was prepared to concede some sacrifice of principle, and self-defence is the key to the first steps along the road to collectivism. The emergency measures of August 1914, particularly the limitations on trading and contraband, were obvious and rather unimportant examples. The requisitioning on 3 August of all shipping in waters adjacent to the United Kingdom, in practice about one-fifth of the total merchant tonnage, was essentially a military move, and had the effect of creating a greater free-for-all, and more opportunities for profiteering, among the owners of the remaining ships.[8] More important was the Defence of the Realm Act, the very embodiment of the theory of national self-defence: it did not itself, in its original form, involve any solid collectivist experimentation with industry or society, but it was, as it were, the unsubstantial awning under which the bits and pieces of collectivist organization could be built up.

In 1914 Britain's railways were a skein of tangled threads compared with Germany's well-knit pattern based on sound military design; but by the time Prussia had completed her lightning conquest of France in 1870, authority in Britain was alerted to the fundamental strategic importance of efficient railway organization. Accordingly the Regulation of the Forces Act of 1871 provided that in the event of war the railways would be put at the disposal of the Government, and in 1896 a Railway War Council was established.[9] On 4 August 1914 the railways passed into the control of the Government, to be run as a unified system by the

Railway Executive Committee, of which the official chairman was the President of the Board of Trade. The individual railway companies were guaranteed the same level of profits as they had enjoyed in 1913; receipts were pooled and the Government, instead of making separate payments for troop movements, from time to time put into the pool the amount by which it fell short of the earnings of 1913 – in 1916, for instance, about £6 million.[10] Since, furthermore, the Railway Executive Committee consisted of the general managers of the principal lines, and since the President of the Board of Trade scarcely interfered with the acting Chairman, who was Herbert Walker of the London and North Western Railway, this measure could not be called nationalization as understood by the committed socialist. Looking back on a year's working, this is how the arrangement was seen in a resolution unanimously adopted by the Trades Union Congress:

That in view of the fact that to meet the great national emergency with which the country was faced in August last it was found to be necessary to place the whole railway system of Great Britain under unified Government control, and having regard to the admitted success from the military point of view, which has attended this step in the interests of the community, this Congress reaffirms its conviction that the complete nationalization of British railways would prove to be in the interests of the community generally. Further, in view of the partial, vague and unsatisfactory character of the present arrangements between the railways and the State, this Congress calls upon the Government before relinquishing its present control to introduce legislation having for its object the effecting of complete national ownership of the railways, to be administered with the aid of an advisory Committee (upon which the employees shall have elected representatives), under a Minister of Railways responsible to Parliament.[11]

The railways were administered 'not by the government, but for the government'.[12] None the less, the theory of private enterprise had taken a knock in that profits to shareholders were pegged far below what they would have been had the companies been free to cash in on the war situation, and in that free competition had been superseded by unified control. The measure passed into effect without a murmur from the most confirmed

Liberal; the real decision, after all, had been taken in 1871.

Contemporary military thinking was, naturally, as alive to the value of certain strategic materials of war as it was to the value of effective rail communications. Much of the near-hysteria which surrounds international politics in the pre-war years was caused by the feeling that technology had so speeded up war as to make a quick trigger-finger essential. Shortly before the outbreak of war the British Army had adopted the new explosive, tri-nitrotoluol (TNT), the other standard explosive being picric acid.[13] The way in which the potential advantage in supplies of strategic materials which Britain derived from an empire on which the sun never set was diminished by her lack of the scientific expertise necessary to exploit them has already been discussed. Of tin and mica she had such abundant supplies that these commodities could, if necessary, be used as media of exchange with the United States and other neutral countries. Coal and steel, normally, were also in abundance, but in time of war had to be carefully husbanded. For iron ores, nitrates, copper and aluminium, Britain relied heavily on North America, and here she would be governed by shipping capacity and availability of credit. The quest for ferro-chrome and certain special steels and irons took her even farther out of the comforting rays of the imperial sun: there was a real danger that the principal sources, Norway and Sweden, might fall under the dominion of the enemy. Optical and chemical glass, potash, spelter and tungsten, and a range of scientific instruments and electrical goods came from the land of permanent darkness.[14]

Between 3 and 5 August 1914, the War Office leapt into action, prohibiting the export of benzol, coal-tar toluol, phenol, nitrotoluene, and other chemicals essential to the manufacture of high explosive. In November all supplies of toluol in the country were requisitioned, but to mollify continuing laissez-faire sentiment a very generous price was paid. At the same time the Defence of the Realm Consolidation Act (which became law on 27 November) gave the Admiralty and the War Council the right to take possession of factories employed in war production or of their output. A more direct, though extremely minor, piece of Government interference in a section of industry not covered by this Act came in December, when distillers were compelled to recover all toluene in excess of three per cent before marketing benzol or naphtha. By this time there was already tremendous competition in the United States for American nitrates and metals: the timorous War Office expedient of appointing an American banking firm as its purchasing agents had all the effectiveness of one little dyspepsia pill combating a perforated ulcer, for British manufacturers continued their own ruthless competition for raw materials, mercilessly bidding up prices against each other. The War Office at the same time put great trust (with some reason, it should be said) in the skilled purchasing ability of the large private firms with which it had had a long association.[15] By the end of 1914, however, it was apparent to the clear-sighted, of whom there were few, that the only way of ensuring that British factories got the necessary materials at reasonable prices was for the Government to assume responsibility for purchase, supply, and distribution. Its own agents kept pressing the War Office to adopt a system of advance bulk purchase and, soon after his appointment on 26 September as Director of Army Contracts, U. F. Wintour circulated a memorandum which to a remarkable degree anticipated the measures which eventually, through sad experience, had to be implemented.[16] Sir Hubert Llewellyn Smith of the Board of Trade referring in an important note of 23 January 1915 to the domestic manufacture of munitions, raised even wider issues:

It is ... probable that we shall ultimately find some form of compulsion necessary in order to ensure both that effective priority shall be given to Government work on existing contracts and sub-contracts, and also that new Government contracts (and sub-contracts) shall be accepted and given priority as compared with private orders already booked. Nothing but compulsion could relieve the contractors from the obligations of their private contracts, and in many cases they would welcome such compulsion. It should, therefore, be carefully considered whether the matter can be dealt with by existing regulations under the Defence of the Realm Act or whether new legislation or new regulations would be necessary for this purpose.[17]

The increasing difficulties of the early weeks of 1915 necessitated more and more direct buying abroad and stimulated spectacular action at home in connexion with one commodity in which supply suddenly ran desperately short: sandbags. All new sacking from the Dundee mills and all old sacks were requisitioned, the usual generous prices being paid. Nevertheless, old-guard resistance to wider governmental control, or even to a general policy of buying ahead, remained unsurmountable.[18] The upshot was the great shell crisis.

The near-monopoly of the German chemicals industry meant that, in addition to explosives, Britain ran dangerously short of dye-stuffs. It was because of this that the Government, acting on the advice of a Committee on Chemicals which it had set up at the outbreak of war, decided upon the ambitious scheme of floating a national joint stock company to manufacture aniline dyes. Itself a somewhat half-baked compromise between Government sponsorship and private shareholding, the scheme very nearly failed in face of the resolute opposition of private manufacturers; a complete fiasco was enthusiastically anticipated by the *Economist*, which, under the editorship of F. W. Hirst, was a bastion of economic orthodoxy. Through Government subscription of £1,700,000 British Dyes Ltd was kept in being till the end of the war, when it was amalgamated with Messrs Levinstein Ltd.[19]

Before the war two-thirds of Britain's sugar supply came in the form of beet sugar from Germany and Austria. In this case Government intervention, in the form of the appointment of a Royal Commission on Sugar Supply with executive powers to purchase and distribute sugar on behalf of the community, was rather more successful than it had been with dye-stuffs.[20] Here, in theory, was a great advance on the nervous fumblings of the War Office in face of a similar problem, and in practice it was highly successful in that, though prices did rise, domestic supplies of sugar were remarkably well maintained. The arrangement, however, was as much in the interests of the sugar traders, otherwise threatened with a loss of their livelihood, as of the community at large. A leading article in the Labour Party newspaper, the *Daily Citizen*, read the lesson of the Sugar Commission and preached another one:

Thus in the hour of its supreme need does the nation turn to the collectivist experiments urged for so many years by the Labour movement. And the experiments are not found wanting. They are abundantly and brilliantly vindicated. Is it too much to hope that the experiment will now be extended from sugar to wheat? Is it too much to hope that these experiments will still be remembered when these dark, anxious days are at an end? If it be necessary for the State to guard the poor from exploitation now, will it not be sound policy to continue the experiment during what we hope will be the long years of unbroken peace?[21]

Leaving the long years of unbroken peace aside, the *Daily Citizen* was justified in showing concern for the problem of wheat supply. For fifty years the British had been turning their backs on arable farming, so that in 1914 four-fifths of the wheat consumed had to be imported from abroad. Although there was as yet no truly serious interference with shipping, bread prices had shown an alarming rise in the first days of war, and the possibility of a flour famine was not one to be lightly dismissed. The War Emergency Workers' National Committee suggested to the Board of Agriculture that the entire home wheat crop should be commandeered. Contemporary opinion in Government and Civil Service circles is admirably summed up in the reply from the Assistant Secretary of the Board:

Having regard to all the circumstances of the case, the Board think that so long as the price of wheat remains moderate it would be unwise to interfere with the free play of competition.[22]

In fact, although the Government left the domestic market to its own devices it did interfere in the international market, purchasing between November 1914 and February 1915 three million quarters of wheat in the United States and Argentina.[23] So strong was the continuing prejudice against the Government undertaking business activities that the whole transaction was carried out in total secrecy.

Government interference in the world sugar market was in the interests of the sugar traders; its interference in finance was, as much as anything, in reply to the demands of the financiers. As a precedent the infringement of the principle of free currency was important, but in reality what the Government was trying to do was to restore to free working a fiscal mechanism which had jammed up under the impact of war; its policy was 'less an interference with the economic system than an attempt to restore a damaged part to normal working'.[24] The war hit the financial world in the solar plexus. The normal flow between Central Europe and the West abruptly halted; city men suddenly found themselves called upon to meet unexpectedly heavy commitments, or else found that they were stuck with fistfuls of bad debts, while, at the same time, the normal sources of loans had dried up. What was needed was a quick transfusion of liquid cash, and this was what the Government provided in the Currency and Bank Notes Act of 6 August.

According to classical political economy the amount of currency circulating in the country should be governed strictly by the amount of gold held in the country, but it was accepted that, since some proportion of the currency would be constantly in use and could not therefore be presented for conversion into gold, the Bank of England could safely issue notes which exceeded by a strictly defined amount the total value of its gold deposits; this strictly defined amount, issued, as it were, on trust, was called the fiduciary issue. The Bank of England was now given permission to increase the fiduciary issue at the same time as the Treasury began the printing of its own £1 and 10s notes. Theoretically Britain remained on the Gold Standard; the new currency notes were legally convertible into gold, and there was no prohibition upon the use of gold for payment of external debts. But so little did holders of currency notes avail themselves of their legal right, and so big were the practical difficulties of transferring large-scale gold payments in time of war – virtually impossible without Bank of England or Treasury assistance, which naturally was not forthcoming – that the traditional working of the Gold Standard was effectively suspended.[25]

Closed as an emergency measure, the Stock Exchange did not open again until January 1915, and then only under very restricted conditions. Yet orthodox opinion seems to have been more impressed by the Stock Exchange being open at all than by the limitations imposed upon it. It was left to the Fabian *New Statesman* to stress the importance of the innovation of Government control of capital issues and direction of investment towards projects believed to be in the national interest.[26] The Government farther imposed restrictions and even prohibitions upon foreign lending. All this is central to the theory of the collectivist planned economy, yet at the time it passed, save in the eyes of a few shrewd socialistic observers, as an *ad hoc* defensive policy upon which no long-term construction should be placed.

There is one other very obvious way in which the war challenged orthodox political economy, and that was through the prodigious expenditure which it involved. Very early on, the Government gave up any attempt to make separate allocations to military or naval expenditure, but simply asked Parliament to make farther grants in aid of the total war effort: such lax prodigality would have brought shudders to Cobden, Bright and Gladstone, pillars of an earlier and more careful era. By July 1915 the war was costing £3 million a day, and over the entire war period national expenditure multiplied sixfold. The National Debt, about the abolition of which the younger Pitt, first prime ministerial disciple of Adam Smith, had once had some deluded notions, rose from £650 millions in 1914 to £7,435 millions in 1919. None the less, over a year of warfare elapsed before any onslaught was made on the old tax structure.

The various scarcities of the early months merge into the associated problem of high prices. Hoarding had been a feature of the early days of the war; in reply the Board of Trade armed itself with the power to requisition at reasonable prices foodstuffs 'unreasonably withheld'.[27] It also went so far as to draw up, in collaboration with the grocers, a list of recommended maximum prices. But the two measures signified no more than an amiable intention, if even that, since little or no attempt was made to put them into practice. By the beginning of 1915 Labour organizations and newspapers were strongly voicing demands for Government control of basic foodstuffs and their prices. The *New Statesman* remained icily detached from its proletarian fellows: the remedy for high prices, it said, with breath-taking perspicacity, was peace, or else, possibly, an extension of the co-operative movement, but certainly not centralized control. It showed no special enthusiasm for the panacea humbler socialists were advocating, Government control of all shipping, though it did favour more energetic organization and control of internal transport: 'more drastic measures,' it agreed, 'may presently be called for.' All such hints and proposals merely aroused the hearty contempt of *The Times*.[28]

The whole question boiled up into the important House of

Commons debate of 11 and 17 February 1915. J. R. Clynes and other Labour speakers pressed the Government at the very least to institute control of prices. Asquith, it will be recalled, defended Government inaction on the highly unimpressive ground that present conditions were no worse than those prevailing in the aftermath of the Franco-Prussian war. The President of the Board of Trade, Walter Runciman, followed him with an unequivocal defence of the doctrine of private enterprise.[29] One might almost suspect them both, were they not such earnest believers, of parodying the laissez-faire cause. The Government's rejection of the nostrum of price control again got the hearty approval of *The Times*.[30]

Most interesting of all was the speech made by the Conservative leader, Bonar Law. It was a difficult speech to follow, the speech of a man not quite clear about his own attitudes. At times he seemed to upbraid the Liberal Government for not going far enough in its modest measures of State interference, yet in conclusion he seemed, for the time being, to be against such interference. A brief aside during the last sentences of the speech suggests that Bonar Law had at least been reflecting that Toryism did not have quite the same organic association with laissez-faire as Liberalism:

British-owned ships are under British control, and we have just as much right – I do not know whether this is good Tory doctrine or not – to seize this part of the national organization as I believe we have, if the necessity arises, to seize every able-bodied man in the country. From that point of view I am not in disagreement with the hon. gentlemen opposite. But I do say that no such case has arisen yet, and that until the evil becomes much greater than it is any attempt to exercise control in that way would be found perfectly futile. It would be very different in any case. But I repeat that there is a limit to the profit which we can allow to be made out of this war, and if that limit is reached, I would be at one with those who say that the House of Commons ought to step in.[31]

This wondrously vague piece of Tory soul-searching stands as a good example of how little progress the ideas of collectivism, despite isolated successes in exceptional instances, had made by February 1915. However, many of the basic issues which take us on beyond the universally accepted demands of self-defence had been aired, and the one major consequence of this House of Commons debate was the setting up of two Committees of Investigation into Coal Supply.[12] The reports did not come till April, but they then carried farther the challenge to laissez-faire.

[III] THE PRESSURES OF NECESSITY

One of the major sources for the history of the development of State control during the First World War is the massive *History of the Ministry of Munitions* written up from the inside at the end of the war. It prints many valuable memoranda and other original documents which give a particularly good picture of the attitudes of leading Civil Servants: parts of the *History*, indeed, were withheld from the public until after the Second World War. At the same time much of the commentary is written in the mood of extreme economic orthodoxy which characterized the Lloyd George ministry in the years immediately after the war. Necessity, it is insisted again and again, was the mother of State control. Talking of the State factories set up under the first Munitions Act, it declared that they 'owed their inception not to any definite plan or policy of State monopoly but to the immediate stress of practical necessity'.[13] It shrewdly explained the way in which State control increased by what it fed on:

Once any measure of control had been undertaken the forces pressing for complete control became stronger and were ultimately irresistible. Partial control was unjust as well as unsuccessful, and control of supply created monopolies which had to be met by controlling prices.[14]

The overall attitude of the writers is revealed on the first page of the seventh volume when they say, 'It appears probable that experience of State control during the war has retarded rather than hastened the spread of State socialism.'

The basic and non-polemical trend of the argument of the munitions historian is supported by a distinguished contemporary economic historian, who has written:

There was no one at this time to present the theoretical case for direct State action, and the controlled economy was not seen and planned as a whole, but allowed to grow, regulation upon regulation, as specific needs arose.[35]

With the second, and more important, part of this statement there can be no quarrel whatsoever; the first part requires slight amendment. From March 1915 to December 1916 more and more publicists put forward with strengthening conviction what might not unfairly be called 'the theoretical case for direct State action', until one could say that in the autumn of 1916 there was probably, in informed public opinion, a majority to be found in favour of such action. Admittedly newspaper leading articles are particularly difficult source materials to deal with: one has always to reckon with the possibility that some of the most pungent ones may have been written by a junior sub with a hangover, and it is quite often impossible to derive any sense at all from the less pungent ones. Fluctuations in opinion are especially discernible in the *Manchester Guardian*, edited by one of the greatest Liberal radicals of the generation, C. P. Scott; these may well have been a genuine expression of the Liberal dilemma. As the war wore on the *Guardian* spoke more and more strongly and consistently in favour of State control. In *The Times*, which was given wide editorial freedom, though owned by the first of the great Tory press Lords, Lord Northcliffe, the fluctuations can be explained as part of the Tory duality already mentioned. The historical value of *The Times* does not reside so much in its leading articles – too often an uncommunicative blend of balance and bigotry – as in the authoritative articles by eminent outsiders which it carried. A Liberal line more old-fashioned than that of the *Guardian* was followed by the *Daily News* (edited by A. G. Gardiner), the *Nation* (edited by H. W. Massingham) and the *Economist,* the last-named being essential to an understanding of the direction in which received economic attitudes were blowing.

By the third month of 1915 the inadequacies of British war production held the field of public discussion. The champion of collectivist radicalism, Leo Chiozza Money, contributed a shrewd article to the *New Statesman* entitled 'Power of Production First':

Opinions are very much in the melting-pot at this time, and all sorts of queer things are bubbling up to the surface in our United Kingdom.

We may excuse the appearance during the process of no small amount of froth. There are hasty concessions to Conscription, to Protection, to Big Navies, to Railway Nationalization, to the Control of Supplies, and even indeed to the rankest Socialism. So many cherished opinions, whether right or wrong, are without stable foundation that there may be plenty of surprises in store for all political parties when the Great War has at last come to an end, and the nation dissolves its organization for war to resume the disorganization of peace.[36]

In writing thus, Money was both premature in suggesting that there was as yet any real organization for war and undeceived in his forecast of the final outcome after the war.

The Defence of the Realm (Amendment) Act (No. 2) of February 1915 put into practice the suggestions made two months previously by Sir Hubert Llewellyn Smith, and involved a revolutionary extension of the Defence of the Realm Consolidation Act of November. It was possible for economic traditionalists to swallow the powers granted to the Admiralty and the War Office in connection with firms which were already in the munitions business; but the application of these powers, as necessary, to all other factories and workshops capable of conducting warwork was altogether a much larger mouthful. *The Times* gave its blessing to what it headlined as 'A Step in Government Control', but the *Manchester Guardian*, talking of 'Socialism in War', and 'another great advance towards the temporary nationalization of industries', expressed uneasiness. Nine days later the *Manchester Guardian* published a more favourable leading article, entitled 'War Socialism', which called for the further step of control of profits.[37] Limitation of profits was in fact a bait which, from the time of the Treasury Conference, the Government began to dangle in front of the Labour movement.

An atmosphere of crisis overhung April and May; there was universal anxiety over the shell shortage after the publication in the middle of April of Sir John French's long and factual dispatch on Neuve Chapelle, and anger after the publication of Colonel Repington's *Times* report on 14 May. The appointment of a special Munitions' Committee under Lloyd George was welcomed by *The Times* as a solution 'for which *The Times* has repeatedly pressed'. The *Manchester Guardian* called for 'some of the discipline and organization of Germany',[38] and other papers made much of the shining example set in this respect by the enemy country. From both *The Times* and the *Mail* there was much heated agitation for 'mobilizing the whole nation' or for 'national service'.

Growing pressure of opinion and the failure of the existing Government to come to grips with the problems of war would almost certainly have brought a change in ministry within months; the immediate shell scandal blown up by Colonel Repington made it inevitable within weeks; the violent and irreconcilable quarrel at the Admiralty over the ill-fated Dardanelles expedition between the First Sea Lord, Admiral Fisher, whom the Conservatives admired, and the First Lord of the Admiralty, Winston Churchill, whom they loathed, pinned it down to days. Only the back-bench Liberals seemed to be taken by surprise. On Monday 17 May the 'lobbies and smoke-rooms' were 'full of dismal prophecies', and two days later, when the decision to bring in the Conservatives had been announced, there was an indignant meeting of Liberal M.P.s, who were mollified, however, within twenty minutes by Asquith.[39] Too much should not be made of the change in personnel involved in the construction of a coalition ministry. It is true that Asquith's closest political friends, men like McKenna and Runciman, were the most zealous upholders of private enterprise, and that, on the whole, the new Conservative ministers were more prepared to approach war-time difficulties empirically, but the real boost that the Coalition gave to the forces of collectivism was that as an all-party ministry, and manifestly a war ministry, it could with much greater impunity pass measures which were in violation of beliefs previously firmly held by most Liberals and Conservatives alike.

As a symbol of the intention to grapple firmly with the munitions problem a new ministry was created, the first appearance of the most typical, and often the most fruitless, by-product of the collectivist process. There followed the Munitions of War Act, described by an American contemporary as 'perhaps the most decisive step in the state control of industry taken during the war'.[40] Primarily the Act dealt with the labour shortage, but State control of labour was paralleled by State control of profits. Most important of all, the new ministry went straight ahead with the establishment on its own account of National Factories, of which there were sixteen by the end of July and 250 by the end of the war, most of them built during 1915 and 1916.[41]

The sight of the Government at last rolling up its sleeves was hailed with delight in most of the press, though the *Manchester Guardian* hankered after something at once more radical and more tender towards the susceptibilities of the business classes:

We confess we should have thought it simpler and better for the Government to have dealt with munition works as they did with the railways, taking over the entire concern and allowing to existing owners a handsome income as owners and remuneration as managers.[42]

The Times canvassed another proposal for dealing with both the labour shortage and the demands of the Western Front, the compilation of a National Register. Although the *Economist* countered with a trumpet blast of individualism, the Government took up the suggestion at the end of June, and National Registration Day was duly held early in August. To the *New Statesman* this was a turning point, bringing an end to the four months of repentance and good resolutions which had followed upon the utter disorganization of the first stages of the war.[43]

We have concentrated, rightly, on the munitions crisis and the labour problem associated with it, for this was the first great force which pushed politicians, reluctant to go beyond the obvious provisions for national self-defence, towards positive collectivist action. But at the same time as the dramatic changes were being heralded with all the pomp and circumstance of which Lloyd George was master, discontent with high prices was bubbling away and slowly working its own change in the alchemy of administrative activity. Scarcity of labour had caused the setting up of the Committee on Production, but the Committee's own Fourth Report makes it clear that fear of profiteering was a strong motive for turning the thoughts of its members towards ideas of State control.[44] The Committee of Investigation into Coal Prices, which consisted of Mr Vaughan Nash, C.B., Professor W. J. Ashley, Mr A. W. Flux, and three M.P.s, declared resoundingly in its April report that the ordinary capitalist distribution 'has broken down in the extraordinary circumstances of the present winter'; that immediate direction and control were essential, and that it might even be necessary for the Government to

assume direct control of the output of the collieries of the United Kingdom, with a view to regulating prices and distribution in accordance
with national requirements during the continuance of the present
war.[45]

The more conservative reports of the other coal committees reinforced the Government's own prejudices in the matter, and it
went no farther, even after the ministerial reconstruction, than
imposing domestic price control, although there were calls from
many camps, including that of the extreme suffragettes, for
nationalization.[46]

Agitation over food prices brought a modest but growing governmental response. In April 1915 all the insulated spaces on
British steamships on the Australian and New Zealand sea-routes
were commandeered; in December all insulated spaces, irrespective of the sea-route served, were taken over; and at the close of
the year a Requisitioning Committee was set up with powers to
requisition entire ships.[47] Comment in the press varied between
vague advocacy of a national policy on food purchase and distribution and very firm rebuttals of any such thing. Government
spokesmen still continued openly to extol the virtues of the un-
regulated market, though agitation over high rents had also
brought the Increase of Rent and Mortgage Interest (War Restrictions) Act, which in effect pegged rents of houses with rateable values not exceeding £35 in London, £30 in Scotland and
£26 elsewhere to their 1914 level.

None the less, it is in the summer of 1915 that the long discussion of the rising cost of living blends with the second great
positive force of necessity which eventually pushed the country
a long way farther along the road to State control: the physical
shortage of food, and the need to maximize home production.
In June 1915, a Committee on Agriculture was set up under the
chairmanship of Lord Milner, right-wing die-hard and enthusiastic social-imperialist. Its first report, published in July, put forward
a number of sensible recommendations amounting to a national
agricultural policy. Unhappily the Government, believing that it
had now mastered the submarine menace, made no attempt to
put them into practice. The second report, presented in October,
suggested the creation of County War Agricultural Committees
to give directives to farmers in the locality as to the most efficient

use of their available resources.⁴⁸ The Committees were duly appointed; but, lacking clear leadership from the Board of Agriculture, then headed by Lord Selborne, outstanding among the covey of incompetent administrators which was the parting gift from the old world of Edwardian England to the new world of total war, they achieved very little. The theories which, when put into practice eighteen months later, gained great praise for the Lloyd George ministry were actually fully hatched by the autumn of 1915; there lacked only the political will to set them to work.

Late 1915 and early 1916 are a time of stalemate as far as the growth of collectivism is concerned. Attention was concentrated on the National Register, the Derby Scheme, and conscription. It was for these topics that the *Economist* reserved its individualist fire, demonstrating incidentally that if Liberals were out of touch with the economic needs of the war, they were also heroic in their defence of the rights of conscience, now beginning to suffer in face of the aggrandizement of the State. There was, too, the breach in the dyke of classical political economy opened at another point by the budget of September 1915: it was a breach no bigger than a man's finger, but the waters, once let through, would not easily cease. In prefacing his budget proposals, McKenna expressed the fear that they would 'satisfy neither the strict Free Trader nor the scientific Tariff Reformer'; the natural working of free trade, he said, had in any event been spoiled by the war. The sentences which marked the first swing in British policy towards protectionism since the Repeal of the Corn Laws in 1846 sounded pretty innocuous – an effect which was heightened by the highly humorous intèrjection of the Labour member, Will Crooks, faithfully recorded in the *Hansard* report:

I put forward now, however, a list of articles the importation of which may properly be restricted by means of duties, in time of war, on both the grounds I have mentioned, namely foreign exchange and luxuries. So far as the duties do not put an end to importation, they may be a source of revenue not to be neglected. The articles to which I refer are motorcars and motor-cycles, and parts thereof, cinema films –. (Mr W. Crooks: 'Poor old Charlie Chaplin') – clocks, watches, musical instruments, plate glass, and hats. . . .
On each of these articles I propose an *ad valorem* duty of 33⅓ per

cent, or its equivalent, in the form of a specific rate, that is to say, on weight instead of on price.[49]

Only one back-bench Liberal, Thomas Lough, a former junior minister and chairman of a prosperous grocery concern, put up a spirited defence of the divine right of free trade. A concurrent breach in the principle of free currency was involved in the Treasury decision, in face of the fall in value of the pound to 4·50 dollars, to support the rate of exchange by the purchase of British-held American securities.[50] Early in 1916 the free trade hole was enlarged by the introduction of 'safeguarding', further protectionist tariffs said to be necessary to safeguard essential British industries.

The continued extravagance of the War Office and its reluctance to make use of its compulsory powers gave rise to the sick joke: 'No price is too high – for the War Office to pay – when honour and freedom are at stake.' But the direction in which opinion was swinging can be seen in the report of a Board of Trade Departmental Committee on Prices appointed in June 1916, a key document in the study of collectivism during the First World War.[51] The full report was extremely conservative in tone, going no farther than the recommendation that, if necessary, there should be farther Government requisitioning of shipping, and that bulk buying of meat by the Government (originally conceived as part of the programme of feeding the vast armies) should be extended. But an actual *majority* of the Committee (seven out of twelve) added the following memorandum:

... The present circumstances, being altogether exceptional, lend themselves readily to the inflation of prices and the making of large profits, and we think the evil cannot be effectively checked short of Government action, which must be wise and well considered, but at the same time far-reaching. The Government, we think, should more and more enlarge its purchases of meat and bacon from outside sources, and, where possible, become the sole purchaser, and should insist upon the purchasing public getting the full benefit of advantageous buying.

We think the recommendations should also have dealt with the home supplies of meat, bacon and milk. In many cases far too much profit is being made by the home producers, and we are of opinion that reasonable prices should be fixed. There is no new principle in this. The

Board of Trade, which has taken wide action in respect to the price of coal, is now extending its powers. There has been legislative action affecting the rents of houses. The Government has taken over the whole woolclip of the United Kingdom at a price determined by reference to the prices of the previous year. We know of no adequate reason why the public control of prices should not embrace the primary foodstuffs produced at home. In regard to the milk industry, for instance, a Committee of men and women acquainted with the conditions of the trade might be appointed to regulate prices, taking all the factors fully into account, and endeavouring to act fairly as between farmers, the distributors and the public.

We believe that machinery could be set up by Parliament which would eliminate from milk prices any element of extortion and encourage more efficient organization in distribution.[52]

Among the seven who signed this memorandum there were two Labour M.P.s, W. C. Anderson and J. R. Clynes (who were both, in addition, members of the I.L.P.), one trade union leader, Tom Shaw, and a member of the executive of the Fabian Society, Mrs Pember Reeves; but the other three, Sir Gilbert Claughton, Chairman of the London and North Western Railway and a director of Barclays Bank, D. Drummond Fraser, a banker and economist, and Thomas Brodrick, were all men who had heretofore held economic opinions of unimpeachable orthodoxy. As nearly as such things can be calendared, the summer of 1916 was the time when, as far as intelligent opinion is concerned, the tide of collectivism was definitely in flood.

[IV] INTELLIGENT OPINION

From the later decades of the nineteenth century, industry had been combining into larger units than would have been thought proper in mid-Victorian times. If in some respects the growth of industrial combinations was halted by the war, the value of large-scale production and minimized competition was at the same time made abundantly clear to capitalists. In 1915 the five main London transport undertakings decided to pool their resources, and this was given the sanction of Parliament. It was in the same year that the main London milk distributors linked themselves together in the United Dairies Limited.[53] The most important sign of the co-operative, if not combinative, impulse among businessmen was the founding in the summer of 1916 of the Federation of British Industries, which described itself as:

the latest and most important development of the Trade Organization movement in the United Kingdom. For many years past the manufacturers in many of the leading industries of the country have experienced the advantages to be gained by co-operation and association for the protection of their common interests in organizations devoted to their particular trades. The exigencies of wartime conditions added impetus to this movement and led to a large increase in the number of trade associations, with the result that practically every industry and the majority of trades within each industry, now have associations to assist and to foster the manufacture of British goods.

For this scheme of organization to be complete it was seen that British manufacturers and producers required the co-ordinating assistance of a National Association, which would concentrate and weld together the efforts which each trade exerted through its trade associations so that manufacturers might be enabled to speak and act in a manner commensurate with their strength and importance. The national needs during the war, and still more, the problems which would have to be faced when the war was over, necessitated the formation of a strong central organization representative of British manufacturers and producers as a whole.[54]

In time of war the impulse towards combination, co-operation, and rationalization helped to reinforce the movement towards State collectivism. Although at the end of the war the literature of the Federation of British Industries burst into a chorus of hatred against collectivism and all its works, for the period of war there was no hint of this attitude in F.B.I. publications. Other writers used the need for industrial rationalization as an argument in favour of State action. At the same time the glories of war gave a great stimulus to the theories of social imperialism. The two lines of thought form the basis of an interesting series of articles published in *The Times* during July and August 1916, and shortly republished, with an introduction by Lord Milner, as *The Elements of Reconstruction*. 'Reconstruction' is the theme word and the two anonymous authors are looking forward to a solution, after the war, to the problems of industrial organization: they claim that in that solution must be combined the experience gained in both the wartime national factories and the new private trusts and combines, and the lessons of German State socialism tempered by elements of British guild socialism.[55]

The amalgamation which had just taken place of the two great chemical firms, Brunner Mond and Co., and Castner Kellner and Co., is referred to approvingly, and the writers suggest that there should be 'a still more comprehensive crystallization', with 'the British Empire itself as an active and contributory partner in the ultimate combination'. *The Elements of Reconstruction* goes on to insist on the necessity of 'one national plan', and to contrast the old 'chaotic world of individualistic business run for unchecked private profit' with the proposed new 'system of amalgamated businesses in which the public interest is the controlling shareholder'.[56] The whole approach is well summed up in the following passage:

Without any preachment or propaganda we all find ourselves today drifted into a virtual agreement upon the reasonable course of economic development. It is a development towards nationalization; so far we go with the Socialist, but it is a development not by the Socialist's panacea of 'appropriation' at all, but by amalgamation, by co-ordination and co-operation, and by bringing the State into partnership, and an increasing partnership, in the big businesses that result from these amalgamations, by developing the crude beginnings of the 'controlled establishment', by the *quid pro quo* of profit-sharing and control in the national interest in exchange for the national credit and a helpful tariff.

It is not one of the least of the compensations for this war that it has necessitated experiments upon an otherwise impossible scale in the handling and rationing of the people's food and drink, and upon the conversion of private into quasi-public businesses.[57]

The writers were obviously impressed by, and sympathetic towards, guild socialism, which they say has done valuable work in 'preparing the minds of large masses of workers for industries upon a national scale'. Among the wilder proposals, that for parliamentary constituencies drawn on an occupational rather than a geographical basis (firmly stepped on by Lord Milner in his preface) has guild socialist overtones. If there are also about the whole programme faint shades of an incipient fascism – there must be an end, the authors say, to 'the pitiful old struggles' in the labour world[58] – the basic impression is of men of high intelligence and right-wing sympathies who have arrived at a considered rejection of all the old dogmas of laissez-faire.

Meanwhile, W. H. Dawson, the historian, was compiling a collection of essays on *After War Problems*, which, because of wartime delays, was not published till 1917. In his introduction Dawson talked of 'the deadly doctrine of laissez-faire'.[59] None of his contributors was quite so forthright, though Sir Joseph Compton-Rickett, Free Churchman, Liberal M.P. and former coal-owner, in a chapter on 'Organization of the National Resources' called for the cautious extension of collectivism. 'The growth of communal control and of State ownership,' he concluded, 'will probably secure the best of Socialism for us without its inherent weakness.'[60] A chapter on 'National Efficiency' by William Garnett emphasized the necessity for State encouragement of science. While thinkers of the political right and centre were becoming converted to some kind of collectivism, spokesmen of the left were consolidating their prepared positions. At the 1916 Labour Party Conference all sections of the movement united behind Philip Snowden's resolution on the financing of the war, which called for nationalization of railways, mines, shipping, banking and insurance.[61]

It is necessary now to turn again to the very practical and pressing problem of food shortage and food prices, another matter governed by a vital development in the outside war: the German resumption in October 1916, after an interlude designed to appease American sentiment, of submarine warfare. Now a 'decisive step'[62] was taken with the appointment of a Royal Commission 'to inquire into the supply of wheat and flour in the United Kingdom, to purchase, sell and control the delivery of wheat and flour on behalf of His Majesty's Government, and generally to take such steps as may seem desirable for maintaining the supply'. An important parliamentary debate on food prices took place on 16 October. Barnes, for the Labour Party, accused the Liberals of a 'mournful, lingering feeling of regret' for laissez-faire, which he said was 'as dead as Queen Anne'. Runciman, for the Government, had already poured derision on the idea of a Food Controller or Minister of Food, but he got no praise from the *Economist*

which, with the departure of F. W. Hirst, had switched to the new
tunes. 'The advocates of stricter control and stronger measures,'
it said, in reporting the debate, 'had the best of the argument.'
Turning to prophecy, it forecast that in a year's time nine-tenths
of the country's food would be under Government control.[63]

Poor Runciman was shortly eating his words: on 15 November
he had to announce that the Government had decided to appoint
a Food Controller. 'We have been driven bit by bit, against our
will,' he explained, 'to suspend the easy flow of purely voluntary
action.'[64] The problem was to find someone to take on the job,
but that was not easy, as the Government visibly shook before a
number of thunderous onslaughts, the most telling of which was
that of Winston Churchill:

It has been a question of driving bit by bit, inch by inch driving the
Government along the path which necessity in the end has forced them
to enter upon . . . I believe that before the end of this War, unless it
comes to an unexpected end, all shipping will certainly be taken over
by the Government and regulated in one form or another, no doubt
through its existing owners. I believe that all important employment
will be regulated by the State for the purposes of the War. I believe
that ration tickets for everything that matters will be served out to
every one of us. I believe that prices will have to be fixed so as to secure
to the poorest people in this country who are engaged in fighting this
War as comrades with us, the power of buying a certain modicum of
food sufficient to keep up physical war-making efficiency, at prices
which are not outside the scope of the wages they receive, whatever
those wages may be . . . All this will come. It can all be avoided quite
easily. We have only got to send across and say we want to give in and
all these difficulties can be avoided. But . . . all this kind of thing will
undoubtedly be done, and more than we can think of now will be
done, by the desperate resolution of the British nation not to be
balked of its object. But why not do these now? Why not do them
now while there is time? No one is stopping the Government except
themselves.[65]

The Government food policy had got no farther than the Order
of 21 November, which enforced price control for milk, when
recurrent trouble in the South Wales coalfield forced its hand
in another direction. Various proposals for control of the coal-
mines had been canvassed in the press throughout the autumn

though *The Times* put it about that the Government was restrained by a tenderness towards coal-owners who were generous contributors to Liberal Party funds.[66] However on 29 November a new Defence of the Realm regulation made provision for the taking over of the South Wales mines on 1 December. The regulation specifically envisaged the extension of this control, if and when necessary, to other mining areas. The ideas of collectivism, then, were very much in the air in December 1916; but there was a strong feeling that the Government was showing laxity in failing to channel them into definite action. It is in this atmosphere that the great political crisis breaks; to it we must now, briefly, turn.

[V] THE UNDERTONES OF POLITICS

According to one economic historian, the political crisis of December 1916, and the replacement of Asquith by Lloyd George, 'formed a watershed in the conduct of the war'.[67] E. V. Morgan puts the matter more circumspectly:

The turning point, so far as there could be any single one, was the resignation of the Asquith Ministry and the accession to power of Mr Lloyd George.[68]

As shorthand statements these serve well enough, though they cry out for the obvious qualification that strong pressure for collectivist action had been building up for many months before December 1916, and had, indeed, already achieved many striking successes. Furthermore, in many of its policies the new ministry was as ham-handed and inadequate as its predecessor. Asquith, in fact, was in greater degree an obstacle to the type of centralized control the war made necessary than Lloyd George was an instigator of it. It is tempting, none the less, to see the vanquishment of Asquith solely as a victory for the forces of collectivism. There is more truth in this than the old-fashioned historian with the blood of political battle pounding in his ears would have us believe, but it is a truth that must be integrated into the complicated background murmur of politics.

The new Cabinet of May 1915 contained twelve Liberals, eight Unionists, one Labour member and Lord Kitchener; the Irish Nationalists had been offered, but declined, representation. It was bigger by two than the old Cabinet: there was a Minister of Munitions (Lloyd George), and Lord Lansdowne, aristocratic heir to the great Whig tradition of liberal rationalism though an ultra-Conservative in his hostility to Irish Home Rule, was included as Minister without Portfolio. In February 1916, the further addition was made of a Minister of Blockade. To counterbalance this growing cumbrousness of the Cabinet machine, one important step was taken towards modernizing the parliamentary system: a temporary Act was passed freeing ministers from the eighteenth-century requirement that upon appointment they must resubmit themselves to the electorate. As a token recognition of the need to reorganize the political control of the war, the War Council was reconstituted in June as the Dardanelles Committee: the name itself expresses the significance of the Dardanelles expedition – pressed by Churchill, Lloyd George and Hankey (Secretary of the War Council), resisted by Sir John French and the generals on the western front – as the major military storm centre of the period. Yet the executive decisions remained in the hands of the large and unwieldy Cabinet, an arrangement which *The Times*, calling for 'a smaller cabinet sitting every day', attacked as early as September 1915.[69] In November the Dardanelles Committee became the War Committee of six leading politicians, organized on a more formal basis; the Cabinet was still the ultimate authority. As there was no place for him in the six, Churchill resigned from what he called 'well-paid inactivity' and joined his regiment in France.[70] Then Sir Edward Carson, who advocated a more vigorous attempt to open up an eastern front at Salonika in the Balkans, resigned on policy grounds. As a violent Ulster Unionist, he had never been very well disposed towards Asquith, and he now became a powerful opponent.

Ministerial woes had been greatly increased by the incompetence of Sir John French and of Lord Kitchener: Arnold Bennett, dining at the McKennas', was informed 'that nobody *could* be worse at the War Office than Kitchener. He wasn't even a brute.'[71] Asquith's solution was to divest the War Secretary of his additional Staff functions, to give them, along with the title of Chief of the Imperial General Staff, to Sir William Robertson, and to replace French as Commander-in-Chief by Sir Douglas Haig. While these changes marked clear gains in the British military potential against the German, they also strengthened the military at the expense of the politicians. Asquith could not, however, escape as easily as this from the mounting criticism of his political leadership. Between the introduction of conscription for single men and universal conscription, there was a first-class crisis, when the provisional Conscription Bill introduced by the Government had to be withdrawn because of the hostility it met in a secret session of the House of Commons. In March 1916 Christopher Addison, Liberal M.P. and crony of Lloyd George, noted in his diary:

There appears to be a movement among the Conservatives to try and get L. G. to take a strong line and they are even prepared to go the length of recognizing him as P.M.[72]

From outraged Ireland came further slings and arrows when the Dublin Easter Rising made it clear that the more excitable Irish patriots were not prepared to wait upon the parliamentary game at Westminster. The incident was a shattering one for British Liberalism, and it brought the resignation of the Irish Secretary, Augustine Birrell, who had clearly been taken entirely by surprise. After an ill-conceived spell of repression (including fourteen executions), Lloyd George was sent to negotiate. He showed great skill in a difficult situation, though also, his enemies said, more than a dash of his proclivity for being all things to all men; be that as it may, many Liberals *believed* that Lloyd George had produced a viable settlement, and that it was the fault of Asquith that it was not put into effect.

In May *The Times* was calling for a reconstruction of the Government.[73] Kitchener's death necessitated a slight Cabinet reshuffle: Grey was recruited to the House of Lords, and Lloyd George, after some misgivings over the diminished powers now enjoyed by that Office, became War Secretary; E. S. Montagu took Lloyd George's place at the Ministry of Munitions, and Lord Curzon was added to the War Committee. On balance Asquith's position was weakened, for Kitchener, if stupid, had been loyal, and Grey had been a valuable right-hand man in the Commons. Public criticism of military strategy was muted, but within the innermost circles of politics men like Carson, Churchill and Lloyd George were genuinely uneasy about the way the war was going, particularly over the failure to open up an effective eastern front. According to Christopher Addison the last straw for Lloyd George was the way in which Rumania, unsupported by the Allies, was allowed to fall under German dominion.[74] That there was a good deal of overt criticism of the weakness of Asquith's control of domestic policies we have already seen. The actual issue which provoked the final crisis, that of a reform in the executive machinery of war government, was both a banner behind which the two lines of criticism could march without appearing disloyal or subversive, and a matter of substance in its own right; it was also a useful lever by which Lloyd George could apply the pressure of personal ambition. In September Asquith had tried, unsuccessfully, to appease the critics, by experimenting with a pair of Cabinet committees – one for war, one for finance. In an earlier period – in the middle of the Crimean War, say – the situation would have been resolved by an open vote in the House of Commons. Now that the war emergency had set the seal on the long process whereby such decisions were steadily being removed from the direct purview of Parliament, this was practically out of the question. To that extent denunciations of the backstairs intrigues which took place at the beginning of December are anachronistic. In any case the Government was a coalition, and bound to collapse if it lost the support of its Conservative members, though the Conservatives could not withdraw their support till they saw a viable alternative.

It is on this point that the coming-together of Lloyd George and Bonar Law is crucial. The two had nothing in common but their faults; in their virtues – Lloyd George's greatest was his warmth and generosity of spirit, Bonar Law's his austere honesty – they were poles apart, and for years Bonar Law had nursed a cordial detestation of the man he regarded as a ranting demagogue. The first mediating figure was Carson, but the man who did most to bring about the vital juncture was Sir Max Aitken, the owner of the *Daily Express*. In bringing together two men who had a basic common purpose by overcoming the prejudice of one of them, there was nothing very sinister. Less agreeable was the way in which Aitken's *Express* as well as Northcliffe's *Mail* helped to whip up a crisis atmosphere in a manner unfavourable to Asquith. Even so, these powerful organs of mass communication were not really going far beyond what many intelligent commentators believed to be necessary; they were in fact acting, in however distorted a form, as the agents of a change necessary to the safety and well-being of society at a time when the normal electoral process had been disrupted.

Lloyd George made his move on Friday, 1 December, proposing to Asquith that the war should be run directly by a reduced War Committee, which would take day-to-day decisions without reference to the larger Cabinet; Asquith would continue to have the name and forms of the Prime Ministership, but he would be excluded from this committee, of which Lloyd George would be the chairman. Lloyd George was without doubt chiefly motivated by a concern for the successful prosecution of the war; at the same time he cannot have been unaware that his proposal in effect meant the supersession of Asquith by himself. Asquith was not keen on the idea, but the impression he derived on Sunday, 3 December that the Unionists would not back him made him decide that evening to give way. The next day, accordingly, Lloyd George began making his plans, while *The Times* raised Asquith's temperature with an article saying that in the new arrangement he would be a complete nullity. Had this been channelled by Lloyd George through Lord Northcliffe (the owner of *The Times*), as Asquith believed, there would be more validity in the accusations often levelled against the press lords and against Lloyd George. In fact the article was written by Geoffrey Dawson, editor of *The Times*, who had seen Carson the day before; if anyone comes badly out of the incident it is Carson (not to mention Asquith, who demanded that Lloyd George should denounce the article). The article is best viewed as a reasonably independent-minded commentator's attitude to the crisis.[75]

Asquith might well have been more disturbed by the same morning's *Manchester Guardian*, which in the course of a vigorously anti-Asquith leader said of his ministry: 'Nothing is foreseen, every decision is postponed. The war is not really directed – it directs itself.'[76] In supporting Lloyd George's scheme, C. P. Scott could see as clearly as Dawson that it effectually meant the eclipse of Asquith. The *Guardian*'s final remedy was in keeping with its high ideals, though not with the dire necessities of war: it suggested a general election.[77]

Asquith, indignant with Lloyd George, indignant with *The Times*, and misadvised by McKenna and his laissez-faire friends, informed Lloyd George that his projected system was unworkable. Lloyd George replied with his resignation. The following day (Tuesday 5 December) the Conservative members of the Cabinet pressed Asquith either to resign or to accept their own resignations. Asquith, therefore, went to the King with his own resignation, his friends telling him that, since none of his rivals was strong enough to form a ministry, he would soon be back. In fact Bonar Law, Lloyd George and their close associates were now concerting their final moves. Though Lloyd George was clearly going to be the dominant figure in any alternative ministry it was agreed that, if strategy demanded it, Bonar Law (who was summoned by the King that evening) should become Prime Minister. Bonar Law endeavoured to persuade Asquith to join a new Government, preferably as Lord Chancellor. After a first refusal on Tuesday evening, Asquith seemed more amenable the following afternoon when a meeting was held in the King's presence between Asquith, Bonar Law, Lloyd George, Balfour and Henderson; but later in the day Asquith stated categorically that he would not serve under Bonar Law or indeed under anyone else. Obviously a ministry headed by a Conservative (Bonar Law) and lacking the support of the Liberal leader (Asquith) would be weaker and less viable than one led by a Liberal (Lloyd George) and supported by the Conservative leader (Bonar Law). On Bonar Law's advice, therefore, the King on Thursday 7 December invited Lloyd George to form a ministry, and he, after his famous 'doping séance' with the leaders of the Labour Party, in which he got their support in return for a series of more or less extravagant promises, accepted the King's commission that evening.[78]

The final political consideration in Lloyd George's triumph was the support he got from Labour, and, more important, from a large section of the Liberal Party. It was here that Asquith and his friends miscalculated. On the Monday Addison and a fellow Liberal M.P., Kellaway, had initiated a canvass on behalf of Lloyd George, which revealed that Lloyd George had forty-nine out-and-out supporters, and that 126 others would support him if he could form a Government.[79] The potential patronage of the prime ministerial candidate was clearly an important influence, but the figures, taken in conjunction with the opinions expressed by the *Manchester Guardian* and the *Economist*, are also of interest in showing the existence, prior to the final *dénouement*, of a substantial body of Liberal discontent with Asquith's leadership. One of the reasons for this was certainly the Irish issue. Criticism was put in its most extreme form by the *Manchester Guardian* in the following words:

> Mr Asquith permitted the Home Rule agreement negotiated by Mr Lloyd George to be torn up along with Government's pledges on which it was based.[80]

But the main reason turns us again towards the basic explanation of the change of ministry as the political summation of changes in economic and social attitudes which had already taken place. The *Guardian* expressed the belief that the new Government in contrast to the old, would not shrink from State control of mines, shipping, and 'any other industry vital to the war . . . or to the food of the people':

> Who shall say that, if mightily conceived and boldly carried out, such a mobilization of our national resources may not be decisive in its effects on the war? At least such an attempt will be well worth making, and we have good hope that it may be made.[81]

The *Economist*'s epitaph on the Asquith ministry was that 'the country was always ahead of the Government'.[82] Lest the *Guardian* be thought a naïve and uncritical supporter of Lloyd George, it is worth noting that on 6 December it had forecast that Bonar Law would be the new Prime Minister, and that it kept up its advocacy of a general election long after Lloyd George was solidly ensconced in power.

Asquith, having rejected the attempts to include him in the new ministry, retired with his followers to the Opposition benches: they, not Lloyd George, had split the Liberal Party, though it was Lloyd George who confirmed the split by perpetuating his coalition with the Conservatives at the end of the war. The Liberal dichotomy between laissez-faire absolutists and radical social reformers had been apparent before the war, though it had been cast into relative obscurity by Asquith's brilliance as a parliamentary tactician; the war exposed it ruthlessly. Had there been no war the Liberals might have been left with enough time to adapt themselves to the needs of twentieth-century society, to trim their outdated dogmas, and open their ears to the aspirations of the working classes. But time was just what they did not have in 1916; the war had blown the bottom out of the hourglass. Labour, which had seemed so insignificant that up to 1916 the *Liberal Year Book* lumped Liberal and Labour Members of Parliament together in one biographical section of, as it were, 'goodies', and Conservatives and Irish Nationalists in two separate sections of 'baddies',[83] was now showing its mettle as a party whose collaboration was essential to the success of the war effort, a party, therefore, which was in a position to profit to the utmost from Liberal divisions. Sadly recognizing hard facts, the *Liberal Year Book* for 1919 (the first since 1916) put Liberal and Labour Members in separate tables.[84] Looked at through the telescope of the historian of broader social movements, the advance of the Labour Party and the retreat of the Liberal Party represent the gains of collectivism at the expense of laissez-faire. But for the war the process might have been somewhat different; as it was, by the time Liberals were in a position to cry 'Keynes' or 'Beveridge' at the trifling follies of the other two parties, it was too late.

NOTES TO CHAPTER FIVE

1. *New Statesman*, 14 February 1914, 30 May 1914, and 8 May 1915.
2. Trades Union Congress, *Annual Report 1915*, p. 287.
3. Labour Party, *Annual Conference Report 1916*, p. 35.
4. *The Times*, 22 May 1908.
5. For a brilliant analysis see B. Semmel, *Imperialism and Social Reform*, 1960. Semmel, however, grossly exaggerates when on page 234 he attributes working-class enthusiasm for the war in 1914 to gratitude for the social reforms given them by the imperialists.
6. See W. J. Braithwaite, *Lloyd George's Ambulance Waggon*, 1957.
7. See W. Beveridge, *Power and Influence*, 1953.
8. H. L. Gray, *War Time Control of Industry*, New York, 1918, p. 140.
9. S. J. Hurwitz, *State Intervention in Great Britain*, 1949, p. 156.
10. L. C. Money, *The Triumph of Nationalisation*, 1920, pp. 120–1.
11. Trades Union Congress, *Annual Report 1915*, p. 79.
12. *The Times History of the War*, Vol. VI, pp. 183–4.

13. *Hist. Min. Mun.*, Vol. VII, pt. 1, p. 5; Vol. II, pt. 4, p. 11.
14. ibid.
15. ibid., Vol. VII, pt. 2, p. 6.
16. Quoted in Vol. I, pt. 1, p. 70.
17. ibid, pp. 58-9.
18. E. V. Morgan, *Studies in British Financial Policy, 1914-22*, 1952, pp. 38-9. *Hist. Min. Mun.*, Vol. VII, pt. 1, pp. 6-7.
19. *Economist*, 23 January 1915. J. M. Rees, *Trusts in British Industry, 1914-21*, 1922, pp. 160-1.
20. *Board of Trade Journal, 1914*, p. 808.
21. *Daily Citizen*, 5 October 1914.
22. War Emergency: Workers' National Committee, *Report 1916*, p. 3.
23. P.P., 1915, LXXXVI, Cd. 8438.
24. Morgan, pp. 36-7.
25. W. Ashworth, *An Economic History of England, 1870-1939*, 1960, pp. 266-7.
26. *New Statesman*, 23 January 1915.
27. Morgan, p. 36.
28. *New Statesman*, 16, 23 and 30 January 1915. *Times*, 18 January 1915.
29. *House of Commons Debates*, 11 February 1915.
30. *The Times*, 12 February 1915.
31. *House of Commons Debates*, 11 February 1915.
32. Gray, *War Time Control of Industry*, p. 61.
33. *Hist. Min. Mun.*, Vol. VII, pt. 1, pp. 6-11 and *passim;* Vol. VIII, pt. 1, p. 34.
34. Vol. VII, pt. 1, p. 9.
35. Morgan, *Studies in British Financial Policy*, p. 35.
36. *New Statesman*, 6 March 1915.
37. *Hist. Min. Mun.*, Vol. I, pt. 2, p. 57. *Times*, 10 March 1915. *Manchester Guardian*, 10 and 19 March 1915.
38. *The Times*, 12 May 1915. *Manchester Guardian*, 12 May 1915.
39. C. Addison, *Politics from Within*, 1924, Vol. I, p. 58.
40. Gray, p. 30.
41. L. C. Money, *Triumph of Nationalisation*, p. 49. *Hist. Min. Mun.*, Vol. VIII, pt. 1, pp. 40-8.
42. *Manchester Guardian*, 2 July 1915.
43. *The Times*, 24, 26 May, 23 June 1915. *Economist*, 5 June 1915. *New Statesman*, 14 August 1915.
44. *Hist. Min. Mun.*, Vol. II, pt. 2, pp. 68-70.
45. P.P., 1915, X, Cd. 7866.
46. *Suffragette*, 10 September 1915.
47. Gray, p. 144. See generally, A. Salter, *Allied Shipping Control*, Oxford, 1925.
48. P.P., 1915, X, Cd. 8048, Cd. 8095.
49. *House of Commons Debates*, 21 September 1915.
50. Morgan, p. 41.
51. P.P., 1916, XIV, Cd. 8358.
52. ibid, p. 17.
53. *Report of Advisory Committee on London Traffic;* P.P., 1920, XXI, Cmd. 636, p. 10. Departmental Committee on Prices; P.P., 1916, XIV, Cd. 8358, p. 12.

54. Federation of British Industries, *What It Is and What It Does*, n.d. (1923?), p. 1.
55. *The Elements of Reconstruction*, 1916, p. 38.
56. ibid., pp. 38-9, 43.
57. pp. 47-8.
58. pp. 66-71, 57-8.
59. W. H. Dawson (ed.), *After War Problems*, 1917, p. 10.
60. ibid., pp. 116-20.
61. Labour Party, *Annual Conference Report 1916*, p. 135.
62. Gray, p. 205.
63. *Economist*, 21 October 1916.
64. *House of Commons Debates*, 15 November 1916.
65. ibid., 16 November 1916.
66. *The Times*, 22 November 1916.
67. S. Pollard, *The Development of the British Economy, 1914-50*, 1960, p. 42.
68. Morgan, *Studies in British Financial Policy*, p. 91.
69. *The Times*, 1 September 1915.
70. ibid., 13 November 1915.
71. Bennett, *Journals*, p. 156 (11 March 1916).
72. Addison, *Politics from Within*, p. 246.
73. *The Times*, 2 May 1916.
74. Addison, *Politics from Within*, p. 268.
75. On this paragraph see T. Jones, *Lloyd George*, 1951, pp. 83-7, and the sources cited there.
76. *Manchester Guardian*, 4 December 1916.
77. ibid., 6 December 1916.
78. On this paragraph see Jones *loc. cit.*
79. C. Addison, *Four and a Half Years*, 1934, p. 274.
80. *Manchester Guardian*, 7 December 1916.
81. ibid., 8 December 1916.
82. *Economist*, 9 December 1916.
83. *Liberal Year Book 1914*, pp. 39-76; *1915*, pp. 40-77; *1916*, pp. 41-78.
84. *Liberal Year Book 1919*, pp. 42-73.

CHAPTER SIX

Seasons of Discontent: 1917–1918

[1] SOCIETY AND SHORTAGES

1917, IN a war of ironic equivocation, was the most equivocal year of all. American entry ensured ultimate victory for the West, but for some who were that way inclined it later stirred the bitter reflection that Britain could no longer win a European war without external subvention;[1] although a great moral and, in time, economic boost for the Allies, its immediate effects were to increase Allied difficulties in that America now required her shipping for her own transport purposes, and directed her resources towards her own newly forming armies. President Wilson brought with him a firm and sincere moral ideal, which gave great comfort to troubled liberal consciences in Britain; but it also provided ready-made cant for British politicians of the older balance-of-power tradition. It can even be argued that American entry prolonged the war, giving the West European statesmen a blank cheque upon which they obediently pencilled President Wilson's ideals (elaborated in 1918 as the Fourteen Points), adding, in small writing, their own objective of unconditional surrender. The Russian Revolutions sent tremors of excitement through the Left, but their upshot was dissension in the Labour movement and a hardening of the reactionary influence of the Right. Allied co-operation – the Supreme War Council was established in November – did help to strengthen the call for international action as a post-war safeguard to eternal peace; but Anglo-French relations were never in reality completely free of jealousy and suspicion.

Old economic theories were abandoned, indelible outlines for future social reform drawn, yet working-class discontent and industrial unrest reached a peak. Real care and attention were for the first time lavished on industrial and scientific reconstruction and much was written on the need for Britain to be economically competitive at the end of the war; but as she fought the war, former customers, cut off from supplies of British manufactured goods, developed their own industries and ceased to be customers even of the most competitive-minded British manufacturer. The old heavy industries were enjoying their last frantic burst of prosperity: soon they would be depressed industries. By the spring of 1917, Germany's submarine campaign was hitting British shipping hard, so that in addition to trying to speed up her own shipbuilding programme she appealed to America and Japan to increase theirs. At the end of the war the world had too many ships for its needs: Britain's unchallenged naval supremacy was gone for good, and her ship-building industry was becalmed in economic doldrums. Sir Maurice Hankey and a number of the younger naval officers put it to Lloyd George that the submarine challenge could be met by sending British ships out in convoy: Lloyd George was enthusiastic, but Admiral Sir John Jellicoe and the top naval brass said that the suggestion was out of the question. When the Prime Minister insisted on trying the new expedient there was a steady fall over the summer of 1917 in the loss of shipping tonnage.[2] By the end of the year the new investments in scientific and technological research had paid dividends in the form of submarine detection by high-frequency sound-waves and destruction by depth-charges and paravanes,[3] so that the running danger was under control; the major damage, however, had already been done. If Jellicoe and his colleagues had wished to burlesque themselves as obscurantist fuddy-duddies denying the younger generation the leadership it deserved, they could scarcely have been more successful.

The remark is even more desperately true of the Generals on the Western Front. The year's campaigns opened with the French spring offensive led by the youthful Nivelle (no shining example to his elders, it must be admitted), which brought such a disastrous burden of casualties as to provoke mutinies along the French front and permanently scar French morale. Sir Douglas Haig resolved that the year so badly begun should end in a blaze of definitive glory to be achieved by what was officially known as the Ypres Campaign of 1917 (the third Ypres Campaign of the war), but what became emotionally lodged in the British mind as 'Passchendaele'. The rights and wrongs of Haig's strategy need not detain us here; if he has been unfairly savaged by his opponents, his reputation has not been completely salvaged by his apologists, the most recent of whom admits the emptiness of one of most favoured defences of the General: that he was trying to take the weight off the French.[4] What is certain is that the campaign was fought over territory which was nothing less than a swamp, low-lying land which had been subject to unusually heavy rainfall and whose normal drainage system had been shattered by constant shelling, that it cost 244,897 casualties[5] and achieved microscopic military gains. The new year, despite Russia's virtual withdrawal from the war at the end of 1917, began rather better with a dramatic British break-through at Cambrai, which brought the ringing of bells from church steeples at home; unfortunately the resources needed to follow this up had been squandered at Passchendaele. In March the Germans completely reversed the picture by achieving a forty-mile penetration into the Allied lines; a second offensive in April opened a thirty-mile breach and at its direst moment it was the occasion of Haig's famous Order of the Day of 11 April. There was a further German advance in May. All of this, while never properly exploited by the Germans because of exhaustion and difficulty in maintaining communications, added up for the British to three months of anxious tension which not even the censorship could muffle. From May the war news got steadily better and in the summer the tunnel war at last broke out into a war of movement.

At no time during the First World War was there any widespread privation in Britain, and what might justly be called 'shortages' were only really apparent in 1917, when scarcity of sugar, potatoes, margarine (butter was often quite unobtainable) and coal brought a new phenomenon on the civic scene, the queue. (Beveridge in the study of *British Food Control* which he wrote later for the Carnegie Foundation was out by over six months when he declared that the first food queues, 'due to exceptional circumstances', appeared in October[6] – the proud Civil Servant has here got the better of the impartial historian.) Here is an account from the *Observer* of 8 April 1917:

The usual week-end potato and coal scenes took place in London yesterday. At Edmonton 131 vehicles were lined up at the gates of a coal depot at nine o'clock in the morning, while the crowd numbered several hundreds. There were also bread and potato queues of such a length that the police had to regulate them, and newcomers had to inquire which was the particular queue that they wanted. During last week the Edmonton District Council sold over fifty tons of seed potatoes.

In South London trolleymen with coals were besieged by people who had requisitioned all types of receptacles, including perambulators, wheelbarrows, go-carts and trucks, while others brought sacks, baskets and boxes. At a railway coal-siding the would-be purchasers assembled soon after seven o'clock in the morning and the queue of waiting women and children extended to a great length within an hour or so. Several policemen regulated the crowd, who first had to secure tickets at the coal merchant's office and then make their way to the siding, where the coal was served out to them directly from the railway trucks.

At Wrexham a big farm-wagon laden with potatoes already weighed into shillingsworths was brought into the square by agriculturalists who at once proceeded to sell them to all comers. The wagon was surrounded by hundreds of clamouring people, chiefly women, who scrambled on to the vehicle in the eagerness to buy. Several women fainted in the struggle, and the police were sent for to restore order.

Farnborough, Kent, was yesterday besieged by people who heard that a farmer named Staples had a large quantity of potatoes for sale at 1s. per gallon . . .

Although Lloyd George, succeeding where Asquith had failed, had appointed a Food Controller in the person of Lord Devonport, formerly H. E. Kearley, a self-made magnate of the retail trade, and had established a Food Ministry in Grosvenor House, where the lavish pink flesh of the Rubens murals was covered up to avoid offence to the young girls recruited as typists, any temptation to attribute a magical quality of reform to the Lloyd George Ministry, or to see the change of Government as the inevitable expression of a general will towards more efficient conduct of the war, is easily dispelled by a consideration of Lord Devonport's record. His egregious incompetence is a standing testimony to the influence of personality in history. Devonport had a fixation about what he called 'flaunting', and his first efforts were directed against the display in shop windows of luxury foodstuffs. There followed prohibitions against the feeding of game and the consumption of crumpets and sugar icing, and restrictions upon the kind of food that could be eaten in tea-shops between 3 and 5.30 pm. At times, according to Beveridge, the Food Ministry chiefs would sit in inquisition upon specimens of bakery and confectionery, solemnly deciding whether or not they conformed to the law's demands, the specimens later providing a sumptuous tea for the typists of the sugar department.[7]

As prices rose (to a shilling for a quartern loaf in the case of bread) and shortages developed, Government control of distribution appeared more desirable than ever. The new Food Controller's response was to publish on 3 February 1917 an appeal for voluntary rationing; by what was in effect a sort of Derby Scheme for food, each citizen was to restrict himself to four pounds of bread (or three pounds of flour), two and a half pounds of meat, and three-quarters of a pound of sugar per week:[8] as with the Derby Scheme compulsion was held in the background as a threat which could be applied if necessary, and supervisory powers were vested in local food committees. The scheme, apart from its reliance on public good will, had no basis in reality; the poor still ate far more bread and far less meat than provided for here – it was not uncommon for an agricultural labourer to consume up to fourteen pounds of bread a week – and sugar was already almost unobtainable in many places. At the beginning of May a Royal Proclamation on the saving of grain was read on successive Sundays in churches and chapels throughout the land, and a food economy campaign directed by a leading Conservative extrovert, Kennedy Jones, and assisted by Harry Lauder, was launched.[9] The entire effort more resembled a gigantic music-hall act than a serious effort to deal with the country's food problem.

Lord Devonport's one other contribution was the introduction, followed shortly by the abolition, of a system of meatless days; neither he nor the Government had the stomach for compulsory rationing. On 30 May he resigned; as neither Bob Smillie, the miners' leader, nor Addison, who since Lloyd George's accession had been at the Munitions Ministry, was willing to take on the job,[10] Lord Rhondda was summoned from the Local Government Board. Rhondda was a man of entirely different mettle, 'spare, dark, sensitive, with the look of a mystic' where Devonport had been 'well-fed, florid, grumpy and gruff'.[11] He forthwith secured from the Cabinet approval for the principle of registration for

sugar: the country was divided into 2,000 districts, each with a
local food office to which the householder sent in an application
form for a card which would entitle him to half a pound of sugar
a week, though he could have more if it was available in his
locality. Imperfect the scheme undoubtedly was, but it was not
even put into practice until the end of the year; the fear was that
the introduction of even so rudimentary a form of rationing would
damage civilian morale and give encouragement to the enemy.[12]
When it was finally decided to implement sugar registration,
there was, as might be expected, the urbane opposition of *Punch*.
In a cartoon entitled 'David in Rhonddaland', David (who looks
a little like Lloyd George) is having a trying conversation with
the Mad Grocer (who looks a little like Lord Rhondda):

> *David:* I'm often away from home. How do I get sugar?
> *The Mad Grocer:* You don't: you fill up a form.
> *David:* But I *have* filled up a form.
> *The Mad Grocer:* Then you fill up another form.

Government action had in various places been anticipated by
private and local initiative: the Birmingham Co-operative Society,
for instance, introduced its own system of sugar cards in July
1917. Lord Rhondda's directive of August setting up statutory
Food Control Committees throughout the country gave a further
stimulus to progressive local authorities, such as those at
Gravesend, Pontypool and Birmingham, to go ahead with their
own rationing schemes.[13] Imports of tea, which had been maintained at about 15,000 tons per month between 1913 and 1916, fell
drastically to about 6,000 in the summer of 1917, causing more
queues and local rationing. Even with local schemes it was still
possible for the footloose shopper to amass considerable quantities
of scarce commodities. Sympathy for a woman who fainted in a
tea-queue in Cardiff soon evaporated when it was discovered that
she already had half a stone concealed about her person.[14]
    The Times of 10 December 1917 listed the following as in short
supply in London: sugar, tea, butter, margarine, lard, dripping,
milk, bacon, pork, condensed milk, rice, currants, raisins, spirits,
Australian wines. A week later it reported:

The food queues continue to grow. Outside the dairy shops of certain multiple firms in some parts of London women begin to line up for margarine as early as 5 o'clock on Saturday morning, some with infants in their arms, and others with children at their skirts. Over a thousand people waited for margarine at a shop in New Broad Street in the heart of the city, and in Walworth Road in the south-eastern side of London the queue was estimated to number about 3,000. Two hours later 1,000 of these were sent away unsupplied.[15]

In some areas workers were taking time off to relieve their wives who had been queueing for long spells. The biggest grievance of all was the high price of bread, already a shilling for a four-pound loaf (more than twice the pre-war price) in the spring of 1917. In September the Government, with the assistance of a subsidy, fixed the price at ninepence; from November there was also a subsidy for potatoes.[16]

Christmas 1917 was heralded by appeals from the new Director of Food Economy, Sir Arthur Yapp, for austerity, and was succeeded by stories in the press of a 'meat crisis' or even a 'meat famine'. Provision had been made for retail price control in September 1917, and many butchers were said to be closing their shops in protest at the prices decreed by the local food committees. The Government brought a new word into everyday language when, at the end of February, it imposed upon London a system of rationing for meat depending upon the clipping of 'coupons' from the customer's ration card. From 7 April meat rationing of this type was applied to the whole country, and in May the weekly ration was reduced to three-quarters of a pound. Universal rationing (by registration card, not coupon) followed for tea and butter.[17]

In December 1916 and January 1917, domestic rail services were slashed, and prices increased by as much as 50 per cent; newspaper prices doubled in February (*The Times* from one penny to twopence, the *Daily Mail* from a halfpenny to a penny). But food remained the principal item in the vastly increased cost of living: the average weekly food bill for the 'standard' working-class family (4·57 units and 1·2 supplementary earners) had risen in June 1918 to 47s 3d, the average weekly total bill to 75s 5d. With the emphasis on essentials, increases were proportionally greater for unskilled than for skilled workmen. The Board of Trade reckoned on an 81 per cent increase in the cost of living for the unskilled workman's family as between July 1914 and June 1918; for the skilled workman's family, the figure was 67 per cent.[18] Prices of meat (about double pre-war prices in the summer of 1917), bread and potatoes flattened out somewhat with Government regulation from the autumn of 1917, but other items, bacon for instance (1s 8d per pound in July 1917), continued to rise steeply. Bread, from December 1916, was 'Government Bread', which at first meant no more than that it contained a high (and beneficial) quantity of husk. Later all sorts of foreign substances, such as potato flour and bean flour, were introduced; certain combinations were found to go 'ropey' in warm weather.[19] Upon this bread the civilian, from late 1917 onwards, spread margarine manufactured under the direction of the Ministry of Food, and with it he drank the anonymous blend, Government Control Tea.

Shortages and standardization of available foods contributed to the process of communizing social experience and telescoping class; on the whole, however, it would seem that the much-advertised culinary innovations, such as haricot-bean fritters, savoury oatmeal pudding, barley rissoles, and nut rolls[20] were aimed at those middle- and upper-class households where protein consumption in pre-war days had been high. Mrs Peel in her *Eat-Less-Meat Book*, published in 1917, pointed the contrast between the pre-war menu of a modest middle-class household and that of a labourer. The middle-class menu ran:

FRIDAY. *Breakfast:* fish cakes, sardines, fried bacon, bread, butter, marmalade, tea, coffee. *Dinner:* rabbits, potatoes, gooseberry tart, rice pudding, cream, sugar. *Tea:* bread, butter, jam, cakes, tea. *Supper:* cheese, biscuits, bread, butter, cakes, cocoa.

SATURDAY. *Breakfast:* fish, sardines, fried bacon, bread, butter, marmalade, tea, coffee. *Dinner:* beefsteak, potatoes, cauliflower, queen of puddings, rice pudding, cream. *Tea:* bread, butter, marmalade, cakes, tea. *Supper:* cheese, biscuits, bread, butter, cakes, cocoa, milk, coffee.

SUNDAY. *Breakfast:* bacon, poached eggs, bread, butter, marmalade, tea, coffee. *Dinner:* roast beef, Yorkshire pudding, roast potatoes, rice pudding, gooseberry tart, cream, sugar. *Tea:* bread, butter, jam, cakes, tea. *Supper:* cheese, biscuits, bread, butter, cake, cocoa, milk.

MONDAY. *Breakfast:* bacon, sardines, bread, butter, marmalade, tea, coffee. *Dinner:* cold beef, salad, potatoes, sponge cake, custard pudding, rice. *Tea:* bread, butter, cakes, marmalade, tea. *Supper:* eggs, biscuits, bread, butter, cakes, cocoa, milk.

TUESDAY. *Breakfast:* fried bacon, poached eggs, bread, butter, marmalade, tea, coffee. *Dinner:* cold beef, salad, hashed beef, potatoes, stewed fruit, rice pudding. *Tea:* bread, butter, cakes, marmalade, tea. *Supper:* cheese, biscuits, bread, butter, cakes, cocoa, coffee, milk.

WEDNESDAY. *Breakfast:* fried bacon, sardines, bread, butter, marmalade, tea, coffee. *Dinner:* roast mutton, jelly, potatoes, cabbage, gooseberry tart, pancakes. *Tea:* bread, butter, cakes, jam, marmalade, tea. *Supper:* cheese, biscuits, bread, butter, cakes, cocoa, milk.

THURSDAY. *Breakfast:* chicken and tongue mould, bread, butter, marmalade, tea, coffee. *Dinner:* cold mutton, potatoes, salad, curry, rice pudding, stewed fruit. *Tea:* bread, butter, cakes, jam, marmalade, tea. *Supper:* cheese, biscuits, bread, butter, cakes, cocoa, milk.

Wealthier middle-class families, Mrs Peel added, would, for the adults, have had a late dinner. The trend during the war was for more and more people to have their main meal in the middle of the day.

The labourer's pre-war menu read as follows:

FRIDAY. *Breakfast:* bread, cheese, tea. *Dinner:* potatoes, bread, tea. *Tea:* bread, butter, tea.

SATURDAY. *Breakfast:* 'dip', bread, butter, tea. *Dinner:* sausages, bread. *Tea:* bread, cocoa, jam, tea.

SUNDAY. *Breakfast:* bacon, bread, toast, tea. *Dinner:* meat, potatoes, Yorkshire pudding. *Tea:* bread, pie, tea cakes, tea.

MONDAY. *Breakfast:* bacon, bread, tea. *Dinner:* bacon, bread, tea. *Tea:* bacon, bread, tea.

TUESDAY. *Breakfast:* bread, meat, tea. *Dinner:* meat, bread, tea. *Tea:* meat, bread, tea.

WEDNESDAY. *Breakfast:* bacon, bread, tea. *Dinner:* meat, bread, tea. *Tea:* eggs, 'dip', bread, tea.

THURSDAY. *Breakfast:* bread, butter, tea. *Dinner:* meat, bread, 'dip', tea. *Tea:* meat, bread, butter, tea.[21]

For all classes the hardships of austerity, such as they were, were made grimmer by the intensification of German bombing raids. The worst raid of the whole war came on 13 June 1917, when 162 people were killed and 432 injured, and the autumn that followed was so full of menace that Londoners took to the practice of sheltering in the Tubes, while some of those who could afford it moved to the safer locations of Bath or Bournemouth. The last raid took place over Kent on 17 June 1918, when there were no casualties. Altogether, between January 1915 and April 1918 there were 51 Zeppelin raids, causing 1,913 casualties, and between December 1914 and June 1918 there were 57 aeroplane raids, causing 2,907 casualties. Total civilian casualties were 5,611, including 1,570 fatalities, of whom 1,413 were killed in air attacks.[22] The town which suffered most of all was Dover, especially in the autumn of 1917 when the attacks came in waves lasting twenty to thirty minutes. Dug-outs were constructed and the caves at each end of the town developed into shelters, so that by the end of the year there was accommodation for about 25,000 people. Householders who so desired were supplied with materials for building shelters in the chalky slopes of their own gardens.[23]

For air-raid victims in all parts of the country a dribble of assistance was provided by the National Relief Fund, which also continued to make payments to unemployed boarding-house keepers in the East Coast resorts.[24] Attacks by air and sea apart, some domestic employments were not without risks of their own: deaths from poisoning were not uncommon among those handling explosives, and there were occasional explosions, the worst being that of January 1917 in a munitions factory at Silvertown in east London, which resulted in considerable loss of life:

Looking down the Thames I saw a high column of yellow flames rising, as I thought, from the river . . . The sky . . . became overspread with the loveliest colours . . . The phenomenon lasted, I should think, several seconds. Its disappearance was accompanied by a terrific explosion, rising and shattering and dying away with an angry growl.[25]

Nerves were frayed, tempers tried; discontent mounted. Yet, even discounting press stories of working-class affluence, real gains were made. It is difficult to discern a clear pattern of earnings at this stage of the war, but by its end wages had doubled, had, in other words, kept ten or twenty per cent ahead of the rise in cost of living. At the same time wage rises often lagged well behind the most recent rise in the cost of living, and households with a large number of non-wage-earners were extremely hard hit. When the Working Classes Cost of Living Committee reported in 1918 that the working classes, as a whole, were in a position to purchase food of substantially the same nutritive value as in June 1914, this was perhaps almost as much a condemnation of pre-war conditions as a tribute to wartime reorganization. The Report comments fairly cautiously:

Indeed our figures indicate that the families of unskilled workmen were slightly better fed at the later date, in spite of the rise in the price of food. This conclusion is more than confirmed by the reports we have obtained from the Medical Officers to the Education Authorities in the great cities. From London it is officially reported, after inspection of all the children entering the school, that 'the percentage of children found in a poorly nourished condition is considerably less than half the percentage of 1913'. A similar improvement is shown by the figures furnished by Birmingham, Bolton, Bradford, Bristol, Glasgow and Nottingham. The general impression, especially of the poorer children, is favourable, and the view that parents are now better able to give their children the necessary food is borne out by the information we have received as to the number of meals provided to 'necessitous children' by the local education authorities. It is only in very exceptional cases that education authorities are supplying anything like as many meals as before the war; in most places the number has fallen to about half (Nottingham, Stoke, and Sheffield) and a quarter (London and Bolton), and in some places (as in Birmingham and Liverpool) it is hardly necessary to provide meals at all. The last available figures for England and Wales, those for 1917, compared with the estimated number for 1914, show a decline by about four-fifths in the country as a whole.[26]

Other evidence accumulated by the Board of Trade and the Ministry of Food cuts various ways. Even when the meat ration was at its most exiguous, it was found that 'a certain part of the population, especially in Scotland and in some country districts, did not choose, or could not afford, to purchase the full amount to which their ration entitled them.'[27] On the other hand the reluctance of purchasers in other areas to take such lowly products of the butcher's art as black pudding, a traditionally North-country and Scottish dish, soon meant that they were released from rationing. There is a similar implication, and perhaps there are other more dubious ones, in the Ministry of Food circular of 26 June 1918:

In order to utilize to the best advantage imported meat which may not be suitable for issue to the public in its original form, the sale of beef sausages has been permitted without any coupon.[28]

The warning for the historian is an old one: that it is dangerous to take British society, whether in eating habits or anything else, as geographically homogeneous. Certain areas of Scotland, with a long history of hard times, were still almost medieval in their austerity. However, the wartime pressures of rationing and State control were towards greater uniformity among classes as well as regions. Under State-directed distribution, prime home-killed joints for the first time found their way to poorer areas, where price control made them accessible to local housewives; a proportion of frozen meat ended up in the West End.

For the rich there were other interferences with normal pleasures. Petrol was very strictly rationed, and restrictions were placed on restaurant meals. The first Public Meals Order of 5 December 1916 limited day meals to two courses, and evening meals to three courses – not at all harsh considering that cheese did not count as a course, and soup only as half a course. In April 1917 rationing by weight was introduced in restaurants, and in the last stages of the war coupons were clipped in restaurants as well as in shops. 'The profiteers . . . are still with us,' Blumenfeld noted in his diary in March 1917. One notorious instance, brought about by the search for substitute foodstuffs, was the great wave of profitable speculation in beans and peas at the beginning of the year.[29] Conspicuous consumption was still apparent, much jewellery on view, and dress sales higher in 1917 than in 1915. Theatres continued to prosper famously, and not just in London.

Gilded upper-class life, strikingly depicted in the war novels of Ford Madox Ford, continued remarkably unchanged. Colonel Repington entered some interesting confidences in his diary:

Lady Ridley and I discussed what posterity would think of us in England. We agreed that we should be considered rather callous to go on with our usual life when we were reading of 3,000 to 4,000 casualties a day. But she said that people could not keep themselves elevated permanently on some plane above the normal, and she supposed that things around us explained the French Revolution and the behaviour of the French nobility.[30]

Upper-class life continued, but there were changes. The two

most obvious developments were the blows struck by wartime taxation at the landed interest, and the intrusion of businessmen into the political élite. The first interpretable figures after the war show a decline in the proportion of wealth and income held by owners of land,[31] and an acceleration in the breaking up of the great landed estates.[32] In neither case was the process new, but war deaths had multiplied the burden of death duties. The mass entry of the businessmen can very precisely be pinned to the change of Government in December 1916.[33] Certain organs of the press had for some time been calling for 'a businessman's government', and the social climate, as with other changes associated with Lloyd George, was favourable to his innovations in governmental personnel. There was nothing new about the businessman in politics: politics from Victorian times to 1914, we have seen, had been very much the politics of a class welded out of the old aristocracy and the newer aristocracy of industrial wealth; but to reach high office the businessman had had to climb a political ladder. If the first distinctive characteristic of Lloyd George's ministerial businessmen was their numerical strength, the second was that in a large number of cases they had served little or no political apprenticeship at all. In this category were Sir Albert Stanley, manager of the London Underground and General Omnibuses Combine, Joseph Maclay, a Glasgow shipowner who refused to take a seat in either House of Parliament, Lord Rhondda, a coal-owner, Lord Devonport, an ennobled shopkeeper, Sir Alfred Mond, a chemicals manufacturer, Sir Frederick Cawley, Albert Illingworth and R. E. Prothero. Two further considerations enhance the significance of this new recruitment to government office: first, it coincided with a great extension in the powers and functions of government, and secondly, it was bolstered and consolidated by the great patriotic prestige which businessmen had acquired in this war of machines and industrial systems.

The other striking, though numerically slight, modification in the composition of the political élite was one which has been touched on already in a different connexion, the rise of the Labour politician. Clynes, Barnes, Roberts, Henderson, all came from unimpeachable working-class origins, though it is perhaps more important to note that they had all, in contrast to many of the new businessmen, served a very definite apprenticeship in politics. The political Labour movement since the end of the nineteenth century was the obvious vehicle for the ambitious member of the working classes. Arthur Henderson, the first to reach Cabinet office, had done sterling work as general secretary of the Labour Party. The new infusion did not necessarily strengthen the country's political leadership – in some cases it manifestly weakened it – but it did publicize the ideal of the professional: Maclay was made Shipping Controller because he knew about ships, Devonport Food Controller because he knew about the buying and selling of food, Barnes Minister of Pensions because he knew about working-class hardship. An older principle had prevailed when in the general shuffle of May 1915 Asquith had appointed Henderson President of the Board of Education, for which he had no obvious qualifications. The ideal of the professional extended from parliamentary politics into administration and the Civil Service. As ministries and government departments expanded, Lloyd George again drew upon industry for his top personnel.[34] This specific movement, designed for the purposes of waging war, interacted with a much greater one: the rise within industry of the managerial class. At the end of the war the salaried segment of the community had greatly expanded.

On the whole the wartime trend was towards increased centralization of power, though there was much local initiative in such matters as Air Raid Precaution and food rationing. One of the commonest administrative devices of the war was the local committee or tribunal, with powers over matters varying from the determination of the genuineness of a young man's claim to have a conscientious objection to war, to the ploughing of pasture land. Representatives of labour and the odd *nouveau riche* tradesman figured on these committees, but by and large their régime marked an Indian summer of power and glory for the traditional local bigwigs. Otherwise the war certainly did create a strong breeze of egalitarianism. In the hustle of wartime living many of the more formal symbols of position were quietly abandoned: top hats and butterfly collars disappeared.[35] Many of the more tangible products of position became unobtainable: petrol rationing after August 1916 steadily drove that luxury toy, the motor-car, out of sight. In the Army the badges of officerdom made too obvious a target for enemy snipers, so officers adopted a uniform not very dissimilar from that of their men. The Army did its best to maintain the rigidities of hierarchical distinction, but could not destroy altogether a unity kindled in upheaval and shared danger. More positive were the self-confidence and sense of purpose engendered in a working class which waged many successful battles against authority, and which had its sons lauded as saviours of their country. A decline in the numbers of servants, and of sempstresses and workers in the women's luxury trades, meant a deflation of one of the main bolsters of class-distinction. Political recognition of the rise of the working class and of the female sex was embodied in the Representation of the People Act of 1918, which as well as giving women householders and wives of householders the vote – provided they were over thirty – gave the vote to all men over twenty-one.

[II] THE TEMPER OF LABOUR

The reasons for the extreme working-class discontent of 1917 were varied, and differed in emphasis from place to place; among them were the Conscription Acts, and the manner in which they were applied by over-zealous military authorities, the Munitions Acts, with 'leaving certificates' still a special grievance, the attempts by private employers to extend dilution, high prices, bad housing, and the resentment of skilled workers who found themselves overtaken in the wage race by unskilled. It was in 1917 that the method of working-class action through shop stewards and unofficial representatives, developed on Clydeside and elsewhere in the earlier years of the war, began to react positively with rapidly growing working-class resentment. First news of the Russian Revolution in March 1917 caused great excitement in all corners of the Labour movement, but above all to the advocates of workshop organization. Stress and strain of war, and the sight of much affluence, often just out of reach, were other less tangible agents of unrest.

A hundred years of British history seem to have taught that while the poor are steadily diminishing in numbers, slums are always with us. Since 1913 when it was estimated that the country required a hundred or a hundred and twenty thousand houses, not only had very little been done to meet this requirement, but, with the suspension of much normal building activity, and the congregation of hordes of people in the munitions centres, the situation had actively deteriorated. Thus, although the problem was not a new one, it now came into sharp focus, a grim contour running strongly or faintly across every chart of domestic grievances, a manifest evil when politicians were calling for sacrifice in the name of a better order. It so happened, as with the Royal Commission on Venereal Diseases which, though appointed before the war, delivered its pronouncements into the receptive wartime atmosphere, that the Royal Commission on Housing in Scotland, appointed in October 1912, reported in 1917. Its words on Glasgow need no gloss:

In the older tenements or 'lands', the passages are often dark, narrow, and foul-smelling. Some passages are T-shaped, and at the farther end it is necessary to light a match in the daytime in order to distinguish the doors. Those doors and the partitions are so poorly constructed that there is no privacy even within the houses.

In other cases there is a single long passage traversing the tenement, with doors on either side giving access to different houses (in certain 'back lands' in the Cowcaddens Ward in Glasgow there are as many as ten or twelve houses opening off one passage). With this arrangement through ventilation is impossible.

There is one instance in the Anderston district of Glasgow in which a whole street of high tenements, with damp and dark sunk flats below the level of the street (which is only 19 feet wide), has been wedged into a V-shaped space between two important converging thoroughfares. One witness described the area as follows: 'The sunk flat houses even in a hot dry summer remain damp and unwholesome. The stairs down to these houses are almost invariably dark and dirty, the passages pitch dark on the brightest day, so that only by feeling along the walls can one discover the doors. The bulk of the houses are of the made-down type, very dark lobbies (now lighter by night than day owing to the Corporation's recommendation that incandescent burners be put on the stairhead lamps) . . . In all these closes the stairs are filthy and evil-smelling, water-closets continually choked, and foul water running down the stairs, sickly cats everywhere spreading disease. . . . One street is known as 'The Coffin Close', so bad is its repute – narrow stairs, and dark twisting lobbies, with no light and absolutely no air.[16]

The Commission of Enquiry into Working Class Unrest of June 1917 remarked on bad housing conditions in other parts of Britain. Those at Barrow, a munitions centre where population had expanded greatly, were described as 'a crying scandal':[37] of such new houses as had been made available since the outbreak of war, almost half had been built by the armaments firm of Vickers. In Wales and Monmouth, it was reported:

> ... the workers feel deeply discontented with their housing accommodation and with their unwholesome and unattractive environment generally. The towns and villages are ugly and overcrowded; houses are scarce and rents are increasing, and the surroundings are insanitary and depressing. The scenery is disfigured by unsightly refuse tips, the atmosphere polluted by coal dust and smoke and the rivers spoilt by liquid refuse from works and factories. Facilities for education and recreation are inadequate and opportunities for the wise use of leisure are few.[38]

Housing was a background cause of the rising ire of the working classes.

In the foreground stood the more obvious wartime problems. Before its fall the Asquith Government had been negotiating for official trade union support for the extension of dilution to work other than that connected with the manufacture of war materials, but had failed to win over the Amalgamated Society of Engineers. The desire to maximize national productivity in all commodities was now inextricably bound up with, and overshadowed by, the desire to release as many fit men as possible for service in the armed forces. When, therefore, the new Government again proposed dilution for private work in March 1917, it followed this up on 3 April with the withdrawal of the 'trade cards' scheme, which had been a great triumph for the Amalgamated Society of Engineers, in giving them control of the call-up of their own skilled men. In place of the 'trade cards' scheme the new Ministry of National Service operated a 'schedule of protected occupations', and began to accelerate the release of skilled men for military service; greater use was made of the substitution schemes of September 1916, which had established yet another set of special local committees, this time charged with the task of finding unfit substitutes for militarily fit men.[39]

Before any enactment had been made in regard to the dilution issue, a Rochdale engineering firm saw fit to cash in on what it believed to be the Government's intention, and began to introduce dilutees into its own private work: an immediate strike followed (3 May). But while the mailed fist of military authority at once punched some of the strikers into the Army, the gloved hand of government extracted a fine from the firm, a recognition of the justice of the strikers' case. Meantime national and local grievances throughout the country produced the unofficial 'May strikes' which began on 10 May and lasted for a fortnight. The gloved hand predominated this time, for although eight leaders were charged under the Defence of the Realm Acts the charges were dropped, and the Government agreed that all outstanding complaints would be dealt with by negotiation between Government and trade union leadership; again unofficial action had brought a formal gain.[40]

On 13 June the Government appointed a series of Commissions of Enquiry into Industrial Unrest in eight separate areas in Great Britain. The problem was so urgent that reports were to be furnished within three weeks, though in fact the eight reports and separate summary were not published till 17 July. In the north-east, the commissioners found high food prices the most general cause of complaint. Any image of working-class affluence in this part of the country is severely shaken by their report:

The high prices of staple commodities have undoubtedly laid a severe strain upon the majority of the working classes, and in some instances have resulted in hardship and actual privation. It is no doubt true that in some industries wages have risen to such an extent as largely to compensate for the increased cost of living, but there are workers whose wages have been raised very slightly, if at all, and some whose earnings have actually diminished, and on these the high food prices have borne heavily.[41]

Resentment was aggravated by the belief that high prices were largely due to profiteering and a lack of courage on the part of the Government in dealing with the matter. Leaving certificates and other aspects of the Munitions of War and Defence of the Realm Acts also aroused hostility.[42]

In the north-west area the investigators reported that high food prices were the main cause of unrest: the cost of living, they said, had gone up by 70 to 75 per cent, and the cost of food by 102 per cent, while wages at the most had risen by 40 to 50 per cent, and in some cases not at all. Other sources of anger and irritation were bad housing, military bumbledom, and weak beer which, to make matters worse, was available only at inconvenient hours.[43] The Commissioners for Yorkshire and the East Midlands found food prices and profiteering the basic grievances. They also reported a marked distrust among ordinary working men of the Government and of the official trade union leadership; the latter, the commissioners said, helped to explain the strength of the shop stewards. As a remedy they recommended a programme of social legislation, to which one of the investigators, J. J. Mallon, socialist warden of Toynbee Hall, added a rider calling for higher taxation of the wealthy.[44] In the west Midlands, London and the south-east, the south, the west and Scotland, where there was a strong conviction as to the prevalence of profiteering, food prices were again the chief grievance. While a rather wordy report by the commissioners for Wales elaborated upon the poverty of the whole texture of Welsh social and economic life, the London report contained specific references to a sense of 'inequality of sacrifice' and want of confidence in the Government, and the Midlands report to anger over the leaving certificates' system.[45] The only true note of optimism was that contained in the Scottish report which declared that 'on the whole, the aggregate weekly incomes of industrial workers keep pace with the cost of living.'[46]

The squabble between the Amalgamated Society of Engineers and the Government over the extension of dilution to private work was meantime continuing. Since the revelations of the Commissions on Industrial Unrest suggested that Addison, though undoubtedly a man of progressive sympathies, might be better employed elsewhere than at the Ministry of Munitions he was, in October, moved to the new post of Minister of Reconstruction, while Churchill returned to front bench politics as Minister of Munitions; almost immediately he dropped the contentious proposal for private dilution, and abolished the equally contentious leaving certificates. Free mobility of labour was not thereby restored: D.O.R.A. Regulation 8B of April 1915, which had been designed to prevent employers from enticing workers from one factory to another, remained in force, and a new regulation was introduced prohibiting a worker engaged on one class of work from changing to a different class.[47] None the less there were real concessions to working-class sentiment. Labour's belief in itself and its determination to voice its grievances and aspirations were well demonstrated at the 1917 congress of the T.U.C., which, the *Observer*[48] commented, marked the beginning of a change of mood throughout the entire Labour movement. Arthur Henderson and Sidney Webb completed their draft of a new constitution for the Labour Party, which, while retaining something of the old federal quality, sought by making provision for the establishment of local constituency parties to give it a more homogeneous national basis, turning the ramshackle structure into something more like the efficient mass electoral machine necessary, if Labour were to compete successfully with other political parties. The new constitution which, in addition, committed the Party to a clear socialist objective, came before the Labour Party conference in January 1918, and, after a second conference, was finally adopted.[49]

The new Labour Party constitution marked a consolidation in the strength of the formal, political, and official aspect of the Labour movement. The informal, unofficial and mainly industrial aspect had further successes of its own, which, once again, involved the official industrial leadership. On 26 November 1917, a strike broke out at Coventry over the non-recognition of shop stewards; the trade union leadership was forced to intervene, and in December the position of the shop stewards was recognized in the 'National Shop Stewards Agreement'.[50] Although the worst governmental restraint on mobility of labour, the leaving certificate, had been abolished, the employers in July 1918 developed on their own account a system of 'embargoes' designed to avoid a costly bidding among themselves for scarce labour: further unofficial strikes, again beginning in Coventry and spreading through Birmingham to most of the Midlands, culminated successfully in the withdrawal of the 'embargoes'.

For the Government, the essential problem was to 'comb out' yet more men for the armies of the western front, so drastically depleted in the Passchendaele offensive. The problem was put before the leaders of the Labour movement at the 'Man

Power Conference' which sat between 3 and 5 January 1918; so great was the need for the complete sympathy of the Labour movement, and so strong the muddled aspirations which President Wilson had kindled, that on the last day of the conference Lloyd George made a formal pronouncement of his war aims. On 6 February there came a new Man Power Act which made a bonfire of most of the remaining exemptions from military service. A national conference of shop stewards condemned this measure out of hand, and the trade union leadership kept the Government engaged in delicate negotiation, but the news of German victories in March crumbled away resistance, even among unofficial agitators. A more drastic Military Service Bill of 9 April which brought a further cancelling of exemptions had no effective opposition to face, but, when in June, the Government attempted to extend the War Munitions Volunteer Scheme, which came very close to industrial conscription, trade union resistance was so great that the proposals were withdrawn.[51] The distinction between military and industrial conscription may, philosophically, be a nice one: if men at the front are forfeiting liberty and life, is it morally just that men in the factories should have freedom to strike, and to push up wages? Some of those who resisted military conscription gave as one of their reasons the likelihood that military conscription would lead to industrial conscription. Matters would undoubtedly have been simpler for the Government if it could have gone even farther than the harsh and bitterly contested restrictions which it introduced, and it is, above all, a tribute to the growing strength of the British Labour movement that nothing which really resembled industrial conscription was introduced in this country. At a time when so many sawdust ideals were collapsing, it was as well that the substance of industrial freedom was not irreparably damaged.

Beneath the surface discontent, for which there were real enough reasons, there were equally real, and more enduring, achievements. Most obviously eye-catching was the success in office of leading members of the Labour Party, though even this could serve to unsettle disgruntled spirits. G. N. Barnes was modestly competent as Minister of Pensions, till he replaced Arthur Henderson in the War Cabinet; J. R. Clynes won many plaudits, first as Under-Secretary at the Food Ministry, then as

Food Controller. In politics a revolution was taking place akin to that in seventeenth-century England, when by cutting off the King's head and running the country themselves the Parliamentarians made nonsense for ever of the Stuart claim that there were mysteries of State which only a King could deal with; so too had Henderson, Clynes, Barnes and Roberts made nonsense of the tale that, good as Labour chaps might be on wages and hours of work, they were not fit to govern. The *Observer*[52] predicted that in ten years time Clynes would be Prime Minister of a Labour Government; actually there was a Labour Government in six years, and Clynes just missed being Prime Minister.

[III] CHANGING MINDS

The propaganda techniques of the First World War were afterwards the subject of many exhaustive and more or less hostile studies. In one of the best of these Professor H. D. Lasswell offered the following definition:

It refers solely to the control of opinion by significant symbols, or to speak more concretely and less accurately, by stories, rumours, reports, pictures and other forms of social communication. Propaganda is concerned with the management of opinions and attitudes by the direct manipulation of social suggestion rather than by altering the conditions in the environment or the organism.[53]

From the start propaganda had to be directed at the fairly routine tasks of recruiting, saving, economizing and so on. When the Ministry of National Service was founded one of its main functions seemed to be the purchase of space in the press from which to exhort the older members of the community to offer their services for domestic war work: in one advertisement a young soldier addresses one of his elders in a familiar phrase which had now taken on an admonitory connotation: 'It's a business of blood for me; it's business as usual for you.' To boost the War Savings Campaign of the latter part of the war, use was made of Whistler's 'Portrait of the Artist's Mother': however, to make sure that people got the message, it was felt to be necessary to ruin the painting by printing across it the words, 'Old Age Must Come'.[54]

But beyond these relatively innocuous matters, propaganda was required, in the words of Professor Lasswell,

to mobilize the animosity of the community against the enemy, to maintain friendly relations with neutrals and allies, to arouse the neutrals against the enemy, and to break up the solid wall of enemy antagonism.

It was to the last three objectives rather than the first that the Secret Propaganda Bureau at Wellington House devoted most of its energies; for mobilizing the animosity of British society, there was from 1914, right through 1916, a plethora of preachers, politicians, and pressmen, who scarcely needed the encouragement of the Governmental agencies. Till late 1916 the propaganda machine practically ran under its own steam, churning out a miscellaneous array of slogans, both idealistic and vicious; after 1916 the Government had deliberately to prime the machine by feeding these by-products back into it.

How deep a change there was in the attitudes of ordinary men and women towards the war in 1917 is impossible to determine. From the start there had been stories of working men – apart from articulate syndicalists and shop stewards – who declared that, since society had never done anything for them, the war was no cause of theirs.[55] Yet even in the I.L.P., the strongest of all pacifist and anti-war organizations, patriotic enthusiasm, moral pressure, and conscription were strong enough to ensure that the majority of the eligible members of the party went into the army: in Bradford, historic birth-place of the party, the absent membership in 1918 was accounted for as follows – 429 in His Majesty's Forces, nineteen in His Majesty's Prisons, with, in addition, twenty-nine conscientious objectors on Alternative Service.[56] Even the Glasgow socialist paper *Forward* ran a weekly column of extreme jingoism by 'Rob Roy' (Dr Stirling Robertson). On the whole, therefore, it would seem that almost everyone was touched by war fever. 1917 was not so much marked by disillusionment as by discontent. But there was a touch of despair too, as the scale of the terrible bleeding of the war began to seep into the national consciousness: diarists who had once been full of cheery predictions as to the early end of the war are now wondering if it will ever end at all.[57]

Control of propaganda was undoubtedly one facet of warfare to which the Lloyd George ministry was temperamentally better suited than the Asquith ministry. Lloyd George's innovation was a Department of Information whose function it was to supervise four subdivisions: Wellington House, which continued to provide material for domestic and for neutral consumption; a Cinema Division devoted to the exploitation of this first of the twentieth-century mass media; a Political Intelligence Division charged with ascertaining the state of public opinion throughout the world; and a News Division which was responsible for filtering war news through to the British public. The head of the Department of Information, first C. H. Montgomery of the Foreign Office, then Colonel John Buchan, had the assistance of an Advisory Committee containing three leading newspapermen, Lord Northcliffe (later, when he went on a mission to America, replaced by Lord Beaver-brook), Robert Donald (editor of the *Daily Chronicle*) and C. P. Scott; just as Lloyd George believed that for shipping control you needed a ship owner and for food control a shopkeeper, he saw that for propaganda you needed newspapermen. Subsequently, as a further step in the co-ordination of government policy and propaganda, a member of the Cabinet, Sir Edward Carson, was given supervisory powers over all propaganda matters, and further reorganization in February and March 1918 resulted in the creation of a Ministry of Information under Lord Beaverbrook.[58]

These developments came none too soon as discontent and war weariness began to temper hysterical enthusiasm. A special War Aims Committee, on which Asquith served along with the man who had displaced him, was formed to combat the growth of pacifist sentiment;[59] almost at the same time the most famous propaganda achievement of the whole war was launched, the story that the Germans were converting the bodies of dead soldiers into lubricating oils, pig-food, and manure. Credit for this invention again belongs to private enterprise – that of *The Times*. For the Government Lord Robert Cecil merely contributed the remark, when questioned about the story, that *The Times* 'is a reputable newspaper'. Dummies of a leaflet designed to circulate the story were considered by Wellington House and, according to Mrs Masterman, rejected. None the less *someone* in the Department of Information must have acted, for very shortly just such a leaflet was available. Headed, *A 'Corpse-Conversion' Factory*, and subtitled 'a Peep behind the German Lines', it began:

Out of their own mouths, the military masters of Germany stand convicted of an act of unspeakable savagery which has shocked the whole civilized world, including probably, now that the truth has come out, many of the German people themselves. Attila's Huns were guilty of atrocious crimes, but they never desecrated the bodies of dead soldiers – their own flesh, as well as the fallen of the enemy – by improvising a factory for the conversion of human corpses into fat and oils, and fodder for pigs.

That is what the autocrats of Prussia have done – and admitted. 'Admitted' is too mild a word. They have boasted of it. It is an illustration of their much-vaunted efficiency! A sign of their pious Kultur! Proof of the zeal to waste nothing! Further evidence of the Kaiser's self-imposed deification! 'There is one law, mine!'

How was the discovery made? Quite simply. Herr Karl Rosner, the Special Correspondent of the Berlin *Lokalanzeiger* on the Western front, made the announcement in his published dispatch of 10 April.

The pamphlet then gave a reproduction of the dispatch in the original German, followed by an English translation. One or two oddments of circumstantial evidence were added, and various expressions of horror from such notabilities as the Chinese Ambassador in London.[60] Actually if the German dispatch meant anything it meant that the corpses of horses were being utilized, and the whole story was finally and formally exploded in the House of Commons in 1925. It made a great impression at the time, and it left its odour behind it: when tales first came through early in the Second World War of Hitler's gas chambers, Fleet Street would not print them, saying that it wanted no more corpse-conversion stories.

One of the most notorious of the Ministry of Information propaganda films, *Once a Hun, always a Hun*, was much criticized in Parliament by Mr Leif Jones, for too nakedly revealing the economic interests of many of the businessmen employed at the Ministry. Two German soldiers are first shown in a ruined French town meeting a woman with a babe in arms whom they strike to the ground. The two soldiers gradually merge into two commercial travellers now seen in an English village after the war. One enters a small general store and shows the shopkeeper a pan. The shopkeeper is at first impressed, but his wife enters and reveals the 'Made in Germany' inscription underneath. She calls in a policeman who orders the German from the shop. The final words on the screen point up the message, 'there can be no trading with these people after the war'.[61]

In the changed atmosphere of 1917, new propaganda initiatives were required. Up till this point in time Liberals had been very much alone in cheering themselves upon such stirring visions as 'the emancipation of the German people' and 'the war that will end war', occasionally receiving a contemptuous glance from *The Times* which felt that there were sterner tasks on hand than consideration of the post-war settlement of Europe.[62] H. G. Wells received rather more encouragement since it was a concomitant of his theories that there should first be the *tabula rasa* of a war to the finish, and he was able to publicize openly his theories of a Peace League which would make future wars impossible. Other individuals and groups were working along similar lines, but felt it politic not to raise their voices too loudly. Of all discernible agencies of opinion probably the Fabian Society stands up best to close examination of its attitudes to the war, accepting that, because it was there, the war must be fought, but eschewing the glorification of the present one for the careful study of the avoidance of future ones. Its plans for international government were put before members and before the rather exclusive readership of the *New Statesman*. Other plans were worked out by a handful of dissident Liberals, who, along with Lord Bryce, the chairman of the Atrocities Committee, were known as the Bryce group; these plans were kept secret to avoid the charge of pacifism. Even when a League of Nations Society was formally constituted on 3 May 1915, under the chairmanship of the Liberal M.P. Sir Willoughby H. Dickinson, it carried on its propaganda in whispers, distributing its literature by personal contact. The *Manchester Guardian* was enthusiastic, but admitted the difficulties of promoting ideas generally associated with cranks and sentimentalists.[63]

Throughout 1917 and, indeed, 1918, the Conservative press remained unimpressed by, and sometimes hostile to, the concept of a League of Nations. But Lloyd George, whose vision hitherto of the ending of the war, as expressed in his war speeches, had been confined to the dealing of a 'knock-out' to Germany, or, more cryptically to the statement that 'this war will come to an end when the Allied Powers have reached the aims which they set out to attain when they accepted the challenge thrown down by Germany,'[64] recognized in it a good new plank with which to replace the shivering timbers of his propaganda wagon. Moreover, the entry into the war of America, where League of Nations sentiment, mustered by the unimpeachably patriotic League to Enforce Peace, and extolled by President Wilson, was strong, made the whole idea respectable, and in fact a necessity if amity between the new allies was to be maintained. The coming of Wilson, hailed by the *Daily News* on 3 April as 'the authentic voice of humanity', following so quickly upon the news of the Russian Revolution which seemed to herald the fall of the secret Liberal ogre, Russian autocracy, gave a tremendous boost to British Liberal idealism. Growing consciousness of the futility of the continuing slaughter moved that hardened reactionary, Lord Lansdowne, to circularize the Cabinet with a memorandum on a negotiated peace as early as November 1916, and he put forward his proposals publicly a year later. While other Conservatives referred to German feelers for a negotiated peace as 'peace plotting' or 'peace offensives', one of them, Lord Robert Cecil, to whom the latter phrase has been attributed, was becoming convinced by the horror around him that some sort of League of Nations must be formed at the end of the war. The Union of Democratic Control, whose main objectives were the early ending of the war and the establishment of parliamentary control over foreign policy rather than the sponsorship of a League of Nations, detected in the latter part of 1917 a 'turning of the tide', a greater willingness to listen to ideas which a year before would have been branded as 'defeatist' and pro-German.[65]

The new mood of the Labour movement has already been referred to; by making use of the work done by the I.L.P., which had long since produced its own plans for a 'League of Peoples', and by the U.D.C., whose war aims the Labour and Trade Union Conference of December 1917 took over *en bloc*, it now began to show a more sophisticated interest in the problems of war and peace. In August Arthur Henderson had been squeezed out of the War Cabinet because he favoured the holding of an international socialist conference at Stockholm, to be attended by German as well as Allied and Neutral delegates, but since Barnes moved into his place and G. J. Wardle into Barnes's place, Labour representation was undiminished. British Labour and the American President were the twin millstones which ground a declaration of war aims from Lloyd George. His first point was that Britain had no aggressive aims, no desire for 'the break-up of the German peoples or the disintegration of their State or Country'. To this he added three others: that 'the sanctity of treaties must be re-established', by which he meant that while there was 'no demand for war indemnity, such as that imposed on France by Germany in 1871', there must be 'complete restoration, political, territorial and economic, for the independence of Belgium, and such reparation as can be made for the devastation of its towns and provinces; . . . secondly, a territorial settlement must be secured, based on the right of self-determination or the consent of the governed'; lastly, Lloyd George said, 'we must seek by the creation of some international organization to limit the burden of armaments and diminish the probability of war,' a rather vague proposition which is glossed by the subheading inserted in the published version of the speech, 'A League of Nations.'[66]

That there was a change in public attitudes is made clear by the lessening hostility to such organizations as the U.D.C., and by the great success which attended the first mass meeting sponsored by the League of Nations Society once it dared to come out from under cover in the spring of 1917.[67] The old cries of honour and duty were wearing a little hoarse, the memories of the outrage inflicted upon Belgium rather hoary; it was becoming difficult for the human frame to bear all the slaughter and sacrifice and not believe that it was for something which was at the same time bigger, and more precise. Lloyd George sensed this in introducing his war aims speech:

When men by the million are being called upon to suffer and die, and vast populations are being subjected to the sufferings and privations of war on a scale unprecedented in the history of the world, they are entitled to know for what cause or causes they are making the sacrifice. It is only the clearest, greatest and justest of causes that can justify the continuance even for one day of this unspeakable agony of the Nations. And we ought to be able to state clearly and definitely not only the principles for which we are fighting but also their definite and concrete application to the war map of the World.

By adopting, at the instance of its most persuasive politicians, the phrases and slogans coined earlier by a minority of Liberals, largely to allay their own uneasiness, a whole nation was able to maintain the righteous quality of its war effort; unhappily the new righteousness went hand in hand with the old; a new world of virtue, yes, but punishment for the wickedness of Germany first.

[IV] THE ART OF DISENCHANTMENT

One area which became remarkably immune to anti-German hysteria was the front line: F. H. Keeling reported that few of the men around him felt much anger over, or sympathy for, Nurse Cavell; a similar detached scepticism towards other reported German activities in Belgium was reported by C. E. Montague and other front-line soldiers.[68] What deep hostility there was seemed rather to be directed towards the French, the allies with whom, to the misfortune of European peace, we were largely at odds throughout the inter-war years.[69] After the war there came a whole shoal of literature of disillusion written by ex-servicemen. In *Disenchantment* C. E. Montague movingly described the sordid tunnel existence which called

on all ranks of troops in the actual line to put up with a much diminished chance of survival, only the barest off-chance if they stayed there year after year. While they lived it was inflicting upon them in trenches a life squalid beyond precedent. And that same evolution had pressed back the chief seats of command into places where life was said to contrast itself in wonderful ways with that life of mud and stench and underground gloom.[70]

Those early volunteers who had a simple old-world religious faith were probably most immune to the numbing influence of trench life; but they and their faith were extinguished in the Battle of the Somme. Before going over the top Second Lieutenant J. S. Engall wrote to his parents that he had taken Communion the previous day with dozens of others who were going over with him, and that he had never attended a more impressive service:

I placed my soul and body in God's keeping, and I am going into battle with His name on my lips, full of confidence and trusting implicitly in Him. I have a strong feeling that I shall come through safely; but nevertheless should it be God's holy will to call me away, I am quite prepared to go: and . . . I could not wish for a finer death; and you, dear Mother and Dad, will know that I died doing my duty to my God, my Country, and my King, I ask that you should look upon it as an honour that you have given a son for the sake of King and Country.[71]

Engall perished, as did thousands like him; for those who survived it was difficult not to doubt King, Country, or God. Another who fell had already written, 'Any faith in religion I ever had is most frightfully shaken by things I've seen.'[72] For a man whose enthusiasms had been social, not religious, one year was enough to turn enthusiasm sour: as F. H. Keeling put it to the Fabian historian, R. C. K. Ensor: 'I hope this bloody war is going to end soon – of course there is no chance of that, but the sooner the better.'[73]

Worst of all for the future of British society was the divide which yawned between, on the one side, the civilian fed on the sentimental mush of books like A. J. Dawson's *Somme Battle Stories* and the paper victories of the Press Bureau, aware of and almost inured to, colossal slaughter, but oblivious to the real tortures, physical and mental, of trench warfare, and on the other the soldier who was enduring them. At home there were air attacks, shortages; but these were the flickering of a match compared with the hell of the Western Front. At home there appeared to be affluence; there certainly was profiteering. As early as February 1916, F. H. Keeling pointed the bitter contrast:

Broadly speaking, the English either volunteer for this hell or else sit down and grow fat on big money at home. The contrast between the two fates is too great.[74]

Alienation of soldier from civilian is not the only cross-fissure which opened in British society. Lloyd George was borne to power on a justified reaction against the bungling of his predecessor; the bungling, exaggerated by the Northcliffe press in its constant reference to 'the old gang', seemed to be proven beyond doubt by the strictures of the Committee of Investigation into the

Dardanelles fiasco,[75] which were given the widest prominence in
the same newspapers. In May 1918 Asquith associated himself with
a bitter attack on the Lloyd George Ministry launched by Sir
Frederick Maurice. Even more serious than the feuding among
politicians was the feuding of politicians against generals, the
hostility between Haig and Lloyd George being common knowledge. Curiously the Liberal press rallied to Haig, showing the
same touching faith in him, as the expert in matters in which they
themselves were inexpert, as they had shown in Kitchener.[76]

For the period of the war this is all rather nebulous, just a face
at the window occasionally troubling the mind. It was the aftermath that brought disenchantment knocking boldly at the door;
most of the bitterest words were reflected in the grim tranquillity
of the post-war years. Contemporary records, such as Henry
Williamson's War Diary[77] or the parts of Charles Edmonds's *A
Subaltern's War* which were written in 1917, suggest that though by
the end the soldier was wearied and sceptical, to call him disil-
lusioned would be to add the sin of exaggeration to the folly of
generalization. Looking back Edmonds's reflection was: 'The soldiers were not "disenchanted", for war had never offered them an
enchanting prospect: they were just "fed up".'[78] Even Montague
in 1917 was content to write the usual vacuous rubbish in introducing the war drawings of Muirhead Bone:

It is a trench to gladden the connoisseur's heart. How the men must
have worked whenever they were not fighting – and digging is less
dear than fighting in the soul of youth – in order to model this perfect
line of defence and offence – its shapely firing-step and clean-cut vertical
walls and massively squared traverses! Here is no gaping V-shaped
ditch to collect the enemy's trench mortars and invite his wandering
whizz-bangs in. And the men know it. You walk along the trench and
see a just pride, as well as confidence, in their faces. It is noon now, and
some of them are blowing on hot tea to cool it, or eating out of their
dixies a hot stew of meat, potatoes and peas. It has not always been thus
in an English firing-trench. The English only learn war, in each of their
wars, by degrees. But now they have learnt it. The day is fine, and other
men are asleep, basking like cats, in a state of beatitude, on little sunny
shelves and bunks cunningly sculptured out of the trench's firm clay
walls. One little knot of men off duty are bending over a comic paper
at a corner . . .[79]

But from the rarer and more sensitive spirits, poets and artists, disillusionment, well before the ending of the war, was already bodying forth. While Rupert Brooke just lived long enough to hymn the heartfelt praises of a generation going to war, Wilfred Owen just lived long enough to utter the bitter despair of the same generation coming out of the same war. Nothing expresses more movingly the alienation of one generation from another than his *Parable of the Old Men and the Young*:

> So Abram rose, and clave the wood, and went,
> And took the fire with him, and a knife.
> And as they sojourned both of them together,
> Isaac the first-born spake and said, My Father,
> Behold the preparations, fire and iron,
> But where the lamb for this burnt-offering?
> Then Abram bound the youth with belts and straps,
> And builded parapets and trenches there,
> And stretched forth the knife to slay his son.
> When lo! an angel called him out of heaven,
> Saying, Lay not thy hand upon the lad,
> Neither do anything to him. Behold,
> A ram caught in a thicket by its horns;
> Offer the Ram of Pride instead of him.
> But the old man would not so, but slew his son . . .[80]

The War did not create a new movement in the arts, but it fostered what was barest and grimmest in 'modernism' and mocked the canons of the older schools. In Britain, as on the continent, the main characteristics of the modern movement were already established well before 1914; they were in a sense a product of the same restlessness and aspiration which led the peoples of Europe to welcome the war when it came. Britain had her futurists and her vorticists, her symbolists, and, in the theatre, her social realists. None the less there was a very strong tide of resistance apparent in the successes of the Georgian reaction in which poets such as Laurence Binyon stressed the traditional forms, and in the derision poured upon Roger Fry's attempt to mount an exhibition of Post Impressionist Art. But to deal with modern war only the techniques of modern art were adequate; what gilded Edwardian society had rejected, battered post-war society came slowly to accept. Not that there was complete continuity with pre-war developments in the arts any more than anywhere else; here too it was true that, where illusions had helped to ease the road to war, the war shattered these illusions. One of the major tenets of futurism was its faith in the dynamic of war; one of its younger British exponents, C. R. W. Nevinson, returned from the war with that faith destroyed.

It is in the latter part of 1917 that the letters of the young artist and serviceman, Paul Nash, begin to show intense anger against the war and its civilian proponents. One letter to his wife written in November 1917 is eloquent of the effect of the war upon him both as soldier and painter.

We all have a vague notion of the terrors of a battle, and can conjure up with the aid of some of the more inspired war correspondents and the pictures in the *Daily Mirror* some vision of a battlefield; but no pen or drawing can convey this country – the normal setting of the battles taking place day and night, month after month. Evil and the incarnate fiend alone can be master of this war, and no glimmer of God's hand is seen anywhere. Sunset and sunrise are blasphemous, they are mockeries to man, only the black rain out of the bruised and swollen clouds all through the bitter black of night is fit atmosphere in such a land. The rain drives on, the stinking mud becomes more evilly yellow, the shell holes fill up with green-white water, the roads and tracks are covered in inches of slime, the black dying trees ooze and sweat and the shells never cease. They alone plunge overhead, tearing away the rotting tree stumps, breaking the plank roads, striking down horses and mules, annihilating, maiming, maddening, they plunge into the grave which is this land; one huge grave, and cast up on it the poor dead. It is unspeakable, godless, hopeless. I am no longer an artist interested and curious, I am a messenger who will bring back word from the men who are fighting to those who want the war to go on for ever. Feeble, inarticulate, will be my message, but it will have a bitter truth, and may it burn their lousy souls.[81]

That the war was not entirely negative in its effects on the arts we saw when discussing developments in the world of music. The history of the British War Artists is one of the finest chapters in the war, and a true tribute to the genuineness of the conviction, so often voiced, that in fighting this war Britain was fighting on behalf of civilization. The idea of sending Muirhead Bone as the first War Artist emanated early in 1916 from a former literary agent-employed in Wellington House. Bone's Exhibition of January 1917 became the first of a series given by the band of 'Official War Artists'.[82] It was during the darkest days of German victories in March 1918 that the Ministry of Information produced the massive and visionary scheme of a whole collection of war paintings, to be painted without hindrance or guidance by the best young talent then serving in the war. As Masterman – now head of the Literature and Art Department, as Wellington House had become upon the creation of the Ministry – later wrote:

We had to hunt the world to find the men we desired. We discovered Henry Lamb as Medical Officer in Palestine, Wyndham Lewis and D. P. Roberts in the Artillery in France, John and Paul Nash serving in the infantry in the battles round Ypres, Stanley Spencer a private (forbidden to sketch) in the hills round Salonika and his brother Gilbert as a Red Cross orderly in a hospital of Sinai.[83]

In putting opportunity before so many young men the scheme did immeasurable service to the future of British painting. That the resistance of the Treasury, which wanted to know 'how the painting of pictures which could only be exhibited after the war could be defined as British propaganda', was overcome was in large measure due to Masterman and Arnold Bennett, who had the powerful support of Lords Beaverbrook and Rothermere.[84] Thus laissez-faire in the arts was challenged as elsewhere, the State rising, in the words of the art critic P. G. Konody, 'to art patronage on an unprecedented scale'.[85] In return the State got as undeceived a view of the war as ever Goya's portraits were of his sitters. In an exhibition of 1917 entitled *Modern War*, Nevinson exhibited the subsequently famous, 'Illustration: Mitrailleuse', of which Sickert, a leader among the older generation of English artists, wrote:

Mr Nevinson's 'Mitrailleuse' will probably remain the most authoritative and concentrated utterance on the war in the history of painting.[86]

The scene depicted in bold simplified form is a grim and harrowing one, horror rather than heroism is the keynote. The Leicester Galleries Exhibition of May 1918, 'Void of War', by Paul Nash, was perceptively summarized by Arnold Bennett:

Lieutenant Nash has seen the Front simply and largely. He has found the essentials of it – that is to say, disfigurement, danger, desolation, ruin, chaos – and little figures of men creeping devotedly and tragically over the waste. The convention he uses is ruthlessly selective. The wave-like formations of shell-holes, the curves of shell-bursts, the straight lines and sharply defined angles of wooden causeways, decapitated trees, the fangs of obdurate masonry, the weight of heavy skies, the human pawns of battle – these things are repeated again and again, monotonously, endlessly. The artist cannot get away from them. They obsess him; and they obsess him because they are the obsession of trench-life.[87]

Of the most outstanding of the paintings on view, Konody wrote, 'I cannot think of a picture that interprets the whole terrible meaning of war as completely and convincingly as Lieutenant Paul Nash's little oil painting "Void"'.[88]

The highest product of a society, the products of its creative workers, are of the highest importance to the historian of that society. The art and poetry, tentative some of it still, of austerity and disillusionment appearing at the end of the war led on to some of the greatest creative work of the 1920's, to Eliot and his *Waste Land*, to Ben Nicolson and his nihilistic abstractions. But the vision of despair of the artist, the disenchantment of the literary soldier, are not necessarily representative of society as a whole, or even of all returning soldiers. Their attitudes, in so far as they had any, were only crystallized in the years which followed the ending of the war.

NOTES TO CHAPTER SIX

1. C. E. Montague, *Disenchantment*, 1922, p. 169.
2. Edmonds, *Short History of the First World War*, pp. 224–6.
3. *Report of British Association*, 1919, pp. 14, 273–4.
4. J. Terraine, *Douglas Haig, the Educated Soldier*, 1963.
5. The figures are for the period 31 July to 10 November, Edmonds, p. 252.
6. W. Beveridge, *British Food Control*, Oxford, 1928, p. 195.
7. ibid., pp. 33, 35, 36.
8. *The Times*, 3 February 1917.
9. Beveridge, *Food Control*, p. 37.
10. R. Smillie, *My Life for Labour*, 1925, p. 220. C. Addison, *Politics from Within*, p. 300.

11. McDonagh, *In London During the Great War*, p. 205.

12. Beveridge, pp. 172 ff.

13. ibid., pp. 196–7. A Briggs, *History of Birmingham*, II, 1955, p. 205.

14. Beveridge, p. 208.

15. *The Times*, 17 December 1917.

16. Beveridge, pp. 111, 155. *House of Commons Debates*, 25 July 1917.

17. Beveridge, pp. 142 ff., 205 ff.

18. *Report of Working Classes Cost of Living Committee* P.P., 1918, VII, Cd. 8980, p. 7. A. L. Bowley, *Prices and Wages in the United Kingdom, 1914–20*, Oxford 1921, pp. 32 ff.

19. *The Times*, 29 June 1917.

20. See esp. C. S. Peel, *The Eat-Less-Meat Book*, 1917, pp. 109–169.

21. ibid., p. 23.

22. Official figures, printed in *Observer*, 12 January 1919.

23. S. Coxon (ed.), *Dover during the Dark Days*, 1919, pp. 170–84.

24. *Report on the Administration of the National Relief Fund to 30 September 1918;* P.P., 1919, XXVI, Cmd. 16, p. 4.

25. McDonagh, p. 169 (20 January 1917).

26. P.P., 1918, VII, Cd. 8980.

27. E. M. H. Lloyd, *Experiments in State Control*, Oxford, 1924, p. 230.

28. Beveridge, *British Food Control*, p. 211.

29. Blumenfeld, *All in a Lifetime*, p. 81 (15 March 1917). Beveridge, p. 37.

30. C. Repington, *The First World War 1914–18*, 1920, Vol. II, p. 3 (21 July 1917).

31. C. Clark, *National Income and Outlay*, 1937, p. 94.

32. *The Times*, 21 April 1922.

33. For a wider perspective see W. L. Guttsman, 'The Changing Social Structure of the British Political Elite, 1886–1935' and 'Aristocracy and the Middle Classes in the British Political Elite, 1886–1916', in *British Journal of Sociology*, 1951 and 1954.

34. *Hist. Min. Mun.*, Vol. VII, pt. 1, p. 8.

35. Blumenfeld, p. 38: 'I looked up today at the tops of omnibuses, and counted fifteen omnibuses and not a single top hat.' (28 September 1915).

36. P.P., 1917–18, XIV, Cd. 8731, p. 4.

37. ibid., Cd. 8663, p. 31.

38. ibid., Cd. 8668, p. 23.

39. G. D. H. Cole, *Trade Unions and Munitions*, pp. 134, 142–4.

40. ibid., pp. 145–6.

41. P.P., 1917–18, XIV, Cd. 8662, p. 2.

42. ibid., pp. 2–6.

43. ibid., Cd. 8663, pp. 14, 16, 24, 25.

44. ibid., Cd. 8664, pp. 2–3, 6, 7.

45. ibid., Cd. 8665, pp. 3, 8; Cd. 8666, pp. 2–5; Cd. 8667, p. 4; Cd. 8668, *passim*; Cd. 8669, p. 3.

46. Cd. 8669, p. 3.

47. Cole, *Trade Unions and Munitions*, p. 151.

48. *Observer*, 21 October 1917.

49. Labour Party, *Report of Annual Conference 1918*, pp. 102, 140.

50. Cole, *Workshop Organization*, p. 71.

51. **Cole**, *Trade Unions and Munitions*, pp. 139–40, 155–6.

52. *Observer*, 30 June 1918.

53. H. D. Lasswell, *Propaganda Technique in the World War*, 1927, p. 9.

54. Hardie and Sabin, *War Posters*, p. 12.

55. McDonagh, *In London during the Great War*, p. 91.

56. *Bradford Pioneer*, 1 March 1918.

57. e.g., Blumenfeld, p. 62 (8 May 1916). McDonagh, p. 200.

58. *House of Commons Debates*, 5 August 1918. G. Bruntz, *Allied Propaganda and the Collapse of the German Empire in 1918*, 1938, pp. 22–4.

59. Bruntz, p. 19.

60. *A 'Corpse-Conversion' Factory*, n.d. (1917?). See L. Masterman, *C. F. G. Masterman*, pp. 292–3.

61. Lasswell, p. 45.

62. *The Times*, 2 July 1915, 4 December 1915.

63. H. Winkler, *The League of Nations Movement in Great Britain, 1914–1919*, New Brunswick, 1952, pp. 50 ff. *Manchester Guardian*, 31 October 1916.

64. Speech at Glasgow, 29 June 1917.

65. H. Hanak, 'The Union of Democratic Control during the First World War', in *Bulletin of Institute of Historical Research*, November 1963.

66. D. Lloyd George, *The Allied War-Aims*, 1918.

67. Winkler, p. 54.

68. Keeling, *Keeling Letters and Reminiscences*, p. 248 (11 November 1915). Montague, *Disenchantment*, p. 31. L. Housman (ed.), *Letters of Fallen Englishmen*, pp. 123, 128 ff.

69. See esp., R. Graves, *Goodbye to All That*.

70. Montague, p. 31.

71. J. S. Engall, *A Subaltern's Letters*, 1918, pp. 119–20.

72. *Letters of Fallen Englishmen*, p. 150 (March 1916).

73. Keeling, p. 238 (11 August 1915).

74. ibid., p. 290 (27 February 1916).

75. P.P., 1917–18, X, Cd. 8490.

76. e.g. *Daily News*, 5 October 1918.

77. H. Williamson, *A Soldier's Diary of the Great War*, 1929.

78. C. Edmonds, *A Subaltern's War*, 1929, p. 205.

79. C. E. Montague, *The Front Line*, 1917, pp. 4–5.

80. W. Owen, *Poems*, 1920, p. 9. c.p. Siegfried Sassoon's 'They' – *The War Poems of Siegfried Sassoon*, 1919, p. 47.

81. P. Nash, *Outline, an autobiography and other writings*, 1949, pp. 210–1.

82. L. Masterman, *C. F. G. Masterman*, p. 286.

83. ibid., p. 303.

84. ibid., pp. 303–4.

85. *Observer*, 14 December 1919.

86. C. R. W. Nevinson, *Modern War*, 1917, pp. 22–3.

87. Leicester Galleries, *Exhibition No. 258, May 1918*, pp. 4–5.

88. *Observer*, 19 January 1919.

CHAPTER SEVEN

Science and Collectivism

[I] SCIENCE, TECHNOLOGY AND THE WAR

THE PROBLEMS of definition involved in a historical study of collectivism, socialism, nationalization, etc., are considerable; but they are nothing compared with the complex usage of words like science, technology and invention. Let it be understood first of all that by science is meant natural science, as does the plain man when he speaks of 'the wonders of science': he means television sets, not parliaments, though the systematic study of parliamentary institutions may be termed by its practitioners a social science. Science, as it is used here, then, is first defined by its subject matter: it is concerned with the phenomena of the physical universe. It is defined, secondly, by its method, which is empirical and systematic, and directed ultimately towards the establishment of general laws which state the relationship between different natural phenomena. The object of science thus described is simply knowledge: man's pursuit of the truth about his own environment. That this is a rarefied and detached pursuit is sometimes stressed by talking not of 'science', but of 'pure science'. But the product of this rarefied pursuit, knowledge of the workings of some aspect of the physical world, can clearly be of the utmost use to mankind. The man who applies his knowledge of scientific laws and his training in scientific empirical investigation with the aim of creating a precise material benefit is the applied scientist. The application, day in and day out, of the discoveries of the pure scientist and of the applied scientist to a particular economic use, to a particular industry or branch of an industry, gives rise to an important, but more limited, body of knowledge, technology. The skilled technologist may refine and develop the techniques of his own subject, but he will remain essentially orientated towards immediate use, rather than towards the establishment of abstract relationships or definitive truths.

There is an obvious line linking science to applied science to technology. In seeking a definition for invention we have to move on to a different track. The scientist or technologist is of necessity a man of some considerable acquired knowledge: invention is open to the most ignorant among us, though it is most likely to spring from someone with a scientific or technological background. George Stephenson, the pioneer of the steam locomotive, had no formal scientific or technological instruction, but he took good care that his son, who successfully developed this new means of traction, should be better prepared. It is still possible to conceive of a circumstance in which necessity might genuinely be the mother of invention; but more likely than not technology and science would be its father and grandfather. None the less, invention is essentially *ad hoc* and the laws governing it are chancy; it can make its own separate and direct contribution to technology and to industry.

Wars are not fought over the great truths of the universe, and, in immediate consequence at least, are more likely to hinder than help the progress of pure science. What a war will do, however, is to provide a stimulus to the development and application of existing ideas, that is to technology and to applied science; a war will release purse-strings and encourage politicians to found institutions for the practical applications of science; a war, itself the great creator of necessity, will foster an atmosphere favourable to invention. In the broad sweep of science history one can see that, while industry and technology owe an obvious debt to science, there is something of a two-way flow; that improvements at the level of technology and industry sometimes help to advance the frontiers of pure science – the laws of thermodynamics, for instance, owe something to the practical development of the steam engine. It is always possible, therefore, that in the flurry of wartime activity some advantage may rub off upon the pursuit of pure science.

Most of the governing advances in twentieth-century science had been made before the outbreak of war. In nuclear physics the discoveries of the great physicist J. J. Thomson in the nineties had led on to the construction of a model of the atom by his even greater protégé, Ernest Rutherford, just before the war. In theoretical physics the continental scientists, Einstein and Planck, had formulated the relativity and quantum theories respectively, though neither theory, as yet, had a very wide currency in Britain. The same was true for the new psychology, involving such concepts as the subconscious and the *libido*, pioneered by Sigmund Freud, though some knowledge of it had penetrated to bright young Edwardians, such as those one encounters on the early pages of Aldington's *Death of a Hero*. In biochemistry, the imperialist science of our own day which is fast invading the realms of anatomy, botany and genetics, the pioneer work was being done, in face of great obstacles, by Gowland Hopkins. The wartime food shortage, and the dietary problems which it involved, did bring the Government to some vague interest in this branch of science; it naturally had little interest in relativity, the subconscious, or the putative shape of the atom. Even the potential of the developments in applied science and technology, which in fact have revolutionized human life throughout the world, were scarcely appreciated in the Britain of 1914: the headship in chemicals, 'the central industry in modern civilization,'[1] had been allowed to pass to Germany; wireless telegraphy had had a popular coup in assisting the arrest at sea of Dr Crippen the murderer, but was otherwise scarcely exploited to the full; in manufacture and use of the internal combustion engine Britain lagged behind the European continent and America.

Government emergency action in other fields at the outbreak of war was paralleled by the setting up of a Government Chemical Products Supply Committee under Lord Haldane

to consider and advise as to the best means of obtaining for the use of British industries sufficient supplies of chemical products, colours and dye-stuffs of kinds hitherto largely imported from countries with which we are at present at war.[2]

From its labours there sprang the not very successful national dye company. Lack of urgency in scientific matters in the period of 'Business as Usual' is highlighted by the way in which one of Rutherford's most precious assistants, Lieutenant Moseley, was allowed to take part in the Gallipoli landings, where he was killed; it is difficult to imagine the nation today being quite so prodigal of its scientific brainpower. In May 1915 a deputation of professional scientists from the Royal Society and other learned societies urged upon the Presidents of the Board of Trade and Board of Education, the need for

Government assistance for scientific research for industrial purposes, the establishment of closer relations between the manufacturers and scientific workers and teachers, and the establishment of a National Chemical Advisory Committee for these purposes.[3]

The Government was now very seriously worried by its 'embarrassment of . . . many necessities', its dangerous nakedness in the production of optical glass, dye-stuffs, magnets, 'countless drugs and pharmaceutical preparations', tungsten and zinc.[4] The President of the Board of Education, Pease, at once announced to the Commons his plan for a central body of wider purpose and powers than the proposed National Chemical Advisory Committee. Pease, like Haldane, was a casualty of the first Cabinet crisis: both deserve credit for the White Paper issued in July by Arthur Henderson, outlining a form of 'permanent organization for the promotion of industrial and scientific research.'[5] This organization, formally established by an Order in Council of 28 July, took the traditional form of a Committee of the Privy Council assisted by an Advisory Council, which, of course, did the work. The Advisory Council met for the first time on 17 August; it was allocated £25,000 for its first year's work, £40,000 for its second. From 1 December 1916 the Committee of the Privy Council for Scientific and Industrial Research was reorganized as a separate government Department with a Minister, in the shape of the Lord President of the Council, responsible to Parliament. (The Lord President was, however, responsible for an awful lot of other things as well.) A few months later a further step in the consolidation of centralized control of scientific research was taken when the National Physical Laboratory was transferred from the Royal Society to this newly christened Department of Scientific and Industrial Research (D.S.I.R.). One hundred years before, Lord Liverpool's ministry had sought release from the physical and spiritual ills which afflicted the country at the end of the Napoleonic wars by providing one million pounds for the building of new churches. Now in the latter part of another world war Parliament again passed a 'Million Act', the money this time to be devoted to scientific research. A new deity was being enthroned.[6]

While the original Privy Council committee was being formed, the Admiralty set up its own Board of Invention and Research. Although the presidency was given to the ex-First Sea Lord, Fisher, the Board contained some eminent scientists, including Professor J. J. Thomson, Sir Charles Parsons, and Dr G. T. Beilby, and had a consulting panel of twelve university science professors. Its functions were described thus:

(*a*) To concentrate expert scientific inquiry on certain definite problems, the solution of which is of importance to the naval service;

(*b*) To encourage research in directions in which it is probable that results of value to the navy may be made by organized scientific effort;

(*c*) To consider schemes or suggestions put forward by inventors and other members of the general public.

The Ministry of Munitions, too, had an Inventions Panel. The general public responded with enthusiasm, bombarding the panel with schemes for catching Zeppelins by magnetism, and for death rays powered by the mysterious agency of 'electricity'.[7]

Although the Medical Research Committee, an institution which under its later designation of Medical Research Council ranks more closely in importance with the D.S.I.R., had its origins in the 1911 National Insurance Act and was set up in August 1913, it was really the war which got it off the ground; it did not in fact present a report till the year 1914–15.[8] The reports thereafter are full of all the enthusiasm of writers who believe that not only civilization, but science is on the march; the war, they declare, is 'a great stimulus' providing 'unequalled opportunities for study and research, of which the outcome may bring lasting benefits to the whole future population'; diversion of resources to war problems, they claim, has meant no loss to medical science. Through the Medical Research Committee work of the utmost value on dysentery, typhoid, cerebro-spinal fever, and new antiseptics was indeed accomplished. Then the box of tricks, so useful in time of war, was banged shut. The first post-war report dolefully lamented that since the Armistice medical research had 'disintegrated' for lack of funds. None the less, although pruning of public expenditure was the order of the day, it was clear that the Government did not wish to chop the committee off completely: the will to permanence was expressed in the change of title, from 1 April 1920, to Medical Research Council.[9] On the whole, indeed, opinion at the end of the war was in favour of the further institutionalization of science, and a large number of committees on scientific problems were set up under the auspices of the Ministry of Munitions or the Ministry of Reconstruction.

Moving away from the more obvious forms of Government sponsorship of science, let us look at the way in which the war accelerated existing technological developments, or fostered invention. Before the war the motor vehicle was a luxury item, made, as likely as not, abroad; it was (apart from the motor bus) scarcely used at all commercially. The military had, however, long appreciated its potential, and, after the Boer War, Britain, like France and Germany, had adopted a subsidy plan to ensure supplies in time of war, while at the War Office there was a permanent Mechanical Transport Committee, subsequently the Mechanical Transport Branch, under the Director of Supplies and Transport. Starting with the subsidized vehicles and their drivers, the War Office finally, by a process which has already been exhaustively analysed in connection with the growth of collectivism, requisitioned the whole output of all factories able to produce suitable machines, of which a great variety, ranging from lorries and ambulances to, eventually, tanks, were developed.[10] The domestic motor car industry, as such, came to a standstill; but productive capacity was greatly increased and perceptive observers could see that the new developments were pregnant with possibilities for the future. This was especially true now that parturition could proceed behind the safe screen of the 33⅓ per cent McKenna Duty.

The most famous of all the technological innovations of the First World War was the tank, to use the original code name which soon became universal. The idea rose with two different groups towards the end of 1914, one inspired by Winston Churchill at the Admiralty, the other centred on Sir William Tritton, Managing Director of the Lincoln firm of William Foster & Co., who had been asked by Admiral Bacon of the Admiralty to construct a tractor capable of laying its own bridge for crossing trenches.

In April 1915 the two groups came together, and in August the project was transferred to the Ministry of Munitions. By September, Foster's had produced the prototype of the first tank, called 'Little Willie'; this was replaced by 'Big Willie', which, when given different tracks, was renamed 'Mother'. 'Mother' was ready for tests in January 1916; secrecy was preserved by a deliberate policy of treating the whole matter as a joke.[11] The introduction of the tank was at first resisted by the War Office and by Kitchener, who called it 'a pretty mechanical toy', and its surprise value was thrown away in ineffective deployment on the Somme, but eventually the tank played an important part in breaking the frozen claw of trench warfare. The tank is a good example of an invention, spawned by many brains, nurtured in an environment of technology, but called forth by the necessity of war; what is in some ways an even more interesting one was the invention by Lieutenant-Colonel P. Nissen, a civil engineer with the Royal Engineers, of the Nissen hut, which went a long way to meeting the basic needs of shelter for the vast concentrations of troops behind the lines in France. Camouflage was a French idea, taken up in this country by the Royal Academician, Solomon J. Solomons.

As with land-bound motor vehicles before 1914 there was a certain limited apprehension of the military potential of aircraft, and the National Physical Laboratory, in addition to its regular grant of £7,000 per annum, received a special sum for aeronautical researches.[12] Both the army and the navy had their own air services, the Royal Flying Corps and the Royal Naval Air Service, with a Joint Air Committee under the Committee of Imperial Defence to secure co-operation. German air attacks in 1915 provoked demands for a unified policy of defence and retaliation, paraded in the Northcliffe press and focused on a by-election fought, and allegations made, by Mr Pemberton Billing. The curious division of labour, evolved in February 1916, that the navy was responsible for hostile aircraft till they reached the coast, and then the army thereafter, was scarcely satisfactory. A new Air Committee under Lord Derby was formed, but it was weakened from the start by internal rivalries and jealousies, and by its own lack of executive authority; a Committee of Investigation did, however, exonerate the Royal Flying Corps from the charges made against it by Billing and others. In May the Air Committee was succeeded by a stronger Air Board presided over by Lord Curzon, but, still short of executive powers, it failed, in particular, to pull the Admiralty into line. It was Lloyd George's New Ministries Act which reorganized the Board on a statutory basis, with a new President, Lord Cowdray, ranking as a minister. In November 1917, the Air Board became the Air Council, with a new Secretary of State for Air, in the person of Lord Rothermere, who had succeeded Lord Cowdray as President.[13]

In the early stages of the war, the main military function of aeroplanes was reconnaissance over the enemy lines, though a number of raids upon civilian centres were also undertaken. Such raids were greatly extended in 1917 while the defensive role of the air services was at all times constantly before the eye of the domestic population. By the end of the war there was widespread interest in the possible civilian uses of aircraft. In April 1918 the Government formed a Civil Aerial Transport Committee under Lord Northcliffe, and two leading manufacturers, Holt Thomas and Handley Page, anxious to exploit their new productive capacity, proclaimed their plans for the development of civil aviation.[14] The stimulus to what was virtually a new industry was enormous. At the outbreak of war the British air services had possessed a total of 272 machines; in October 1918 the R.A.F. had over 22,000 effective machines. During the first twelve months of war the average monthly delivery of aeroplanes was 50; in the last twelve months it was 2,700. Before the war Britain had been heavily dependent on other countries for aero-engines, so much so that in the Aerial Derby of 1911 only one of the eleven machines had a British engine. 'By the end of the war, however, British aero-engines had gained the foremost place in design and manufacture, and were well up to requirements as regards supply.' The total horse-power in the last twelve months of the war was 'comparable with the total horse-power of the marine engine output of the country'. Advances in performance were even more striking. The aeroplanes sent out with the B.E.F. in 1914 had a maximum speed of 80 miles per hour, a rate of climb from ground level of 300 or 400 feet per minute, and were equipped with engines of 60 to 100 horse-power. In 1918 the fastest machines could reach 140 miles per hour and had a rate of climb from ground level of 2,000 feet per minute. The Handley-Page V/1500, which had its first test flight in May 1918, was capable of developing over 1,300 horse power. The maximum flying height had been raised from 5,000 to 25,000 feet. Three days before the armistice two Handley Page bombers stood fully equipped awaiting the order to start for Berlin.[15]

Wireless likewise proclaimed its potential during the war: it was of especial use in maintaining communications along the far-spread front lines, though on the Eastern front the Russians so mishandled the medium that they provided a valuable intelligence service to their German enemy. In stressing the importance and future possibilities of wireless, the *Observer*, in January 1919, pointed out that but for this means of communication Germany would have been completely cut off from the outside world in the latter stages of the war. It was during the war that the first British valve transmitters, a big advance on the earlier disc, arc, or alternator transmission, were installed, mainly for wireless contact between the ground and planes on reconnaissance. As supplies from the main pioneer companies in this field, Marconi, Edison, Swan and A. C. Cossor, were insufficient, contracts for radio valves were given to the main manufacturers of electric light bulbs, the General Electric Company Ltd., the British Thomson-Houston Company, Ltd., and the British Westinghouse Electrical and Manufacturing Company Ltd. The commitment of these three companies to the nascent radio industry was, by the end of the war, so great that it was they who exerted some of the strongest pressure on the Government to permit broadcasting in the post-war years. The first actual broadcasters were in many cases men who had gained experience of wireless during the war: Arthur Burrows, employed by the Government to monitor the wireless transmissions of the Central Powers, H. J. Round, who operated wireless direction-finding stations on the East Coast, and Peter Eckersley, a wireless equipment officer in the Royal Flying Corps.[16] Burrows saw most clearly the future uses of wireless, for broadcasting of speech and music instead of merely for telegraphic communication: in 1918 he forecast 'the concert reproduction in all private residences of Albert Hall or Queen's Hall concerts, or the important recitals at the lesser *rendezvous* of the music world.'[17] The one important technological advance in radio springing from the needs of war was the development of the thermionic valve: just as important were the development of vested commercial interests in the future expansion of radio, the training of a small group of dedicated enthusiasts, and, on the other side, the firing of the public imagination with the romantic possibilities of this medium of communication.

The same sort of impulses were at work in the other technologies affected by the war. The central importance of the chemicals industry provoked the Government action which has already been examined. The electrical industry benefited immensely from the enormous power demands of the other war industries, and between 1914 and 1919 the capacity of municipal and company generating stations nearly doubled.[18]

In the first fumblings of its food policy the Government made little use of existing scientific knowledge, though Runciman, as President of the Board of Trade, did, before the collapse of the Asquith Ministry, invite a committee of the Royal Society to conduct a survey of British food supplies. The agricultural policy instituted at the beginning of 1917 was based on the principle that the calorific value of grain is much higher if eaten direct rather than fed to livestock and eaten as meat. Scientific evidence that alcohol was at its deadliest when steadily accumulated through a day's solid drinking was adduced in favour of the afternoon closure of public houses. Full exploitation of scientific knowledge only began after Lord Rhondda's appointment as Food Controller; thereafter the Royal Society Committee acted 'practically as a scientific consultative committee in all matters of food supply', and Sir William Thompson was appointed Scientific Adviser to the Food Ministry. A special Food Investigation Board of the Department of Scientific and Industrial Research investigated problems of food preservation.[19]

These various matters show the interaction between science and the war effort, but the biggest scientific advance of the whole war era, the artificial disintegration of the atom, had nothing whatever to do with the demands of the war. Rutherford had for a time left his work on nuclear physics to devote his talents to the problems of submarine detection – without any striking success. Early in 1918 he returned to his laboratory in Manchester to resume his own researches, and it was here that he brought about what has proved the most portentous scientific achievement of the century. Further investigations into Rutherford's discoveries required apparatus on a massive scale, so that nuclear physics, which had previously had no obvious social relation, was now brought into direct contact with the engineering industry. All of this added up to give a new scientific orientation to British society at the end of the war, just as economic developments gave an orientation towards collectivism.

It is an oversimplification, D. S. L. Cardwell has judiciously pointed out, to talk of the 'impact' of science on society: 'science is not an alien, external force like famine pestilence or conquest, it is a characteristic of our society.'[20] There are three sectors of society in which science is a particularly active characteristic: industry, education and thought (taking the last term to cover the highest philosophical speculations on the universe and its god or gods as well as every-day attitudes and prejudices). In the first sector, the war demonstrated more convincingly than ever before that science paid dividends – the dividend for the moment was national survival, but for the future it could be national or private profit. Before the war, science, one professor said, 'was a proper occupation for the leisure of an English gentleman'. The war unequivocally made it a proper full-time occupation for a growing professional and white-collar class: in the National Factories especially, the scientific worker enjoyed a marked rise in status.[21]

Science, religion and radicalism had been the three major forces behind such education as there was in the early nineteenth century. 'Britain's strength depends on sea power and school power,' Sir Michael Sadler had declared in the 1890s. But the lesson had constantly to be relearned; the Board of Education *Reports from Universities and University Colleges* for 1913–14 announced:

Among the many important national functions in which the university institutions will have a large share will be that of meeting the scientific needs of our industries on a scale which will enable this country to compete on equal terms with the best equipped of its rivals.[22]

In company with other committees on the teaching of modern

foreign languages, a committee on science teaching was a feature of the educational reconstruction programme of the last year of the war,[23] and it became very much the fashion to stress the role of education in a science-conscious society.[24]

Science in the mid-nineteenth century helped to foster the confident belief that man had the physical world at his feet, that the universe held no mysteries which could be withheld from him. The Darwinian thesis, though ultimately destructive of revealed religion, served at first to stimulate and highlight religious and philosophical disputation. Gladstone could happily integrate evolution into the existing framework of his religious belief; Disraeli nailed his colours to what became an enduring cliché:

What is this proposition now put before us with a glib assurance the most astounding? It is this: is man an ape or an angel? My Lord, I am on the side of the angels.

Men like John Stuart Mill rallied to the development of human reason as an alternative absolute to revealed religion. But in the early twentieth century Freudian psychology, with its revelation of the importance of the subconscious, and the quantum and relativity theories, involving what to the pedantic mind would seem to be contradictions and absurdities, took the stuffing out of Reason as well as of Religion. What was critical was the concatenation of these theories and the senseless havoc of war, which brought, as it were, a double-dose of Doubt. John Galsworthy, the novelist, put it jocularly:

Everything being now relative, there is no longer absolute dependence to be placed on God, Free Trade, Marriage, Consols, Coal or Caste.[25]

E. L. Woodward, the historian, put the matter more seriously:

Man was now left to himself, yet he was not even master of his own intelligence and will. It would appear that he was free only to laugh, and the echo of this laughter down the corridors of time was not a pleasant sound.[26]

So it seemed to a sensitive mind in the years after the war. For the less darkly sensitive the larger vision opened by scientific advance was the contrary one of developing material prosperity, tempered by that of ever more horrific weapons of war.

More relevant to the main purpose is the manner in which the advancement of science contributed to the growth of the collectivist idea. To the scientific mind the pre-1914 economic system (though it might be justified by other higher considerations) could scarcely be justified on grounds of efficiency, more especially since it had made so little provision for scientific research. By contrast the powers assumed by the State in 1917 did enable it for the first time to attempt a scientific allocation of the resources of the community. Developments in electricity supply, of its essence suited to large-scale production, and, later, in broadcasting, simply cried out for State action.[27] It would be nonsense to suggest that during the war all scientists became collectivists, or even that most of them had any thoughts on the subject, but certainly the most articulate of them, that is to say the scientists who played a part in opinion-forming, inclined in this direction. When the 1919 President of the British Association, the Hon. Sir Charles Parsons, asked whether the coal owners and, as he said, 'our masters the miners' were to remain free 'to waste or conserve at their own sweet will, or to exploit as they please, this necessity of the country's existence', he showed himself to be no socialist; yet he was in favour of nationalization of the coal mines. Left to themselves, he said business men produce 'slums and millionaires'.[28] Others, like Professor Frederick Soddy, went a good deal farther:

The uses already made of science show how necessary it is that a new social order be developed before a million times more awful powers are unleashed by man. So far the pearls of science have been cast before those who have given us in return the desolation of scientific warfare and the almost equal desolation of unscientific government. In the world that is to come the control of financiers, lawyers, politicians, and the merely possessive or acquisitive must give place to a system in which the creative elements must rule . . . Common ownership of the acquisitions of science is the only path of progress.[29]

As elsewhere, the reaction was a two-way one. The growth of science fostered the growth of the collectivist ideal; the establishment of collectivist policy in the last two years of the war fostered the growth of science. The founding of the Department of Scientific and Industrial Research was the symbol of collectivism applied to science just as the founding of the Ministry of Shipping was the symbol of collectivism applied to shipping. The new ministries of the war period, especially the first of them, the Ministry of Munitions, took a special interest in the techniques and potentialities of science.[30]

[II] RECONSTRUCTION

Many of the motive forces behind the wartime collectivism – egalitarianism in a time of high prices, the desire for scientific efficiency, the needs of self-defence, and the two great shortages of munitions and of food – have already been examined. Now a closer look must be taken at a word which was being bandied about in 1915, and which, from the summer of 1916, was on every politician's lips: 'reconstruction'. The idea of reconstruction rose naturally from the ideals of August 1914, and from such declarations as Lloyd George's 'Great War' speech of September 1914. It appeared early because, after all, the war was expected to end early. As the war went on and on it became more and more necessary to stress the radical nature of the reconstructed society which would arise from the carnage. Asquith had equipped his Government with a standing Reconstruction Committee of Cabinet ministers with a small Secretariat attached. In March 1917 the Cabinet Committee was replaced by a committee of experts with Lloyd George as nominal chairman and Edwin Montagu as vice-chairman and executive head, and this in turn was replaced, despite adverse comment in press and Parliament, by a Ministry of Reconstruction.[31] The scientific approach of the new Ministry was stressed:

The country is for the first time equipped with a Department not devoted to research in the field of the physical sciences, but to research into questions of political science and to the encouragement of action on the lines of the results ascertained.[32]

Reconstruction, in the words of the War Cabinet, was 'not so much a question of rebuilding society as it was before the war, but of moulding a better world out of the social and economic conditions which have come into being during the war.'[33] The first foreshadowing of social reconstruction, the extension of war pensions, grew directly out of the military war and its very high casualty rate, and the Act of November 1915 was more striking as evidence of the continued enshrinement of laissez-faire principles than of any dramatic shift in social policy. That shift comes only with the new Act of late 1916 and the creation of a Ministry of Pensions, both of which were concerned as much with the disruptions and flux in domestic employment as with the military situation, for the 1911 Act was now extended to cover all persons employed in trades relating to the war effort. On 26 February 1917 a more generous schedule of war disablement and widowhood pensions was introduced, with rates varying, for privates, from 27s 6d per week down to 5s 6d, with allowances for children.[34] The widely publicized reconstruction programmes of 1917, in which education and housing had star billing, were in part designed to allay war-weariness and discontent. All through 1917 and 1918 work continued on the most ambitious administrative reconstruction of all, the abolition of the Local Government Board and the creation of a Ministry of Health.

As with so many other reforms carried out by the Lloyd George Ministry, the idea of a Ministry of Health was already being discussed before the fall of Asquith. But it was the new President of the Local Government Board, Lord Rhondda, who put the shoulder of political purpose and enthusiasm to the idly turning wheel of vague speculation. Rhondda invited Dr Addison to take charge of an inquiry into the problem,[35] and himself, after two months' work, submitted an important Memorandum to the War Cabinet:

(1) Public opinion is now keenly aroused on the existing deficiency and inefficiency of our public medical services, especially for maternity and infant welfare. There is a widespread insistent demand for improvement. The working of the Insurance Act has shown what can be achieved by a systematic provision of medical services, but these are admittedly inadequate, particularly for the crucially important needs of women and children. . . .

(2) There are several other grave difficulties resulting from the existing chaos in our health services, e.g. in providing medical services for discharged soldiers and their widows and orphans, in the obstacles

hampering the development of the needed specialist services for insured persons, large numbers of whom are discharged soldiers; in the constant drag on the improvement of tuberculosis services; and in the quarrelling over the maternity and infant welfare schemes ... These and other crying evils can only be remedied by the immediate establishment of one Central Ministry of Health, in place of the two or three separate and competing Government Departments, which at present separately supervise various elements in the national health problem.

(3) ... All that is wanted is a three-clause Bill establishing a 'Ministry of Health and of Local Government,' to supersede the Local Government Board and transferring to it the medical and sanatorium functions (but, for the present, no others) of the English and Welsh Insurance Commissions, and giving to it the necessary powers coupled with provisions of adequate Exchequer funds ...

(4) The Bill would be popular and would raise no party controversies. It would be essentially a war emergency measure for making possible the immediate development of the maternity and infant welfare and other services above described, for which public opinion is already clamouring, and which have become doubly needed by reason of the war havoc, and doubly urgent if they are to be started before the difficulties of demobilization render such an initial step both too late and impossible. It is, therefore, earnestly desired that this small but supremely useful step be sanctioned forthwith, so that the Bill may be introduced in the House of Lords at once, with the promise of substantial Exchequer grants.[16]

Before succumbing to Lloyd George's pleas that he should take over the Food Ministry, Rhondda extracted a promise from the Prime Minister that a Ministry of Health would indeed be brought into being.[17] Thereafter the project languished for a time, but in 1918 it became one of the major preoccupations of the Ministry of Reconstruction, now in the hands of Dr Addison. In addition to the necessary inter-departmental communications, Addison held a series of conferences with the local authorities, members of the medical profession, and the insurance committees and approved societies engaged in the administration of the National Health Acts. After general agreement had been reached upon the need for a Ministry of Health, discussion centred on the problem of the Poor Law system administered by the Local Government Board, the most troublesome aspects of which were thrashed out by a Committee presided over by Sir Donald

Maclean. Eventually a draft Bill, introduced into the House of Commons four days before the Armistice, was drawn up by the Home Affairs Committee of the War Cabinet. Its purpose as explained by Addison was to bring together under one body of men and one Minister the chief government departments concerned in matters affecting the health of the people.[38]

Resistance to this great measure, especially from the mandarins of the Local Government Board, was strong enough to force its withdrawal. The new Bill, introduced early in 1919 and given a third reading in April, had the grave defect of leaving untouched the piecemeal health powers of the local authorities.[39] Yet in its modest way it did represent one important aspect of the positive effect of the war on social policy, well summed up by Addison in his speech on the second reading:

If we wanted an illustration of how necessary it was to bring our practice into accord with our knowledge, we have it before us at the present time, because in this matter our practice is far behind our knowledge. Somehow or other we hear of these things, they sink into our minds, and we go away and forget them. For years attention has been drawn to the fact that we have in our children, in our elementary schools, armies who are physically defective or have defective vision, etc. We have them of every age and in every year, not a company or a brigade or a division, but an army. Every year they go and lose themselves in the mass of the population. We forget them until suddenly some great national event occurs which brings it up to us in its reality. That was the case in the War. Then we saw those generations of children we had heard of so often who were represented in the military age by hundreds of thousands of men who were physically unfit and could not pass the very moderate standard of physical fitness which the army required. Then it was revealed as a source of national weakness, which is very great in time of emergency, but it is just as much a source of national weakness in time of peace.[40]

The war, Addison is saying, did not create a body of knowledge and theory which was not there before, but it brought a violent awareness of the need to apply it, especially through the revelation that about one recruit in three was medically unfit. The war, one might say, brought the level of social practice up to somewhere near that of social knowledge.

In education, nevertheless, the first effects of the war were far from favourable; Government plans for greatly increased expenditure on educational grants announced in the King's speeches of 10 March 1913 and 10 February 1914, were 'arrested by the outbreak of war'.[41] But in theory, if less obviously in practice, education benefited greatly from the notions of 'reconstruction' and the desire to improve national efficiency and competitiveness prevalent from the summer of 1916. The Board of Education Report for 1915–16 was prefaced by a panegyric on the importance and glorious future of education. The Report for 1917–18 declared that the war

has certainly brought a clearer and wider recognition of the value of education, and, while showing the defects and short-comings of our system, has produced the resolution to improve it.[42]

The implementation of this resolution was placed in the hands of H. A. L. Fisher, Vice-Chancellor of Sheffield University, and, in December 1916, the first professional teacher to hold political responsibility for education as President of the Board of Education. The actual realities of juvenile education were laid bare in March 1917 in the Final Report of the Departmental Committee on Juvenile Education in relation to Employment after the War (appointed in April 1916) which, however, after exposing the early withdrawal of children from school in order to employ them in strenuous and often futureless 'war work', went on to postulate the replacement of

the conception of the juvenile as primarily a little wage earner ... by the conception of the juvenile as primarily the workman and citizen in training.[43]

Fisher himself submitted a short, succinct report to the Cabinet calling for massive State subvention of education.[44] While theorizing abounded, war conditions did bring one practical advance: in those areas and amongst those families where greater employment had brought greater prosperity, there was a growing tendency to enroll children for secondary schools.[45]

In August 1917 Fisher put his proposals for the first major Education Act since 1902 before the House of Commons. It was the negative impulse of the war which he stressed: his Bill was prompted by deficiencies which have been revealed by the War; it is framed to repair the intellectual wastage which has been caused by the War; and should it pass into law before peace is struck it will put a prompt end to an evil which has grown to alarming proportions during the past three years – I allude to the industrial pressure upon the child life of this country – and it will greatly facilitate the solution of many problems of juvenile employment, which will certainly be affected by the transition of the country from a basis of war to a basis of peace.

On the positive side he referred to the 'increased feeling of social solidarity which has been created by the War' and remarked that the acceptance of conscription 'means that the boundaries of citizenship are not determined by wealth and that the same logic which leads us to desire an extension of the franchise points also to an extension of education'. State compulsion, he concluded, was essential for the protection of the rising generation against the 'injurious effects of industrial pressure'.[46] Fisher's proposals to consolidate the administration of education roused the hostility of the local authorities; his decision to prohibit completely the system of part-timers, and his intention of introducing compulsory continuation classes, were strongly opposed by industry, especially the coal owners and the farmers; it was also argued that his Bill involved the suppression of the individual and of the rights of parents, and, finally, that Parliament anyway had no mandate for such sweeping changes.[47] As with the Ministry of Health Bill, so too the Education Bill had to be withdrawn. Introduced in new form early in 1918, it passed its third reading in July.

As enacted, the measure called upon the local education authorities to formulate and submit to the Board of Education complete schemes covering all forms of education for their districts, combining where necessary with the authorities in adjoining districts. A universal minimum leaving age of fourteen was to be enforced, and there were to be compulsory day continuation schools for those between fourteen and eighteen not undergoing suitable alternative instruction. All fees in public elementary schools were to be abolished. Standards in higher classes were to be improved, physical training was to be encouraged, there was to be special provision for handicapped children and for nursery schools. The intention was to have a comprehensive system which would give all children and young persons the opportunity to enjoy the advantages of whatever form of education was best suited to their particular capacities.[48]

One of the gravest blows to education struck by the war was the loss of teachers in action. Fisher proposed that henceforth three-fifths of the cost of teachers' salaries should be met by the Board of Education, so that the earnings of elementary school teachers could be doubled. A separate Superannuation Act brought a trebling of teachers' pension benefits. Although the Board of Education still maintained the standard British doctrine that 'in material prospects the teaching profession can never hope to compete with other professions', elementary school teaching was now economically sufficiently attractive for it to become a middle-class rather than a working-class profession.[49] A shortage of graduates was another obvious consequence of the war: because of enlistment in the army, attendance at Oxford University, for instance, had fallen from 3,181 in 1914 to 491 in 1917.[50] Fisher was anxious to secure an expansion of university education in the post-war years, and again realized that this could only be achieved by direct provision of Government funds. Accordingly the University Grants Committee was appointed in 1919 as an autonomous agency for channelling State finance to the universities.[51] In 1920 two hundred State Scholarships were instituted.

Under the Ministry of Reconstruction, a Committee on Adult Education was appointed which reported that, after the obvious interruption to adult education work at the beginning of the war, the volume of educational activity in 1917 was larger than in pre-war years.

The awakened interest has been shown in the courses of lectures, study circles, and classes arranged by a large number of organizations. A large part of this activity has been directed towards the study of the historical background and causes of the war, but attention is now being turned to the problems of Reconstruction. We are informed that organizations find great difficulty in coping with the demand for knowledge on these questions.[52]

A subsequent report remarked that 'one of the most valuable fields of activity is the army itself'. The seeds of the awakened interest in learning, the committee reckoned, were to be found in the throwing together in closer association than had been usual in civilian life of men of varied antecedents, experience and outlook, whilst the war,

the issues involved, the changes it has precipitated, the problems which are arising out of it, have led many who previously thought but little about the larger problems of life and society to seek knowledge and understanding.[53]

The reasoning here is possibly a little specious; reading between the lines, one might rather say that the intense frustration and boredom of military training, the sense of vital years slipping fruitlessly by, gave the men an interest in the army educational facilities which they might otherwise have scorned. From the earliest stages of the war certain camps had provided such facilities, and by 1917 all eighteen-year-old recruits were given compulsory teaching of citizenship, history, elements of economics and natural science.[54] The committee recommended that the various bits and pieces of educational instruction should be organized into one unified educational service – a recommendation implemented in the Second World War.

[III] THE TURNING OF THE SCREW

Lloyd George's original proposal to Asquith had been that a smaller and more effective War Committee should have day-to-day executive authority over the conduct of the war. The traditional Cabinet would continue to exist, albeit in the administrative background rather than in the executive foreground. His final solution, facilitated by Asquith's refusal to co-operate, was to merge the War Committee and the Cabinet into a War Cabinet of five: Lloyd George, as Prime Minister, Lord Curzon, as Lord President of the Council, Lord Milner and Arthur Henderson, as Ministers without Portfolio, and Bonar Law, Chancellor of the Exchequer and Leader of the House of Commons. All but Bonar Law, therefore, were freed from departmental responsibilities. That the Prime Minister now ceased to hold the leadership of the House of Commons was a further sign of the declining influence of that House over government; Lloyd George's parliamentary attendances became extremely rare, and at one stage at the beginning of the following year it was indignantly pointed out that there was nobody on the front bench save a Junior Lord of the Treasury. To avoid the dangers of confused decisions ill-remembered afterwards, which had attended upon the old system, a minute-taking Cabinet Secretariat was established. While the executive was drastically weeded down in size, new offices sprouted in copious profusion, giving the ministry a total numerical strength of eighty-eight, which was nearly twice that of pre-war days. As about sixty of the new ministers and junior ministers were in the House of Commons, unkind parallels were drawn with the eighteenth century and the days of jobbery and placeholding.

We have already glanced at the way in which the new bureaucracy dealt with the pressing problem of food distribution. As a prelude to rationing meat retail price control had been introduced in September 1917. At the same date the Government took a 'long step in socialistic policy'[55] by instituting a flour subsidy at a rate of £50 million a year designed to bring down the price of bread to 9d. a quartern loaf. A potato subsidy followed in November. To hold down the prices of other commodities the Food Ministry ran the gamut of all possible expedients: complete control of the entire process of production and distribution, control of wholesale only, or control of retail only. Prices were determined by what Beveridge described as a mixture of 'costings, conference and compromise'. The tangible consequence was a constant stream of food control orders made under the authority of D.O.R.A. which, bound together, make a fat section of the Parliamentary Papers for the session 1917–1918.[56] The irrepressible individualist, Thomas Lough, declared to the House of Commons in February 1918 that, in despair of reading or counting the orders of the Ministry, he had taken to weighing them and had found that on one day alone he had received half a pound's worth. Vigorous action was taken against contravention of the food control orders, and in the last months of war and the first months of peace there was a total of 65,000 prosecutions, with penalties ranging from the £5,500 fine imposed upon a potato profiteer to the £10 fine imposed upon a man who expressed his dissatisfaction with his wife's cooking by throwing his dinner into the fire.[57]

Distribution was only one aspect of the food problem; production was another. It is very much to the credit of the Lloyd George Government that, after possessing itself of an energetic President of the Board of Agriculture, Rowland Prothero, it at once took up and put into practice the various projects which since 1915 had been floating in an administrative vacuum. First moves were made in December 1916, and these, a judicious mixture of carrot and stick, were consolidated in the Corn Production Act of April 1917: farmers were guaranteed minimum prices for wheat and oats for a period of five years; agricultural labourers were given a minimum wage; and the Board of Agriculture took to itself powers of entry and enforcement of proper cultivation. Within the Board, a Food Production Department (Food Production Committees in the case of the Scottish and Irish Boards) was established in January with special responsibility for increasing the productivity of existing arable land, and for bringing new land under cultivation by drainage and other methods.[55]

The existing and highly ineffective County War Agricultural Committees were called upon to appoint County Agricultural Executive Committees of not more than seven members, which were then stiffened by the inclusion of additional members appointed by the Board of Agriculture, and blessed, apart from minor reservations, with the Board's own emergency powers. In February and March 1917, the Executive Committees undertook a massive survey designed to reveal the amount of additional land which could be brought into cultivation in the spring: the total estimates amounted to 300,000 acres in England and Wales, and 50,000 acres in Scotland. They issued instructions to farmers cn methods of cultivation, and, if these were not obeyed, dispossessed the recalcitrant occupier, either running the farms themselves or letting them to new tenants. The 1918 programme worked out by the central departments was a still more ambitious one, calling for an increase in arable of 2,700,000 acres in England and Wales, and 350,000 acres in Scotland, over the figures for 1916. To each Committee a quota of this was allocated, it being left to the Committee to give directions to individual farmers. In urban areas the Committees co-operated with the local town or urban district council in providing town-dwellers with allotments which they could cultivate in their leisure time. Allotments were a characteristic feature of the First World War, as of the second and the years which followed it; the allotments of 1917 and 1918 played their part in the universal blurring of class lines – the gardening proletarian was well on the high road to middle-class respectability.

Already in December 1916 there were, in the operations of the Sugar Commission and the Wheat Commission, precedents for the bulk-buying of imports. Under the Lloyd George ministry this approach to the problem of food supply was vastly extended, and, what is more, integrated into a buying machinery which served not only Britain, but her West European Allies, all of whom were by now largely dependent on the North American continent. The basic co-ordinating agency was the Inter-Ally Council of War Purchase and Finance,

the apex of a complex structure which, almost unnoticed, has effected an unparalleled economic revolution by transferring the import of all foodstuffs from private hands into Government control.[59]

Four main bodies, the Wheat Executive, the Sugar Commission, the Meats and Fats Executive, and the Oil and Seed Executive, each with their headquarters in London, and each linked to a countervalent export body in America, undertook purchase and allocation of food supplies to the Allies. At home the efforts to stimulate farm production were followed up by the Ministry entering the domestic agricultural market as a buyer on a similar scale.[60]

Shortage of food had been one of the great pressures of necessity first making its weight felt in 1915; the other, shortage of munitions, had been rather more competently dealt with before December 1916. The extremely useful, though ill-written and self-congratulatory *War Cabinet Report for the Year 1917*, published in 1918, suggested that 'whilst no exact demarcation line can be fixed,' a 'broad definition' would be that prior to the cabinet crisis 'industries essential to war needs had been taken under Government control', and that

In the same way 1917 may be described as a year in which State control was extended until it covered not only national activities directly affecting the military effort but every section of industry – production, transport and manufacture.[61]

The Ministry of Munitions was an upstart and an aggressionist: less set in its ways than such older departments of state as the War Office, it was an ideal instrument for direct Government action, and the aggrandisement of its spheres of interest after December 1916 is in itself symbolic of Government intention. The Ministry assumed responsibility for the supply of aircraft to both Army and Navy, the development of agricultural machinery, the supply of fuel oils, and the control of the manufacture, use and distribution of sulphuric acid. By October 1917 there were 143 National Factories in operation, all dealings in metals were under national control, and the Government was directly fostering the home production of tungsten from colonial ore and of iron and steel from British mines, which were themselves taken over in September. A special department, established in March 1917, was devoting its energies to the development of domestic sources of non-ferrous metals, such as tin, zinc, lead and wolfram.[62]

Coal, as a consumer commodity whose price rocketed in the early stages of the war, had been a subject for State interference in 1915. This apart, the supply of coal was central to the whole structure of Britain's industrial effort, and, indeed, was of great importance to Britain's military allies. Labour troubles in South Wales had brought Government control of the mines there. After a grim winter of domestic fuel shortages and further labour troubles, the Cabinet early in 1917, extended control to the entire coal industry, for this purpose creating at the Board of Trade a special Department under a Coal Controller. The financial arrangements were similar to those operating in regard to the railways, only more complicated: a levy on earnings above prewar created a fund used to compensate those owners whose earnings fell below prewar, or whose mines were closed altogether by the Coal Controller. Still not quite what a socialist would call nationalization, the arrangement did give the Government a stronger hand than it had in the railways; this it used with striking success in a scheme which, by ensuring that each community drew its needs from the nearest, rather than, as had happened under free enterprise, from a far coalfield, saved 700 million ton-miles per annum. Negotiating directly with the miners, the Coal Department conceded a wage increase of 1s. 6d. a day, operative from 17 September 1917.[63]

The War Office purchases in 1916 of the home and the Australian and New Zealand wool clips had been aimed at the specific problem of the provision of military clothing. But once it had established a monopoly or near-monopoly of purchase, the Government found itself implicated not only with military contractors, but with the ordinary textile manufacturers engaged in the home and export trade. To reconcile their needs with its own monopoly the Government evolved a complicated rationing scheme of quarterly allowances of wool based on former scales of consumption. In mitigation of the reality of Government control, supervision of the scheme was vested in a Board of Control sitting at Bradford, the heart of the wool and worsted trades, and composed of representatives of employers and employees, as well as of the Army Contracts Department; but the Board was chaired by a Government-appointed Director of Wool Textile Production. U. F. Wintour, Director of the Army Contracts Department, instituted a similar policy for hides and leather, while in August 1917 the Ministry of Munitions took possession of the year's flax crop. In the cotton industry, increasingly deprived of its raw material, crisis point was reached by June 1917. A Cotton Control Board was set up with the task of preserving the industry from total disruption through a policy of rationalization. A basic standard of 60 per cent of pre-war capacity was enforced; firms permitted to work above this contributed a levy to be used in the interests of the industry as a whole, and its workpeople. All this added up to a mechanism of economic planning and allocation of priorities of a sort never before possessed by a British Government.[64]

There was one other major sector of commercial enterprise which felt the tightening screw of state control after December 1916: shipping. Until December less than half the total British tonnage and practically none of the great liners had been requisitioned by the State; under the new Ministry of Shipping almost every ship was taken over, so that the Shipping Controller, working in conjunction with a committee of management of the big shipowners, was now able to organize and re-distribute the

nation's ships in the most economical manner. For each consignment of freight the shipowners, whose high profits had been a
known scandal, were paid Blue-Book rates, the basis determined
early in the war which gave a fair margin over pre-war figures;
any profit made on the transaction went to the Treasury. Control
of shipbuilding, at first vested in the Shipping Controller, was
tightened in May 1917, when a separate department under Sir
Eric Geddes, who was given the title of Controller of the Navy,
was made responsible for this.[65] Inland, a Canal Control Committee was appointed in March 1917 to run the more important
canals not owned by the railway companies.

Who exactly thought up and carried out these experiments in
State control? Lord Salter (Arthur Salter), Director of Ship
Requisitioning at the Admiralty Transport Department, which
provided the nucleus of the Ministry of Shipping, modestly de-
precates any attempt to give credit to individuals and refers to
'the logic of events and the impelling necessity of the situation'.[66]
At the top of the political tree Lloyd George was nothing of a
theorist, very little of a planner; his concern was to get things
done, his strength that he would give a hearing and a trial to all
suggested means towards this end. From the summer of 1916
there were floods of suggestions from politicians and publicists of
all descriptions. Most of the direct initiative however, came from
men within the Civil Service. The real pioneers of bulk purchase
in this country were the 'whirlwind trio' at the Army Contracts
Department, E. M. H. Lloyd, 'the brains behind the throne',
E. F. Wise, 'director of offensive and defensive operations' and
U. F. Wintour.[67] Having done their good work in jute, textiles
and leather, these three officials moved over to the Ministry of
Food, where they were joined by one of the greatest administrators
of the age, William Beveridge. Certainly the Civil Servants, like
the politicians, were responding to implacable external pressures;
but it is also important that the responses of men like Lloyd,
Beveridge, Salter, Josiah Stamp at the Inland Revenue and Sir
Hubert Llewellyn Smith at the Board of Trade, were the right
ones. And many of them, having had first-hand experience of the
operations of State collectivism in time of war, came to feel that
these operations could with advantage be continued in time of
peace.

In the end the experiments in State control triumphantly vindicated themselves, making an indispensable contribution to the winning of the war, although some were conducted in a feeble and half-hearted fashion. There was, too, an obvious tendency to regard the creation of a new Ministry, or a new Department, with its attendant bureaucracy, as in itself a panacea; the principle of the paramountcy of the national interest was at times confused with the principle of jobs for the boys. One experiment which notoriously failed was the establishment of a Ministry of National Service with the simple purpose of making 'the best use of all persons, whether men or women, able to work in any industry, occupation or service'. The first Director-General of National Service, Neville Chamberlain, formerly Lord Mayor of Birmingham, was not lacking in energy: he had taken possession of a London hotel, assembled a large staff, and begun to organize work before the Act establishing his Ministry was passed. Although some connecting link between recruiting (the responsibility of the War Office) and allocation of labour (mainly the responsibility of the Ministry of Munitions) was obviously desirable, it was difficult to see where the functions of National Service differed from those of the recently-established Ministry of Labour. Chamberlain found himself doing little more than running an appeal for National Service Volunteers, who were to take on civilian jobs and release more men for the forces. This sudden burst of voluntaryism at a late stage in the war simply added confusion to the problems of labour policy. 'What National Service wants,' the New Statesman declared rudely, 'is not a hotel, but a mortuary chamber and a post-mortem'.[68] Chamberlain shortly resigned, 'because,' said one writer, 'he had nothing to do.'[69] Upon the accession of Sir Auckland Geddes the Ministry was reorganized and given a general responsibility as 'the War Cabinet's General Staff on Man-Power'. With specific tasks in regard to military recruiting, it had thereafter a more obvious and respectable raison-d'être.

With over nine-tenths of the country's imports being bought directly by the State, with 240 National Factories in operation and large sectors of economic and social activity under direct State supervision, people by 1918 were becoming inured to the idea of State collectivism. 'As the war continued,' wrote Evelyn Wrench, we became increasingly accustomed to restrictions of every sort. When the fourth anniversary came, Government control was so much part of our lives that we found it difficult to jump back in our minds to the pre-war world in which we lived in July 1914.[70]

Informed observers tended to the belief that some at least of the socialistic experiments would be worth maintaining after the war; making the best of a bad job the Anti-Socialist Union changed its name to the Reconstruction Society.[71] The leaders of private industry were remarkably silent while the war lasted, contenting themselves with singing the praises of large-scale industrial organization. The philosophy of the Federation of British Industries was that in modern conditions 'the group, the society, and the collective effort are authoritative'.[72] Overt hostility to State control did not burst out till October 1918 when the war looked to be all but won:

Among the business community there is practical unanimity of agreement that there should be as little interference as possible on the part of the State in the future Governance of Industry.[73]

At the same time the lessons so painfully learned over the previous years could not so suddenly be jettisoned, and the same writer recognized 'that the re-settlement of the industries of the country on a peace basis is a task so huge that it could not satisfactorily be left to unguided private effort'.[74] Officially the Government verdict was that the 'war has brought a transformation of the social and administrative structure of the state, much of which is bound to be permanent'.[75]

NOTES TO CHAPTER SEVEN

1. J. D. Bernal, *Science in History*, 1954, p. 569.
2. P.P., 1916, VIII, Cd. 8336, p. 8.
3. ibid.
4. ibid., pp. 7-8.
5. P.P., 1914-16, L. Cd. 8005.
6. Cd. 8336, pp. 3, 8-9, P.P., 1917-18, XI, Cd. 8718, pp. 3, 49. P.P., 1918, IX, Cd. 9144, p. 3.

7. *Report of British Association 1919*, p. 139. *House of Commons Debates*, 21 May 1917.

8. P.P., 1914–16, XXXI, Cd. 8101.

9. ibid. P.P., 1916, XIV, Cd. 8399; 1917–18, XVII, Cd. 8825; 1919, XXVI, Cmd. 412, pp. 5, 7; 1920, XXI, Cmd. 1088, p. 5.

10. *The Times History*, pp. 283–4. Fairlie, *British War Administration*, p. 89.

11. *Engineering*, 12 September 1919, p. 334. *Report of British Association 1919*, p. 263. Addison, *Politics from Within*, p. 133.

12. Cd. 8336, p. 6.

13. *Report of the War Cabinet for 1917;* P.P., 1918, XIV, Cd. 9005, pp. 56–66.

14. Fairlie, p. 119. *Observer*, 17 November 1918.

15. *Report of British Association 1919*, pp. 15, 258.

16. ibid., pp. 158, 269–270. S. G. Sturmey, *The Economic Development of Radio*, 1958, pp. 22–5, 34–5. A. Briggs, *The Birth of Broadcasting*, 1962, p. 37.

17. Quoted by Briggs, p. 38.

18. *Report of British Association 1919*, pp. 18, 165.

19. P.P., 1916, IX, Cd. 8421. Beveridge, pp. 99, 194 ff. P. Starling, *The Nation's Feeding*, 1919, pp. 12–13. Cd. 9144, p. 4.

20. D. S. L. Cardwell, *The Organisation of Science in England*, 1957, p. 2.

21. *Report of British Association 1919*, p. 166.

22. P.P., 1914–16, I, Cd. 8137.

23. P.P., 1918, IX, Cd. 9011 and Cd. 9036.

24. See e.g. *Bulletin of Federation of British Industries*, 14 February, 9 May and 12 September 1918.

25. J. Galsworthy, *A Modern Comedy*, 1929.

26. E. L. Woodward, *Short Journey*, 1941, p. 123.

27. *Report of British Association 1919*, p. 17. *Coal Conservation Sub-Committee Interim Report;* P.P., 1917–18, XVIII, Cd. 8880. *Departmental Committee on Electric Power Supply* (Williamson Committee); P.P., 1918, VIII, Cd. 9062. *Departmental Committee on Broadcasting;* P.P., 1923, X, Cmd. 1951.

28. *Report of British Association 1919*, p. 142.

29. *Daily Herald*, 30 January 1920.

30. Money, *Triumph of Nationalisation*, p. 53.

31. *Report of War Cabinet for 1917;* P.P., 1918, XIV, Cd. 9005, pp. 199 ff.

32. ibid., p. 202.

33. ibid., p. xix.

34. *House of Commons Debates*, 26 February 1917.

35. Viscountess Rhondda *et al.*, *D. A. Thomas, Viscount Rhondda*, 1921, p. 264. *House of Commons Debates*, 7 November 1918 (col. 2338).

36. Printed in Rhondda, pp. 266–7.

37. ibid., p. 268.

38. Cmd. 325, pp. 290 ff. *House of Commons Debates*, 7 November 1918.

39. A. Newsholme, *The Ministry of Health*, 1926, pp. 93, 137–8, 150–1. P. Abrams, 'The Failure of the Social Reform, 1918–1920' in *Past and Present*, April 1963, p. 51.

40. *House of Commons Debates*, 28 February 1919.

41. *Report of Board of Education 1914–15;* P.P., 1916, VIII, Cd. 8274, p. 1.

42. P.P., 1917–18, XI, Cd. 8594, pp. 1–4. P.P., 1919, XXI, Cmd. 165, p. 3.

43. P.P., 1917–18, XI, Cd. 8512, p. 5. See above p. 119.

44. H. A. L. Fisher, *An Unfinished Autobiography*, 1940, pp. 103–4.

45. *House of Commons Debates,* 19 April 1917.

46. ibid., 10 August 1917.

47. ibid., 13 March 1918. Fisher, pp. 106–8.

48. *Report of War Cabinet for 1918*, Cmd. 325, pp. 295 ff.

49. Cmd. 165, p. 2. Fisher, pp. 104–9. H. and M. Wickwar, *The Social Services,* 1949, p. 273.

50. Fairlie, *British War Administration,* p. 242.

51. Fisher, p. 116.

52. P.P., 1918, IX, Cd. 9107, p. 6.

53. P.P., 1918, IX, Cd. 9225, p. 3.

54. ibid.

55. Gray, *War Time Control of Industry*, p. 24.

56. Beveridge, *Food Control,* pp. 162–81. P.P., 1917–18, XXVI.

57. F. Coller, *A State Trading Adventure,* 1925, p. 75. Beveridge, pp. 237–8.

58. *Report of War Cabinet for 1917*, Cd. 9005, pp. 156–9, on which the next paragraphs are based.

59. ibid., p. 170.

60. Beveridge, pp. 162–81. Coller, pp. 59–152.

61. Cd. 9005, p. 130.

62. ibid., pp. 67–79.

63. On this paragraph see R. A. S. Redmayne, *The British Coal-Mining Industry during the War,* Oxford, 1923, pp. 257 ff.

64. H. D. Henderson, *The Cotton Control Board,* Oxford, 1922. *Economist,* 11 August 1917. *Memorandum on War Office Contracts;* P.P., 1917, XX, Cd. 8447, pp. 17–20.

65. A. Salter, *Allied Shipping Control,* Oxford, 1921, pp. 2 ff.

66. A. Salter, *Memoirs of a Public Servant,* 1961, p. 87.

67. Coller, *A State Trading Adventure,* pp. 66–7.

68. *New Statesman,* 21 July 1917.

69. Fairlie, p. 254.

70. E. Wrench, *Struggle 1914–20,* p. 333.

71. *Daily Express,* 20 May 1918.

72. Federation of British Industries, *What It Is and What It Does,* p. 3.

73. *Bulletin of Federation of British Industries,* 12 October 1918.

74. ibid.

75. *Report of War Cabinet for 1918*, Cmd. 325, pp. 214–15.

CHAPTER EIGHT

The End of the War

THE SECOND Battle of the Marne of July 1918 was the first faint sign that the ascendancy had definitely passed to the Allies, and the news of the advances which followed brought a distinct lightening of domestic discontents, which had been exacerbated by the first wave of a drastic influenza epidemic. Earliest indications of the disease had appeared in the Grand Fleet at Scapa and Rosyth in April and May, and, at about the same time, among the British troops in France. In May there were a few civilian victims in Glasgow, but the massive simultaneous outbreak throughout the country did not come till the end of June. This first wave reached its crest in the second week of July, being shortly followed by a second wave which came to a peak in the first week of November. A final wave appeared towards the end of January 1919, and reached its crest in the last week of February. Total deaths were 151,446 (140,989 civilians), the highest relative to population for any epidemic since the cholera outbreak of 1849.

Virulent influenza appeared throughout the world in 1918–19, and attempts to relate it to British wartime privations are not completely satisfactory. In Britain, for the first time since the institution of public health records, the poor suffered no more than the rich. In the wealthy boroughs of Chelsea and Westminster the mortality rate ran at 6·1 per thousand and 5·2 per thousand respectively; in the poor boroughs of Bermondsey and Bethnal Green it ran at 5·6 and 5·1 per thousand respectively. The Scottish rate was 4·3 per thousand, with no significant variation between town and country, rich area or poor. If these statistics show anything, then, with a kind of sepulchral irony, they suggest that the conditions of resistance to disease as between social classes were now more equal than ever before. Where the epidemic was selective was in its high incidence among young adults – an unusual feature, which, however, was as true of neutral countries as of war-weary Britain.¹

Two events demonstrated the high pitch which tensions had reached in the last summer of the war. In the fantastic Old Bailey trial, in which Pemberton Billing, M.P. was prosecuted for libelling a dancer, Maud Allan, as a sexual pervert, the egregious defendant secured acquittal and public acclaim by alleging the existence of a 'Black Book', compiled over twenty years by German agents, and containing the names of many prominent British men and women, with a catalogue of their sexual weaknesses. The other event was the strike of 12,000 policemen on 31 August over non-recognition of the newly-established National Union of Police and Prison Officers, the dismissal of a union official, and a demand for a wage rise of one pound a week, with an additional 12 per cent war bonus. By the end of the day, however, Lloyd George had wooed and won the men with the usual specious promises.²

By early October it was noted that:

London is more crowded today than at any time in the memory of the present generation, and now that the war news is so magnificently encouraging it is a brighter London too. . . . The hotels are full; there are queues at the best and most popular restaurants; the shops are reaping a rich harvest; and the theatres and music-halls are enjoying a boom.³

A week later McDonagh remarked that: 'All the talk is about the expected imminent collapse of the Germans'.⁴ While the word 'Armistice' was being bandied in the press, the Bill completing the political emancipation of women was enacted: its single important clause read:

A woman shall not be disqualified by sex or marriage for being elected to or sitting or voting as a Member of the Commons House of Parliament.

On the evening of Saturday, 9 November, Lloyd George was guest at the Lord Mayor's Banquet; although the more ostentatious forms of gluttony were avoided, the feeding was lavish enough to provide the right setting for the knowledgeable rumours that the war was nearing a victorious close. Regretting that he had no more positive news, Lloyd George none the less confidently declared that, 'The issue is settled'. Even so, the announcement of the Armistice on Monday, 11 November, came with a certain unexpected suddenness.

This morning at eleven o'clock I was startled by the booming of maroons, fired from police and fire brigade stations, the loud reports of those near at hand being faintly re-echoed by others far off. As it is six months since these warnings of an air raid have been heard in London (our last bombardment by the enemy having occurred in May), I wondered what they could now imply, so early in the morning. Looking through my window I saw passers by stopping each other and exchanging remarks before hurrying on. They were obviously excited but unperturbed. I rushed out and inquired what was the matter. 'The Armistice!' they exclaimed, 'The War is over!'

I was stunned by the news, as if something highly improbable and difficult of belief had happened. It is not that what the papers have been saying about an Armistice had passed out of my mind, but that I had not expected the announcement of its success would have come so soon, and, above all, be proclaimed by the ill-omened maroons. Yet it was so. What is still more curious is that when I became fully seized of the tremendous nature of the event, though I was emotionally disturbed, I felt no joyous exultation. There was relief that the War was over, because it could not now end, as it might have done, in the crowning tragedy of the defeat of the Allies. I sorrowed for the millions of young men who had lost their lives; and perhaps more so for the living than for the dead – for the bereaved mothers and wives whose reawakened grief must in this hour of triumph be unbearably poignant. But what gave me the greatest shock was my feeling in regard to myself. A melancholy took possession of me when I came to realize, as I did quickly and keenly, that a great and unique episode in my life was past and gone, and, as I hoped as well as believed, would never be repeated. Our sense of the value of life and its excitements, so vividly heightened by the War, is, with one final leap of its flame today, about to expire in its ashes. Tomorrow we return to the monotonous and the humdrum. 'So sad, so strange, the days that are no more!'[5]

Many others undoubtedly shared this reflective frame of mind. Captain Henry Williamson, now based in England, included one last entry in his diary:

Thank God the end of the awful blind waste and brutality of war has come, and let us pray it may never return. . . . I am feeling rather ill and depressed, in spite of all the rejoicing around me; immeasurably relieved, glad to be alive, and glad we have won; but tired and a little sad.[6]

In that other society, the fighting line, there was even less enthusiasm.[7] But for the nation at home, Mrs Peel's fancy was a not impertinent one:

It seemed almost as if one heard a dead silence and then that the whole nation gave a sigh of relief. A few moments later the people had gone mad.[8]

On the packed tram on which McDonagh travelled in to town the passengers were 'obviously deeply moved, whether they were chattering and laughing or self-absorbed and silent', but another observer preferred Mrs Peel's epithet, 'London' he said, 'was a city gone mad'. Boy Scouts raced around on bicycles sounding the all clear; shops shut, schools released their children; Big Ben, silenced by the war, chimed: newspaper bills, banished by war economy, appeared to blazon the news, 'Fighting has ceased on all Fronts'. The grey November day turned to drizzle by the afternoon, but that could not abash what McDonagh described perceptively as 'the urge to do something ridiculous', to have, one might say, the last-but-one fling in a four-year intoxication.[9]

Not only did everyone seem bent on bursting their throats in an effort to contribute to the din, but everything that could be banged, blown and rattled seemed to have been pressed into service for a like purpose. I could distinguish the hooting of motors, the ringing of handbells, the banging of tea-trays, the shrilling of police whistles, and the screaming of toy trumpets in the resulting infernal orchestra. Among the many ludicrous incidents to be observed were a colonel in uniform squatted on the top of a motor-car sounding a dinner-gong and a parson marching at the head of a group of parishioners singing lustily with a Union Jack stuck in the top of his silk hat.[10]

The war seemed to be ending just as it had begun; it was like August 1914 all over again. A vast crowd gathered in front of Buckingham Palace chanting, 'We-want-King-George!' After being duly rewarded by the royal appearance, the concourse sang 'Land of Hope and Glory', followed by 'Tipperary'. Similar scenes of rejoicing took place throughout the country. At the same time Parliament's adjournment for a service of thanksgiving in Westminster Abbey was no mere formality, but a

genuine expression of the religious element ever present in the
war fever: in Birmingham people who had learned so patiently
to queue for foodstuffs now queued outside the Cathedral for
an opportunity to take part in one of the three separate services
which had to be held there.[11] Optimism for the future was again
as high as ever it had been among the Brookes, the Keelings, and
the Gordon Carruthers's[12] of 1914. Asquith on 2 November had
returned to an old theme in hailing the 'last act' in 'one of the
greatest dramas in history':

It is not too much to say that it has cleansed and purged the whole
atmosphere of the world.

Speeches everywhere elaborated the theme: addressing a meeting
in Victoria Square, Birmingham, on the evening of Armistice
Day, the Lord Mayor, Sir David Brooks, declared:

today is the greatest day in the history of our country, and it marks the
beginning of a new era in human development. . . . We must take care
to use this great opportunity aright so that the world may be better and
not worse by reason of the overthrow of the old order.[13]

In the last entry in his war diary, McDonagh wrote of the in-
auguration of 'an era of peace and security, after years of care
and worry'.[14]

The atmosphere was one of high hopes for a better world;
but they went hand in hand with an inward-looking jubilation
at the triumph of British arms. There was a real sense of religious
dedication and thanksgiving; but it partnered a most unholy
hatred of the defeated enemy. Not long before, A. J. Balfour had
declared of them, 'Brutes they were when they began the war,
and brutes they remain,' and this was an attitude the ruling
politicians were happy to perpetuate, as thoughts turned towards
the holding of a general election. The existing Parliament had
been in being for very nearly ten full years; the recent Representation of the People Act had completely altered the basis of the
electoral franchise; Liberals of independent mind had hankered
after a general election even in the course of the war, and the
Labour Party had begun flexing its muscles from the time of the
ratification of its new constitution. But not only did Lloyd George

decide upon an early election, he decided to fight it in concert with his allies in the war-time coalition. Sensing, apparently, that the days of the old Liberal Party were numbered, he ignored Asquith's speech of 2 November calling for Liberal reunion, and instead singled out a small group of amenable Liberals for the honour of endorsement as coalition candidates. These candidates, along with a balancing group of Conservatives, were granted what Asquith, with topical sarcasm, called the 'coupon', a joint letter of support signed by Lloyd George and Bonar Law. The coupon, as Mr. T. Wilson has pointed out, was simply the outcome of a tactical bargain between Lloyd George and the Conservatives, designed to secure for him a body of Liberal supporters at a time when he was 'declaring war on the greater number of Liberal candidates'; it was not, as is often said, determined on the basis of attitudes taken up in the Maurice debate .[15]

Labour members of the coalition were offered the opportunity of sharing in the political spoils of military victory, but a delegate conference on 14 November decided that the Party should withdraw from the Government and contest the election as a separate unit.[16] The argument for staying in was made most convincingly by J. R. Clynes, and on one view it is arguable that it might have been better had Labour remained in a position from which to exert some influence over immediate post-war policies. However, given the need to reintegrate completely the anti-war and pro-war elements, to establish the Party convincingly as the rallying point for progressive and internationalist opinion, and to assert its indisputable existence as a national political party, the decision, which Clynes, in contrast to a few time-servers like G. N. Barnes, loyally obeyed, was a wise one.

Parliament was dissolved on 25 November, and the election was scheduled for 14 December. The five major aims upon which Lloyd George and his associates campaigned chimed well with the many-belled tolling of public sentiment. They were: getting the soldier home as quickly as possible; fair treatment for soldier and sailor; punishment for the Kaiser; making Germany pay; better social conditions for the people of Britain. The first two aims and the last had been to the fore in a famous speech made by Lloyd George at Wolverhampton, two days before the dissolution of Parliament: in reply to his own question, 'What is

Lib platform

H-heroes

our task?', he had declared: 'To make Britain a fit country for heroes to live in'. But as the campaign hotted up it was the frothy mischief of the other two aims which boiled over the top. The *Daily Mail* kept the flame high by publishing daily, in the same sort of black box it had used for hounding foreign waiters in the early part of the war, statistics of British casualties. Lloyd George declared that the Kaiser would be brought to trial; G. N. Barnes put the campaign firmly on the level of gutter-press apoplexy when, in reply to a questioner, he declared, 'Myself, I am in favour of hanging the Kaiser'. The fair reparation for war damage in France and Belgium of which Lloyd George had spoken in his war aims speech eleven months previously had now become the bubble demand for 'the whole cost of the war'; Sir Eric Geddes, one of the leaders of the generation of business experts and political incompetents of 1916, produced the delightful metaphor of 'squeezing Germany till the pips squeak'.[17]

Two other issues adorned the campaign. The Labour Party in its election manifesto went out of its way to stress its hostility to the institution of conscription. On 10 December, J. H. Thomas, railwayman's leader, pulled off a considerable dramatic success by reading out a letter written, he said, by a British general which advocated permanent conscription. Lloyd George urbanely replied (with his war-time experiences in mind he may well have meant every word he said) that he could not be held responsible for the opinions of every British general, but coalition candidates were subsequently subjected to strong heckling on this subject. When the *Daily News* came out with the claim that 'a vote for the Coalition is a vote for conscription', Lloyd George was forced to the categorical assertion that this was 'a calculated and characteristic falsehood'. In denouncing his opponents, especially the Labour Party, as being tainted with Bolshevism and Pacifism, the coalitionists gave more than they got. Russia could be pointed to as the dread warning when Lloyd George indicted the Labour Party as being 'run by the extreme pacifist, Bolshevist group': pacifist, to the earnest student of the popular press meant a 'funk-hole Cuthbert'; Bolshevist meant a bloodthirsty bearded cossack: but the contradiction apparently went unnoticed.[18] An especially bitter campaign was waged in East Leicester, where Ramsay MacDonald, despite the fact that the local I.L.P. was one of the two strongest in the country, lost his seat. The unpopularity of internationalist ideas, for all the talk of a League of Nations and of a better world, was driven home by the defeat in West Derbyshire of the Earl of Kerry, son of Lord Lansdowne: to lose a Unionist seat in this election was quite an achievement, shared by only seven others.[19] The strength of jingoistic fervour was most clearly demonstrated by the defeat of Asquith, although his Conservative opponent had not in fact been allotted a coupon.

From the first moment it became known that the coalition was going to fight an election as a unity, and in haste, the Liberal opponents of Lloyd George talked of the 'stampede election'. J. M. Keynes carved a permanent niche for this portraiture of the election in his *The Economic Consequences of the Peace,* published in 1919. Professor Mowat has stressed the quietness and sobriety of the contest and the appearance of rival candidates on common platforms, and concludes that 'it is probable that the temper of the campaign has been exaggerated'.[20] 107 out of 707 seats were in fact uncontested. None the less, contained in what Keynes intuitively grasped and so self-consciously embellished, there were profound truths: the general election of 1918 was probably the most critical, and certainly, in the Parliament it produced, the most unfortunate, in Britain's modern history. That the election was held in haste had one supremely important consequence – the failure, despite the parade of soldiers' voting rights and the holding up of the count till 28 December, to secure the suffrage of more than one soldier in four. To many soldiers, already bitten by the bug of disenchantment, the idea of voting, so the *Daily Mail* Parliamentary Bureau in Paris reported, was just a joke; the majority of the others, most of whom did not in practice get the opportunity, intended to vote Labour; the report, so obviously contrary to the political interests of the *Daily Mail,* seems reliable.[21] Altogether between fifty and sixty per cent of the electorate recorded their votes, and rather more than half of those – 5,091,528 in all – voted for the coalition, giving it 484 members, of whom 338 were Conservatives. The line between 'Coalition Unionist' and 'Unionist' *tout court* was not always a very distinct or a very valid one: there were at any rate yet another 44 Conservatives in the House so that, when it became clear that the Irish Sinn Fein candidates were not going to take their seats, the total Conservative contingent amounted to about three-fifths of the entire House of Commons. Labour, for the first time, became the largest opposition party with 59 members. The Asquith Liberals, or 'Wee Frees', secured only 26 seats, though polling more than a million and a quarter votes.

It is the dominant Conservative wall that most deserves analysis into its component bricks, and especial interest attaches to the 168 new members who had had 'something very much like a complimentary ticket to Westminster', as J. M. McEwen, whose brilliant statistical analysis of the election does much to demonstrate the validity of Keynes' flamboyant remarks, puts it.[22] The first remarkable point is that this election ratified and reinforced the changes in the political élite adumbrated in the ministerial appointments of 1916. Traditionally Unionist representation had been dominated by landowners or by businessmen of national eminence: thus of new members returned in January 1910, those in county constituencies were mainly (65 per cent) local men, while those sitting for boroughs were mainly (64 per cent) non-local. Among the new Conservative M.P.s of 1918 it was in the borough constituencies that local men predominated (82 per cent), while the counties now had a majority of outsiders (54 per cent). What these statistics represent is a great swelling in the number of local businessmen on the benches of the powerful Unionist Party; most of them had little or no experience of national politics. The other striking feature about the new Unionist members was that less than a quarter of them were under forty, whereas nearly one half of the re-elected Unionists had been under forty at the time of their own first entry into Parliament. The average age of the whole Parliament was 51 years, 7½ months. The Labour Party representation was not of much higher calibre. The tide of patriotic fervour was so high that MacDonald, Jowett and Henderson were each defeated by members of the jingoistic Labour splinter-group, the National Democratic Party. Only three I.L.P.-financed candidates were returned, all newcomers to Parliament, and the local Labour Parties, which were being formed under the terms of the new constitution, produced a mere seven successful candidates. The mass of the Parliamentary Labour Party consisted of trade union candidates of a solid and uninspiring cast: twenty-five of them were candidates of the Miners' Federation.[23]

It was an old Parliament, and it was an inexperienced Parliament; it was not one with which men returning from the war would find any very close sense of identity. 'Only 68 of the newly elected Unionists,' J. M. McEwen points out, 'had been in uniform during the war, and it should not go unremarked that 27 of them held the rank at least of lieutenant-colonel or its equivalent.'[24] Yet it was still possible to see the election results, not as a massive triumph for reactionary and inexperienced Toryism, but as an overwhelming mandate for Lloyd George to proceed with his reconstruction plans for a better society. 'When the sweeping Election victories were announced in the closing days of 1918,' wrote Evelyn Wrench, 'I was convinced that we were about to witness the greatest constructive job of social reform carried out in our lifetime.'[25]

[II] PLUS ÇA CHANGE...

However genuine Lloyd George's own hopes that he might fulfil his promises and carry through just such a job, he and his colleagues expected to be faced first with a hard battle against the industrial dislocation and unemployment likely to follow hot on the heels of the war. From the analogy of the Napoleonic and Boer wars it was argued that there must be no immediate or indiscriminate demobilization of Britain's vast armies. It was the same pessimism as had been evident in the first days of war, as much the product of an unbalanced insecure society as the hysterical enthusiasm which then, as now, went with it. The first serious planning for orderly demobilization was initiated in the pregnant summer of 1916 when Edwin Montagu was put at the head of a Demobilization Sub-committee of the Cabinet Reconstruction Committee. In August 1917 Montagu's Sub-committee came under the auspices of the new Ministry of Reconstruction, and it was here, with the co-operation of the War Office, the Admiralty, the Air Ministry and the Ministry of Labour, that the master plan was drawn up.[26] With the basic objective of averting mass unemployment it was decided that the priority of a man's release should be based, not on the length of his service, but on the ability of industry to absorb him. Individuals, not whole units, would be demobilized. Accordingly each serviceman was allotted to one of five categories, of which only two, and the Government stipulated that these should be numerically very small, were to be demobilized at once. Within each category, it was agreed, preference should be shown to married men, to those with long records of service, and to those who had served long in the firing line. When the Armistice did come, the Government had to bear in mind that, despite the popular upsurge of emotion, the war was not yet technically at an end, and that it might be desirable to maintain a considerable force in the field in order to secure an acceptable peace treaty; such a force would be less necessary if the Government intended to stand by its more idealistic utterances on the subject of war aims, but it did not; nor did public opinion seem to wish it to do so.

The two favoured categories of servicemen were the 'demobilizers' – those whose services were essential to expedite the demobilization of everybody else – and the 'pivotal men' – those who were vital to the industries of 'reconstruction' and whose employment, it was reckoned, would help to create further jobs. The Ministry of Labour made a selection of businesses and professions which might be regarded in this light, then special authorities within each occupation decided which individual men should be deemed 'pivotal'. To assist in determining allocation to the other three categories use was made of the labour exchanges, where employers seeking the return of specific men filled in a form giving the serviceman's full name, unit, regiment, and theatre of war or command. Each serviceman had to state on a civil employment form which was also filed at the labour exchange whether or not he had received an offer of employment; if he had not he was entitled to request that a particular employer be approached on his behalf. In those cases where the employer's form and the serviceman's form corresponded, a slip was torn from the latter and returned to the man's commanding officer. The relatively lucky individual concerned thus became a 'slip man' and entered the third category, those who were to be released after the start of general demobilization in accordance with priorities determined by the Ministry of Labour on the basis of the relative importance of each trade or profession to the national welfare. There remained a fourth category of those who, though without definite offers of jobs, were normally employed in industries which, being central to the reconstruction effort, were likely to provide work immediately, and a fifth category of all other 'non-slip' men who would be released in the order of importance of their normal civilian occupation.[27]

Partial demobilization did not begin till 9 December, almost a month after the Armistice. Each man now selected in accordance with the grand plan was sent first to a camp behind the lines from whence he proceeded across the Channel to a dispersal station in his own home district. Here the various formalities took about twenty-four hours, in the course of which he acquired a railway warrant, a ration book, an out-of-work donation policy, a civilian clothes allowance and 28 days home leave, together with pay and ration allowances for that period. The out-of-work donation policy was a considerable advance upon the original niggardly intention to use the four-year-old charity-based National Relief Fund to subvent those servicemen who, despite the Government's best-laid demobilization schemes, might find themselves jobless. Without being called upon to make any contribution himself, the ex-serviceman was entitled to benefits of 24s (raised to 29s four days before the general election) for each week he was without employment, with 6s for a first child under fifteen and 3s for each additional child; payments however were restricted to a maximum of twenty weeks out of the first fifty-two following upon demobilization.

At the end of the twenty-eight days furlough, the serviceman became technically demobilized. He was not discharged but transferred to the Z Reserve, thus giving some colour to the conscription scare which arose during the election, and creating much disquiet in the weeks which followed. More than that, the whole scheme was grotesquely misconceived. At its root there was a responsible desire to avoid mass misery and unemployment, but in its effects it demonstrated power rather than responsibility, the prerogative of unenlightened bureaucracy. There was no attempt to deal positively with the problem of the provision of employment, that was left entirely to individual employers. The *Herald* commented satirically on the lot of the serviceman:

We leave the matter of finding him employment to the owners and we present him with cash and promises, which work out to an average of about 9s a week for fifty-two weeks, provided he is unemployed for twenty of them. It is superb, immense. None but an imperial people, victorious against its enemies, but overcome with emotion and thankfulness before its returning heroes could have done it.[28]

The negative endeavours of the scheme simply created a rising curve of unfairness: the man last in was the man most likely to have retained contacts with his civilian employment and therefore most likely to be first out; the man first in was likely to have lost all contact with former employers, and therefore likely to be last out. Even before the unfairness became apparent, the delay in beginning and continuing with demobilization seemed bad enough.

In calling for the men to be sent home at once the *Herald* was not alone:

Munition-making has stopped; motorists can joy ride; the King has a drink; society has had its victory ball and is settling down to its old job of pleasure making.[29]

The Government tried to meet the criticism with three distinct moves. On 13 December it introduced a scheme whereby a serviceman then on leave in Britain, though not yet demobilized, could take up an offer of employment from a pre-war employer if endorsed by the advisory committee of the local employment exchange, always provided that the soldier's service headquarters agreed that he was not indispensable to the armed forces. This 'contracts system', as it was called, though it might secure the release of a few more men, had the main consequence of adding yet another element of chance to the lottery of demobilization, and only served to inflame existing discontent. On 19 December it was announced that the payment of war gratuities would commence forthwith: each man was entitled to a lump sum, ranging from £5 for a private to £15 for a warrant officer, class I, with an additional 10s for each month after the first year of service overseas and 5s for each month after the first year of home service. On the same day Lloyd George appointed Sir Eric Geddes to co-ordinate the demobilization work then being administered by fourteen separate departments.[30]

The new year opened with the publication of the Government's explanation of the slow rate of demobilization: the needs of the army of occupation overseas, and the economic situation at home, it was explained, were paramount considerations; general demobilization had not yet been ordered and only 'pivotal' men, and coal miners, since the country had run into a serious coal crisis, were then being released; apart from this, French and British railway, shipping and port facilities were inadequate.[31] The explanations failed to satisfy those men who were in the most heart-rending position of all: on the point of re-embarkation for France at the termination of a period of leave. On Friday, 3 January, 10,000 soldiers at Folkestone demonstrated against this fate, and the following day 2,000 men demonstrated at Dover. Claiming that the trouble was mainly over the operation of the 'contracts system' the War Office decided to extend the facilities by which men on leave might procure or complete contracts. But the injustice of the system was merely underlined, for those who were not able to profit by the relaxation were ordered back to their units forthwith. At Brighton 8,000 soldiers took part in a mass meeting of complaint on 6 January, and on the same day and the day following, there were demonstrations in Whitehall. Soldiers appeared in lorries with placards which read: 'We won the war. Give us our tickets'; 'Get a move on Geddes'; 'No more red tape'; 'We want civvie suits'; and 'Promises are not piecrust'. Support for the servicemen was forthcoming from all sections of the press, from the *Daily Express* ('Get on or Get out, Geddes') as well as the *Herald*, and from many civic groups, including the Birmingham City Council, which denounced

the incapacity, circumlocution, and general disorder with which the question of demobilization is being dealt with by government departments, leading to general dislocation of business and great disadvantages to the men.[32]

The Army Council brought the contracts system to an abrupt end; then Winston Churchill, War Minister in the Government as it was recast after the election, announced what was in effect the jettisoning of the whole demobilization plan in favour of something nearer to a first-in first-out system, by which all but 900,000 men would be released. From 1 February, in a move to lessen the divide which every day was growing more bitter between soldier and citizen, pay rates in the army of occupation were increased. All this was more reasonable and more equitable, but it congealed into a solid spectre a number of uneasy shadows that had been flitting around for some time. First the fear of deeper military commitment in Russia – a fear, which, at a personal level, had almost certainly influenced the soldiers' demonstrations at the beginning of January; and second the fear of conscription. When the Government sought to give Parliamentary sanction to the retention of 900,000 conscripts beyond, if necessary, the conclusion of a peace treaty, it ran into an ingrained opposition which has endured for fifty years: in an intriguing debate, William Adamson, the Fifeshire miner who now led the Labour Party in the Commons, argued for a 'free' system in which voluntarily enlisted soldiers would be paid a wage on a par with the average earnings of the industrial worker.[33] The opposition of a few coalition members was not sufficient to prevent the measure passing on 6 March. Outside protests continued, both on the Russian and the conscription issue, but as the new demobilization plans were rapidly executed hostility faded. None the less the average serviceman could scarcely but have a feeling of resentment over the handling of his release from military duties; in February 1920 there were still 125,000 men awaiting demobilization.

While society waited for the men to come home, or ignored their very existence, there were a few modest fruits of victory upon which to sustain the joys of the Armistice.

The right to make cakes and pastries of every kind and to cover them with sugar or chocolate or both was restored to Britons on 7 December, 1918, as was the right to eat an unlimited quantity of these or other cakes at afternoon tea.[34]

Pre-war flour returned; street lights blazed again; there was a double meat ration for Christmas 1918. But rationing continued: for meat till November 1919, for butter till early 1920, and for sugar till November 1920. There were still many prosecutions for violation of the food control regulations, coal was in very short supply, and, worst of all, prices of nearly everything took a sharper upward turn than at any time since 1914.[35] Dislocation of trade prolonged scarcities, the burst of speculative investment which began shortly after the Armistice fostered inflation, the sanction of patriotism no longer restrained the would-be profiteer. Shortage of housing and pressure on urban centres brought an extreme rise in rents in 1920.

Wages rose rapidly too, giving rise again to the familiar paradox: a short-term sense of grievance in working-class households concealing a very real long-term gain. A bricklayer in full employment (he suffered, and continued to suffer, from the highly seasonal nature of his employment), earning an average weekly wage of 42s 10d in July 1914, was earning 79s 2d in July 1919, and 100s 7d in July 1920; his labourer's earnings at the same three points in time were 29s 1d, 65s 2d, and 87s 4d. In the engineering and shipbuilding trades a patternmaker's average wage rose from 42s 1d in August 1914, to 86s 8d in February 1920; a riveter earning 37s 9d in August 1914, earned 74s 9d in April 1919, and was earning 80s 5d a year later; the corresponding figures for a labourer were 22s 10d, 58s 3d, and 63s 11d. A compositor working in Sheffield (where wages were lower than in a larger town) was on average paid 36s a week in July 1914, 72s in 1918, and 89s 6d in July 1920. Engine-drivers, earning about 42s a week in 1914 were earning up to 90s in August 1919; firemen had risen from 26s to 66s. The trend towards greater proportionate increases in the poorer-paid employments can be clearly seen in the worst paid of all manual occupations: the agricultural worker who averaged 13s 4d in 1914 was by 1920–21 earning 46s a week. The average income of all working-class families between 1914 and 1920 rose by 100 per cent, which more than cancelled out a rise in the cost of living of 75 per cent. But there were pockets of extreme hardship; large families were hit all round, and above all by soaring milk prices which in the winter of 1919–20 reached $8\frac{1}{2}$d a quart, twopence up on the first winter of peace. A special committee on milk prices reported that

> numerous returns from Food Committees conclusively prove that consumption is being seriously reduced, and inquiries show that in the case of large families of young children the prices are proving a very great hardship.

Many hardships, real and imagined, combined to make 1919 a

year of strikes. As in the first year of war, so in the first year of peace: the watchdogs of the Clyde barked first. Acting in effective unity, the Clyde Workers' Committee and trade union leaders of the older type pressed their claim for a forty-hour week as the best method of absorbing the returning servicemen. A complex of circumstances contributed to the dramatic events which followed: on the labour side the syndicalist tradition kindled anew by revolution accomplished in Russia and attempted in other parts of the world; on the Government side a manifest fear of Bolshevism and its world-wide off-shoots, and a confirmed suspicion of Glasgow as an eternal trouble centre; on both sides the snapping of nerves tautly stretched, and now deprived of war's intoxication. The earlier Clyde strikes had been spontaneous and broad-based, but now, when the war was won and the peace in grave danger of being lost, there was greater working-class solidarity than ever. When the leaders of the forty-hours movement called a general strike on Monday, 27 January, they succeeded completely in all the principal factories: three mass demonstrations took place on the 27th, the 29th and the 31st. The third the Government anticipated by concentrating troops, tanks and machine guns on the city; the actual 'battle of George Square', however, was fought with policemen's truncheons – the police by all accounts being the aggressive party – fists, and bottles of fizzy lemonade. On 1 February the tanks moved in upon the deserted battlefield; the strike continued for a further ten days. A dozen of the leaders were arrested, but only against two could a successful charge be made out, and that scarcely implied any deep subversion of the established order: Willie Gallacher and Emanuel Shinwell were imprisoned for 'inciting to riot'. Looking back ruefully many years later Gallacher unwittingly exposed the whole situation: 'We were carrying on a strike when we ought to have been making a revolution', he wrote. All talk of the likelihood of revolution in Britain in 1919 is quite beside the point, as J. M. Keynes again perceptively observed.[16]

While agitation on Clydeside was met with a demonstration of force, the simultaneous threat of the Miners' Federation to call a strike was met by the appointment of a special statutory Commission with full miners' representation, to investigate the condition of the coal industry. The tanks had conquered a pitch from which the strikers had already retired; the Commission was to produce a report which the Government had no intention of implementing. But the miners were meantime prevailed upon not to strike. A Lancashire cotton-workers' strike in June passed off without great incident. A second London police strike on a rather small scale broke out in August, followed by a more serious one, accompanied by much rioting, in Liverpool: again the armed forces were called in. Most serious of all was the national railway strike which began on 29 September. Although the Government was able to deploy its wartime emergency powers, when the strike ended on 5 October the railwaymen had won their main point, abandonment of a proposed wage cut. From 20 September there was a major strike among the iron-moulders, and this was less easily disposed of – it continued in fact for four months.[17]

Strikes made the headlines, blown up by the press into windy extravaganzas about anarchism and Bolshevism. Since the other critical topic which came nearest home was that of Ireland where the internal war, so clearly presaged in 1914, had by January 1919 effectively begun, newspapers in this first post-war year presented a strikingly similar appearance to those of the last pre-war year. Society, believing itself launched on a voyage to a new and better world, seemed after all to have merely been on the Greenwich ferry.

[III] TYING UP THE LOOSE ENDS

For all that, there were developments of substance, a knitting up of loose threads which added another broad band to the unfolding pattern of social advancement. First in significance is the Housing and Town Planning Act of July 1919, the summation of wartime developments which can, more justly than in any other sector of the social services, be termed revolutionary. House-building had practically ceased during the war, creating a gap so vast that a mighty dynamo would be required to get a spark across it. Commissions of investigation had brought out the iniquity of existing housing conditions. The Government itself stood committed to building 'Homes fit for Heroes'. Heroes and others, in a time of galloping inflation, had become used to the idea of controlled rents. That private enterprise could provide the necessary 600,000 houses was dubious; that it could provide them at the sort of rents people expected to pay was out of the question. While the Salisbury Committee on *Housing in England and Wales*, which reported in October 1917, had tentatively canvassed the idea of intensified State action, the Royal Commission on Housing in Scotland had already indicated the only solution, a massive public initiative in house-building.[38]

The Act, therefore, called upon the local authorities to conduct within three months, and from time to time thereafter, surveys of the housing needs of their areas, to draw up plans for dealing with these needs, and to submit the plans for approval to the Ministry of Health. The first critical feature of the Act is the undertaking given that when these plans had been approved all losses incurred in carrying them out, save for the tiny driblet of a penny rate which the local authorities were to levy, would be borne by the Exchequer. The State, in other words, was assuming direct financial responsibility for a large sector of the future homes of the working classes. The second distinctive feature of the Act is the scheme drawn up for determining the rents to be charged in these new houses. The existing controlled rents of working-class houses were to be taken as a general guide but rents could be varied both above and below this line according to the amenities of the house and, more important, the tenant's capacity to pay. Though it was expected that by 1928 it would be possible in most cases to charge an economic rent, the principle of subsidized accommodation for those most in need was to be maintained. That costs under the Act were sometimes needlessly high was rather the fault of the way in which it was operated than of the Act itself: in providing for the building of local authority housing up till 1921 at a rate equivalent to 70,000 houses a year, let at rents ranging from about 5s a week in rural areas to about 12s a week in parts of London, the Act was not unsuccessful.[39] In that the Minister had powers to insist that the new houses should have fitted baths the Act did help, albeit modestly, to fuel the general movement towards the diffusion of a common material standard throughout society. This for the time being was more important than the long-term consideration that as long as there was both private and public housing, the boundary of the municipal housing estate would tend also to be a boundary of social class.

Aesthetically the houses were not always a great success, and in Scotland their construction marked a departure from the eminently sane, though grossly abused, tradition of tenement dwelling.

Dr Addison did not entirely circumvent private enterprise. The Housing (Additional Powers) Act, which followed rapidly behind the major Act, permitted a small lump sum subsidy for houses built by private enterprise, provided they conformed to certain conditions as to size. Although the finger which the State in 1915 had laid on fast-rising rents had opened out into two copious hands, the original problem had not disappeared. Acts of 1919 and 1920, while permitting substantial increases in controlled rents, extended the scope of control to cover houses built before the summer of 1919 which had rateable values of up to £105 in London, £90 in Scotland, and £78 elsewhere.

The Housing Act of 1919 and the Education Act of 1918 are the two major examples of the burgeoning of collectivist social action during the war era. A third is the Unemployment Insurance Act of 1920. The wartime additions to the rather limited 1911 Act have already been noted, as has the post-war 'out-of-work donation', which, despite the contempt of the *Herald*, had a certain significance – paid to both ex-service men and women, and war workers, and having no insurance basis whatever, it broke the tight bonds of the existing National Insurance structure. The principal Act of 1920 developed the idea of including nearly all wage-earners within its embrace, but sought to assert the strict insurance principle – the embrace was to be that of a Victorian father. Included were all wage-earners save for non-manual workers earning more than £250 per annum, Civil Servants, soldiers and schoolteachers, and farm labourers and domestic servants. A weekly contribution of 10d per week for men, shared, as in the 1911 Act, between employee, employer and the State, yielded an unemployment benefit of 15s per week for a maximum of 15 weeks in any one year, provided a minimum of twelve contributions had been made, and provided that though capable of work the applicant had been genuinely unable to find any. The confines of the scheme may seem more obvious than the breadth of commitment in fact assumed by the State; but when the melting snows of mass unemployment poured in after 1921, it was the confines which were easily swept away. It is true that

the major extensions of social benefits in the twenties owed more
to adverse economic circumstance than to the intentions of the
framers of the 1920 Act; but the Act itself was very much the
product of wartime developments, and of the desire to mitigate
the economic dislocation expected as the aftermath of war.

The wartime experiment of running the railways as a consolidated national service rather than as a series of private profit-
making agencies was widely held to have vindicated itself
triumphantly, and in 1919 a Bill for the establishment of a Ministry
of Ways and Communications with powers to buy up, by Order
in Council, all railways, canals and docks, was introduced. But
in the struggle between the Good Fairy Reconstruction and the
Bad Fairy Bolshevism, the purchase clauses dropped off, and the
putative Ministry of Ways and Communications shrank to a
mere Ministry of Transport. When Government control finally
expired in 1921, the 130-odd railway companies of pre-war days
were grouped into the Big Four, the London and North Eastern,
the London Midland and Scottish, the Great Western, and the
Southern. Important safeguards for the community were preserved in the form of a new Railway Rates Tribunal, and in
elaborate, though not very effective, conciliation machinery for
dealing with labour disputes.

Even where there was no Government-imposed amalgamation,
the phase of accelerated private industrial combination clearly
detectable during the war reached its culmination at the end of
the war. In the first half of 1919 the 43 chief banking concerns
of 1914 became the Big Five, with a powerful hold on British
trade and industry. Lever Brothers took a further gulp at their
smaller competitors; Vickers Maxim amalgamated with Metro-
politan Carriage Works; a group of financiers acquired and
greatly extended Guest, Keen and Nettlefolds.[40] So manifest were
these developments that the Government appointed a Committee
on Trusts to investigate them.[41] A minority consisting of Ernest
Bevin, the trade union leader, J. A. Hobson, W. H. Watkins, and
Sidney Webb, the Fabian, concluded that in certain industries
combination had gone so far as to render them ripe for public
ownership. J. M. Rees, who wrote a study of the problem based
on the report of the Committee, reached a similar conclusion.[42]
The collectivists indeed were now happily having it both ways:

a highly fragmented industry had to be nationalized because it was inefficient; a highly concentrated one because it was a menace.

On the other side of industry there was a counterpart to industrial combination in the amalgamation and consolidation of trade unions which took place in the immediate post-war years. The Iron and Steel Trades Confederation had been established in 1917; the Amalgamated Engineering Union was established in 1920; and the Transport and General Workers' Union in 1921. In part these amalgamations, though they did not go anything like the length desired by the advocates of industrial unionism, marked a permanent triumph over the old sectionalism which had been submerged in the wartime 'unofficial' struggles. The new-found unity, purpose and confidence were expressed in the creation in 1921 of a permanent General Council to replace the old Parliamentary Committee of the T.U.C. Trade union membership figures which had reached $6\frac{1}{2}$ million in 1918 soared to $8\frac{1}{3}$ million by 1920.

After looking at the advances made by labour in the earlier part of the war, we turned to the advances made by women. The stop-go nature of the legislation of 1919 is illustrated in the last chapter of the story of the emancipation of women which falls within our purview. In November 1918, just before the election, an Act was rushed through making women eligible to stand for Parliament. After the election the Labour Party introduced a Women's Emancipation Bill to remove every remaining legal inequality between men and women. The Bill passed all stages in the Commons, but the Government had it defeated in the Lords, bringing in instead its own Sex Disqualification Bill which duly became law. This weaker measure opened jury service, the magistracy and the legal profession to women, and gave them qualified entry to the upper reaches of the Civil Service; it was made clear that there was in law no barrier to their full membership of the ancient Universities of Oxford and Cambridge. Political emancipation was indeed, as the suffragists had always said it would be, followed by a spate of social and economic legislation affecting women. But the new Affiliation Orders Act of 1918 was by no means abandoned in its generosity: it increased the five shillings maximum maintenance allowance of the Bastardy Laws Act of 1872 to ten shillings.

[IV] CUTTING THEM AGAIN

That the collectivist idea which had been applied so potently to
the problems of housing and unemployment insurance would not
be strong enough to secure the prolongation or extension of the
wartime control of the major sectors of industry could not have
been clearly foreseen at the time of the Armistice: indeed the very
concept of reconstruction had seemed to imply some such control.
However, with the return to peace, private enterprise recovered
its voice. The day after the Armistice, Sir J. Walton unleashed in
the House of Commons a tirade against the Government bureaucrats: 'every trade and industry that they have touched they have
hampered and injured'.[43] One day later the Executive Committee
of the F.B.I. turned its sights upon the National Factories and
declared that they must not be used 'for the purpose of State
trading under conditions which will inevitably be unfair to private
enterprise'.[44] An impressive array of industrial chieftains gathered
on 16 January 1919 in a joint meeting of the F.B.I., the Associated Chambers of Commerce of the United Kingdom, the Mansion
House Association on Railway and Canal Traffic, the Traders'
Traffic Conference, the Pressed Brick Manufacturers' Association,
the Furniture Warehousemen and Removers' Association, the
Horticultural Traders' Association of Great Britain and Ireland,
the National Federation of Fruit and Potato Trades' Association,
and Messrs. Butterley and Co. Ltd., to pass a unanimous resolution against nationalization of the railways.[45] As the war receded
behind the golden horizon of the post-war boom the anti-collecti-
vist sentiment of the employing class hardened, though there continued, in the light of recent experience, to be reservations and
qualifications. Thus although the Executive of the F.B.I. at its
meeting on 26 March 1919 was clearly worried by what it called 'the
present strong efforts to commit the country to a policy of nationalization', and set up a special committee to watch the situation,
it also remarked that 'some measure of national control might
conceivably be a good thing in some industries'.[46] However, in
the F.B.I. Report on Nationalization, published in 1919, the
reservations were minimal, the old principles supreme:

We would begin by laying it down as a general proposition that centralized management by a Government Department is fatal to commercial efficiency and enterprise. . . . We desire to record our emphatic opinion that in dealing with industries or public services of whatever class, whether local or national, any further extension of state monopoly should be avoided. . . .[47]

The anxiety betrayed in these activities and resolutions was justified, for from 3 March the Royal Commission on the coal industry, appointed to avert a miners' strike, was effectively putting private enterprise on trial. The Commission consisted of four members appointed by the Government, the Hon. Justice Sankey (Chairman), Arthur Balfour, Sir Arthur Duckham, and Sir Thomas Royden; four members appointed by the Miners' Federation of Great Britain, Robert Smillie, Herbert Smith, Frank Hodges, and Sir Leo Chiozza Money; two members agreed between the Government and the miners, R. H. Tawney and Sidney Webb; and three members appointed by the coal owners, R. W. Cooper, J. T. Forgie, and Evan Williams. In an interim report published at the end of March, the four Government nominees declared:

Even upon the evidence already given, the present system of ownership and working in the coal industry stands condemned, and some other system must be substituted for it, either nationalization or a method of unification by national purchase and/or by joint control.[48]

A separate interim report of the miners' representatives along with Tawney and Webb, found that

in the interests of the consumers as much as in that of the miners, nationalization ought to be, in principle, at once determined upon.[49]

The three coal-owners' representatives made no pronouncement at this stage on these larger issues, confining themselves to the more mundane question of wages.[50]

In the second stage of the Commission's inquiries weighty considerations were put forward both for and against nationalization; what is striking is the number of the former which were based on the wartime experience. E. H. Davies of the Mines

Department of the Board of Trade was enthusiastic about the Coal Transport Reorganization Scheme operated during the war; Sir Richard Redmayne, Secretary to the Coal Controller, while unsure about nationalization, favoured 'collective production' and regarded the existing system as 'extravagant and wasteful';[51] William Blane, a mining engineer and large-scale employer, who worked in the War Office between 1915 and 1919 as Assistant Director of Army Contracts, supported the principle of nationalization, as did Arthur Greenwood,[52] successively Lecturer in Economics at Leeds, Assistant Secretary to the Ministry of Reconstruction, and Labour Parliamentary candidate, and A. E. Davies, General Manager of the Banking Corporation. When A. J. Hobson (not to be confused with J. A. Hobson, the economist, who favoured nationalization[53]) on behalf of the Council of the Associated Chambers of Commerce declared that the nationalization of the telephone had introduced what he called a 'forty per cent factor of inefficiency' he was controverted by F. J. Pearson,[54] Assistant Accountant-General for the Post Office, and Sir William Slingo, Engineer-in-Chief to the Post Office.[55] The most illuminating remark of all was that of Sir Keith Price, a businessman who had been brought into the War Office in November 1914, who believed that in wartime Government control had worked well, but 'in peace time the reverse would be the case'.[56]

The second stage concluded with the presentation by the Commission of four separate reports.[57] First there was that of Sankey alone,[58] which in advocating State ownership was fully supported in the separate report presented by Money, Smillie, Smith, Hodges, Tawney and Webb.[59] The third report, that of Sir Adam Nimmo (who had replaced Forgie who became ill), Sir Allan Smith (who replaced Royden), Balfour, Cooper, and Evan Williams, was categorically opposed to nationalization.[60] A fourth report was presented by Sir Arthur Duckham, who although opposed to nationalization, advocated 'district unification'.[61] The verdict was perhaps only a degree or two clearer than mud; it did incline towards nationalization. That such a consummation was devoutly to be rejected was announced to Parliament by Lloyd George on 18 August. Coal Control ended on 31 March 1921, though the Mining Industry Act of 1920 had meantime created a special Mines Department of the Board of Trade with the powers

relating to mines and quarries formerly exercised by the Home
Office and additional ones which permitted it to make schemes for
the drainage of mines and to establish a welfare fund by a levy of
1d a ton on coal produced.

Controls now fell thick and fast as autumn leaves.[62] The
Treasury waged a war of attrition against the Ministry of
Food, whose continued existence was fully justified by the
scarcity and inflationary conditions of the immediate post-
war years. It and the Ministry of Munitions were abolished in
March 1921. The liquor licensing situation was stabilized by the
Licensing Act of August 1921, which, while ending the régime of
the Liquor Control Board and returning full jurisdiction to the
local justices, applied the new licensing hours to the whole country
instead of just to the wartime controlled areas. The administration
of the State schemes at Carlisle and Gretna was transferred to the
Home Office. The permanent limitation on drinking implied in
the 1921 Act was adventitiously reinforced by the coming into
effect in 1920 of the 1913 Temperance (Scotland) Act, which
permitted local option: polls were held in 584 out of 1,215 areas
yielding the following results: 'no change' in 511 areas, limitation
in 37, and 'no licence' in 36.

The return to economic orthodoxy was most completely
demonstrated in the reports of the Balfour Committee and the
Cunliffe Committee. The former, while divided on the question of
free trade, with a strong minority advocating a general 10 per
cent tariff, was firm in its advocacy of a rapid demolition of State
control;[63] the latter cheerfully pinned its faith in the Bank Charter
Act of 1844 and recommended an eventual return to the Gold
Standard.[64] It recognized, however, that the internal circulation
of gold sovereigns had gone for good, as indeed it had. In its
decontrol policies the Government was actuated by the belief
that it was doing the best thing for the stimulus of post-war
industry. Exclusively wartime measures obviously had to go,
and the sooner the better. However, the hope and encouragement
stirred in collectivist breasts by the wartime innovations could not
be permanently stilled; correspondingly the fears aroused among
last-ditch individualists could not be allayed either. A Conservative Party leaflet of 1919 claimed to the credit of the Government in time of war that it had 'carried on war industries',

'controlled other industries', 'organized shipping' and 'organized food supplies'.[65] But a leaflet of 1920 declared:

Nationalization has never been tried on a large scale in this country, and where it has been tried – in Germany and Bolshevik Russia – it has proved a hopeless failure, compared with individual enterprise.[66]

The Federation of British Industries was able in the same year to bring home the full horror of nationalization by quoting M. Constantin Grunwald, General Secretary to the Russian Manufacturers' Association in London, as saying:

You cannot get nails in the Soviet shop, but a boy will be standing in the street offering you those same nails in a surreptitious way.[67]

Although on its final accounts the Ministry of Food actually made a small profit, *The Times*, whistling to keep its courage up, misleadingly reported the facts under such headings as 'State Trading Losses', 'Auditor's Strong Criticisms' and 'A Record of Waste'. Similarly the economic successes of the Carlisle experiment were grossly travestied.[68]

Till the late summer of 1920, Government, industry and society enjoyed boom conditions, then came the crash that led into the long inter-war depression. The index number of prices, standing at 192 in 1918, 206 in 1919, 265.1 at the peak in April 1920, collapsed to 155 in 1921 and 131 in 1922. The froth was off the pint, and what lay underneath was worse than anything purveyed under liquor control. Old markets had gone, others had shrunk; the world had too many ships, preferred oil to coal, was trying to operate the delicate nineteenth-century supply and demand mechanism when the conditions in which that had worked not too badly had been irreparably shattered. Unemployment, which averaged 3·1 per cent in the latter half of 1920 rose to 13·5 per cent in 1921 and 13·8 per cent in 1922. The Government reacted in the worst possible way: 'reconstruction, when not dropped into the dustbin, was put on the shelf'.[69] In the passion for economy of 1921, even the Fisher and Addison Acts were affected. It became clear that there was no prospect at all of the school-leaving age being raised to fifteen; such continuation

classes as had been formed were slowly strangled. Similarly the
Addison policy was effectively terminated in July 1921, when a
limit of about 170,000 was set on the number of houses to be
allotted a subsidy. Providing homes fit for heroes had become too
expensive; 'the heroes would have to go without'.[70] Heavy and
continuous unemployment certainly forced upon the Government greater and greater responsibility for providing unemployment benefits in which the insurance element was mere myth.
But for the man who would have preferred the Government to
create work for him this was no great boon.

Reconstruction turned to retrenchment, the land fit for heroes
became the waste land. What of the world outside, now that the
war to end war, the war to make the world safe for democracy,
was over? What of the cries for hanging the Kaiser, the promises
to make Germany pay? The Peace Treaty concluded at Versailles
on 28 June 1919 did as much as was humanly possible to reconcile these different objectives. Hanging the Kaiser was out of the
question as Lloyd George probably knew in advance of the
general election, since the Kaiser had fled to Holland where his
hosts were not willing to give him up. But Article 231 of the
Treaty declared that Germany was to pay reparations for the entire
cost of the war. Articles 1 to 26 established the dream of all pro-
gressives, and the noblest product of the war, a League of
Nations. Some men of the Left certainly were critical of what they
called a 'League of Victorious Allies' when what they wanted was
a 'League of Peoples', by which they meant a league representative of all shades of opinion within a country, not just of governments; but before long the whole Labour Party was united in its
championship of, to misquote what Mr R. A. Butler has said in a
different connexion, 'the best League we've got'. Within the
Conservative Party Lord Robert Cecil became an enthusiastic, and
eventually somewhat lonely, publicist for the League. But in 1919
a Conservative leaflet welcomed it in the words 'out of evil
cometh good'.[71]

There was a Peace, and there was a League of Nations. Yet
there was no peace, and the nations were divided. There were
revolutionary insurrections followed by reactionary repression
throughout the world. Allied forces were still involved in Russia.
The 'troubles' had broken out in Ireland. In the summer of 1920 it

appeared that the Government was about to intervene on the side
of Poland in the Russo-Polish war: an extraordinary demonstration of labour hostility to such a 'crime against humanity', induced
second thoughts.[72] If the country had not become pacifist it had
certainly become war-weary. The desire to hang the Kaiser, never
gratified, became a matter of shame, like an unsated debauch.

Three quarters of a million men were killed in the war, nearly
two million wounded. That in itself was a serious physical loss and
a deep wound in the social consciousness. Disillusionment had
broken upon the more sensitive at various times during the war;
the majority remained in a state of intoxication, or, for those in
the armies, in a state of suspended judgement. On the whole hopes
were high in 1918, and even in 1919, as to what great goals might
now be achieved. Waiting for an interview in the Warden's
lodgings of All Souls, E. L. Woodward, a good representative
of the middle-class volunteer of 1914 (when he was in his mid-
twenties), who later become a distinguished and level-headed
historian, reckoned that the survivors of his generation,

would be able to use in peace their experience learned in war. I thought
that the future was in our hands; that we should get the support of those
immediately younger than ourselves; that our elders would listen to us,
and, for very shame, be ready to give us a directing control over the
management of affairs.[73]

In fact the election of 1918 had already entrenched the elderly in
power, and the elderly enacted the policies of retrenchment. The
grains of disillusionment were sown in the mudflats of war, but it
was the post-war let-down which brought on the harvest of
bitter rice. Woodward constructed moving words upon the
bitterness he came to feel,

in the first few years after the war, about the hollow words used too
often at the unveiling of war memorials. Glib words about the 'Great
Sacrifice'. I know that in many cases these words were used with deep
feeling by men who had lost their own sons. They became almost a
cliché in the oratory of politicians. Laurence Binyon's noble words
'they shall not grow old as we who are left grow old' took on an ironic
meaning in the mouths of speakers who were well content to grow old
and fat, and who had never asked the dead whether they had chosen to

die young in order to avoid old age. As time went on, I began to dislike more and more the celebration of Armistice Day. I wished that all the formal ceremonies might be abandoned, and that this commemoration of the dead could be left to those for whom it had some personal meaning. Darkness is not better than light, death is not better than life; no praise from comfortable men can bring the dead back to the sun they loved. It was too easy for the older generation to find a convenient anodyne in the formal politeness of a two-minutes' silence, in the weaving of wreaths, in the provision of adequate pensions for widows and orphans.[74]

This was a disillusionment which could not but be shared by men of all classes, as Government promises collapsed and industry went into stagnation. It marked the post-war decade. Yet it was only clearly and articulately expressed by a handful of middle-class poets and prose-writers. The working classes had always had their battles to fight. Owning so little in 1914, they had lost so much less over the war period. They and society as a whole had many gains to enter in the ledger along with the losses.

NOTES TO CHAPTER EIGHT

1. Local Government Board, *Report of Medical Department 1918–1919*; P.P., 1919, XXIV, Cmd. 462. *Report on Influenza Epidemic of 1918–1919*; P.P., 1920, X, Cmd. 700. *Report on Influenza Epidemic in Scotland 1918–1919*; P.P., 1919, X, Cmd. 282.

2. McDonagh, *In London During the Great War*, pp. 232 ff. *The Times*, 5 June 1918. R. Groves, 'When 12,000 London Policemen went on Strike' in *Socialist Outlook*, 22 January 1954.

3. *Daily News*, 10 October 1918.

4. McDonagh, p. 321 (17 October 1918).

5. ibid., p. 325 (9 November 1918), p. 327 (11 November 1918).

6. H. Williamson, *A Soldier's Diary of the Great War*, p. 252 (11 November 1918).

7. C. Edmonds, *A Subaltern's War*, p. 204. Montague, *Disenchantment*, p. 31. See the imaginative description in R. Aldington, *Roads to Glory*, 1930, pp. 35–45.

8. C. S. Peel, *How We Lived Then*, p. 173.

9. Wrench, *Struggle 1914–20*, p. 352. McDonagh, p. 328. See also C. E. Playne, *Britain Holds On, 1917–18*, 1933, pp. 392–5.

10. McDonagh, p. 329.

11. Briggs, *History of Birmingham*, p. 225.

12. In Alec Waugh's novel *The Loom of Youth*.

13. Quoted by Briggs, *History of Birmingham*, p. 225.

14. McDonagh, p. 333.

15. T. Wilson, 'The Coupon and the British General Election of 1918' in *Journal of Modern History*, March 1964.

16. G. D. H. Cole, *History of the Labour Party since 1914*, 1948, p. 83.

17. *The Times*, 24, 31 November, 10, 12 December 1918.

18. *Manchester Guardian*, 11, 13 December 1918. *Daily News*, 11, 12 December 1918. *The Times*, 14 December 1918.

19. See J. M. McEwan, 'The Coupon Election of 1918 and the Unionist Members of Parliament', *Journal of Modern History*, 1962, pp. 294 ff.

20. C. L. Mowat, *Britain Between the Wars*, 1955, p. 5.

21. *Daily Mail*, 30 December 1918.

22. McEwan, p. 295. The figures cited in the following sentences are taken from McEwan's valuable article.

23. Cole, *History*, pp. 83-8.

24. McEwan, p. 300.

25. Wrench, *Struggle 1914-20*, p. 423.

26. *Report of Ministry of Reconstruction to 31 December 1918;* P.P., 1918, XIII, Cd. 923:, p. 1. *Report of War Cabinet for 1918;* P.P., 1919, XXX, Cmd. 325, p. 301.

27. On these and the next two paragraphs see S. R. Graubard, 'Military Demobilisation in Britain following the First World War', in *Journal of Modern History*, 1947, pp. 297 ff., and sources there cited.

28. *The Herald*, 23 November 1918, quoted by Graubard.

29. ibid., 7 December 1918.

30. *The Times*, 20 December 1918.

31. ibid., 1 January 1919.

32. Quoted by Graubard (on whose article the preceding paragraph is based), p. 302.

33. *House of Commons Debates*, 27 February 1919 (cols. 677-8).

34. Beveridge, *British Food Control*, p. 269.

35. A. L. Bowley, *Prices and Incomes 1914-20*, p. 35.

36. Gallacher, *Revolt on the Clyde*, p. 221. J. M. Keynes, *The Economic Consequences of the Peace*, 1919, p. 237. Cp. 'Revolution Averted' in R. Graves and A. Hodge, *The Long Week End*, 1940.

37. Mowat, *Britain between the Wars*, pp. 38-40.

38. *Housing in England and Wales;* P.P., 1918, XXVI, Cmd. 9087. P.P., 1917-18, XIV, Cmd. 8731.

39. See esp. M. Bowley, *Housing and the State*, 1945, pp. 15-25.

40. *Report of Committee on Trusts;* P.P., 1918, XIII, Cmd. 9236.

41. ibid.

42. J. M. Rees, *Trusts in British Industry 1914-21*, 1922, pp. 252-5.

43. *House of Commons Debates*, 12 November 1918.

44. Federation of British Industries, *Annual Report 1918-19*, p. 12.

45. *Bulletin of the Federation of British Industries*, 16 January 1919.

46. ibid., 31 March 1919.

47. Federation of British Industries, *The Control of Industry: Nationalisation and Kindred Problems*, 1919, pp. 2, 4.

48. P.P., 1919, XI, Cmd. 84, p.5.

49. P.P., 1919, XI, Cmd. 85, p. 3.

50. P.P., 1919, XI, Cmd. 86.

51. P.P., 1919, XI, Cmd. 359, pp. 79–89, 222–40.

52. P.P., 1919, XII, Cmd. 360, pp. 950, 545–8.

53. ibid., pp. 473–6.

54. Cmd. 359, pp. 174, 181–2.

55. Cmd. 360, p. 474.

56. ibid., p. 1001.

57. P.P., 1919, XI, Cmd. 210.

58. p. 5.

59. p. 27.

60. p. 35.

61. pp. 56–7.

62. See R. H. Tawney, 'The Abolition of Economic Controls 1918–21' in *Economic History Review*, 1943, on which this paragraph is based.

63. P.P., 1918, XIII, Cd. 9035, pp. 25–6, 44–53, 67–8.

64. P.P., 1919, XIII, Cmd. 464, p. 3.

65. National Union of Conservative Associations, *The Government Record in War and Peace*, 1919.

66. National Union of Conservative Associations, *Labour and the Labour Party*, 1920.

67. *Bulletin of Federation of British Industries*, 19 January 1920.

68. Beveridge, p. 330. Shadwell, *Drink in 1914–22*, pp. 127–8.

69. Tawney, p. 8.

70. M. Bowley, *Housing and the State*, pp. 22, 26.

71. National Union of Conservative Associations, *The League of Nations to prevent War*, 1919.

72. Cole, *History*, pp. 103–7.

73. Woodward, *Short Journey*, p. 114.

74. ibid., p. 116.

CHAPTER NINE

After the Deluge

---

[1] DADDY, WHAT DID THE GREAT WAR DO TO YOU?

WHERE HISTORY differs as a scholarly pursuit from a science is in the inability of the historian to conduct anything in the nature of a controlled experiment. In summarizing analytically the material presented chronologically in the course of this book, we find that there are not many topics in which we can say this or that was caused by the war, *and nothing but the war*. If we attempt to list the bed-rock direct consequences of the war, we shall find that we are dealing as much with the *method* by which the war affected society as with the actual effects in society.

The direct consequences, which we can limit to seven, reacted with a multiplicity of other forces creating a tremendous range of side effects and indirect consequences. First and second are the obvious tangibles, the loss of life and limb, and the destruction of what contemporary writers liked to call 'treasure'. Third is the wholesale disruption caused by the war in the old mechanism of international trade and finance. Fourth is the huge physical demand of the war for manpower and machines, which, given, of course, the deeper pressure of the will to survival, created an irresistible pressure for the reorganization and reorientation of society; what forms the reorganization took, what lessons were learned from it, depended on other circumstances, but the immediate and eventual ramifications were immense. Fifth is the way in which the war, in one sense the ultimate expression of the German challenge to British supremacy, brought to Britain a sharp sense of her deficiencies and a sharp determination to remedy them. Sixth is the mass of domestic problems piled up by the war's interruption of normal social development. Seventh is the scale, horror, and excitement of the war, calling forth all sorts of different responses from all sorts of different people, and necessitating the mobilization, not just of men and machines, but of minds, which in turn created all kinds of reactions and by-products.

The loss of 745,000 of the country's younger men (leaving aside the unknown proportion of the 1·6 million wounded who were gravely mutilated) amounting to about 9 per cent of all men under 45, meant a definite alteration in the population balance, which can be presented with reasonable statistical precision, but whose full emotional effects cannot be precisely assessed. In 1911 there were 155 males aged between 20 and 40 per thousand of the population in England and Wales; in 1921, for every thousand of the population, there were only 141. The balance of females over the age of 14, therefore (discounting any other minor factors involved), rose from 595 per thousand in 1911 to 638 per thousand in 1921, and the proportion of widows per thousand of the population rose from 38 to 43.[1] There is no exact measure of the quantity of personal agony concealed behind these figures, but society, in later years, exhibited all the signs of having suffered a deep mental wound, of having undergone a traumatic experience, to which the agony and the slaughter, as well as the more generalized horror over the destruction of an older civilization and its ways, which we shall consider in a moment, contributed. In the inter-war years the birth rate declined even further than it had in Edwardian times, but although the loss in the war of potential fathers was a contributory factor a later Royal Commission concluded that it was not in itself a significant one.[2] Other by-products of the war – the wider diffusion of contraceptives or the pruning of large family establishments for example – reacted within the broader trend. Already by 1921 the average number of children under 14 per family had declined from 1·29 to 1·12, bringing the important incidental consequence of a raising of living standards.[3]

Much was written in the years after 1918 on 'the lost generation'. We have seen the statistical basis – one in ten of the generation aged between 20 and 45 during the war, missing. What the figures do not make so clear, but what has often been pointed out, is that the missing were the cream of the generation, the first volunteers, the junior officers; out of Oxford University's total roll of service of 14,561, 2,680 were killed.[4] A faint touch of myth, perhaps, was mixed with the grim reality, which was mainly stressed by those articulate men who had themselves been Oxford men, junior officers, early volunteers. Society, very hesitantly, was turning towards the idea of choosing the occasional leader elsewhere than from the university officer class, but there is no doubt that much of the political weakness of Britain in the inter-war years can be attributed to the paucity of young talent of quality. To avoid getting one's generations hopelessly mixed, it is worth recalling that the survivors of the lost generation were men like Clement Attlee and Harold Macmillan, who reached political eminence in the forties and fifties, when they were not noticeably deficient in colleagues of high calibre. Where the loss of the tithe of a generation did also seem to make itself felt – this is problematical ground – was in the weakening of any possible mediatory agency between the old generation, entrenched in power by virtue of the Coupon Election, and the young generation which grew up in the maelstrom years of the war.

While the wartime damage to Britain's capital assets (with the notable exception of shipping) was not of great significance, the immense financial cost of the war, through the high taxation which it necessitated and the inflationary trend which it created, did have powerful social effects. First of all the trend towards the compression of disposable incomes intensified, drawing classes closer together, making it difficult for the upper classes, and very nearly impossible for the middle classes, to maintain the lavish standards of pre-war days. Secondly the landed classes received the final series of blows, which, in combination with other political developments, finally knocked them out of their political and social primacy. Thirdly, as the 'tax line' dropped to incomes of £130 at the same time as working-class earnings began to rise above this figure, it virtually ceased to exist as the sort of social demarcation that it had been in Edwardian times. The sale of War Savings Certificates was another financial expedient which contributed to this spreading of the pale of respectable citizenship.

The dislocations of the old international economic system were extremely serious for a trading nation such as Britain and created problems which helped to give rise to mass unemployment in the inter-war years. But the immediate effect was to demonstrate the falsity of many of the economic dogmas associated with that system. Despite the effective departure from gold, the economy not only survived, but was able to produce enormous sums of money for the prosecution of the war. It almost began to look as though economics could be the servant of man, rather than man the servant of economics. The same conclusion could be drawn from the vast experiment in state control developed step by step to meet the needs of war. The lesson was not immediately learned: what was wrong with Britain in the twenties was that she suffered from what the war had done, and failed to profit from what the war had taught – her governments were composed of sadder but not wiser men. But the story does not end there. In the first place the precedents had been set, establishing in fact a new measure of tolerance for large-scale State intervention. Thus the collectivist measures which were enacted at the end of the war, the big ones like the Housing Act and the Unemployment Insurance Act, and, later, the setting up of the B.B.C., and the little ones like the establishment of the Forestry Commission in 1919, created little stir. In the second place ideas which could in pre-war years be laughed off as Utopian fantasies, denounced as contrary to economic law, or displayed as evidence of the sinister intentions of socialism, had been put to work and had been seen to work. In the years after the war, as the country entered upon economic depression and mass unemployment, more and more political thinkers began to argue that escape could only come through the revival of some of the policies of the war years. In 1927 four young Conservatives, Robert Boothby, Harold Macmillan, John de V. Loder and the Hon. Oliver Stanley pointed out that:

The war period shattered preconceived economic notions, proved possible theoretic impossibilities, removed irremovable barriers, created new and undreamt-of situations. Yet by far the greater part of the legislation which today governs trade and industry dates from before that period. We are surely entitled to ask whether it is now adequate to meet the vastly changed conditions of the modern economic era.[5]

Under the impact of the great crash of 1931 collectivist economic policy was greatly extended in the thirties; it became dominant in the nineteen-forties, and although there have been slight relaxations since then, no serious politician today, save perhaps Mr Enoch Powell, would contemplate a return to the orthodoxy of Edwardian Britain.

The shortage of manpower contributed along with the other shortages to the wartime extension of State control, but its main effects were more subtle. The working class as a social class, though suffering many hardships and grievances, derived a number of permanent advantages from their favourable market position – wage rates were doubled, the average working week was reduced from 55 hours to 48 – and, more important still, they got a taste of the better material comforts of modern civilization. That the working class made as much as it did of its favourable situation was in large measure due to the efforts of the organized labour movement, which was already developing in strength and cohesion before 1914; but the need of the Government for the co-operation of the leaders of the labour movement in maximizing the war effort meant that they also gained immensely in prestige and status, even to the extent of taking Cabinet office. The political side of the movement, the Labour Party, was strengthened sufficiently for it to be able to wring advantage from the divisions and weaknesses in the Liberal Party. The working man, in factory or mine, or conscripted into the army, not only was, but was seen to be, fully implicated in the country's survival. A handful at least of politicians and opinion-makers began to stress his claim upon a fuller citizenship, making this claim a major motivation behind the extension of the franchise in 1918, and one among several behind the social legislation of the same period.

The gaps in the home front left by men summoned to the fighting front had to be filled, and they could only be filled by women, and, to a lesser extent, by children. The manner in which the situation was exploited owed much to the experience the women's leaders had derived from the pre-war suffrage movements; it is also true that before the war the doors to a number of professions were already slowly opening. Yet it is difficult to see how women could have achieved so much in anything like a similar time-span without the unique circumstances arising from the war. Almost certainly when the time came for a further Reform Act in the great series extending back to 1832 they would, or some of them would, have been included in the new franchise, and the vote would no doubt have assisted the fight for further economic, social and civic freedoms. But the war brought opportunity in concentrated and varied form, and from the stock of patriotic bombast paid the women a valuable bonus: men and women joined together to praise women's contribution to the war effort, bringing a confidence in their new role to women, and an acceptance of it among men, which might otherwise not have been easy to create.

The straight demand for mighty weapons of offence and defence inevitably gave a great prestige to science and a stimulus to technological, if not scientific, research. At least as important an influence on public and private research, however, was the sense of insecurity and desperate challenge brought home to British society by the war. In the really major advances of twentieth-century science the war was totally irrelevant, and Sir Charles Parsons rightly pointed out that

the work of the scientists during the war has perforce been directed more to the application of known principles, trade knowledge, and the properties of matter to the waging of war than to the making of new and laborious discoveries.[6]

Yet even from such work there came developments – aviation and broadcasting being two of the most striking – of the utmost importance for society in time of peace. The two major features of the process were the desire of commercial companies to exploit the new technological potential they had developed for purposes of war, and the creation, through the drama of war, of a popular interest in, and appetite for, such developments. It must, however, always be borne well in mind that science is international, and that the influence of war was often very secondary to the influence of, in particular, the United States of America.

The interruption by the war of normal domestic, social and economic development undoubtedly contributed to the economic ailments of the inter-war years. At the same time by inflating such problems as housing and education to enormous size it brought them within the vision of the most myopic politician. The will to action was enhanced by the contemporary collectivist experience, by the need to appease the working class and the desire to accord its members some of the privileges of citizenship, and above all by the present supreme struggle which brought out Britain's defects in the physical well-being of her people, as it had exposed her weaknesses in scientific equipment. Here is part, the major part, of the explanation for the burst of social reform at the end of the war. We must qualify it by recollecting what the Wickwars[7] stress in discussing the Addison Housing Act, that the collectivist 'tendency was already at work before the war of 1914'. They then add that 'the end of the war gave an illusion of dramatic suddenness to what might otherwise have been a gradual and almost imperceptible process'. But in this book, following Miss Marion Bowley,[8] I have described the Housing Act in its scope and provisions as revolutionary. In reality, there is no conflict: the problem is the same as that involved in the new freedoms gained by women – no doubt they would have come eventually as an 'almost imperceptible process', but in fact, because of the war, they came in a sudden burst. Similarly, by an only slightly less direct train of causation, the Housing Act, and the other social legislation, in the form in which it actually came, was a consequence of the war.

But what were the consequences of these pieces of social legislation? Here we run up against the complicated chemistry of social improvement in modern society, which involves 'a rare and fascinating phenomenon, the rise of a new standard of living, the pursuit of which has made a profound difference to the poverty-stricken of all classes'.[9] Once it has started, this phenomenon is to some extent self-perpetuating, but at its centre are the material products of scientific advance and the extension of collectivist social welfare. The importance of the reconstruction legislation of the war period is that it forms the basis of this subsequent extension, and thus makes a large contribution to the overall process. Although the Addison Housing Act was stifled, half a million houses were built under its important successor, the Wheatley Act of 1924, which greatly extended the subsidy policy. Similarly, some of the ideals of the Fisher Education Act, destroyed in 1921, were restored after 1924. Many of the other wartime developments – the growth of women's spending power, for example – fit into the chain-reaction; by accelerating pre-war trends, they create still greater acceleration.

Our final direct consequence of the war is a multiple one. The war was exciting as well as horrible. Where the world was not really, as Blumenfeld put it, 'topsy-turvy', people tended to want to believe that it was; the wish became the father to the thought, and the thought became acceptable. Early twentieth-century Britain had been a disturbed society, but those who openly railed against its conventions were a small minority: the emotional excitement of this greatest of all wars gave a certain universality to the concept of change, gave a moral sanction to the disruptions and transformations demanded by the physical needs of war. When enthusiasm flagged, propaganda stepped in. For the ordinary citizen, despite dark liberal talk of truth being the first casualty of war, the poison did no more than prolong the emotional debauch a little longer than it might otherwise have lasted, leaving behind little but a bad taste and perhaps – among ex-soldiers at least – a certain healthy scepticism of the printed word: 'whatever your pastors and masters tell you had best be assumed to be just a bellyfull of east wind'.[10] Pastors indeed did their own cause great harm by their pulpit propaganda.

The havoc of the war, in the apt word of E. L. Woodward, had a 'scorching' effect on the minds of British intellectuals:

The novels and poems of D. H. Lawrence, the early novels of Aldous Huxley, Lytton Strachey's *Eminent Victorians*, Mr Keynes's *Economic Consequences of the Peace* bear evidence of minds 'scorched' by war, and reacting against a nervous strain which was almost unbearable. The strain was caused not by any doubt about the issue of the war, but by the very fact of a European war and the breakdown of accepted standards.[11]

Woodward obviously regretted the disappearance of old virtues; he obviously disliked the tone of, say, Lytton Strachey's closing description of the service of remembrance held for the martyred Victorian hero General Gordon:

The service was conducted by four chaplains – of the Catholic, Anglican, Presbyterian, and Methodist persuasions – and concluded with a performance of 'Abide with me' – the General's favourite hymn – by a select company of Sudanese buglers. Every one agreed that General Gordon had been avenged at last. Who could doubt it? General Gordon himself, possibly, fluttering, in some remote Nirvana, the pages of a phantasmal Bible, might have ventured on a satirical remark. But General Gordon had always been a contradictious person – even a little off his head perhaps, though a hero; and besides he was no longer there to contradict . . . At any rate, it had all ended very happily – in a glorious slaughter of twenty thousand Arabs, a vast addition to the British Empire, and a step in the Peerage for Sir Evelyn Baring.[12]

To attribute the cynicism of Lytton Strachey or the mystical hatred for industrial civilization of D. H. Lawrence solely, or in any sizeable degree, to the experiences of the war would be ludicrous. The serious attack on Victorianism began in the 1890's and developed under the leadership of Shaw, Wells, Davidson, Fry and many others in the Edwardian period but it was in the nature of the war, murderous beyond all proportion to moral or material gains made, to foster scepticism, irony, irreverence.

Of religion not a great deal has been said so far, since no clear trend really emerges till the end of the war. It was in keeping with the exaltation of the times that the churches should be well patronized during the war, and they seemed a natural focal point of Armistice celebration and thanksgiving. Ministers of religion had embarked with enthusiasm upon the 'Holy War'. 'The Church', as the Minister of St Giles Cathedral, Edinburgh, recalled,

to an unfortunate degree, had become an instrument of the State and in too many pulpits the preacher had assumed the role of a recruiting sergeant. Almost every place of worship throughout the length and breadth of the land displayed the Union Jack, generally placed above the Holy Table, while some had great shields carrying the flags of all the allied nations. The first thing I did myself when I went to St Paul's, [Greenock] was to have a huge Union Jack and the national flag of Scotland displayed upon the east wall of the chancel. Being young, and owing to the inflamed feelings of the times, I said many things from my pulpit during the first six months of my ministry that I deeply regret. It is no excuse to say that many preachers were doing the same thing. I still feel ashamed when I recall declaiming on one occasion – about the time of Haig's 'Our Backs are to the Wall' message – that anyone who talked of initiating peace negotiations with the rulers of Germany was a moral and spiritual leper who ought to be shunned and cut by every decent-minded and honest man! This monstrous and stupid utterance, of which the Press got wind and duly lauded, so moved one of my patriotic hearers, the Manager of the Greenock Docks, that he startled the congregation by involuntarily shouting 'Hear, hear!'[13]

But sensitive believers were already secretly in revolt. C. F. G. Masterman, formerly a staunch Anglican, complained to his wife that a service at Westminster Abbey seemed like an activity at Wellington House, and remarked that the only religious leader who emerged with credit was the Pope, because of his appeal to the warring nations, and that the body which came through best was the Quakers.[14] After the war there was an immense reaction against the fervour and bigotry which had displayed itself in its most nauseating forms during the war. The brutal horror of the military war had a direct effect on religious belief: in February 1918 Masterman, in his diary, was musing upon the possibility that

God is a devil who rejoices in human suffering. He may be. There's no evidence to show He isn't.[15]

Many other long-term forces are involved in the decline of organized religion, not the least of them being the failure of the churches, from the time of the industrial revolution, to capture the interest of the proletariat. If anything, there did seem during the war to be a positive attempt to meet this situation, as Churchmen asked 'why should it be the exception rather than the rule for the workers to feel that the Church is their home?'[16] In the social reorganizations of the war, the Churches, though they may have been assisted towards interdenominational unity through the sharing of ministers, were, on the whole, adversely affected, especially from the breaking-up by war-service of the old close-knit dissenting communities.[17] The extent to which, in the perspective of three decades of change, the Churches suffered, can be seen from Rowntree's 1935 survey of York:

the number of adults attending church has fallen from 17,060 in 1901 to 12,770 in 1935, notwithstanding the fact that during that period the adult population of the city has increased from 48,000 to 72,248. . . .

In 1901 adult attendances amounted to 35.5 per cent of the adult population; in 1935 it amounted to only 17.7 per cent.[18]

The direct 'scorching' of the war reacted with the indirect consequences of the social transformations wrought by the war and with the broader trend of intellectual scepticism to create one great denominator, 'a widespread impatience of authority as such,'[19] which was both a part of, and an influence on, the social climate of the inter-war years. It could be seen in the 'new morality',[20] it could be seen in the decline of 'deference', it could be seen in religion. But, alas, it had only a negative influence on politics: that was the supreme equivocation bequeathed by the war, and the key to the tragic aspects of Britain's inter-war history.

[II] THE NEW SOCIETY

Geography, naturally, did not change much between 1914 and the 1920's (Southern Ireland gained independence at the end of 1921). In the twenties, however, a new population drift from the areas which in 1914 held the main concentrations of industrial power towards the Home Counties and the South East becomes apparent. While the population of London and the Home Counties increased by 18 per cent between 1921 and 1937, that of the Midland Counties increased by only 11 per cent, that of the West Riding, Notts and Derbyshire by only 6 per cent, the Lowlands of Scotland by only 4 per cent (although the Scottish birth rate was higher than the English) and that of Lancashire by less than 1 per cent. The population of South Wales declined by 9 per cent, and that of Northumberland and Durham by 1 per cent.[21] This trend was the geographical expression of the depression in coal mining and the old heavy industries, which accounted for the high and steady figure of 1½ million unemployed throughout the decade, and of the growth (though insufficient growth) of the new light, science-based industries. London and its motorized traffic problem had already caused concern before the war, and it already had its extensive environs inhabited by 'suburbans'; but it was in the twenties that the great development of commuterland – Hendon, Morden, Wembley, etc. – began, so that the total population of Greater London rose to over eight millions. Before the war it was London with its sweated trades which housed the most notorious swamps of poverty while the miners and the skilled workers in the heavy industries had been the most prosperous members of the working classes.

Clearly the movement towards the new technologies was inevitable, and signs of it were apparent enough well before 1914. It can be argued that, apart from the wider interruption of international trade, the war had an adverse influence in that it brought a final intensive development and exploitation of the old industries, when there should instead have been a steady conversion to new industries.[22] There is some, but not a lot of, force in this, since the war did also bring a stimulus to the new industries. What was ironic about the wartime industrial experience was the great, and justified, sense of power and importance it gave to the miners and heavy engineering workers, who were then, after the war, to find themselves working in conditions of falling demand. And although that same experience demonstrated not just the value of science-based industry but also the uses of Government direction and control, no attempt in the twenties was made towards sending new industry where it was required to absorb unemployment. So the pattern established itself: a prosperous, bustling south producing a tremendous range of new consumer goods; a decaying north.

The war had a dissolving effect on the class structure of Britain, the elements working the change being both economic – taxation especially – and emotional: the sense of 'topsy-turvydom', the sense of common citizenship. But Britain was still, as it is today, very much a class-conscious society. At the top the landed class, which had been the dominant component of the political élite of Edwardian times, moved into political, though not so obviously into economic and social, eclipse. Much attention, in the first years of peace, was focused on the extensive land sales which took place: 'England is changing hands', became a stock remark. By March 1919 about half a million acres were on the market, and by the end of the year over a million acres had been sold. In 1920 sales were still greater, with the Duke of Rutland making the pace by selling off about half of his Belvoir estate, 28,000 acres in all, for £1½ million.[23] One firm of estate

Upper class + wer

THE NEW SOCIETY 341

agents claimed that within a single year land equal in area to an English county had passed through their hands.[24] There were three main reasons for these sales. They could first of all be simply the continuation of a policy initiated at the beginning of the century whereby the landowner sought to consolidate his income by selling off outlying holdings; that is to say, financial impoverishment was not necessarily involved. Second, however, there was the question of high taxation, initiated as far as the landowner was concerned in the years before 1914, but greatly extended during and at the end of the war, when the 1919 budget raised death duties to 40 per cent on estates of £2 million and over. The frequent deaths in battle of young aristocrats made the burden of death duties even greater than it might otherwise have been. Third was the fact that, because of wartime exploitation of agriculture, land values had greatly risen, while rents had not; by selling, the landowner could put the increased value straight into his pocket. Economically, then, the position of the land-owners was not too serious: they

emerged into the inter-war period still in residence in their country seats, with their territorial empires considerably reduced, but with their incomes – once debts had been cleared and reinvestments made – probably much healthier than they had been for very many years.[25]

But their feudal dominance of the countryside was almost at an end, as their own tenants took the opportunity presented by the land-sales to set themselves up as owner-farmers. The sale of urban land, opening the door to the small domestic landlord, and to a new type of property developer, took place at the same time as the sale of landed estates. Town houses, now that the upkeep of large establishments was so difficult, were sold too, symboliz-ing the movement of aristocratic high society away from the centre of the London political stage.[26]

The new flow of political power within the topmost class was given its first big boost by the events of December 1916, and was ratified in the 1918 general election. It was expressed in the notorious energy with which Lloyd George created new peer-ages – 98 between 1917 and 1921, his fall from office unfortunately preventing him from completing his century – in the passing over of Lord Curzon in favour of the 'countrified businessman'

Stanley Baldwin for the Prime Ministership in 1922, and in the formation of the influential 1922 Committee of Conservative backbenchers – most of them businessmen. It was, naturally, a matter of deep regret to aristocrats like Lord Henry Bentinck who believed that the Conservative Party was being 'thoroughly commercialized and vulgarized', and Plutocracy 'ennobled, decorated, knighted and enriched'.[27] The upper class, then, is still, as in Edwardian times, a composite class, but the balance has moved definitely from the landed to the business interest. It was this class, or the younger members of it, which, drawing upon the hectic hedonism of the war, created the gay high-life associated with the ninteeen-twenties. It was this class which occupied the literary attentions of Aldous Huxley, and of John Galsworthy, the chronicler of the fortunes of a Victorian business family. Galsworthy, making a not very funny joke at the expense of social investigators who talked of the ten per cent below the poverty line, said that he was concerned only with the ten per cent above the property line.[28] Inequality in the division of income and wealth was still very marked, but not quite as marked as before the war: in 1910 1·1 per cent of the population took 30 per cent of the income; in 1929 1·5 per cent took 23 per cent of the income, and two thirds of the wealth was owned by 2½ per cent of the population. Bowley and Stamp, in their analysis of the national income as it was in 1924, pointed out that, while in 1911 individuals with incomes above £5,000 drew 8 per cent of the aggregate national income, in 1924 those earning £9,500 (the equivalent, given the rise in prices between 1914 and 1924) drew only 5½ per cent. They then proceeded to the very cautious summing up:

When the full effects of taxation are taken into account the real income available for saving or expenditure in the hands of the rich is definitely less than before the war. The sum devoted to luxurious expenditure is (allowing for the rise of prices) definitely less than in 1911, but it is still sufficient to bulk large in the eyes of the public, since it is concentrated in small areas, enlarged by the spending of visitors from overseas and advertised by the newspapers.[29]

When we move into the middle classes, the outstanding and incontrovertible statistical fact is the increase over the war period in the salaried class from under 1·7 millions in 1911 to over 2·7 millions in 1921, a rise from 12 per cent to 22 per cent of the occupied population.[30] The figures themselves are inflated because of the inclusion in this category of low-paid shop assistants, clerks, etc., and the expansion is exaggerated because the classification in 1921 was rather more rigorous. None the less the growth is striking. Itself a social phenomenon of outstanding importance, it reflects the expansion of four important groupings in the community: the professions, for whom rising material and welfare standards brought a new demand; the Civil Servants and clerical administrators, needed by the growing bureaucracy; the managerial class required for the running of large-scale modern industry; and those women who held on to the opportunities opened to them during the war (in 1931 there were 5½ million women in employment, 37 per cent of the female population between 14 and 65).[31] The other important feature of note is the decline in servant-keeping among middle-class households. The total decrease in the number of servants in the country over the war period, about a third, is less than is sometimes suggested; despite what observers during the war thought, many women were forced back at the end of the war into this degrading occupation. Still, the decrease that did take place came largely out of the households of the middle classes. In the commuter areas of London the number of resident servants per 100 families declined from 24·1 to 12·4, whereas in the West End it only edged down from 57·3 to 41·3.[32] In the whole of Liverpool the decline was from 13·5 to 8·3; in suburban Wallasey from 22·4 to 14·5.[33]

The decline in servant-keeping helped to weaken the barriers between the middle and lower classes, though a comparison between John Galsworthy's Tony Bicket in *A Modern Comedy* and E. M. Forster's Leonard Bast do not suggest any great change in upper-middle-class attitudes. The 'tax line' had all but disappeared in 1919–20 when there were 7¾ million tax-paying citizens,[34] six times the number in 1914, though this total fell again when the exemption limit was shortly raised to £150 per annum. When Bowley conducted a second social survey in 1924 with the express purpose of finding out whether working-class poverty had diminished since 1913, the problems of deciding which were working-class households and which were not had subtly changed:

In general, our principle has been 'when in doubt, rule out.' In the previous inquiry the inclination seems rather to have been the other way.[35]

The lines of distinction between middle and working class, that is to say, have become much more blurred than before; the feeling is that the clearly definable working class has got a little smaller. This feeling is borne out by the figures in the 1921 census: the total number in the 'wage-earner' category, the main core of the working class, has fallen to under 15 millions,[36] other variables being at least cancelled out by the increase meantime in the population. Carr-Saunders and Caradog-Jones, in their inter-war studies of the social structure of England and Wales, it may be noted here, refused to use the language of social class, belligerently in the first study when they asserted that 'the belief in the existence of social classes . . . is the result of studying social theory of doubtful value and of neglecting social facts',[37] less belligerently in the second, when they merely inquired, 'is it not a misreading of the social structure of this country to dwell on class divisions when, in respect of dress, speech, and use of leisure, all members of the community are obviously coming to resemble one another?'[38]

The working class in 1914 was large and it was poor. In the early twenties it was not quite so large, and it was not quite so poor. Bowley referred to his earlier pronouncement that 'to raise the wages of the worst-paid workers is the most pressing social task with which the country is confronted today', and continued:

It has needed a war to do it, but that task has been accomplished, so far as rates of wages are concerned, though employment has not been permanently possible for all at those rates.[39]

There was the achievement, and there the qualification upon it. Real wages for full-time employment were up by 20 per cent, the average working week down from 55 hours to 48 hours. But there was also, in certain areas, continuous unemployment on an unprecedented scale. Where 11 per cent of the families in Bowley's previous survey had been in primary poverty, the new wage rates should have reduced this figure to 3·6 per cent; because of unemployment the actual figure was 6·5 per cent. In the mining village of Stanley, which had basked in the coal boom of 1913, conditions were actually slightly worse now that coal-mining was a depressed industry: 7·5 per cent in primary poverty in 1924 as opposed to 6 per cent in 1940. In the long view the achievement was much more important than the qualification; but in the meantime the qualification brought much misery.

The great flux in material conditions, mental attitudes, and leisure activities contributed to the blurring of social distinctions. The decline in drunkenness, in itself a most important social fact, also helped to bring working-class behaviour into the area of the middle-class norm. While mentioning 'the immense present-day volume of drinking which takes place', the *New Survey of London Life and Labour* stressed that 'the outstanding points are,

the decrease in the amount of drinking per head, as distinct from the amount spent on drink, and the decreased extent to which actual excess, and the economic and physical effects of excess, are found. The social status of drunkenness has steadily fallen in the eyes of the working-class population. Where once frequent drunkenness was half admired as a sign of virility, it is now regarded as, on the whole, rather squalid and ridiculous'.[41]

A levelling out in the opposite direction was suggested by Mary Agnes Hamilton, writing in 1935 of 'the new morality':

in this respect the practice of the middle classes now tends, with variations of its own, to resemble that previously common enough among what were then called the 'lower orders'.[42]

A similar sort of social communion was to be found in widespread religious non-observance.

The most potent force of all was the growth of the mass media of communication. This was at first treated by the politicians with something of the same fuddy-duddy obscurantism as brought the return of much of the old economic orthodoxy in 1920 and 1921, but was shortly made the occasion for the enlightened application of the wartime collectivist lesson. In March 1919 a wireless telephony (i.e. the broadcasting of speech and sound as distinct from code signals – wireless telegraphy) transmitter was set up at Ballybunion in Ireland by the Marconi Company, and, under the direction of H. J. Round, successful transmissions were made to America. This led to the installation of a more powerful 6-kilowatt transmitter at Chelmsford, where, in addition to the testing of speech and long-distance transmission, short transmissions of musical items were also made. The product of the experimental work at Chelmsford was a standard Marconi transmitter for commercial purposes. In February 1920 a new 15-kilowatt station at Chelmsford began broadcasting two half-hour daily programmes of news items and live and canned music, which were enthusiastically picked up by the owners of receiving sets. The *Daily Mail* gave a lead to popular interest and arranged the celebrated Melba broadcast from Chelmsford of 15 June 1920, which has been widely recognized as 'a turning-point in the public response to radio'. But many vested interests, particularly among the military, regarded these developments as entirely frivolous, and issued grave warnings on the plight of airmen seeking guidance in bad weather who received only musical entertainment. Accordingly the Chelmsford broadcasts were banned, though transmitting and receiving licences continued to be issued to those who could provide testimonials to the seriousness of their scientific interest. Serious or not, there was nothing to stop the owners of receivers listening to broadcasts from Paris and the Hague; from January 1922 the Marconi Company was again allowed to broadcast speech and music, and this it did at Writtle, and at 2 L O – Marconi House in the Strand – where broadcasts of one hour a day began on 11 May 1922. But the Post Office insisted that broadcasts must be broken off every seven minutes to allow a pause for the reception of official messages, a restriction which Professor Briggs has likened to the old prescription that motor cars must be preceded by a man with a red flag. The chief influence on 2 L O broadcasting was Arthur Burrows, who argued that although there should be a large number of items of 'a really popular character' the attempt should also be made to 'lift' the public above its 'present standard of musical appreciation'.[43]

The Marconi Company was not alone in its interest in broadcasting; other companies wished to exploit the new potential which they had developed for war purposes. At a meeting of the Wireless Society of London in 1920 the British Thomson-

Houston Company displayed a radio receiver which could be installed in the home for about £30. By the summer of 1922 both the Metropolitan-Vickers Electrical Company (now Associated Electrical Industries) and the Western Electric Company were preparing to make transmissions. Each had American associations, and it was indeed the tremendous radio boom which took place in the United States at the end of the war (demonstrating the international quality of technological advance), combined with the pressure of the British companies, which helped to bring about the next development, a 'treaty' between the Post Office and the 'Big Six' (the four companies already mentioned, plus the Radio Communications Company and the General Electric Company). The outcome was the British Broadcasting Company, which began operations at the end of 1922, and moved in April 1923 to the home always associated with it, at Savoy Hill.[44] With the Calvinistic Scot, John Reith, as General Manager, and, inside a year, Managing Director, and Arthur Burrows as Director of Programmes, standards were high, but the Company was in essence a commercial company working for private profit through expanding sales of radio sets. The State at first had shown a narrow suspiciousness of broadcasting; but from August 1923, when a Departmental Committee on Broadcasting presented a glowing appreciation of its potential as a medium of mass communication,[45] governmental attitudes began to change. A second Broadcasting Committee, reporting in 1925, declared:

Broadcasting has become so widespread, concerns so many people, and is fraught with so many far-reaching possibilities, that the organization laid down for the British Broadcasting Company no longer corresponds to national requirements or responsibility. Notwithstanding the progress which we readily acknowledge, and to the credit of which the Company is largely entitled, we are impelled to the conclusion that no company or body constituted on trade lines for the profit, direct or indirect, of those composing it can be regarded as adequate in view of the broader considerations now beginning to emerge.[46]

Acting on the Committee's recommendations, the Conservative Government of the day established a public corporation in place of the private company. The founding of the British Broadcasting Corporation, embodying the application of the collectivist method to one of the most potent of the social relations of science, symbolizes very neatly the union of two of the major forces discussed in this book.

A similar comment could be passed on the enactment of the British Cinematographic Films Bill in 1927, which, by instituting a system of quotas and subsidies, was designed to break the American monopoly and encourage the making of British films. The war had taught the value of propaganda and the after-glow of war flames up strongly in report of the Moyne Committee (1936), which described the cinema as

undoubtedly a most important factor in the education of all classes of the community, in the spread of national culture and in presenting national ideas and customs to the world. Its potentialities moreover in shaping the ideas of the very large numbers to whom it appeals are almost unlimited. The propaganda value of the film cannot be over-emphasized.[47]

If it was the propaganda value of films which helped to bring about the necessary legislation for the protection and development of the native industry, it was their entertainment value which most affected British society in the early twenties. More than this, as the *New Survey of London Life and Labour* noted,

The influence of the films can be traced in the clothes and appearance of the women and in the furnishing of their houses. Girls copy the fashions of their favourite film star. At the time of writing [1934], girls in all classes of society wear 'Garbo' coats and wave their hair *à la* Norma Shearer or Lilian Harvey. It is impossible to measure the effect the films must have on the outlook and habits of the people. Undoubtedly they have great educational possibilities which have so far been very imperfectly attained. But the prime object aimed at is not to instruct or 'uplift', but to amuse, and in this object the cinema has proved very successful. It is estimated by the Cinematograph Exhibitors' Association that the aggregate weekly attendances at London cinemas now amount to a third of the population. Certainly today the cinema is *par excellence* the people's amusement.[48]

State intervention also took place in a third technological development greatly stimulated by the war, aviation, whose importance for society, however, was for the time being trivial compared with that of the cinema, or even radio. Holt Thomas's new Aircraft Transport and Travel Company began the first daily air service for passengers and goods between London and Paris in August 1919. Only two or three passengers were carried at a time:

One would walk into the little office where the clerk ... was seated and ask: 'How many have you got for today?' 'Two,' he would answer, with an air of satisfaction. 'And how many for tomorrow?' ... 'Three,' he would reply, with an even greater pride.[49]

The passengers, 'resigned but still apprehensive', would be packed into the 'small aeroplanes like sardines in a tin'.[50] By January 1920 three British companies were operating regular cross-channel services. But despite the Atlantic and Australian flights undertaken in the Vickers 'Vimy' (an adaptation of the wartime bomber) in 1919, which helped to preserve the romantic image which aviation alone brought untarnished from the war,[51] civil aviation simply did not pay. Temporary government subsidies to the three British companies were followed by the establishment in 1924 of Imperial Airways, with a government subsidy and certain government-appointed directors.[52] The major government assistance to the motor-car industry had come in the form of its wartime tariff policy. In 1920 there were 550,000 motor vehicles (including motor-bicycles) on British roads; in 1922, 952,000 and in 1930, 2,218,000.[53]

British society in 1914 was strongly jingoistic and showed marked enthusiasm at the outbreak of war. The strongest single popular sentiment on international politics after 1918 was 'It must never happen again'. There was doubtless nothing very heroic about this and indeed the envenomed European atmosphere of the early twenties suggested that, like it or not, it might very well happen again. Yet the 'war to end war' talk, the early Liberal idealism, the successful economic co-operation which had taken place between the Allies, and the realistic revolt against the possibility of another bloodbath, had produced the ideal represented by the League of Nations. The ideal was bedevilled by the bitter divisions and the cynicism also thrown up by the war, but there can be no doubt that, as represented by the League of Nations Union, it got stronger and stronger in Britain in the inter-war years. Misguided and confused though it was, British society seemed to be seeking something at once finer and more rational than the emotional clap-trap which had led it into war in 1914: thus in October 1933 the electors in the safe Conservative constituency of East Fulham rejected the fire-eating blimp, Alderman W. J. Waldron, in favour of the young Labour candidate, J. C. Wilmot, fighting on a programme of, among other things, disarmament and international co-operation through the League of Nations; and in 1935 eleven million people expressed through the 'Peace Ballot' (or 'Blood Ballot' as the *Daily Express* wittily called it) their belief in the League of Nations.[54] Yet in 1939 this island paradox of Britain once again entered into a world war against Germany. It is to the political basis of the paradox that we must now turn.

[III] THE SAME OLD STATE

The political scientist draws a distinction between 'Society' and its political and administrative organization, 'the State'. A rough and ready way of explaining the paradoxical aftermath of the First World War would be to say that while society had changed, the State had not. Or one could say that the war had thrown the forces of social change and the forces of political change out of joint. A society of new ways and new attitudes had been created. New organs of government, sources of endless self-congratulation on the part of the War Cabinet, were elaborated, yet the Ministry of Reconstruction was denied any really effective executive authority, the Ministry of Health was a mere shadow of what it might have been, and the much-vaunted Haldane Committee on the Machinery of Government, presenting its Report a few days after the election, produced only a rigid and unrealistic blueprint which no one, in any case, made any attempt to put into force.[55] In economics important new lessons were learned, but in the end most of the old structure was restored. In politics old-style Liberalism was destroyed, but, despite the advances of Labour, the supremacy of Conservatism was established for two decades. Other countries had revolutions; Britain had a Coupon Election.

Not that a revolution in Britain was either likely (political and economic tensions were never sharp enough, there were no shattering blows of occupation or defeat) or desirable (Germany with its Weimar and then Nazi 'revolutions' fared far worse than did Britain). But the Coupon Election, in the size and calibre of the Conservative majority which it riveted on the country, was a misfortune. Equally unfortunate was Lloyd George's apparent acceptance that he was the captive rather than the leader of that majority. Thus votes given for Lloyd George and reconstruction, where they were given as such, became votes for Conservatism and reaction. But most votes were given as the last gesture in the long patriotic debauch (the defeat of Asquith is the most vivid piece of evidence of this): the Conservatives, after Lloyd George, 'the man who won the war', could, with justice, claim to be the best patriots; and many of them had the coalition coupon to prove it.

Over the war period there were changes in the composition of the Conservative Party. Ironically, these, if anything, were changes for the worse: Baldwin and Neville Chamberlain, businessmen both, had many admirable qualities, but neither had great gifts of political leadership. Why was there no successful challenge to the low-grade leadership of the inter-war years, even within the Conservative Party? Some of the men who might have raised it were dead. Many survivors, swept by the post-war tide of bitterness and disenchantment, conceived a healthy contempt for politics and all its ways. Men younger still, the generation too young to fight in the war, seemed completely remote from the ageing world of politics. The first inter-war decade was marked by a sceptical and bitter-sweet detachment from politics, the second by a firm and bitter, but utterly futile, commitment to violence and extra-parliamentary action.

These, however, are minor considerations compared with the key political fact at the end of the war, the absence of a strong party of the Left. Consider the Liberal and Labour Parties as two cars on a funicular railway: it was during the war that the Liberal Party, going down, met the Labour Party coming up. The image is not really very apt, since it implies that the Liberal Party was inevitably foredoomed, which was not so. What happened, as we saw, was that the Liberal Party was prevented by the war from gaining the necessary time in which it might have resolved its own internal contradictions. Prior to 1914 one or two Liberals like Arthur Ponsonby and C. P. Trevelyan who disagreed with the

Labour
failure

imperialistic trends in the Party, apparent after Lloyd George's
Mansion House speech of 1911, were beginning to look with
favour on the internationalist aspirations and keener devotion to
social reform of the Labour Party; but their idea clearly was that
Labour should be a subordinate partner to a radically-minded
Liberal Party.[56] At the end of the war these same men flocked into
the Labour Party, largely, they said, on the grounds that it, and
especially its important component part, the I.L.P., was the only
party with anything like a true internationalist spirit, but also
because they now saw no hope of further social reform from any
other party.[57] They were joined by others, enthusiastic upholders
of the war effort, like Leo Chiozza Money, E. F. Wise, the live-
wire Civil Servant from the Ministry of Food, and Christopher
Addison, the Minister of Health whose attempt to build homes fit
for heroes was frustrated by a Government whose concern turned
to maintaining a land safe for investments. These men argued that
socialistic theory had vindicated itself during the war, and regretted its abandonment.[58]

The Labour Party, then, strengthened and consolidated within
itself by developments during the war, also benefited from an
influx of new recruits; and this was just at the time that the
Liberals were bitterly split between the majority trapped in the
Lloyd George coalition, and the 'Wee Frees' who continued to
follow Asquith. The long-term results were immense, but for the
time being neither the twenty-six Asquithite Liberals returned in
1918 (actually, by an irony implicit in the 1916 crisis, the more
reactionary section of the party) nor the 59 Labour M.P.s, inef-
fectually led in the absence of their pre-war leaders, could present
an effective opposition to a Coalition Government with a parliamentary strength of 474. In 1922 the Conservatives dropped
Lloyd George; the election which followed gave Labour 142
seats, the Asquith Liberals 60 and the Lloyd George Liberals 57.
By January 1924 Labour with 191 seats had taken office; arrayed
against it were 259 Conservatives and a reunited (more or less)
Liberal Party of 159.

As a new party regarded with the utmost suspicion in many
quarters, Labour, once again under the able but not very adventurous leadership of Ramsay MacDonald, set itself two tasks: to
demonstrate its fitness to govern, and to establish its independent

status as one of the two major parties of State. It was primarily for the latter reason that no attempt was made to strengthen the Government's parliamentary position by seeking an understanding with the Liberals (who were anyway, in many respects, more out-moded in their political ideas than the Conservatives, especially since their more radical members had joined the Labour Party). The upshot was that, apart from the Wheatley Housing Act, the first Labour Government hardly scratched the surface of the major problems of the day. The Conservatives under Baldwin then aggravated the economic situation by restoring the Gold Standard in 1925; at the same time their attempts to carry out the policies of 'Tory Socialism' roused the opposition of their own right-wing extremists. The ultimate expression of political confusion and economic failure came in the great crisis of 1931 which once again entrenched a solid Conservative majority in power. If there ever was an effective two-party system in Britain, it was not very apparent in the inter-war years; if ever a two-party system was needed, it was needed in the inter-war years. All attempts to form new groupings, planning groups, popular fronts, proved unsuccessful. Finally the Government and the country, determined to avoid the mistakes which had led to the First World War, blundered into the Second World War.

[IV] 1914-1918 AND ALL THAT

The First World War was, to borrow from *1066 And All That*, 'a bad thing', and no one but a callous rogue would wish to deny the validity of the bitterness which followed it; would wish, say, when talking of the emancipation of women to forget that a vote won might coincide with a husband or son lost. But no one but a romantic reactionary would wish to regret the world which disappeared in the deluge of 1914–18. In her *Testament of Youth,* one of the most moving of all descriptions of a private life shattered by the war, Vera Brittain incidentally brings out how the narrow conventions of provincial middle-class life by which girls were confined in pre-war days were also shattered. It is right to stress the hysteria, the phoney religion and the nauseating propaganda; but it is worth remembering that British Governments did at least have the conscience to make provision for conscientious objection, that Walter Long, the Tory squire at the Local Government Board, worked hard to see that conscientious objectors got their legal rights, and that a few crusty individualists did stand up for them.

Doubtless a new age in Britain would have been ushered in more slowly and more agreeably if there had been no war, if social and political forces, spared its distorting effects, had been left to march more closely in unison. But the war is a historical fact, whose consequences, in the end, can only be presented, not argued over. Its greatest significance is as a revelation, not so much of the folly of statesmen, but of the irrationality and love of violence bedded in human society.

NOTES TO CHAPTER NINE

1. The figures, drawn from the Census reports of 1911 and 1921, are presented in convenient form by A. L. Bowley and M. Hogg, *Has Poverty Diminished?*, 1925, p. 3.

2. *Report of Royal Commission on Population*; P.P., 1948–49, XIX, Cmd. 7695, p. 46.

3. Bowley and Hogg, p. 4.

4. Woodward, *Short Journey*, p. 115.

5. R. Boothby, *et al., Industry and the State*, 1927, p. 35. See generally A. Marwick, 'Middle Opinion in the Thirties: Planning, Progress and Political Agreement', in *English Historical Review*, April 1964.

6. *Report of British Association 1919*, p. 10.

7. H. and M. Wickwar, *The Social Services*, 1949 edn., p. 137.

8. M. Bowley, *Housing and the State*, pp. 9–35.

9. H. and M. Wickwar, p. 289.

10. C. E. Montague, *Disenchantment*, p. 94.

11. Woodward, p. 122.

12. L. Strachey, *Eminent Victorians*, 1918, p. 309.

13. C. L. Warr, *The Glimmering Landscape*, 1960, pp. 118–19.

14. L. Masterman, *C. F. G. Masterman*, p. 290.

15. (14 February 1918) quoted in ibid., p. 305.

16. Society for Propagation of Christian Knowledge, *The Church and the People*, 1915.

17. G. Spinks (ed.), *Religion in Britain since 1900*, 1952, pp. 68, 75.

18. B. S. Rowntree, *Poverty and Progress*, 1940, p. 420.

19. National Council on Public Morals, *The Ethics of Birth Control*, 1925, pp. 2–3.

20. ibid.

21. P.P., 1939–40, IV, Cmd. 6153 (Barlow Report), pp. 36–7.

22. M. Abrams, *The Condition of the British People, 1911–45*, 1945, p. 21. Cp. Scott and Cunnison, *Industries of the Clyde Valley*, p. 185.

23. F. M. L. Thompson, *English Landed Society in the Nineteenth Century*, pp. 330–31.

24. C. F. G. Masterman, *England After the War*, 1922, pp. 45–6.

25. Thompson, p. 337.

26. ibid., pp. 335 ff.

27. H. Bentinck, *Tory Democracy*, 1918, pp. 2–3.

28. *A Modern Comedy*, p. x.

29. A. L. Bowley and J. Stamp, *The National Income 1924*, pp. 57–9.

30. ibid., pp. 11–12.

31. R. Strachey (ed.), *Our Freedom and its Results*, pp. 137–8.

32. *New Survey of London Life and Labour*, Vol. II, 1931, p. 465.

33. D. Caradog Jones (ed.), *Social Survey of Merseyside*, 1934, Vol. II, pp. 301, 306 ff.

34. D. C. Marsh, *Changing Social Structure of England and Wales*, 1955, pp. 216–17. Dr Marsh expresses this as one quarter of the population over twenty. It is, of course, a much higher proportion of heads of families.

35. Bowley and Hogg, *Has Poverty Diminished?*, p. 28.

36. Bowley and Stamp, p. 11.

37. A. M. Carr-Saunders and D. Caradog Jones, *Social Structure of England and Wales*, 1927, pp. 71–2.

38. ibid., 1937, p. 66.

39. Bowley and Hogg, p. 20.

40. ibid., p. 36.

41. *New Survey of London Life and Labour*, Vol. IX, 1935, p. 245.

42. *Our Freedom and Its Results*, p. 268.

43. A. Briggs, *The Birth of Broadcasting*, pp. 45, 47–53, 70–9.

44. ibid., pp. 53, 59–68, 82–3, 88, 93–142.

45. P.P., 1923, X, Cmd. 1951, pp. 5–7.

46. P.P., 1926, XX, Cmd. 2599, p. 240.

47. P.P., 1936–37, IX, Cmd. 5320.

48. *New Survey of London Life and Labour*, Vol. IX, p. 47.

49. R. Harper, *The Romance of a Modern Airway*, 1931, pp. 9–10.

50. ibid.

51. J. D. Scott, *Vickers*, 1962, pp. 174–6.

52. See esp. A. Plummer, *New British Industries in the Twentieth Century*, 1937, pp. 156 ff.

53. ibid., p. 103.

54. See Marwick, *Clifford Allen*, pp. 159, 200–1.

55. *Report of the Committee on the Machinery of Government*; P.P., 1918, XII, Cmd. 9230. P. Abrams in *Past and Present*, 1963, pp. 51–52.

56. See esp. A. Ponsonby, *Social Reform versus War*, 1912, and C. P. Trevelyan, *From Liberalism to Labour*, 1922.

57. Trevelyan, *op cit.*

58. C. Addison, *The Betrayal of the Slums*, 1922, *Practical Socialism*, 1926. L. C. Money, *The Triumph of Nationalisation*, 1921.

Bibliography

Place of publication is London unless otherwise stated

I. GOVERNMENT PUBLICATIONS AND OFFICIAL REPORTS

Public General Statutes, 1914–21 (8 vols.).
Sessional (or 'Parliamentary') Papers [cited as P.P.]: 1913 (82 vols.), 1914 (102 vols.), 1914–16 (85 vols.), 1916 (35 vols.), 1917–18 (27 vols.), 1919 (54 vols.), 1920 (52 vols.), 1921 (44 vols.), 1922 (28 vols.).
Report of Departmental Committee on Broadcasting, 1923, X, Cmd. 1951. *Report of Committee on Broadcasting,* 1926, VIII, Cmd. 2599. *Report of Committee on the Cinematographic Films Act* (Moyne Committee), 1936–37, IX, Cmd. 5320. *Report on the Distribution of the Industrial Population* (Barlow Report), 1939–40, IV, Cmd. 6153. *Report of Royal Commission on Population,* 1948–49, XIX, Cmd. 7695.
House of Commons Debates, 5 series, 1913–21.
House of Lords Debates, 5 series, 1913–21.
Official History of the Ministry of Munitions, 8 vols., 1918–22 [cited as *Hist. Min. Mun.*].
Annual Register, 1914–20.
Board of Trade, *Journal,* 1914–20.
Board of Trade (Ministry of Labour after December 1916), *Labour Gazette,* 1914–20.
British Association for the Advancement of Science, *Annual Reports,* 1914–20.
Federation of British Industries, *Annual Reports,* 1917–22.
Federation of British Industries, *Bulletin,* 1917–20.
General Federation of Trade Unions, *Annual Reports,* 1914–20.
Independent Labour Party, *Annual Reports,* 1910–22.
Labour Party, *Annual Reports,* 1910–22.
Labour Year Book, 1916.
Liberal Year Book, 1914–20.
Ministry of Reconstruction, *Reconstruction Problems,* 1918–19.
Trades Union Congress, *Annual Reports,* 1910–22.
War Office, *Women's War Work,* 1916.

II. NEWSPAPERS AND PERIODICALS

Bradford Pioneer
British Citizen and Empire Worker (1916–18)

Common Cause
Daily Chronicle
Daily Citizen (1912–15)
Daily Herald (1920)
Daily Mail
Daily Mirror
Daily News
Economist
Forward
The Herald (1915–19)
Manchester Guardian
Morning Post
Nation
New Statesman
Observer
Punch
Spectator
Suffragette
Sunday Pictorial (1915–18)
The Times
The Worker (1916)

III. OTHER CONTEMPORARY MATERIAL

(The propagandist literature issued during the war, of which there is a fine collection in the Edinburgh University Library, is too immense to be detailed here. Only a few of the most important pamphlets are mentioned.)

Addison, C., *British Workshops and the War*, 1917.
Addison, C., *The Betrayal of the Slums*, 1920.
Addison, C., *Practical Socialism*, 1926.
Aldington, R., *Death of a Hero*, 1929.
Andler, C., *'Frightfulness' in Theory and Practice*, 1916.
Angell, N., *The Great Illusion*, 1910.
Archer, W., *The Great Analysis*, 1911.
Barker, E., *et. al.*, *Why We are at War. Great Britain's Case*, 1914.
Bentinck, Lord H., *Tory Democracy*, 1918.
Booth, C., *Life and Labour of the People in London*, 17 vols., 1902–03.
Bowley, A. L., *The Division of the Product of Industry*, 1919.
Bowley, A. L., and Burnett-Hurst, A. R., *Livelihood and Poverty*, 1915.
Bowley, A. L., and Hogg, M., *Has Poverty Diminished?*, 1925.
Bowley, A. L., and Stamp, J., *The National Income, 1924*, 1927.
Brend, W. A., *Health and the State*, 1917.

Britain Transformed, n.d.

British Labour and the War, n.d.

British Universities and the War, 1917.

Brooke, R., *Collected Poems,* 1918.

Cable, B., *Doing Their Bit,* 1916.

Cable, B., *Between The Lines,* 1916.

Carr-Saunders, A. M., and Jones, D. C., *Social Structure of England and Wales,* 1927 and 1937.

Central Committee for National Patriotic Organisations, *Report,* 1914.

de Chair, Sir D., *How the British Blockade Works,* 1916.

Clifford, J., *Our Fight for Belgium and What It Means,* 1918.

Cole, G. D. H., *Labour in War Time,* 1915.

Cole, G. D. H., and Arnot, R. P., *Trade Unionism on the Railways,* 1917.

Commission on Educational and Cultural Films, *The Film in National Life,* 1932.

A 'Corpse-Conversion' Factory, n.d.

Cosens, M., *Lloyd George's Munitions Girls,* 1916.

Coxon, S. (ed.), *Dover During the Dark Days,* 1919.

Dawson, A. J., *Somme Battle Stories,* 1916.

Dawson, W. H. (ed.), *After War Problems,* 1917.

Donald, R., *Trade Control in War. Things which the British Government has done well,* 1916.

The Elements of Reconstruction, 1916.

Federation of British Industries, *The Control of Industry,* 1919.

Federation of British Industries, *What It Is and What It Does,* n.d.

Fisher, H. A. L., *Educational Reform,* 1917.

Gosling, H., *Peace: How to Get and Keep It,* 1916.

Henderson, A., *The League of Nations and Labour,* 1918.

H.M.S.O., *Great Britain and the European Crisis,* 1914.

H.M.S.O., *Report of Committee on Alleged German Outrages,* 1915.

Hirst, F. W., *The Political Economy of War,* 1915.

Horsfall, T. C., *National Service and the Welfare of the Community,* 1906.

Jones, D. C. (ed.), *Social Survey of Merseyside,* 1934.

Keynes, J. M., *The Economic Consequences of the Peace,* 1919.

Labour Party, *Report of Special Committee on Deportations in March 1916 in the Clyde District,* 1917.

Leeson, C., *The Child and the War,* 1917.

Leicester Galleries, *Catalogue of Exhibitions, 1917–1918.*

Lloyd, E. M. H., *Stabilisation,* 1923.

Lloyd George, D., *The Great War,* 1914.

Lloyd George, D., *When The War Will End,* 1917.

Lloyd George, D., *The Allied War Aims,* 1918.

McCurdy, C. A., *To Restore the Ten Commandments,* n.d.

Mackenzie, F. A., *British Railways and the War*, 1917.
Masterman, C. F. G., *The Condition of England*, 1909.
Masterman, C. F. G., *England After the War*, 1922.
Mathews, B., *We Must Go On To Victory*, n.d.
Metcalfe, A. E., *Woman's Effort*, 1917.
Money, L. C., *Riches and Poverty*, 1905 and 1913.
Money, L. C., *The Triumph of Nationalisation*, 1920.
Montague, C. E., *The Front Line*, 1917.
Moore, H. K., and Sayers, B., *Croydon and the Great War*, 1920.
Murray, G., *Ethical Problems of the War*, 1915.
Murray, G., 'The Pale Shade', 1917.
National Council on Public Morals, *The Declining Birthrate*, 1916.
National Council on Public Morals, *The Cinema*, 1917.
National Council on Public Morals, *The Ethics of Birth Control*, 1925.
National Housing and Town Planning Council, *The Housing Manual*, 1923.
National Union of Conservative Associations, *Leaflets*, 1911–21.
National Union of Women Workers, *Report of Reconstruction Conference October 1915*, 1915.
Nevinson, C. R. W., *Modern War*, 1917.
Nevinson, C. R. W., *The Roads of France*, 1918.
Nevinson, C. R. W., *The Great War – Fourth Year*, 1918.
Newton, A. P. (ed.), *The Empire and the Future*, 1916.
Northcliffe, Lord, *At the War*, 1916.
Oliver, F. S., *Ordeal by Battle*, 1915.
Owen, W., *Poems*, 1920.
Owen, W., *Collected Poems*, 1963.
The Oxford Pamphlets, 1914–15.
Pankhurst, C., *The War*, n.d.
Peel, C. S., *The Eat-Less-Meat Book*, 1917.
Ponsonby, A., *Democracy and the Control of Foreign Affairs*, 1912.
Ponsonby, A., *Social Reform Versus War*, 1912.
Proud, E. D., *Welfare Work*, 1916.
Reeves, Mrs P., *Round About a Pound a Week*, 1913.
Robertson, W. (ed.), *Middlesbrough's Effort in the Great War*, n.d.
Rowntree, B. S., *Poverty, a Study of Town Life*, 1901.
Rowntree, B. S., *Human Needs of Labour*, 1918.
Rowntree, B. S., *Poverty and Progress*, 1940.
Roxburgh, R. F., *The Prisoners of War Information Bureau in London*, 1915.
Sassoon, S., *War Poems*, 1919.
Scott, L., and Shaw, A., *Great Britain and the Neutral Countries*, 1915.
Seddon, J. A., *Why British Labour Supports the War*, n.d.
Selbie, W. B., *Christian Nationalism*, n.d.

Shaw, G. B., *Commonsense About the War*, 1915.
The Sinking of the 'Lusitania', n.d.
Smith, D. H., *The Industries of Greater London*, 1933.
Smith, H. L. (ed.), *New Survey of London Life and Labour*, 9 vols., 1930–35.
Society for the Propagation of Christian Knowledge, *War Time Tracts for the Workers*, 1915.
A Souvenir for Visitors to the British Front, n.d.
Starling, P., *The Nation's Feeding*, 1919.
Sprigg, W. S., *The British Blockade*, n.d.
Strachey, L., *Eminent Victorians*, 1918.
Tillett, B., *Who Was Responsible for the War – and Why?*, 1917.
The Times History of the War.
Trevelyan, C. P., *From Liberalism to Labour*, 1921.
The War Aims of the British People, n.d.
Ward, Mrs H., *England's Effort*, 1916.
Ward, Mrs H., *Towards the Goal*, 1917.
War Emergency: Workers' National Committee, *Report, August 1914–March 1916.*
Wells, H. G., *Mr Britling Sees It Through*, 1916.
Williams, J. E. H., *One Young Man*, 1917.
Worsfold, W. B., *The War and Social Reform*, 1919.
Yates, C., *The Women's Part*, 1918.

IV. LETTERS, JOURNALS AND MEMOIRS

Addison, C., *Four and a Half Years*, 2 vols., 1934.
Addison, C., *Politics from Within, 1911–1918*, 2 vols., 1924.
Asquith, H., *Moments of Memory*, 1937.
Asquith, M., *An Autobiography*, 4 vols., 1922.
Barnes, G. N., *From Workshop to War Cabinet*, 1924.
Beecham, Sir T., *A Mingled Chime*, 1944.
Bennett, A., *Journal 1896–1926*, 1933.
Bertie, Lord, *Diary, 1914–18*, 2 vols., 1924.
Beveridge, Lord, *Power and Influence*, 1953.
Blumenfeld, R. D., *All in a Lifetime*, 1931.
Blunden, E., *Undertones of War*, 1930.
Braithwaite, W. J., *Lloyd George's Ambulance Wagon*, 1957.
Brittain, V., *Testament of Youth*, 1936.
Brockway, F., *Inside the Left*, 1942.
Brownrigg, D., *Indiscretions of the Naval Censor*, 1920.
Buchan, J., *The King's Grace*, 1935.
Chamberlain, A., *Politics from Inside*, 1937.
Cecil, Viscount, *A Great Experiment*, 1941.

Childs, Sir W., *Episodes and Reflections*, 1930.
Clarke, T., *My Northcliffe Diary*, 1931.
Clynes, J. R., *Memoirs*, 2 vols., 1937.
Cockerill, Sir G., *What Fools We Were*, 1944.
Cole, M., *Growing Up into Revolution*, 1949.
Collingwood, R. G., *An Autobiography*, 1939.
Crozier, F. P., *Impressions and Recollections*, 1930.
Edmonds, C., *A Subaltern's War*, 1929.
Elton, Lord, *Among Others*, 1938.
Engall, J. S., *A Subaltern's Letters*, 1918.
Farrer, R., *The Void of War*, 1918.
Fawcett, M. G., *The Women's Victory and After: Personal Reminiscences 1911–1918*, 1920.
Fisher, H. A. L., *An Unfinished Autobiography*, 1940.
French, Lord, *1914*.
Gallacher, W., *Revolt on the Clyde*, 1936.
Gillespie, A. D., *Letters from Flanders*, 1916.
Graves, R., *Goodbye to All That*, 1929.
Grey of Fallodon, Viscount, *Twenty-five Years, 1892–1916*, 2 vols., 1925.
Gwynn, S., (ed.), *The Anvil of War: letters from F. S. Oliver to his brother*, 1936.
Haldane, R. B., *An Autobiography*, 1929.
Hamilton, M. A., *Remembering My Good Friends*, 1944.
Harper, R., *Romance of a Modern Airway*, 1931.
Henson, H. H., *Retrospect of an Unimportant Life*, 2 vols., 1942.
Hendrie, J., *Letters of a Durisdeer Soldier*, n.d.
Hitchcock, F. C., *Stand To: A Diary of the Trenches, 1915–18*, 1920.
Housman, L., *The Unexpected Years*, 1936.
Housman, L., (ed.), *Letters of Fallen Englishmen*, 1931.
Jones, P., *War Letters of a Public Schoolboy*, 1918.
Keeling, F. H., *Keeling Letters and Reminiscences*, 1918.
Kenney, A., *Memories of a Militant*, 1924.
Kirkwood, D., *My Life of Revolt*, 1935.
Lansbury, G., *My Life*, 1927.
Lloyd George, D., *War Memoirs*, 6 vols., 1933–36.
Lockhart, R. B., *Your England*, 1951.
Lucy, H., *Diary of a Journalist*, 1922.
McDonagh, M., *In London During the Great War*, 1935.
McKenna, S., *While I Remember*, 1921.
Montague, C. E., *Disenchantment*, 1922.
Mottram, R., Easton, J., and Partridge, E., *Three Personal Records of the War*, 1929.
Nash, P., *Outline, an Autobiography and other Writings*, 1949.

Nevinson, H. W., *More Changes, More Chances,* 1925.
Nevinson, H. W., *Last Changes, Last Chances,* 1928.
Newton, Lord, *Retrospection,* 1929.
Oxford and Asquith, Earl of, *Memories and Reflections,* 1928.
Pankhurst, S., *The Home Front,* 1932.
Priestley, J. B., *Margin Released,* 1962.
Repington, C., *The First World War, 1914–1918,* 1920.
Russell, Earl, *Portraits from Memory,* 1956.
Salter, Lord, *Memoirs of a Public Servant,* 1960.
Sassoon, S., *Memoirs of a Fox-Hunting Man,* 1928.
Sassoon, S., *Memoirs of an Infantry Officer,* 1930.
Smillie, R., *My Life for Labour,* 1924.
Steed, H. W., *Through Thirty Years, 1892–1922,* 1925.
Tawney, R. H., 'The Attack' and 'Some Reflections of a Soldier', in *The Attack and Other Papers,* 1953.
Warr, C. L., *The Glimmering Landscape,* 1960.
Beatrice Webb's Diaries, 1912–24 (ed. M. Cole), 1952.
Wells, H. G., *Experiment in Autobiography,* 1936.
Williamson, H., *A Soldier's Diary of the Great War,* 1929.
Willoughby de Broke, Lord, *The Passing Years,* 1924.
Woodward, E. L., *Short Journey,* 1942.
Woolf, L., *Beginning Again,* 1964.
Wrench, J. E., *Struggle 1914–1920,* 1935.

V. SECONDARY AUTHORITIES

Abrams, M., *The Condition of the British People 1911–1945,* 1945.
Abrams, P., 'The Failure of Social Reform: 1918–1920', in *Past and Present,* April 1963.
Andrews, I., and Hobbs, M., *Economic Effects of the War upon Women and Children in Great Britain,* New York, 1918.
Andrzejewski, S., *Military Organization and Society,* 1954.
Ashworth, W., *An Economic History of England 1870–1939,* 1960.
Baker, C. W., *Government Control and Operation of Industry in Great Britain and the United States During the World War,* New York, 1921.
Balfour, Lady F., *Dr Elsie Inglis,* 1918.
Barnett, C., *The Sword Bearers,* 1964.
Beaverbrook, Lord, *Politicians and the War, 1914–1916,* 1928.
Beaverbrook, Lord, *Men and Power 1917–1918,* 1956.
Beaverbrook, Lord, *Decline and Fall of Lloyd George,* 1963.
Bernal, J. D., *Science in History,* 1954.
Beveridge, W., *The Public Service in War and Peace,* 1920.
Beveridge, W., *British Food Control,* Oxford, 1928.

Beveridge, W., *Some Experiences of Economic Control in War Time,* 1940.

Beveridge, W., *War and Insurance,* Oxford, 1927.

Bolitho, H., *Alfred Mond, First Lord Melchett,* 1933.

Bowley, A. L., *Prices and Wages in the United Kingdom, 1914–1920,* New York, 1921.

Bowley, A. L., *Some Economic Consequences of the Great War,* 1930.

Bowley, A. L., *Wages and Income in the United Kingdom since 1860,* Cambridge, 1937.

Bowley, A. L., *Studies in the National Income,* 1942.

Bowley, M., *Housing and the State,* 1945.

Briggs, A., *History of Birmingham,* Vol. II, 1955.

Briggs, A., *Social Thought and Social Action. A Study of Seebohm Rowntree,* 1961.

Briggs, A., *Birth of Broadcasting,* 1962.

Bruce, M., *The Coming of the Welfare State,* 1961.

Bruntz, G., *Allied Propaganda and the Collapse of the German Empire in 1918,* 1938.

Bulkley, M. E., *Bibliographical Survey of Contemporary Sources for the Economic and Social History of the War,* New York, 1922.

Cardwell, D. S. L., *The Organisation of Science in England,* 1957.

Carter, H., *The Control of the Drink Trade in Great Britain,* New York, 1919.

Carver, T. N., *Government Control of the Liquor Business in Great Britain and the United States,* New York, 1919.

Chapman, G., *Vain Glory,* 1937.

Clark, C., *National Income and Outlay,* 1937.

Clarkson, J. D., and Cochran, T., *War as a Social Institution,* New York, 1941.

Clephane, I., *Towards Sex Freedom,* 1936.

Cole, G. D. H., *Labour in the Coal-Mining Industry 1914–21,* Oxford, 1923.

Cole, G. D. H., *Trade Unionism and Munitions,* Oxford, 1923.

Cole, G. D. H., *Workshop Organisation,* Oxford, 1927.

Cole, G. D. H., *History of the Labour Party since 1914,* 1948.

Cole, M., *The Story of Fabian Socialism,* 1961.

Coller, F., *A State Trading Adventure,* 1925.

Cook, Sir E., *The Press in War Time,* 1920.

Crowther, J. G., *British Scientists of the Twentieth Century,* 1952.

Curtis, S. J., *Education in Britain since 1900,* 1952.

Dearle, N. B., *A Dictionary of War Time Organisations,* Oxford, 1924.

Dearle, N. B., *An Economic Chronicle of the Great War for Great Britain and Ireland,* Oxford, 1929.

Dearle, N. B., *The Labour Cost of the World War to Great Britain, 1914–1922*, 1940.

Dewar, G. A. B., *The Great Munitions Feat 1914–1918*, 1921.

Dixon, F. H., and Parmelee, J. H., *War Administration of the Railways in the United States and Great Britain*, New York, 1918.

Edmonds, J. E., *Short History of World War I*, 1952.

Edwards, R. S., *Cooperative Industrial Research*, 1950.

Ensor, R. C. K., *England 1870–1914*, 1936.

Fairlie, J. A., *British War Administration*, New York, 1919.

Falls, C., *The First World War*, 1960.

Fayle, C. E., *The War and the Shipping Industry*, 1927.

Gaus, J. M., *Great Britain, A Study of Civic Loyalty*, Chicago, 1929.

Ginsberg, M. (ed.), *Law and Opinion in England in the Twentieth Century*, 1959.

Gollin, A. M., *Proconsul in Politics: a study of Lord Milner in Opposition and in Power*, 1964.

Gorham, M., *Broadcasting and Television Since 1900*, 1952.

Grady, H. F., *British War Finance 1914–1919*, New York, 1927.

Graham, J. W., *Conscription and Conscience*, 1922.

Graubard, S. R., 'Military Demobilisation in Britain following the First World War', in *Journal of Modern History*, 1947.

Graves, R., and Hodge, A., *The Long Week End*, 1940.

Gray, H. L., *War Time Control of Industry*, New York, 1918.

Grier, L., Ashley, A., and Kirkcaldy, A. W., *British Labour Replacement and Conciliation 1914–1921*, 1921.

Groves, R., 'When 12,000 London Policemen went on Strike', in *Socialist Outlook*, 22 January, 1954.

Guttsman, W. L., 'The Changing Social Structure of the British Political Elite, 1886–1935', in *British Journal of Sociology*, 1951.

Guttsman, W. L., 'Aristocracy and the Middle Classes in the British Political Elite, 1886–1916', in *British Journal of Sociology*, 1954.

Guttsman, W. L., *The British Political Elite*, 1963.

Hammond, J. L., *C. P. Scott of the Manchester Guardian*, 1934.

Hammond, M. B., *British Labour Conditions and Legislation during the War*, New York, 1919.

Hanak, H. H., 'The Union of Democratic Control during the First World War', in *Bulletin of Institute of Historical Research*, November 1963.

Hankey, Lord, *The Supreme Command 1914–1918*, 1961.

Hardie, M., and Sabin, A. K., *War Posters*, 1920.

Harrod, Sir R. F., *Life of John Maynard Keynes*, 1951.

Hassall, C., *Rupert Brooke*, 1964.

Havighurst, W., *Twentieth Century Britain*, New York, 1962.

Heath, H. F., and Hetherington, W., *Industrial Research and Development in the United Kingdom*, 1946.

Heard, G., *Morals since 1900*, 1955.

Henderson, H. D., *The Cotton Control Board*, Oxford, 1922.

Hibbard, B. H., *Effects of the Great War upon Agriculture in the United States and Great Britain*, New York, 1919.

Hirst, F. W., *The Consequences of the War to Great Britain*, 1934.

Hirst, F. W., and Allen, J. E., *British War Budgets*, Oxford, 1926.

Howard, M., 'Lest We Forget', in *Encounter*, December 1963.

Hurwitz, S. J., *State Intervention in Great Britain*, New York, 1949.

Jewkes, J., *et al.*, *The Sources of Invention*, 1958.

Jones, T., *Lloyd George*, 1951.

Kirkcaldy, A. W. (ed.), *British Finance During and After the War 1914–1921*, 1921.

Lasswell, H. D., *Propaganda Technique in the World War*, 1927.

Lee, J. M., *Social Leaders and Public Persons*, 1964.

Litman, S., *Price and Price Control in Great Britain and the United States During the World War*, New York, 1920.

Lloyd, E. M. H., *Experiments in State Control*, Oxford, 1924.

McDowall, R. B., *British Conservatism 1832–1914*, 1959.

McEwan, J. M., 'The Coupon Election of 1918 and the Unionist Members of Parliament', in *Journal of Modern History*, 1962.

Mackintosh, J. M., *Trends of Opinion about the Public Health, 1901–1951*, 1953.

Mackintosh, J. P., *The British Cabinet*, 1962.

McVey, F. L., *The Financial History of Great Britain 1914–18*, 1918.

Mantoux, E., *The Carthaginian Peace, or the Economic Consequences of Mr Keynes*, 1946.

Marchant, Sir J., *Dr John Clifford, Life, Letters, and Reminiscences*, 1922.

Marsh, D. C., *Changing Social Structure of England and Wales*, 1955.

Marshall, T. S., *Citizenship and Social Class*, 1950.

Marwick, A., *The Explosion of British Society, 1914–62*, 1963.

Marwick, A., *Clifford Allen: the Open Conspirator*, 1964.

Marwick, A., 'James Maxton, his Place in Scottish Labour History', in *Scottish Historical Review*, 1964.

Marwick, A., 'Middle Opinion in the Thirties: Planning, Progress and Political Agreement', in *English Historical Review*, 1964.

Masterman, L., *C. F. G. Masterman*, 1939.

Meech, T. C., *This Generation, 1900–1926*, 1927–28.

Middleton, T. H., *Food Production in War*, Oxford, 1923.

Morgan, E. V., *Studies in British Financial Policy, 1914–25*, 1952.

Mowat, C. L., *Britain Between the Wars*, 1955.

Nef, J. U., *War and Human Progress*, 1950.

Newsholme, Sir A., *The Last Thirty Years in Public Health*, 1936.

Newsholme, Sir A., *The Ministry of Health*, 1925.

Newsome, D., *Godliness and Good Learning*, 1961.

Nowell-Smith, F. (ed.), *Edwardian England*, 1964.

Ogilvie, V., *Our Times*, 1950.

Peel, C. S., *How We Lived Then 1914–1918*, 1929.

Pelling, H., *Modern Britain, 1885–1955*, 1960.

Playne, C. E., *The Pre-War Mind in Britain*, 1928.

Playne, C. E., *Society at War 1914–1916*, 1931.

Playne, C. E., *Britain Holds On 1917–1918*, 1933.

Plummer, A., *New British Industries in the Twentieth Century*, 1937.

Political and Economic Planning, *The British Film Industry*, 1952.

Pollard, S., *The Development of the British Economy 1914–1950*, 1960.

Ponsonby, A., *Falsehood in War Time*, 1926.

Pratt, E. A., *British Railways and the Great War*, 1921.

Pribicevik, B., *The Shop Stewards' Movement and Workers' Control 1910–1922*, Oxford, 1959.

Redmayne, Sir R. A. S., *The British Coal-Mining Industry During the War*, Oxford, 1923.

Rees, J. M., *Trusts in British Industry, 1914–21*, 1922.

Rhondda, Viscountess, *et al., D. A. Thomas – Viscount Rhondda*, 1921.

Salter, J. A., *Allied Shipping Control*, Oxford, 1921.

Scott, J. D., *Vickers*, 1962.

Scott, W. R., and Cunnison J., *The Industries of the Clyde Valley During the War*, Oxford, 1924.

Scott, W. R., *et al., Rural Scotland During the War*, Oxford, 1922.

Semmel, B., *Imperialism and Social Reform*, 1960.

Shadwell, A., *Drink in 1914–1922, A Lesson in Control*, 1923.

Smith, H. L., *The Board of Trade*, 1928.

Spinks, G. (ed.), *Religion in Britain since 1900*, 1952.

Squires, J. D., *British Propaganda at Home and in the United States from 1914 to 1917*, Cambridge, Mass., 1935.

Stamp, Sir J., *Taxation During the War*, Oxford, 1932.

Strachey, R. (ed.), *Our Victory and After*, 1936.

Sturmey, S. G., *The Economic Development of Radio*, 1958.

Tawney, R. H., 'The Abolition of Economic Controls 1918–21', in *Economic History Review*, 1943.

Taylor, A. J. P., *The First World War*, 1963.

Terraine, J., *Douglas Haig, the Educated Soldier*, 1963.

Thompson, F. M. L., *English Landed Society in the Nineteenth Century*, 1963.

Titmuss, R. M., *Essays on 'The Welfare State'*, 1958.

Welland, D., *Wilfred Owen*, 1960.

Wickwar, H. and M., *The Social Services,* 1949.

Williams, E. N., *Life in Georgian England,* 1962.

Willis, I. C., *England's Holy War,* New York, 1929.

Wilson, T., 'The Coupon and the British General Election of 1918', in *Journal of Modern History,* March 1964.

Winkler, H., *The League of Nations Movement in Great Britain, 1914–1919,* New Brunswick, 1952.

Wolfe, H., *British Labour Supply and Regulation,* Oxford, 1924.

Woolf, L., *After the Deluge,* Vol. I, 1931.

Index